S0-CIG-497

STATE LAW AS ISLAMIC LAW IN MODERN EGYPT

STUDIES IN ISLAMIC LAW AND SOCIETY

EDITED BY

RUUD PETERS AND BERNARD WEISS

VOLUME 19

STATE LAW AS ISLAMIC LAW IN MODERN EGYPT

The Incorporation of the *Sharīʿa* into Egyptian Constitutional Law

BY

CLARK B. LOMBARDI

BRILL
LEIDEN · BOSTON
2006

This book is printed on acid-free paper.

Library of Congress Cataloging-in-Publication Data

A C.I.P. record for this book is available from the Library of Congress.

ISSN 1384–1130
ISBN-13: 978-90-04-13594-9
ISBN-10: 90-04-13594-4

© Copyright 2006 by Koninklijke Brill NV, Leiden, The Netherlands
Koninklijke Brill NV incorporates the imprints Brill Academic Publishers, Martinus Nijhoff Publishers and VSP.

All rights reserved. No part of this publication may be reproduced, translated, stored in a retrieval system, or transmitted in any form or by any means, electronic, mechanical, photocopying, recording or otherwise, without prior written permission from the publisher.

Authorization to photocopy items for internal or personal use is granted by Brill provided that the appropriate fees are paid directly to The Copyright Clearance Center, 222 Rosewood Drive, Suite 910 Danvers, MA 01923, USA.
Fees are subject to change.

PRINTED IN THE NETHERLANDS

CONTENTS

PART II

ARTICLE 2 OF THE EGYPTIAN CONSTITUTION

ACKNOWLEDGMENTS

While researching this subject and writing the book, I necessarily sought advice and assistance of a great number of people. I was constantly astounded by the generosity of the scholarly and legal community. I must first particularly thank Dean Peter Awn and the late Professor Jeanette Wakin, who introduced me to classical Islamic texts and the classical Islamic legal tradition. I am grateful as well to numerous other teachers and colleagues who have shared their knowledge in their diverse fields of expertise: Islamic studies, Middle Eastern politics, comparative law and constitutional law. Among them, I would particularly like to acknowledge Nathan Brown, Richard Bulliet, Kent Greenawalt, Dan Madigan, Brinkley Messick, James Morris, Robert Morrison and Gerald Neumann. Without their assistance, I would not have been able to begin unraveling the tangled skein of Article 2 jurisprudence.

In gathering materials, I was fortunate to have the opportunity to work with the consummately professional librarians at Columbia's Butler Library and Diamond Law Library, and later with the extraordinary librarians at the University of Washington's Gallagher Law Library. Locating Egyptian legislation and court cases provided a special challenge even for these paragons. In acquiring Egyptian legal materials, contextualizing them, and translating them in a manner that captured their nuances, I depended on the generous assistance of Gasser Abdel-Razek at the Hisham Mubarak Center in Cairo, Dalia Blass, Dr. Baudouin Dupret, and Dr. Adel Omar Sherif of the SCC.

A number of people have generously read chapters of this book and commented on them. Tom Cobb, Bernard Haykel, Robert Morrison, Rudolph Peters, and Bernard Weiss have each read the manuscript and have provided invaluable comments. Greta Austin, Mohammad Fadel, Noah Feldman, Jill Hutchings, Ned Scharfenberg and Mark Shulman have all been kind enough to read chapters as well. Their attention has greatly improved this work, and any errors that remain are entirely my own. In the final stages of polishing, I have received research and editing assistance from Bonnell Lombardi, Dana Raigrodski, and Stephanie Rollins. I would like to gratefully acknowledge research funding from the Mellon Foundation, Columbia Law School's Public Interest Law Fellowships, and the University of Washington School of Law.

I could never give thanks enough to my wife, Greta Austin, my children, Chiara and Cecilia, my parents, Bonnell and Rosemarie Lombardi, my sister Brita, and many close friends whose support has been unqualified and has meant so much.

TRANSLITERATION

In preparing transliterations for this book, I have generally followed the system adopted by the *International Journal of Middle East Studies.* I have departed, however, from the practice of the journal when it comes to transliterating Arabic words that are known to English speakers and that are included in *Webster's Third New International Dictionary.* Whereas the journal does not transliterate these, I do. I have also departed from the practice of the journal when it comes to proper names in Arabic. Again, the journal does not transliterate them, but I do, although I have not italicized them. This means that I have not italicized the word Sunnī or names of the Sunnī guilds of law, Ḥanafī, Mālikī, Shāfiʿī, Ḥanbalī, and Ẓahirī, whether they appear in nominal or adjectival form. The only exception to this last rule involves Arab authors who publish regularly in European languages. I will render the names of these figures, such as Adel Omar Sherif, as they do in their own publications.

INTRODUCTION

Over the last thirty years many Muslim nations have drafted or amended their constitutions to require that state law be consistent with *sharīʿa* norms.[1] The adoption and interpretation of constitutional provisions for the *sharīʿa* can be characterized as a form of "constitutional Islamization." This trend raises a number of important questions. What are the historical precedents, if any, for these provisions, and why have Muslim nations recently begun to adopt them? What happens when a country with a "secular" legal system, particularly one influenced by European models, suddenly adopts a *sharīʿa* provision? How do judges in these countries, who often do not have any classical Islamic legal training, go about the difficult task of interpreting and applying the *sharīʿa*? Does the adoption of constitutional Islamization provisions tend to require significant changes to legal systems already in place? Does it tend to drive that country away from or toward evolving international legal norms in the areas of human rights or finance?

Those interested in the phenomenon of constitutional Islamization and its ramifications will find much to ponder in Egypt's recent history. When a new Egyptian constitution was promulgated in 1971, Article 2 provided, among other things, that "the principles of the Islamic *sharīʿa* are *a* chief source of Egyptian legislation" (emphasis added). In 1980, the 1971 constitution was amended and its Islamization provision strengthened. Henceforth, Article 2 provided that "the principles of the Islamic *sharīʿa* are *the* chief source of Egyptian legislation" (emphasis added). In 1985, the Supreme Constitutional

[1] Majority Muslim countries that have, through enactment or amendment, given Islamic legal norms a preferred position in the constitutional scheme include the following: Afghanistan (Afghan Constitution Article 3); Egypt (Egyptian Constitution, Article 2); Iran (Iranian Constitution, Articles 2–4); Pakistan (Pakistani Constitution, Article 227); Qatar (Qatari Constitution, Article 1); Saudi Arabia; and Yemen (Yemeni Constitution, Article 3). The Saudi Basic Law declares both that the *sharīʿa* is binding law and that all legislation repugnant to *sharīʿa* is unenforceable; see Royal Decree No. A/90 Article 1.

Court of Egypt (the "SCC") held that Article 2 as amended required that all Egyptian legislation enacted after the amendment be reviewed for consistency with "the principles of the Islamic *sharīʿa*." Since this seminal 1985 ruling, the SCC has developed a substantive body of jurisprudence applying Article 2—upholding some laws as consistent with the principles of the *sharīʿa* and striking some others down as inconsistent.

Although Article 2 has never been the subject of a book-length study, some scholars over the last 25 years have come to be intrigued by various aspects of Article 2's history or by apparent peculiarities in the Article 2 jurisprudence of the Court. Oussama Arabi, Killian Bälz, Nathan Brown, Baudouin Dupret, Enid Hill, Baber Johansen, Nathalie Bernard-Maugiron, Rudolph Peters, Adel Omar Sherif, and Frank Vogel have written articles that touch upon issues related to Article 2. These works vary in their scope and methodologies. As a result, the authors disagree about how the SCC is interpreting Islamic law in Article 2 cases, what relationship exists between the SCC's theory and other theories of Islamic law, why the SCC has developed its method and finally, what the long-term ramifications of Article 2 jurisprudence will be.

For instance, scholars dispute the relationship of the SCC's theory of Islamic law to other theories of Islamic law. Some scholars have described the Court's Article 2 jurisprudence as reflecting an essentially classical or neo-classical approach to Islamic legal interpretation.[2] Others insist that modernist Islamic legal theory has been the primary inspiration for the Court.[3] Still others have suggested that the SCC's interpretative scheme cannot be easily placed in the Islamic tradition at all and might be considered pseudo-Islamic.[4]

---

[2] See Oussama Arabi, *Studies in Modern Islamic Law and Jurisprudence* (Arab and Islamic Law Series 21; The Hague/London/New York: Kluwer Law International, 2001), 174, 194–200. Compare, however, 199, note 4, which recognizes the problem with defining the SCC's theory as classical or even neo-classical.

[3] See, e.g., Baber Johansen, "Supra-legislative Norms and Constitutional Courts: The Case of France and Egypt," in Eugene Cotran, Adel Omar Sherif, eds., *The Role of the Judiciary in the Protection of Human Rights* (CIMEL Book Series No. 5; London: Kluwer, 1997), especially 369, Frank Vogel, "Conformity with Islamic Shariʿa and Constitutionality under Article 2: Some Issues of Theory, Practice, and Comparison," in Eugene Cotran, Adel Omar Sherif, eds., *Democracy, the Rule of Law and Islam* (CIMEL Book Series No. 6; London: Kluwer, 1999), 535–38.

[4] See, e.g., Killian Bälz, "La construction séculière du droit islamique: la Haute Cour Constitutionelle égyptienne et la 'bataille de voile' dans les écoles publiques," *Droit et Société* 39 (1998), 277–91.

Scholars have also disagreed about the practical effects of Article 2 jurisprudence in the future. Some articles are unabashedly enthusiastic about the Court's theory, arguing that it may represent the beginning of an authentically "Islamic" theory that harmonizes the Islamic tradition with international human rights norms.[5] Others are more cautious, suggesting that Article 2 jurisprudence could be a Trojan horse, which to date has been used for progressive ends but through which regressive policies may later be imposed judicially.[6] Still others suggest that Article 2 jurisprudence might be more or less irrelevant to the evolution of Egyptian law—because, they argue, it tends to reinforce "secular" norms that would be imposed anyway.[7]

In this book, I will wade into the thicket of Article 2 studies and try to answer some of the questions that Article 2 jurisprudence (and the scholarship about it) raises. A monograph-length study provides an author with the space necessary to contextualize Article 2 and Article 2 jurisprudence more fully than is possible in shorter works. It also permits the author to trace the relationship of Article 2 both to earlier theories of Islamic law and to trends in contemporary constitutional jurisprudence in Egypt.

In order to properly contextualize the SCC's Article 2 jurisprudence, I have structured this book essentially as a "biography" of Article 2. This biography will discuss Article 2's ancestors, the general milieu in which it was conceived and born, the specific circumstances surrounding its birth, and the eventual maturation of Article 2 jurisprudence into a distinctive part of the Egyptian legal system.

---

[5] See, e.g., Hatem Aly Labib Gabr, "The Interpretation of Article 2 of the Constitution: Islamic Sharia Principles as a Source of Law," in *Human Rights and Democracy: The Role of the Supreme Constitutional Court of Egypt*, Kevin Boyle and Adel Omar Sherif, eds. (CIMEL Book Series 3; London: Kluwer, 1996), 217–27.

[6] Compare, e.g., Arabi, *Studies*, 18 and Johansen, "Supra-legislative Norms," 376 with Vogel, "Conformity with Islamic Shariʿa and Constitutionality under Article 2: Some Issues of Theory, Practice, and Comparison," in Eugene Cotran, Adel Omar Sherif, eds., *Democracy, the Rule of Law and Islam* (CIMEL Book Series No. 6: London: Kluwer, 1999), 525–44; and Clark Lombardi, "Islamic Law as a Source of Constitutional Law in Egypt: the Constitutionalization of the Sharia in a Modern Arab State," *Columbia Journal of Transnational Law* 37 (1988), 81–122. (As this book will make clear, I have modified my view considerably since writing this article.)

[7] See, e.g., Bälz, "La construction," and Baudouin Dupret, "À propos de la constitutionalité de la Sharīʿa: Présentation et traduction de l'arrêt du 26 Mars 1994 (14 Shawwāl 1414) de la Haute Cour Constitutionelle (*al-maḥkama al-dustūriyya al-ʿulyā*) égyptienne," *Islamic Law and Society* 4 (1997), 98.

Part I provides the background to Article 2. It is comprised of six chapters which discuss the formation of consensus on questions of Islamic legal theory during the classical era, the collapse of that consensus in the modern era, and the appearance in Eygpt of important political factions, each espousing a different theory of Islamic law. Chapter 1 outlines the formation of the Sunnī consensus about Islamic legal authority and methodology. Chapter 2 describes the method that classical jurists used to come up with interpretations of the *sharīʿa*. Chapter 3 discusses the development of a theory that courts in an Islamic state should apply (and rulers should enforce) laws that (a) were consistent with the "rulings of the *sharīʿa*" that the jurists had discovered and (b) did not impede the achievement of social results that jurists had identified as divinely-favored "goals" of God's law. It points out the significance of Islamic state law. By cooperating with the classical jurists and appointing them to serve as legislative advisors and judges, some states, including the Ottoman Empire, were able to endow the law of the state with considerable Islamic legitimacy.

Chapters 4 through 6 turn to the collapse of the classical consensus on basic questions of Islamic legal theory, the rise of competing theories—each trying to become the new "consensus" theory—and the crisis of Islamic legitimacy that this created. Chapter 4 discusses how and why consensus on basic issues of legal theory broke down. Chapter 5 describes some of the new theories of Islamic law that arose in modern Egypt, as different thinkers appropriated classical concepts and vocabulary and re-imagined the proper method both of interpreting the *sharīʿa* and of creating a body of Islamic state law. Chapter 6 discusses how competing Islamist factions in modern Egypt came to champion different modernist visions of interpretive authority and of interpretive method. It also addresses the problems that the breakdown of consensus posed for governments who wished to establish their legitimacy in Islamic terms.

In Part II, this book turns to Article 2 of the Egyptian constitution, which represented a commitment by the government to attempt to establish its legitimacy in Islamic terms. When the government failed to develop an effective program of Islamization that could do this, Article 2 jurisprudence became the means through which the Egyptian judiciary tried to establish a new consensus theory of Islamic law.

When the 1971 Constitution was drafted, it carved out a specific role for the *sharīʿa*. Article 2 of this Constitution stated, "the principles of the Islamic *sharīʿa*" would be one "chief source" of Egyptian legislation. Chapter 7 places the decision to enact Article 2 in its larger context, as part of a broad (albeit short-lived) policy of executive-sponsored Islamization. Shortly after the enactment of Article 2, the government actually began to reach out to Islamists and, tentatively, to prepare Islamic revisions to Egyptian law. Although this plan was considered risky by some, President Sādāt became convinced of its feasibility and utility. As a sign of his regime's commitment, the captive legislature amended and strengthened Article 2 to state that Islamic law would henceforth be "*the* chief source of legislation" [emphasis added]. This language suggested that all Egyptian law would henceforth be required to be consistent with the *sharīʿa.*

After the assassination of President Sādāt by Islamists in 1981, the new president and head of the ruling party dismissed the executive-sponsored Islamization program as quixotic. Notwithstanding the recent amendment of Article 2, the political branches abandoned their policy of revising Egyptian laws to make them more Islamic. However, the judiciary had during the Sādāt years, established considerable independence from the executive. Sensing that the judicial branch might be willing to challenge an apparently unconstitutional policy, Islamists began to bring suits challenging Egyptian laws as un-Islamic and thus unconstitutional under Article 2. At this point, the responsibility for creating and implementing an official government theory of Islamic law moved from the executive and legislative branches to the increasingly independent judiciary.

Chapter 8 describes the Egyptian judicial system that was saddled with the responsibility of deciding Islamists' Article 2 claims. It focuses on the Supreme Constitutional Court (the SCC), an institution that had only been established in 1979. By the mid-1980s, however, it had already established itself as a strong champion of liberal constitutionalism and was incrementally imposing a liberal rule of law in Egypt. The SCC, eager to maintain its growing reputation for integrity and independence, could not afford to be accused of supporting a willful violation by the political branches of a constitutional obligation. At the same time, they had reason to be concerned that any attempt to resolve the question whether (or how) Islamization should take place would do more harm than good.

Chapters 9, 10 and 11 turn to the SCC's emerging interpretation of Article 2. Chapter 9 discusses the SCC's handling of a preliminary question: should the new constitutional court interpret Article

2 at all? As this chapter explains, it was not clear that the constitution permitted them to do so, and it was not clear that, as a policy matter, it made sense for the Court to enter into the increasingly violent debates about the government's failure to carry through with its Islamization policy. In considering whether (or how) to interpret Article 2, the newly-established and still weak Court was naturally concerned about the political ramifications of becoming involved in the heated debates about the role of Islam in Egyptian society. On the other hand, it was also concerned that, if it did not play a role in interpreting and applying Article 2, the demand for Islamization might impede the establishment of a progressive, liberal constitutional rule of law. Ultimately, the SCC compromised by saying that it did not have the authority to review for consistency with "the principles of the Islamic *sharī'a*" any laws that were in force prior to the 1980 amendment of Article 2. However, it had the power to review laws enacted or amended thereafter.

Chapter 10 first discusses the SCC's early Article 2 opinions in which it decided cases with little explanation of its reasoning. This chapter then gives an overview of the theory of Islamic law that the Court has then developed and applied since 1993. In its Article 2 jurisprudence to date, the SCC has systematically borrowed concepts and vocabulary from a range of modernist theories of Islamic law. At the same time, the Court has avoided taking a clear position on some of the most controversial issues of legal theory. In short, the chapter argues that the Court has developed an embryonic 'pastiche' theory of Islamic legal interpretation. That is to say, it has produced a theory that draws widely, but directly, from the Islamic tradition and appeals rhetorically to a wide range of very different Islamist groups. It is, however, a theory that is ambiguous in certain particulars. The SCC has been applying its theory in a way that reflects an implicit preference for liberal development of its theory. It has not, however, explicitly built its liberal assumptions into its theory, and thus, later panels seem to have the freedom to take the theory in different directions.

Chapter 11 provides a series of case studies, which demonstrate how the SCC's theory has been applied. This chapter examines how the justices of the SCC have consistently used the discretion that their theory leaves them to interpret Islamic law in a manner that reinforces the liberal constitutional principles. In its Article 2 opinions, the SCC has been able to use familiar Islamic legal concepts and vocabulary to develop an interpretation of Islamic law that is consistent with and indeed reinforces the evolving liberal rule of law in Egypt.

Chapter 12 looks briefly at the reception of the SCC's evolving Article 2 jurisprudence, both by academics and by lower courts in Egypt. Lower courts have by and large accepted the essential components of the SCC's theory and its general liberal thrust. Nevertheless, these courts have indicated some concerns. In areas where the Court has left its theory ambiguous, they have applied the theory in a way that seems to show more deference than the SCC to classical Islamic norms. Interestingly, although political Islamists disagree with many of the SCC's conclusions, they have to date accepted the legitimacy of the SCC's approach—as demonstrated by the fact that they continue voluntarily to litigate before the Court. This suggests that the SCC has been able to create broad support for a theory of Islamic law that is capable of co-existing with a liberal constitutional philosophy.

The conclusion ties together the two halves of this book by drawing some larger conclusions about Islamic law in the modern world. It argues that the great challenge facing contemporary Islamic legal theorists and political parties is how to deal with the collapse of consensus on questions of Islamic legal theory. In the period during which the classical consensus held sway on questions of Islamic legal theory, Muslim legal thinkers developed a reservoir of sophisticated concepts and vocabulary that allowed them to grapple effectively with questions of morality and effective governance. In the modern era, Muslims have come to agree that the classical method of Islamic legal interpretation and the classical model of the Islamic state are no longer appropriate. There is deep disagreement, however, about what should replace it. Different thinkers have appropriated the insights of classical theory in different ways and refashioned them into many new Islamic legal theories. Different factions have called on states to apply different theories. The result is a situation in which there is a broad desire for Islamization in the abstract, but violent disagreement about what form Islamization should take—disagreement that is rooted in very different ideas about how to interpret the *sharīʿa*.

In at least one country, then, constitutional Islamization has made judges an important new voice in the debates about Islamic legal theory—and particularly on the crucial question of what makes a state law "Islamic." There is no guarantee that other countries will follow the lead of Egypt, or even, for that matter, that later courts in Egypt will continue to embrace the SCC's liberal vision of Islamic legal theory. Nevertheless, the SCC has publicly articulated and applied a decidedly liberal, rights-protecting approach to Islamic legal interpretation. The acceptance of its precedents to date and the constructive dialogue that its approach has generated reveal that Islamic law can realistically be conceived of as a source of liberal legal norms. Under the right circumstances, Islamization can reinforce movements trying to develop the liberal rule of law in the Muslim world.

PART ONE

CLASSICAL ISLAMIC LEGAL THEORY AND THE RISE OF COMPETING MODERNIST LEGAL THEORIES

CHAPTER ONE

THE FORMATION OF THE CLASSICAL SUNNĪ LEGAL TRADITION

Since May 1980, Article 2 of the Egyptian Constitution has declared, "The principles of the Islamic *sharīʿa* shall be the chief source of legislation." Egyptian courts have interpreted this to mean that Egyptian law must be consistent with *sharīʿa* principles. This book will discuss the Supreme Constitutional Court's attempts to interpret and apply Article 2, focusing in particular on its attempt to articulate a practical method of identifying and interpreting the *sharīʿa* norms against which state law would be measured.

In interpreting Article 2, the Supreme Constitutional Court ("the SCC") faced an enormously difficult task. To understand why this should be so, and to understand the solution which the SCC devised, it is important to understand the history of Islamic legal theory and the history of political Islam in modern Egypt. From roughly the ninth to the nineteenth centuries C.E., Sunnī Islamic legal scholars came to agree on a number of basic premises about the nature of God's command and about the ways that humans might best try to understand that command. Working from these common assumptions about authority, epistemology, and hermeneutics, they built up a corpus of subtle and sophisticated Islamic theory. Applying this "classical" theory over the years, generation after generation of jurists contributed to an evolving body of classical Islamic *fiqh*—legal rulings that represented their understanding of God's law, or the *sharīʿa*.

In the modern era, Muslim thinkers began to question some of the assumptions of classical Islamic legal theory and thus questioned the value of the classical interpretations of the *sharīʿa* for the modern world. Nevertheless, they chose not to jettison the rich and sophisticated classical tradition in its entirety. It provided a mine of insights about the nature of revealed law and about the ways in which humans can try to understand such a law. Thinkers tried in different ways to work from these insights, modifying classical techniques to develop a number of different, modern methods of Islamic legal interpretation. In many Muslim countries, including Egypt, Islamist political factions have embraced competing methods of legal interpretation and, thus, competing bodies of Islamic law. They have agitated fiercely, and sometimes violently, in favor of their very different visions of Islamic law. Anyone who wishes to interpret the *sharīʿa* and apply it as law in a modern nation like Egypt must be prepared to address withering criticism and, possibly, resistance from those who favor other visions.

To understand the complexity of the challenge that the SCC faced when it was asked to interpret Article 2, and to appreciate the subtlety of its solution, it helps to have some background in the classical tradition out of which modernist theories of law have developed, some understanding of the way in which modernists have worked with classical concepts to refashion modern theories of Islamic law and, finally, to understand how deeply Muslims in modern Egypt are divided over questions of Islamic legal theory. The next six chapters will discuss the evolution of a classical consensus on questions of Islamic legal theory, the reasons that consensus collapsed, the rise of modernist legal theories and the fracturing of the Muslim polity in Egypt over questions of legal theory.

I. *The concept of the* sharīʿa

The Qurʾān states that God has set down a "*sharīʿa*" which Muslims were obliged to follow.[1] The term *sharīʿa* literally means 'path,' and, early on, Muslims understood this to mean that God had established a body of rules and recommendations and that human salvation depended on their ability to identify and obey these.[2] Over time, Muslim legal thinkers came to conclude that God had placed every conceivable act in a five-part moral scale, ranging from mandatory (*farḍ* or *wājib*), to recommended (*mandūb*), to morally neutral or permissible (*mubāḥ*), to reprehensible (*makrūh*), down to prohibited (*ḥarām*). The *sharīʿa* required humans to perform the mandatory and refrain from the prohibited, and God would punish those who failed to obey these commands. The *sharīʿa* also suggested that wherever possible,

[1] Qurʾān 45:18.
[2] See Norman Calder and MB Hooker, "*Sharīʿa*" in EI2, vol. IX, 321.

humans should perform the recommended and refrain from the reprehensible. God will reward them for doing so (but will not punish them for failing to do so).[3]

Muslim legal thinkers struggled to understand where on the five-part scale every conceivable human action falls, so that they could identify and perform the acts that were mandatory and recommended and abstain from the acts that were prohibited or reprehensible. God had revealed indications of his law to prophets and, some said, in the workings of the world as well. Unfortunately, these indications did not leave a clear or complete picture of God's law, the *sharīʿa.* Thus, debates emerged both about the methods that should be used to interpret God's command and about what, in fact, the *sharīʿa* required.

II. *The development of institutions that shaped interpretation of* sharīʿa: *the madhhabs*

In the centuries after the death of the Prophet Muḥammad, the Muslim community debated how best to acquire an understanding of the *sharīʿa* and how to develop a body of law for the Muslim community. Among the issues that divided religious legal scholars were questions about whether interpretation of God's law should be the prerogative of those with charismatic authority.[4] Another question was whether people could understand the *sharīʿa* simply by observing nature and exercising their reason. The jurists who developed the classical Sunnī legal tradition ultimately rejected exclusively charismatic interpretation and purely rational methods of determining

[3] See, e.g., Muwaffaq al-Dīn Ibn Qudāma, *Rawḍat al-Nāẓir wa-Junnat al-Munāẓir* (Cairo: al-Maṭbaʿat al-Salafiyya, 1385), 16–24; see also the discussion in Wael Hallaq, *A History of Islamic Legal Theories* (Cambridge: Cambridge University Press, 1997), 40, citing Shīrāzī and Ibn Barhān.

[4] There was some question as to whether proper interpretation of God's law might require post-prophetic divine revelation. Some concluded that prophetic revelation of law had died with the Prophet Muḥammad and that Muslims were therefore required to seek knowledge in the revelation and/or human reason. This was to become a central assumption of Sunnī thought. On the development of a theory of cessation of prophecy, see the exhaustive account by Yohanan Friedman in *Prophecy Continuous* (Berkeley: University of California Press, 1989), 49–93.

God's law. According to these scholars, men of discernment should seek signs of God's commands primarily in the texts that recorded the Prophet's revelations, turning only in the second instance to non-scriptural sources such as custom and the laws of the natural world.

The precise origins of Sunnī legal theory remain nebulous.[5] Over time, however, Sunnī jurists began to focus more attention on exploring and explaining the method by which Muslims should interpret the sources that contained the signs of God's commands. Current evidence suggests that the turning point occurred at some point during the third or fourth centuries after the death of the Prophet (the ninth and tenth centuries C.E.), when systematic discussions about Sunnī theories of legal interpretation (*ʿilm uṣūl al-fiqh*) began to appear.[6]

The emergence of a distinctly "Sunnī" tradition of *uṣūl al-fiqh* is connected to the development over the eighth through tenth centuries C.E. of distinctive scholarly associations, the Sunnī *madhhabs*.[7] The *madhhab* is one of the central institutions of Islamic religion and law, and indeed of pre-modern Sunnī Islamic society.[8] As the late

---

[5] Early Muslim jurists, including those who developed the Sunnī tradition, seem not to have focused on developing a systematic legal theory. They interpreted God's law without describing in any detail the methods by which they had reached their legal conclusions. See Norman Calder, "Uṣūl al-Fiḳh" in EI2, vol. II, 886.

[6] For years, the history of *uṣūl al-fiqh* was traced to the seminal work of Muḥammad Ibn Idrīs al-Shāfiʿī (d. 204 A.H./820 C.E.). There is currently considerable dispute over the traditional account. Some have challenged the attribution and dating of works that are usually attributed to al-Shāfiʿī. The seminal argument for a re-dating of the work was made by Norman Calder, *Studies in Early Muslim Jurisprudence* (Oxford: Clarendon Press, 1993). For a modified version of this argument, see Christopher Melchert, "Qurʾānic Abrogation Across the Ninth Century: Shāfiʿī, Abū ʿUbayd, Muḥāsibī, and Ibn Qutaybah," *Studies in Islamic Legal Theory*, ed. Bernard G. Weiss (Leiden: E.J. Brill, 2002), 75–98. Other modern scholars have accepted the traditional attribution and dating but question whether the work was influential. See, e.g., Wael Hallaq, "Was al-Shāfiʿī the Master Architect of Islamic Jurisprudence?" *International Journal of Middle East Studies* 25 (1993): 587–605. Still others suggest that a full understanding of the Sunnī legal development awaits further research into works that may predate those of al-Shāfiʿī. For such arguments, see, e.g., Joseph Lowry, "Does Shāfiʿī have a Theory of Four Sources of Law?" *Studies in Islamic Legal Theory*, ed. Bernard G. Weiss; and Devin Stewart, "Muḥammad b. Dāwūd al-Ẓahirī's Manual of Jurisprudence: *al-wuṣūl ilā maʿrifat al-uṣūl*," *Studies in Islamic Legal Theory*, ed. Bernard G. Weiss, 99–158.

[7] On the development of the *madhhabs*, see generally Christopher Melchert, *The Formation of the Sunnī Schools of Law, 9th–10th Centuries C.E.* (Leiden: E.J. Brill, 1997).

[8] On the question of the way in which the development of the Sunnī *madhhabs* influenced the development of Shiʿite institutions, see Devin J. Stewart, *Islamic Legal Orthodoxy: Twelver Shiite Responses to the Sunnī Legal System* (Salt Lake City: University of Utah Press, 1998).

George Makdisi demonstrated, a *madhhab* functioned, at the institutional level, like a guild of Islamic jurists. A *madhhab* was not licensed by the government. Rather, it was an independent association of jurists. One generation of jurists would teach the next both the interpretive methodology and the accepted substantive doctrines of their guild.[9] Over the centuries, each Sunnī *madhhab* developed official doctrines at the level of interpretive methodology. Because official interpretive methodology required jurists to respect the precedents established over the years by the leading jurists of the guild, guilds also developed official doctrine on some questions of substantive law. Thus, the Arabic term *madhhab* came to be used to refer not only to a juristic guild, but also to the legal doctrine of that organization.[10] Because the term *madhhab* has a doctrinal as well as an institutional component, most contemporary scholars translate the term *madhhab* as 'school' rather than 'guild' of law (and others have left the term untranslated).[11] Understanding the weighty arguments against using the term 'guild,' there is still considerable utility in referring to the *madhhab* as a guild for the purposes of this book. A reader who bears in mind that the *madhhab* was rooted in a guild-like institution will be better equipped to understand the modern developments discussed at length in later chapters. In the twentieth century, political and social developments weakened the institutions of the *madhhabs* and broke their domination of teaching institutions and judicial training. This helped promote the sudden development and dissemination of radically new Sunnī legal theories.

Two important developments helped to shape the *madhhabs* and to establish their crucial role in Islamic society. First, the *madhhabs* began to develop a common approach to Islamic legal interpretation

---

[9] For seminal analyses of the structure, administration and role of the *madhhab*, see the works of George Makdisi, particularly "The Guilds of Law in Medieval Legal History: An Inquiry into the Origins of the Inns of Court," *Zeitschrift für Geschichte der Arabisch-Islamischen Wissenschaften*, 1 (1984), 233–252; "La Corporation à l'époque de l'Islam," *Présence de Louis Massignon: Hommages et témoignages* (Paris: Maisonneuve and Larose, 1987), 35–49; and *The Rise of Humanism in Classical Islam and the Christian West* (Edinburgh: University Press, 1990), 16ff.

[10] See Melchert, *The Formation*, xiv–xvi, cf. Wael Hallaq, *A History of Islamic Legal Theories* (Cambridge: Cambridge University Press, 1999), 158 and 164.

[11] For the decision to continue translating the term as "school," see, e.g., Melchert, *The Formation*, xvii. For an example of a scholar who prefers not to translate the term at all, see Sherman Jackson, *Islamic Law and the State: The Constitutional Jurisprudence of Shihāb al-Dīn al-Qarāfī* (Leiden: E.J. Brill, 1996).

and thus began together to develop a distinctive Sunnī legal tradition. Over time, jurists associated with a number of different guilds came to agree on important principles of epistemology and legal methodology, and they agreed to disagree on certain others. The jurists in these *madhhabs* were thus able to forge a distinct tradition of legal theory and interpretive methodology in which the jurists of these guilds recognized each other's methodology as permissible and accepted that their competing interpretations of God's law must be considered mutually orthodox. Second, four of the *madhhab*s gradually emerged as preeminent in the Sunnī world. By the last quarter of the fifth/eleventh-century A.H./C.E., the jurists associated with the Mālikī, Shāfiʿī, Ḥanafī, and Ḥanbalī guilds had displaced their rivals and became the only generally-recognized institutions for training and licensing jurists. In a recent monograph, Devin Stewart describes the fifth-/eleventh-century developments as follows:

> Through the formation and consolidation of the classical Sunnī juridical *madhhabs*, traditionist jurists were able to gain exclusive control over institutions of Islamic religious education and establish their collective authority for the interpretation of Islamic law. . . . [By this time], their proponents have succeeded in marginalizing or subordinating other groups claiming religious authority, such as theologians, Caliphs and *ḥadīth* experts, and have regularly attempted to prevent other religious groups perceived as heterodox from taking part in the legal system. . . . Only the opinions of scholars who belong to one of the recognized *madhhabs*, and have completed study in a curriculum defined and controlled by the jurists may be taken into account in debate on religious questions. All other opinions, whether supported by evidence or not, are considered heterodox.[12]

According to classical theory, it was the duty of the jurists in these four guilds of law to elucidate God's law as best they could for the Muslim community. Jurists thus studied the records of God's revelation to the Prophet Muhammad, and/or the precedents of legal thinkers of the past in order to develop trustworthy interpretations of God's law. The interpretation of God's law that a classical jurist developed, represented his "*fiqh*" (literally 'understanding' or 'discernment' of God's law). Since *fiqh* represented what humans knew of *sharīʿa*, the words *fiqh* and *sharīʿa* were "sometimes used synony-

[12] Stewart, *Islamic Legal Orthodoxy*, 25.

mously."[13] Nevertheless, it makes sense to keep them distinct. The *sharīʿa* represents God's ideal law. *Fiqh* represents an inherently fallible human interpretation of that law.[14]

III. *The development of competing "orthodox" interpretations of* sharīʿa

Notwithstanding the consolidation of the Sunnī guilds of law, there continued to be considerable disagreement over important questions of methodology. This meant that inevitably, jurists in different *madhhabs* came to disagree with each other on questions of substantive law as well. (That is to say, by embracing approaches to *uṣūl al-fiqh*, jurists came up with different bodies of *fiqh*.) Not only did different *madhhabs* develop different bodies of law, but even jurists within a single guild might disagree on the details of proper methodology or of substantive law. Sunnī Islamic legal theory embraced the diversity of opinion. Classical Islamic legal theory accepted axiomatically that in most cases, humans could never say with absolute certainty which of the opinions was correct. God alone was infallible, and interpretation could only be a probabilistic enterprise. Even a jurist who flawlessly used proper methodology axiomatically accepted that his version of *fiqh* might prove wrong, and a competing version might prove correct. Jurists took comfort in their belief that, all things being equal, God would not punish any Muslim for obeying, in good faith, one plausible version of *fiqh* rather than another—even if it turned out that that a Muslim's chosen version of *fiqh* turned out to be incorrect.[15]

---

[13] See Calder and Hooker, "*Sharīʿa*," 322.

[14] The discussion in this chapter insofar as it distinguishes between *sharīʿa* and *fiqh* is heavily influenced upon the discussions in Bernard G. Weiss, "Interpretation in Islamic Law," *The American Journal of Comparative Law* 26 (1976): 199–205; Bernard G. Weiss, *The Search for God's Law: Islamic Jurisprudence in the Writings of Sayf al-Din al-Āmidī* (Salt Lake City: University of Utah Press, 1992), 1–17, and 93–109. Weiss's works are informed largely by his reading of Shāfiʿī scholars such as al-Ghazālī (d. 1111) and al-Āmidī (d. 1233). For sources describing the way in which other jurists conceptualized the distinction between *fiqh* and *sharīʿa*, see, e.g., Baber Johansen's chapter, "The Muslim *Fiqh* as a Sacred Law," *Contingency in a Sacred Law: Legal and Ethical Norms in the Muslim Fiqh* (Leiden: E.J. Brill, 1999), 1–72; and Muhammad Khalid Masud, *Shāṭibī's Philosophy of Islamic Law* (Islamabad: Islamic Research Institute, 1995), 247–49.

[15] Sunnī legal theorists did, however, develop different explanations for the lack

Although there can be only one *sharīʿa*, there may be several, equally valid versions of *fiqh*. Each of the competing bodies of *fiqh* was considered a legitimate interpretation of God's law, and a person who followed one of these opinions, believing in good faith that it was the correct opinion, would be considered virtuous. The classical jurists' willingness to accept conflicting interpretations of God's law as equally orthodox was a distinctive feature of classical Sunnī Islamic legal thought. In Baber Johansen's words, the jurists' understanding of "orthodoxy" established "normative pluralism within and between schools of *fiqh*." It "thus legitimizes the co-existence of various doctrines and normative systems," and "it allows the peaceful (occasional local outbursts of violence notwithstanding) co-existence of the groups of scholars who sustain these different doctrines and normative systems. . . ."[16]

IV. *Imposing a uniform interpretation of the* sharīʿa *in an "Islamic" state*

The doctrine of mutual orthodoxy created a problem for those who wanted states to establish and apply a single, predictable body of "Islamic" state law. As a theoretical matter, Muslims were required to accept the legitimacy of different interpretations of God's law. To provide stability in a society, however, law must be predictable. If each Muslim was free always to act on his or her preferred interpretation of God's law, then chaos would result. This danger was not lost on classical Sunnī jurists, who concluded that this right to follow a preferred interpretation of Islamic law was a contingent right rather than an absolute one. All things being equal, a Muslim would be permitted to choose from several possible rules of behavior—each rooted in a different interpretation of God's law. According to the classical jurists, however, there were many cases in which all things were *not* equal. In some circumstances, governments could legitimately impose their preferred understanding of God's law as the law of the land—and thus could force their subjects to obey the

of punishment. On this point, see Weiss, *The Spirit of Islamic Law* (Athens, GA: University of Georgia Press, 1998), 116–22, particularly 120, citing al-Ghazālī, Ibn Qudāma, al-Rāzī, al-Āmidī, Ibn al-Ḥājib, and Bihārī.

[16] Johansen, "The Muslim *Fiqh* as a Sacred Law," in *Contingency*, 39.

government's interpretation in preference to their own interpretations. Jurists debated the circumstances under which a ruler could legitimately impose his will. Eventually, many later Sunnī theorists agreed that subjects were morally obliged to obey any state-imposed rule that could be characterized as "*siyāsa sharʿiyya.*" Such a rule was one that (1) did not command Muslims to sin and (2) could reasonably be expected to advance the welfare of the ruler's subjects. As will become clear, classical jurists had precise ideas about what types of rule could be said to meet these criteria.

In the following two chapters, I will describe in more detail the ways in which classical jurists developed their competing bodies of *fiqh*, their interpretations of God's law. Chapter 3 will then describe the types of law that these Islamic jurists believed should be applied by the ruler in an Islamic state.

CHAPTER TWO

DEVELOPING *FIQH*: CLASSICAL SUNNĪ METHODS OF INTERPRETING THE *SHARĪʿA*

After the rise of the *madhhabs*, the classical jurists were entrusted with the task of identifying for the Muslim community the revealed indications of God's command and of determining their implications for people who wished to act in accordance with God's law. This chapter will explore the methods that classical Sunnī jurists used to understand God's commands, as they had been revealed to humans through revelation and, according to some, through the signs of nature. They developed two approaches to legal interpretation that jurists could use to develop their understanding of God's law. *Ijtihād* was a method of reasoning out laws directly from the study of revealed texts. *Taqlīd* was a form of precedential reasoning—deriving laws based on an understanding of texts as interpreted by earlier members of a chosen guild. (Which method a jurist used depended on his qualifications.) Through these methods, each jurist developed his own *fiqh*, a body of norms representing his understanding of God's law.

I. *Classical Sunnī assumptions about authority and epistemology*

In developing their methods of Islamic legal interpretation, the classical Sunnī jurists began with some epistemological assumptions.[1] According to classical Sunnī legal theory, knowledge could be either "necessary" (*ḍarūrī*) or "acquired" (*muktasab*). Necessary knowledge "is either *a priori* or derives from sense perception,"[2] and is said to be

[1] The discussions of epistemology in this chapter rely heavily upon the following works: Aron Zysow, *The Economy of Certainty* (Ph.D. diss., Harvard University, 1984), which approaches Sunnī legal theory from an epistemological paradigm; Bernard Weiss, *The Spirit of Islamic Law* (Athens: University of Georgia Press, 1998), particularly 89–112; and Wael Hallaq in *A History of Islamic Legal Theories* (Cambridge: Cambridge University Press, 1999), particularly 36–83.

[2] Hallaq, *History*, 38.

absolutely "certain" (*qaṭʿī*). Acquired knowledge, on the other hand, is reached through a process of inference.[3] The knowledge that a qualified jurist gleaned through the process of *ijtihād* or *taqlīd* will have been built upon layers and layers of knowledge, some necessary and some acquired, and each such ruling can ultimately be placed on a scale of epistemological certainty ranging from certain (*qaṭʿī*) to "presumptively correct" or "probable" (*ẓannī*).

Rulings that are immediately understood from unambiguous language are treated as knowledge derived from sense perception rather than inference. Accordingly, one could occasionally be "certain" of knowledge gained from a text that is known to speak the truth—such as a text that contains a revelation from God.[4] In cases where texts do not speak unambiguously, however, or where rulings must be derived by analogy to a clear ruling in a revealed text, the jurists accepted that knowledge of the law could be, at best, presumptive. Thus, equally qualified jurists might reasonably come to different conclusions about God's law and, at some abstract level, no one could be absolutely certain which of the competing interpretations was correct.

II. *Using* ijtihād *to interpret the* sharīʿa

Jurists within a *madhhab* were ranked according to their interpretive ability. Different ranks of jurists were expected to use different methods of interpretation. Theoretically, only the most qualified jurists should gain their information about God's law through direct engagement with the texts that recorded God's revelation to the Prophet: the Qurʾān and the *ḥadīth* literature.[5] The process of deriving *fiqh* from direct engagement with religious texts was known as *ijtihād*, and the supremely qualified jurist who was qualified to perform this type of legal interpretation was known as a *mujtahid*.

Ijtihād was often described as a process of deriving *fiqh* from four "sources": Qurʾān, *ḥadīth* literature, consensus (*ijmāʿ*), and juristic

[3] See Zysow, *The Economy of Certainty*, 19–24.
[4] On this point, see, e.g., the discussions in Weiss, *The Spirit of Islamic Law*, 22–23; Hallaq, *History*, 42–45, 82–83, citing al-Juwaynī, Shirāzī, al-Ghazālī, and Bājī.
[5] See the discussion below.

logic (*qiyās*). While accurate, this description does not, by itself, make clear how the process works. It makes sense to discuss in some detail the way in which each "source" helped provide knowledge that was useful in understanding God's law.

A. *Finding commands in revealed texts: The Qur'ān and* ḥadīth *reports*

In the search for *fiqh*, a *mujtahid* would have to start by analyzing texts that purported to record God's revelation to the Prophet Muḥammad. *Mujtahids* started with the Qur'ān, a record of divine words revealed to Muḥammad, in part because they were certain that it represented an absolutely authentic account of God's words.[6] The indubitably accurate Qur'ānic words were not always, however, a clear source of legal guidance. For one, the text simply did not seem to address some types of behavior. It is generally agreed that there are only about 500 Qur'ānic verses with legal content, and these tend to focus more on certain types of law, such as family law, than on others.[7] There were also hermeneutical problems. When the Qur'ān addressed a certain type of behavior, it was not always easy to determine exactly what actions were being addressed and where these actions fell on the five-part moral scale described in Chapter 1. Did a passage condemning wine for its intoxicating qualities condemn wine alone or all intoxicants? And did the condemnation imply prohibition or mere disapproval? To address interpretive problems of this nature, jurists developed sophisticated hermeneutical tools. Their ultimate goal was naturally to identify Qur'ānic passages that were unambiguous and whose meaning was absolutely certain (*qaṭʿī*). Such a text was one whose "sphere of application is so delimited as

[6] This certainty was said to be established through the principle of *tawātur*. On *tawātur*, see Jeanette Wakin, "Interpretation of the Divine Command in the Jurisprudence of Muwaffaq al-Dīn Ibn Qudāma," *Islamic Law and Jurisprudence: Studies in Honor of Farhat J. Ziadeh*, ed. Nicholas Heer (Seattle: University of Washington Press, 1990), 33–52; Bernard Weiss, "Knowledge of the Past: The Theory of *Tawātur* according to al-Ghazālī," *Studia Islamica* 61 (1985): 81–105; Zysow, *The Economy of Certainty*, 11–24; Hallaq, *History*, 60ff.

[7] See, e.g., Hallaq, *History*, 3–4. S.D. Goitein suggests, however, that such a figure may underestimate the legal content of the Qur'ān because it does not take into account the fact that legal verses tend to be longer. See Goitein, "The Birth Hour of Muslim Law," *Muslim World* 50 (1960): 24.

to exclude any possibility of ambiguity,"[8] and it was referred to as a *naṣṣ* (pl. *nuṣūṣ*). Demonstrating further faith in the legal value of revealed texts, Qurʾānic language that was not absolutely unambiguous might nevertheless be sufficiently clear that an interpretation could be considered "probable" (*ẓannī*) and presumptively binding.

The Qurʾān was not the only text that contained revelation. In fact, it was not in practice the most important source of knowledge about God's law. By the time the *madhhabs* began to form, Sunnī-Muslims were coming to accept that the Prophet's example represented a model of correct behavior. They believed that the legal information found in the Qurʾān could fruitfully be supplemented by legal information found in *ḥadīth*s—reports describing events in the life of the Prophet and his companions.[9] Each *ḥadīth* report was supposedly an eyewitness account of the words or deeds of the Prophet or his companions—an account which had been reported by the witness to a listener who then passed on the report to another listener who in turn passed it on down through the generations until it was written down. Although the jurists were confident that the Qurʾān accurately recorded revelations given to the Prophet Muḥammad, they were less confident that all *ḥadīth*s represented trustworthy accounts of prophetic behavior and speech. Third-, fourth-, or fifth-hand reports about the Prophet's actions might not be trustworthy: witnesses might have been mistaken; there might have been an error in transmission; or, indeed, a report might simply have been forged by someone who wished to place his own opinion into the mouth of the Prophet.[10] Jurists thus tried to develop methods of

---

[8] Zysow, *The Economy of Certainty*, 176 n. 77, citing al-Bukhārī; al-Nasafī; Ibn Taymiyya.

[9] There is much controversy about the early history of the *ḥadīth* literature. Much of the debate centers on the conclusions presented in Joseph Schacht's *Origins of Muhammadan Jurisprudence* (Oxford: Clarendon Press, 1950). Building on the earlier work of Goldziher, Schacht argued that few, if any, *ḥadīths* could be accepted as authentic accounts of prophetic behavior. This inspired fierce reactions from Muslims championing the authenticity and accuracy of the *ḥadīth*. See, e.g., M.M. Azami, *On Schacht's Origins of Muhammadan Jurisprudence* (New York: John Wiley, 1985). Some scholars have recently begun to synthesize the competing views. For a summary of the debate and current literature, see David S. Powers, *Studies in Qur'an and Hadith* (Berkeley: University of California Press, 1986), 1ff.; Harald Motzki, "The *Muṣannaf* of ʿAbd al-Razzaq Ṣanʿānī as a Source of Authentic *Aḥādīth* of the First Century, A.H.," *Journal of Near Eastern Studies* 50 (1991): 1–21.

[10] For a summary of some early jurists' concerns about the authenticity of *ḥadīths*, see James Robson, "Ḥadīth" in EI2, vol. III, 24–25; see also Joseph Schacht, *Origins*, 36–52, particularly the quote on 37 from al-Shāfiʿī, *Ikhtilāf al-Ḥadīth*.

determining the authenticity or accuracy of a report.[11] Most of these methods involved a critique of the chain of transmitters—weeding out, for example, chains that included a known liar or a putative transmission between people who were not alive at the same time. It was understood, however, that these criteria were not foolproof. Only the tiny handful of reports that could be validated by the principle of *tawātur* were considered indubitable. The authenticity of other *ḥadīth* reports was less certain. Nevertheless, a *ḥadīth* did not have to be indubitable to be probative of God's will. Less-than-certain reports were graded according to the probability of their being authentic and accurate. Many were considered sufficiently trustworthy that they could be used with confidence for the purpose of developing law.

Even after isolating trustworthy *ḥadīth* reports, jurists faced problems understanding the law that was embedded in these texts. The problem was not acute when the *ḥadīth*s contained explicit prophetic commands. In such a case, the jurist could interpret the commands using the same hermeneutic tools that he used to interpret Qur'ānic commands. Sometimes, however, a *ḥadīth* report contained only an example of a prophetic action. In other words, it described an action which was indubitably correct, but there was no explanation for *why* it was correct. Jurists came up with several approaches to the challenge of identifying the rulings that were implicit in the accounts of prophetic behavior.[12]

As should be apparent from the discussion up to this point, a jurist looking for law in the revealed texts would have to do two things: isolate trustworthy texts; and interpret them. Based on his work, he would be more certain of some rulings than others. His certainty would depend on two factors. First, it depended on the likelihood that the text in which the ruling was found was accurate and authentic. Second, it depended on the jurist's comfort with the clarity of the words in the text. Jurists thus placed rulings derived directly from the revealed texts into four categories.[13] (1) At the

[11] On the science of *ḥadīth* criticism, see J. Robson, "Ḥadīth," 24–26; J. Robson, "al-Djarḥ wa al-Taʿdīl" in EI2, vol. II, 462; For a description of the theoretical issues involved in ḥadīth criticism as perceived by the Shāfiʿī jurist al-Āmidī, see Weiss, *The Search for God's Law* (Salt Lake City: University of Utah Press, 1992), 269–328.

[12] See, e.g., the approach of al-Āmidī described in Weiss, *The Search for God's Law*, 166–79.

[13] The following discussion draws heavily on that of Zysow in *The Economy of Certainty*, 90–91.

highest level were rulings found in texts of certain authenticity whose language was univocal. Such texts (and the rulings found therein) were said to be "certain with respect to both their authenticity and their meaning" (*qaṭʿī al-thubūt wa-'l dalāla*). Such texts left the reader with absolute certainty about what God wanted them to do. To put it differently, they provided the reader with rulings that were "absolutely certain" to be rulings of the *sharīʿa*. (2) and (3) Below these absolutely certain rulings came two subsidiary categories of rulings. The first category was comprised of rulings derived from texts whose authenticity was unquestionable, but whose meaning could not be established with absolute certainty. Such texts were said to be "certain with respect to their authenticity, but only probable with respect to their [precise] meaning" (*qaṭʿī al-thubūt wa-ẓannī al-dalāla*). Of equal value were rulings in a second category: those derived from texts that "are of probable authenticity and whose meaning is certain" (*ẓannī al-thubūt wa-qaṭʿī al-dalāla*). For instance, some *ḥadīths* were absolutely clear in their meaning, but jurists were not positive that these represented accurately what the Prophet said. (4) At the bottom of the epistemological scale came texts that were presumptive with respect to both their authenticity and [precise] meaning (*ẓannī al-thubūt wa-ẓannī al-dalāla*).

Although rulings that fit into the first category were the only ones considered to be absolutely certain, jurists believed that a ruling fitting into either category two or three would be highly likely to be a ruling of the *sharīʿa*. Thus it was considered binding unless the jurist found a more epistemologically secure ruling that contradicted it.[14] Only rulings fitting into the last category were sufficiently uncertain that they could be discounted as a guide to correct action.

[14] The jurists in all guilds except for the Ḥanafī guild consider actions mandated by a text of the first through third levels to be required (*wājib*). The jurists of the Ḥanafī *madhhab* draw a theoretical distinction between actions in the first level, on the one hand, and actions in the second and third levels on the other. They hold that actions of the first sort are absolutely obligatory (*farḍ*), and actions ordained by texts of the second and third levels are merely binding (*wājib*). However, one should not ascribe too much practical import to this distinction. The Ḥanafīs recognized that the probability of a ruling based on a text of the second and third level is sufficiently high that Muslims are absolutely required to perform such rulings. For a general discussion of the categories of *farḍ* and *wājib*, see A. Kevin Reinhardt, "'Like the Difference Between Heaven and Earth': Ḥanafī and Shāfiʿī Discussions of *Wājib* and *Farḍ*," *Studies in Islamic Legal Theory*, ed. Bernard G. Weiss (Leiden: E.J. Brill, 2002), 205–34; see also Zysow, *The Economy of Certainty*, 90–91, 110, 182–83 nn. 82 and 83.

For the purpose of this book, it is important to bear in mind that many modernist Islamic legal theories depart from classical legal theory on the question of whether Muslims are bound to accept as binding rulings that are found in revealed texts but that are less-than-certain with respect to their authenticity, meaning, or both. These modernist theories, including that of the Supreme Constitutional Court of Egypt, depart from the classical position and assert that Muslims are bound only by rulings found in revealed texts that are certain with respect to both their authenticity and meaning. In adopting this position, modernists limit the number of textual rulings that are considered binding and leave more room for utilitarian forms of reasoning.

B. *Establishing the certainty of an interpretation by juristic consensus*

In several *ḥadīth* reports, God promised to protect the Muslim community from error.[15] Most classical Sunnī jurists interpreted this to mean that the Muslim community would never agree upon a mistaken interpretation of law. Accordingly, they reasoned, whenever the entire Sunnī community reached consensus as to the correctness of a ruling, the community could know with certainty that this ruling was a ruling of the *sharīʿa*. Thus, a jurist could come up with a legal ruling that he believed probably reflected God's law. If the qualified scholars unanimously accepted this jurist's proposed ruling, then the ruling ceased to be "probable" and could instead be considered "certain." Scholarly consensus (*ijmāʿ*) thus came to be considered a third "source" of the knowledge about God's law. Consensus was not, it should be stressed, a source from which rulings were derived.[16] Rather, it was a source through which the certainty of a ruling that had already been derived could be definitively established.[17] For

[15] One version of this *ḥadīth* has a sound chain of transmission and is thus reported in several canonical collections of *ḥadīths*. See A.J. Wensinck, *Handbook of Early Muhammadan Tradition* (Leiden: E.J. Brill, 1997), 47–48. Other traditions with a less secure chain of transmission are discussed in George Hourani, "The Basis of the Authority of Consensus in Sunnīte Islam," *Studia Islamica* 21 (1964): 29–31.

[16] On the development and scholarly justifications for this theory, including the role of these *hadīths*, see Hallaq, *History*, 75–81, critiquing the earlier article by George Hourani, "The Basis of the Authority": 13–60.

[17] For discussions of the role that *ijmāʿ* played in the process of Islamic legal

example, through the mechanism of consensus, rulings that are found in revealed texts and that fit into categories two, three or four above might come to have the same epistemological weight as rulings in category one.

There were many scholarly controversies surrounding the proper method of identifying an instance of *ijmāʿ*. For example, did affirmation of a position have to be explicit or could it be inferred from the lack of open disagreement on a point?[18] One particularly crucial debate involved the question of whose agreement counted for the purposes of determining consensus. Most jurists believed that the scholars of a particular generation acted as authoritative representatives of the community, and that the consensus of the scholars of any one generation on a particular point counted as an instance of *ijmāʿ* which precluded future debate on the question. Other jurists, however, such as Ibn Taymiyya, insisted that only the consensus of the first generation of Muslims should be counted as binding *ijmāʿ*; the consensus of later scholars was persuasive, but not binding.[19] Such a position had the effect of limiting the number of laws that could be said to have been settled by *ijmāʿ*, and thus expanded the number of legal issues that remained open to divergent interpretations.

For this book, it is also important to note that Ibn Taymiyya's more restricted definition of *ijmāʿ* was embraced by modernists such as Rashīd Riḍā. (Other modernists discounted the use of *ijmāʿ* entirely.) The implications of adopting this more skeptical attitude towards

---

reasoning, see Weiss, *The Search for God's Law*, 181–258. It should be noted that some Islamic jurists proposed methods besides *ijmāʿ* by which probable laws could be rendered certain. For example, Sunnī jurists believed that inductive corroboration theoretically could serve to turn the merely probable into certain. See Wael Hallaq, "On Inductive Corroboration, Probability and Certainty in Sunnī Legal Thought," *Islamic Law and Jurisprudence: Studies in Honor of Farhat J. Ziadeh*, ed. Nicholas Heer (Seattle: University of Washington Press, 1990), 3–31; Hallaq, "Notes on the Term *Qarīna* in Islamic Legal Discourse," *Journal of the American Oriental Society* 108 (1988): 475–80.

[18] For a summary of some disputed issues, see Weiss, *The Spirit of Islamic Law*, 123–6; Hallaq, *History*, 75–6. For an exhaustive summary and analysis of a thirteenth-century Shāfiʿī jurist's description of the debated issues in a work of *uṣūl al-fiqh*, see Weiss, *The Search for God's Law*, 211–51.

[19] See the discussion in Henri Laoust, *Essai sur les doctrines sociales et politiques de Takī-d-Dīn Aḥmad b. Taimiya* (Cairo: Imprimerie de l'Institut Français d'Archéologie Orientale, 1939), 239–42, citing *Majmuʿat ul-Rasāʾil al-Kubra* 2 vols. (Cairo: al-Sharīfiyya, 1323), I: 17, 82, 266 and *Minhāj al-Sunna al-Nabawiyya fi Naqd Kalām al-Shīʿa wa-'l Qadariyya*, vol. IV, 237–38.

ijmāʿ are serious. As noted already, many modernists have departed from the classical jurists and insist that Muslims are only bound to obey rulings that are absolutely certain or are ratified by consensus. By rejecting any consensus except the consensus of the Prophet's companions, modernists such as Rashīd Riḍā limited the number of rulings that modern Muslims would be obliged to obey.

C. *Extrapolating rulings of the* sharīʿa *by analogy*

The Qurʾān, *ḥadīth* literature and records of scholarly consensus did not explicitly discuss all possible actions. Jurists often had to determine the legal status of actions that were not regulated by clear textual commands. The Sunnī jurists ultimately came to agree that, in such a case, an interpreter would have to move beyond the two scriptural "sources" of *fiqh* and use juristic logic (*qiyās*) to try to reason out the moral status of such an action.[20] Reasoning out laws by *qiyās* was the essence of the *mujtahid*'s task. While I have been using the term *ijtihād* in a broad sense to refer to the process of deriving law through direct engagement with religious texts, some jurists used the term *ijtihād* more narrowly to refer to the process of deriving laws through *qiyās*.[21]

Qiyās was generally associated with analogical reasoning.[22] A *mujtahid* using *qiyās* would begin with a ruling found in a revealed text—

---

[20] The methods by which jurists reasoned out law logically from rulings that had already been established with certainty are extremely complex and often very subtle. My understanding, which is reflected in the following pages, owes much to guided readings of Ibn Qudāma's *Rawḍat al-Nāẓir wa-Junnat al-Munāẓir* (Cairo: al-Maṭbaʿa al-Salafiyya, 1385 A.H./1965–66 C.E.) that were conducted under the late Jeanette Wakin. It also has been informed by recent works of scholarship, including Weiss, *The Search for God's Law*, 551–680; Zysow, *The Economy of Certainty*, 282–458; Malcolm Kerr, *Islamic Reform* (Berkeley: University of California Press, 1966), 66–102; and the many works by Wael Hallaq on the subject, including Hallaq, *History*, 82–115; "Notes on the Term Qarīna in Islamic Legal Discourse," *Journal of the American Oriental Society* 108 (1988): 475–80; "Non-analogical Arguments in Sunnī Juridical Qiyās," *Arabica* 36 (1989): 286–306; "Logic, Formal Arguments and Formalization of Arguments in Sunnī Jurisprudence," *Arabica* 37 (1990): 315–58.

[21] Joseph Schacht, "Ijtihād" in EI2, vol. III, 1026; Zysow, *The Economy of Certainty*, 459–60.

[22] The equation should be made with caution; as Wael Hallaq has noted, juristic *qiyās* incorporates elements of what today might be considered non-analogical reasoning. In some cases, a simplistic equation of *qiyās* with analogy may be misleading. See Hallaq, "Non-Analogical Arguments in Sunnī Juridical Qiyās," 286–306.

for example, an unequivocal Qurʾānic statement that action "x" was forbidden. He would then try to reason out the *ʿilla*, which is the *ratio legis* of the analogy, meaning it is the "attribute or characteristic of the matter under consideration that gives rise to the judgment."[23] Once a jurist had identified the *ʿilla* of the ruling forbidding "x," he could expand the ruling by analogy—saying that any action that shared this *ʿilla* was also forbidden. As Hallaq notes, then, "the analogical argument in law became, in the thought of some theologians and jurists, the archetype of all logical arguments, including syllogistics; the categorical syllogism was deemed to be both epistemologically equivalent and reducible to legal analogy."[24] *Qiyās* is thus often translated as "analogy" by both Muslim and Western commentators.[25]

In the centuries when the jurists in the *madhhabs* were first taking shape, jurists were divided over the degree to which conclusions derived through *qiyās* could be trusted. At the extremes, some asserted that reason could, in limited cases, provide knowledge of the law that was absolutely certain, while others claimed that knowledge gained by reason was so inherently untrustworthy that it should not be used at all.[26] By the time the four Sunnī guilds had established themselves as orthodox, however, a compromise had emerged. Rulings derived by *qiyās* were probative, but they would be considered presumptive rather than "certain"—unless, of course, one of these rulings was ratified by *ijmāʿ*.[27] This compromise did not end all debates about the use of logic to derive law.[28] For example, the type of

[23] Kerr, *Islamic Reform*, 67.

[24] Hallaq, *History*, 83.

[25] See, e.g., Subhi Mahmassani, *Falsafat al-Tashrī fī al-Islām*, trans. Farhat J. Ziadeh (Leiden: E.J. Brill, 1961), 77.

[26] The position that reasoning from "certain" rulings of the *sharīʿa* could, in many cases, provide "certain" knowledge of the law was most commonly associated with jurists who were sympathetic to "Muʿtazilite" theological positions. On the Muʿtazilite school of theology, see D. Gimaret, "Muʿtazila" in EI2, vol. VII, 783ff. The most famous group of jurists opposed to the use of juristic logic in developing *fiqh* were the jurists of the Ẓāhirī guild. For information about the guild and its doctrines, see Ignaz Goldziher, *The Ẓahiris: Their Doctrine and their History*, ed. and trans. Wolfgang Behn (Leiden: E.J. Brill, 1971); Joseph Schacht, "Dāwūd b. ʿAlī b. Khalaf" in EI2, vol. II, 182.

[27] On the incremental move towards compromise, see Hallaq, *History*, 31–33.

[28] Debates about the trustworthiness of logical reasoning continued to be reflected in discussions about the relative importance of rulings derived from texts *vis à vis* those derived through *qiyās*. For example, some jurists believed that opinions from texts of probable authenticity were epistemologically more certain than those derived

reasoning that a jurist could confidently use to narrow analogies and to identify the most plausible ruling was also a subject of heated debate. Given the scripturalist bias of the Sunnī jurists, there was agreement that jurists could be confident of any *ʿilla* that was explicitly mentioned in the texts or was ratified by consensus.[29] Jurists also agreed on the probative value of other formalistic methods of finding an *ʿilla*, such as "logic or language bound hermeneutic[s] favoring literalism over moral substance . . . [or] the simple parataxis of cases, based on some concrete feature or earmark in common between two cases with no concern for causative reasoning, policy, or supervening system."[30] Unfortunately, however, formalist methods of reasoning from revealed texts were often imprecise, and jurists trying to uncover rulings by analogy would come up with several plausible *ʿillas*—each leading to a different legal conclusion. For example, jurists were regularly forced to choose between a broader or narrower *ʿilla*. For example, did the command not to drink wine arise because it was an intoxicant or because it was a *liquid* intoxicant? Faced with such a choice, Sunnī jurists disagreed about which methods, if any, they should use to identify the most plausible *ʿilla*—or, as some would put it, to select between two possible rulings, each of which had been derived by a plausible analogy.

Of particular interest for the purpose of this book was the debate about whether (or how) jurists who were trying to derive a precise law by analogy could make use of information gleaned outside the religious texts. When the *madhhabs* were first forming, some prominent jurists seem to have been willing to base their legal conclusions, in part, on considerations of factors such as the custom of the community or, more important for the purposes of this book, the discernible

---

by analogy to absolutely certain rulings. Others took precisely the opposite position. See, e.g., Frank Vogel, *Islamic Law and Legal System* (Leiden: E.J. Brill, 2000), 53–55, contrasting the position of al-Juwaynī to that of the Ḥanbalī jurists, Ibn al-Qayyim and Ibn Taymiyya.

[29] For example, most jurists believed that the Qurʾān unconditionally explained that wine drinking was prohibited due to the intoxicating quality of wine. By analogy, they concluded that any other beverage that shared the quality of being an intoxicant was also forbidden. See, e.g., Ibn Rushd, *Bidāyat al-Mujtahid wa-Nihāyat al-Muqtaṣid*, 2 vols. (Beirut: Dār al-Kutub al-ʿIlmiyya, 1997), II: 15–16.

[30] Vogel, *Islamic Law and Legal System*, 53. For discussions of various methods of deriving law by analogy, see, e.g., Kerr, *Islamic Reform*, 66–79; Hallaq, *History*, 83–104, Weiss, *The Search for God's Law*, 604–05, 631–32.

patterns of nature. In their reasoning, these early jurists seem at times to be working out the legal status of an action by considering whether the consequences that such an action would be beneficial or harmful for the actors affected directly by the action or, in the alternative, for the public at large.[31] (Following some contemporary legal philosophers, I will refer to this type of reasoning as "utilitarian" reasoning).[32] Other jurists, such as al-Shāfiʿī, eponym of the Shāfiʿī guild, criticized utilitarian approaches to legal reasoning, arguing that they were inherently arbitrary.[33]

Eventually, a compromise emerged. Jurists who supported the use of utilitarian reasoning argued that such reasoning could be integrated systematically into the process of reasoning by analogy as a subsidiary but occasionally determinative factor. In other words, even if the range of possible analogical rulings would be set by formalist methods of identifying the *ʿilla*, utilitarian methods could still be used to determine finally which of the rulings that could plausibly be derived by analogy rulings was most likely to be correct. There were several ways in which utilitarian reasoning could help influence a jurist's choice of competing possible interpretations of God's law.

---

[31] See Rudi Paret, "Istiḥsān and Istiṣlāḥ," in EI2, vol. IV, 256–57; Yves Linant de Bellefonds, "Dūarūra" in EI2, vol. II, 163–64; Gideon Libson, "The Development of Custom as a Source of Law," *Islamic Law and Society* 4 (1997): 137–55 and accompanying sources.

[32] Some prefer the term "consequentialist." See John Finnis, *Natural Law and Natural Rights* (Oxford: Clarendon Press, 1980), 119–24.

[33] See Muhammad b. Idrīs al-Shāfi'ī, *Al-Risāla*, ed. Muḥammad Shākir (Cairo: Muṣṭafa Bābī al-Ḥalabī, 1940), trans. Majid Khaduri, *Treatise on the Foundations of Islamic Jurisprudence*, 2nd ed. (Cambridge: Islamic Texts Society, 1987), 70. When considering the classical Sunnī debates about utilitarian reasoning, it is important to remember always that juristic disputes about the propriety of utilitarian reasoning were not about whether God's law always served the interest of humankind. In theory, all jurists agreed that if one could determine whether the result of an action benefited or harmed those Muslims who were affected by the act, one could gauge God's attitude towards an act (and thus its moral status). Ibn Qudāma, *Rawḍat*, 87. Jurists merely disagreed about whether one could safely foresee all the results of an action or, for that matter, determine whether these actions actually benefited or harmed humans. The critics insisted that only God knew all the long-term results of an action. Furthermore, they insisted that it was hubristic for any humans to think that they could understand what truly benefited them in some larger spiritual as well as physical sense. Thus, even if humans could determine the effects of an action, only God knew for sure whether any particular result constituted a "benefit" to humans. That was, at least, the position imputed to them by later critics of utilitarian reasoning such as Ibn Qudāma. See Ibn Qudāma, *Rawḍat*, 87.

Sunnī jurists proposed a number of different methods of integrating utilitarian reasoning into the process of reasoning out rulings or of understanding how rulings should be applied to new circumstances. Before discussing these methods, it is necessary to become familiar with the conceptual framework which jurists used when describing their methods.

D. *Refining an interpretation of the* sharīʿa *by considering the "goals of the* sharīʿa"

1. *The concept of "goals of the* sharīʿa"

Classical Sunnī discussions of utilitarian reasoning generally incorporated a common conceptual framework and vocabulary. Although the origins of this framework and vocabulary are "obscure," Aron Zysow has suggested that they go back to the work of the tenth-century jurist al-Shāshī.[34] In any case, in the twelfth century C.E., the Shāfiʿī jurist al-Ghazālī drew upon this vocabulary and these concepts in an influential discussion of utilitarianism in his work *al-Mustaṣfā min ʿIlm al-Uṣūl.* Subsequent jurists often drew inspiration from Ghazālī's discussion in their own discussions of utilitarianism.[35]

According to Ghazālī, one can induce from religious texts a number of goals of the *sharīʿa* (*maqāṣid al-sharīʿa*). By goals (sing. *maqṣad*, pl. *maqāṣid*), the jurists meant the production of a result that constitutes a benefit (sing. *maṣlaḥa*, pl. *maṣāliḥ*), or it might be the prevention of a result that constitutes a harm (sing. *ḍarar*, pl. *aḍrār*). Yet how can a jurist identify benefits and harms? First, and most important, it is possible to say axiomatically that the results to which rulings of the *sharīʿa* lead are, in the aggregate, "beneficial" to the people directly affected. From this jurists conclude that a specific result to

---

[34] Zysow, *The Economy of Certainty*, 344, 435 n. 60.

[35] For al-Ghazālī's discussion of the goals of the *sharīʿa* and his understanding of the proper role for utilitarian reasoning, see Abū Ḥāmid al-Ghazālī, *al-Mustaṣfā min ʿIlm al-Uṣūl* (Baghdad: Muthannā, 1970), 2 vols, I: 284–315. For secondary sources analyzing his theory, see Muhammad Khalid Masud, *Shatibi's Philosophy of Islamic Law* (Islamabad: Islamic Research Institute, 1995), 139–42; Zysow, *The Economy of* Certainty, 334–46; Hallaq, *History*, 90; Kerr, *Islamic Reform*, 92. For a general discussion of the doctrine in the works of later jurists, see Ibn Qudāma, *Rawḍat*, 86–87; Weiss, *The Search for God's Law*, 609–13, citing Āmidī; Masud, *Shatibi's Philosophy*, 153 discussing Shāṭibī; Kerr, *Islamic Reform*, 69–70, discussing Qarāfi.

which a ruling of the *sharīʿa* will necessarily lead is a "scripturally defined" benefit. Some jurists went further, however, and suggested that a jurist could survey all the established rulings of the *sharīʿa* and, on the basis of this survey, induce a number of benefits that God generally wants humans to enjoy. A benefit that had been reasoned out through this inductive survey was called a *maṣlaḥa mursala*—which means, literally, an "independent" or "[scripturally] unregulated" benefit. A *maṣlaḥa mursala* is considered to be "independent" of the texts, because it is not the inevitable consequence of a certain law. Rather, it is known to be a benefit because jurists have reasoned out from the implications of the religious texts as a whole that it is a result favored by God.[36]

Scripturally unregulated benefits were placed into a three-part hierarchy. At the top were a handful of benefits that the texts favored so consistently and obviously that a person could know with certainty that these benefits were indispensable to human well-being, and that no law of the *sharīʿa* would ever lead to net long-term loss to them. These were the so-called necessaries (*ḍarūriyyāt*) or universals (*kulliyyāt*). Ghazālī and most subsequent jurists identified only five necessaries: religion, self, property, children, and reason. To these some later jurists added a sixth, honor (*ʿirḍ*).[37] Coming below the necessaries in the hierarchy were a second class of interests known as the "needs" (*ḥājiyyāt*). These needs were not by themselves indispensable to a proper life. Reason revealed that, by promoting the needs, a society will indirectly promote the necessaries. A final category of scripturally defined benefits/interests—the "refinements" (*taḥsīniyyāt*)—completed the scheme. The refinements did not promote the necessaries, but, for the jurists, human reason told them that these "refined" human life.[38]

---

[36] I am indebted to the late Jeanette Wakin for this description of the *maṣlaḥa mursala*.

[37] On the addition of *ʿirḍ* by some jurists, see Zysow, *The Economy of Certainty*, 343–44, and 435, n. 259.

[38] The line between the needs and refinements is hard to draw. Based on his reading of Āmidī, Weiss defines the needs as "non-universal requirements of human well being" and the refinements as "those things that enhance human well-being without being necessary to it." See Weiss, *The Search for God's Law*, 611. Not only would it seem, in theory, to be difficult to distinguish between these two, but jurists seem to have disagreed in practice. As an example of a need, Āmidī cites the benefit to be gained from having a guardian supervise the betrothal and marriage of a

Working within the conceptual framework of "the goals of the *sharī'a*," Sunnī jurists began to explore systematically the parameters of utilitarian reasoning in Islamic law. While some jurists continued to believe that considerations of the scripturally unregulated interests (and thus of public interest) were dangerously subjective, many came to accept that some forms of utilitarian reasoning could legitimately play a role in the process of interpreting God's law.[39] The champions of utilitarian reasoning came up with a number of methods, some of which differed from each other only in subtleties (or terminology), while others differed from each other on a deeper, more fundamental level.[40] For the purposes of understanding modernist legal theories, however (including the one developed by the SCC), it will be sufficient to break the methods down into a simple scheme—listing two particularly important ways which consideration of consequences could be integrated into the legal reasoning. With the caveat that jurists did not always use the same vocabulary to identify these methods, I will refer to these two methods of considering

---

minor female to a qualified suitor. "This does not rise out of unalterable or universal necessity, but it does arise out of a very real concern to assure that the suitor be properly qualified lest he prove to be unsuited as a husband after the girl comes of age." In other words, the presence of a guardian may not be necessary in any particular case, but having guardians as a general ruling serves to prevent harm to the life, property and offspring of a woman by weeding out unqualified suitors. Intriguingly, in his *Rawḍat*, Ibn Qudāma disagrees that the benefit to be gained from having a marriage guardian is protection for the woman from unsuitable marriages. He declares it to be protection for the woman from the shame of publicly seeking sexual satisfaction and considers it to be a refinement. See Ibn Qudāma, *Rawḍat*, 86–87.

[39] For a summary of some of the debates, see Zysow, *The Economy of Certainty*, 335–64; Masud, *Shāṭibī's Philosophy*, 135–64; John Makdisi "Legal Logic and Equity in Islamic Law," *American Journal of Comparative Law* 33 (1985): 63–92.

[40] Juristic discussions about utilitarian elements of legal reasoning are often difficult to follow (and to summarize) because jurists conceptualized the issues differently and/or used different terminology to describe what seem to be essentially similar methods of reasoning. For example, more or less similar utilitarian methods of reasoning might be described by some jurists as an essential part of narrowing the *'illa* and, by others, as a separate step in *qiyās* that took place after *'illa*s had been narrowed. See Zysow, *The Economy of Certainty*, 403–4; see also Hallaq, *History*, 110–11. A few jurists apparently conceived of utilitarian reasoning as a sixth "source" of law separate and apart from the process of reasoning out laws by *qiyās*. See Masud, *Shāṭibī's Philosophy*. Similar types of reasoning might also be referred to by several different names: consideration of appropriateness (*munāsaba*), consideration of necessity (*ḍarūra*), consideration of benefit (*istiṣlāḥ*) or juristic preference (*istiḥsān*) might all effectively refer to the same logical scheme. See, e.g., Zysow, *The Economy of Certainty*, particularly 335–64, 394–419; Weiss, *The Search for God's Law*, 593–680.

consequences when selecting a ruling as the following: consideration of appropriateness (*munāsaba*); and consideration of necessity (*ḍarūra*).

2. *Setting aside a ruling derived by analogy on grounds of "inappropriateness"* Many classical Sunnī jurists were willing to integrate the consideration of public interest broadly and subtly into the process of analogical reasoning, with the result that the rulings that they derived reflected, indirectly, their understanding of public interest.[41] For the sake of convenience, I will select one of the terms that jurists used to identify this type of reasoning, and will refer to it throughout this book as the method of considering the "appropriateness" (*munāsaba*) of competing interpretations of the law.[42]

The consideration of appropriateness did not play a role in every case of reasoning by analogy. The jurists distinguished between rulings that involved questions of faith or ritual and those that regulated human interactions/transactions, such as rulings governing contracts, torts, and so forth. The rulings governing faith and ritual were referred to as *ʿibādāt*. Those governing civil transactions were called *muʿāmalāt*. Consideration of appropriateness played a role only when jurists were trying to derive a ruling within the *muʿāmalāt*. To understand why, it is helpful to consider how a jurist considered appropriateness. It was accepted that every ruling of *muʿāmalāt* promoted one or more of the human interests (or prevented a harm). A *mujtahid* who had decided to use *qiyās* to derive by analogy a new ruling of *muʿāmalāt* might initially come up with several possible analogies—each leading to a slightly different ruling. The jurist then looked for the most apt analogy. Many jurists insisted that, to select between the plausible analogical rulings, the jurist must in part consider how each of the possible rulings would affect the interest of the persons directly regulated by the ruling and, to some extent, the interests of

[41] In EI2, Rudi Paret asserts that this methodology was first systematically discussed in the fifth century. Paret, "Istiḥsān and Istiṣlāḥ," 256. Zysow generally agreed with this: *The Economy of Certainty*, 340–41. Wael Hallaq, however, has recently challenged these conclusions, arguing that this type of reasoning was already being discussed in the fourth century. See Hallaq, "Considerations on the Function and Character of Sunnī Legal Theory," *Journal of the American Oriental Society* 104 (1984): 679–89; Hallaq, *History*, 132.

[42] For a taste of the bewildering variety of names, and subtle approaches to what was, for all practical purposes, *munāsaba*, see Zysow, *The Economy of Certainty*, 357–58.

the public at large. The way in which these considerations affected the choice, however, was indirect.

A jurist considering "appropriateness" would reflect closely on the law with which he was starting and from which he would draw his analogy. He would ask whether this base law promoted any cognizable benefit (*maṣlaḥa*). Having done so, he would survey the possible laws that could be derived by analogy and he would make sure that he eliminated ones that would not serve the same benefit(s) as the base law.[43] This meant that the jurist would select not the ruling that would lead to the greatest amount of benefit (a position that would be, essentially, utilitarian), but rather the ruling that he believed would lead to the same benefit as the original ruling. Although the method of considering appropriateness was apparently controversial, much of the controversy seems not to have centered on the permissibility of using some form of utilitarian reasoning in the deriving analogies. Rather, it focused on the way in which utilitarian reasoning should be performed. Thus, the Mālikī jurist Qarāfī famously said:

> It is commonly said that [consideration of] *maṣlaḥa mursala* is peculiar to us [i.e., the Mālikīs], but if you examine the other schools you will find that when they weigh the similarities and differences between two matters [for the purposes of drawing an analogy], they do not seek scriptural corroboration for the consideration on the basis of which they compare and differentiate, but rather that they are content with mere appropriateness (*munāsaba*), which is none other than *maṣlaḥa mursala*.[44]

3. *Setting aside rulings derived by textual interpretation or analogy on grounds of "necessity"*

What I have called the consideration of appropriateness represented one way in which consideration of human interests could affect a

---

[43] For an analysis of the specific approach proposed by Ghazālī, see, e.g., Hallaq, *History*, 88–90; for that described by the Shāfiʿī scholar Āmidī, see Weiss, *The Search for God's Law*, 604–28; for that of the Mālikī scholar Qarāfī, see Kerr, *Islamic Reform*, 69–70, 73–76; for that of Ibn Taymiyya, see Makdisi, "Legal Logic and Equity": 81–84.

[44] See Shihāb al-Dīn al-Qarāfī, *Sharḥ Tanqīḥ al-Fuṣūl fī al-Uṣūl* (Tunis: 1328 A.H), 346–7. The translation is from Kerr, *Islamic Reform*, 86. Note however, that I have translated "munāsaba" as "appropriateness" where Kerr translates it as "suitability." See also a similar statement in his *al-Dhakhīra* (Cairo: Al-Azhar University Press, 1961), vol. I: 122, trans. in Kerr, *Islamic Reform*, 70.

jurist's interpretation of Islamic law. As already noted, however, it only played a role after the jurist had tried to identify rulings in the revealed texts and records of binding consensus. If he found no unequivocally binding ruling in these sources, he had to try to derive further laws by analogy or some other form of *qiyās*.

Could consideration of public interest ever affect a jurist's interpretation or application of clear rulings found in revealed texts? If a jurist discovered an unambiguous Qur'ānic ruling, might he decide on the basis of public interest that, notwithstanding the clear scriptural command, it might be wrong under extraordinary circumstances to apply this ruling? Some jurists were inclined to say yes. It was clear, however, that this might be a door through which rationalism or subjectivism could enter the law. Recognizing this, jurists struggled to explore whether as a theoretical matter why they might be entitled to carve out a public interest exception to an explicit scriptural law. Those who were inclined to permit such exceptions took care to define carefully the narrow circumstances under which departures would be permitted.

Ghazālī, for example, only permitted departures from applicable scriptural rulings in cases where the jurist could be absolutely certain that applying the law would do "universal" harm to one of the necessaries.[45] According to Ghazālī, such a situation gave rise to a condition of "necessity" (*ḍarūra*) that required the otherwise-applicable ruling of the *sharīʿa* to be set aside. Ghazālī's definition of necessity was extremely narrow. To begin, as noted previously, Ghazālī believed the necessaries to consist only of the human interests in life, property, children, reason, and religion, while some later jurists added honor.[46] A law had to be certain to do "universal" harm to one or more of these specific interests. Furthermore, Ghazālī had a very narrow understanding of "universal" harm. According to him, humans are ill-equipped to evaluate the benefits and harms to which an act may lead. God alone knew all the consequences of an action and God alone could weigh one person's suffering against another's. For this reason, humans should be wary of weighing the harms imposed

[45] See, e.g., Abū Ḥāmid al-Ghazālī, *al-Mustaṣfā min ʿIlm al-Uṣūl* (Cairo: Muṣtafa Muḥammad, 1937), 284–315, particularly 286–87, 294–95. See also the translation of the second passage in Kerr, *Islamic Reform*, 94–95.

[46] On the "necessaries," see note 38 and accompanying discussion.

on some Muslims against harms imposed on others. Ghazālī insisted, for example, that passengers on a sinking ship may not disregard the prohibition against killing and throw one of their number overboard, even if they believe such an action would save the lives of the rest. Similarly, a band of starving Muslims may not draw lots and eat the loser.[47] At some point, however, the results of an action were so obviously and vastly harmful that one could be certain that the general harm outweighs the interests of any particular individual. As an example of such a situation, Ghazālī posited that an invading army of unbelievers had placed a Muslim in front of them. Advancing behind its human shield, the army would destroy an entire Muslim community (including the Muslim who is serving as their human shield). In cases like this, where necessary interests of the whole Muslim community were at stake, the harm to Muslim society would be considered "universal." Accordingly, the prohibition on killing a Muslim must be suspended on grounds of necessity.[48]

4. *A utilitarian road not taken in the classical era: Ṭūfī's utilitarian approach to interpreting the* sharīʿa

Even the jurists who championed the use of utilitarian reasoning in Islamic law remained painfully aware of the possibility that, by accident or design, utilitarian reasoning could become a door through which subjectivism entered Islamic law.[49] Thus, almost all jurists

---

47 Ghazālī, *al-Mustasfā*, 141. See also discussion about this passage in Kerr, *Islamic Reform*, 94.

48 Ghazālī, *al-Mustasfā*, 141–42. See also the analyses of this passage in Kerr, *Islamic Reform* 93–95; John Makdisi, "Hard Cases and Human Judgment in Islamic and Common Law," *Indiana International and Comparative Law Review* 1 (1991): 203–05; and Masud, *Shatibi's Philosophy*, 140–41. The passage in *al-Mustasfā* suggests that necessity can only be invoked if all people harmed by the exception would also have been harmed if the ruling had been applied. In other words, deviating from the normal ruling would only harm people who were going to be harmed anyway. (It thus integrates the idea of pareto efficiency.) How often would such a situation arise? Probably not often, but one situation in which it arises is extremely important. That is the situation in which rebellion against a strong ruler (even an unjust one) would cause harm so widespread that it would cause grievous harm to all the people that the rebellion was theoretically supposed to serve. It is thus possible that Ghazālī's discussion of necessity was important primarily because it helped define the parameters of lawful rebellion.

49 See Paret, "Istiḥsān and Istiṣlāh," 256. See also the discussion of al-Shāṭibī in Hallaq, *History*, 182–187 and accompanying notes.

considered it impermissible to use forms of reasoning that today would be considered purely utilitarian. By "utilitarian" I mean forms of reasoning through which each jurist would determine God's attitude towards an act by considering whether it comported with his own reasoned understanding of the good—an inherently subjective endeavor. According to almost all jurists, then, utilitarian reasoning should take into account only specific types of consequence. It could enter the process of interpretation through carefully circumscribed methods, such as the consideration of appropriateness or necessity.

Even so, at least one jurist, Najm al-Dīn al-Ṭūfī (d. 716 A.H./1316 C.E.), seems to have embraced an essentially utilitarian method of reasoning.[50] Placing as much store in humans' ability to reason from nature as in their ability to reason from texts,[51] Ṭūfī proposed a controversial method of determining the legal status of an act through a purely utilitarian balancing of benefit and harm.[52] If a jurist has to choose between two laws, Ṭūfī proposed that he should select the one that has "as many benefits as possible . . . or the most important one."[53] He justified this approach to legal reasoning by citing a ḥadīth in which the Prophet had allegedly said, "no harm and no retribution" (*lā ḍarar wa lā ḍirār*).[54] For any number of reasons, however, many jurists found this justification uncompelling.[55]

---

[50] On al-Ṭūfī, see Kerr, *Islamic Reform*, 98–102; Hallaq, *History*, 128–29, 150–53; W.P. Heinrichs, "al-Ṭūfī" in EI2, vol. X, 588–89. The description of al-Ṭūfī presented here draws upon these studies.

[51] "And let it not be said that the Law knows better what are man's interests and that therefore his interests can be deduced from the Law's indications. For we have established that regard for these interests is itself one of the indications of the Law, and in fact, the strongest and most specific of them. Let us then give it precedence in order to achieve these interests." Ṭūfī, *Sharḥ al-Ḥadīth al-Thānī wa Thalāthīn*, printed in Muṣṭafa Zayd, *al-Maṣlaḥa fī al-Tashrī' al-Islāmī wa Najm al-Dīn al-Ṭūfī* (Cairo: Dār al-Fikr al-'Arabī, 1953), appendix, 48, trans. in Kerr, *Islamic Reform*, 100–01.

[52] Ṭūfī, *Sharḥ al-Ḥadīth*, printed in Zayd, *al-Maṣlaḥa*, appendix, 41; trans. in Kerr, *Islamic Reform*, 99.

[53] Ṭūfī, *Sharḥ al-Ḥadīth*, printed in Zayd, *al-Maṣlaḥa*, appendix, 46; trans. in Kerr, *Islamic Reform*, 101.

[54] Kerr, *Islamic Reform*, 101, discussing and partly translating Ṭūfī, *Sharḥ al-Ḥadīth*, printed in Zayd, *al-Maṣlaḥa*, appendix, 48.

[55] This particular *ḥadīth* was not considered itself to be of absolutely certain authenticity and meaning. Recognizing this serious weakness, Ṭūfī was forced to argue that circumstantial evidence renders this ḥadīth stronger than its chain of transmitters (the *isnād*) would normally allow. See Ṭūfī, *Sharḥ al-Ḥadīth*, printed in Zayd, *al-Maṣlaḥa*, appendix, 41; cited in Kerr, *Islamic Reform*, 99; see also the discussion in Hallaq, *History*, 151.

Ṭufī's work, on its own, should probably not be taken as evidence for a strong utilitarian tradition in classical Islamic thought. Indeed, it seems to be the exception that proves the ruling that jurists generally wished to restrict utilitarian reasoning and to preclude utilitarian reasoning entirely. After the death of Ṭūfī, his theory found no champions. As Hallaq notes, the juristic rejection of Ṭūfī's proposed approach was so complete that it was consigned to "oblivion . . . for centuries, until it was rejuvenated again in the twentieth century when *maṣlaḥa* became a main axis around which legal reform revolves."[56] Whether or not his thought can be taken as anything other than an aberration in classical theory, however, Ṭūfī has had a tremendous impact on modernist Muslim legal thinkers, such as Rashīd Riḍā, and, through them, on the SCC.

E. *A distinction between universal and particular rulings of the* sharīʿa

Broadly speaking, *ijtihād*, the ideal method of deriving law, was a process of identifying rulings in the text of the Qur'ān and *ḥadīth* literature and, where necessary, supplementing them with new rulings that had been logically extrapolated from the scriptural rulings. A jurist using *ijtihād* would come up with two types of ruling: universal rulings and particular rulings. A ruling based on a scriptural command was universally applicable. That is to says, if a jurist found a situation that fell within the bounds of a precise divine command in a revealed text, then all Muslims were always obliged to obey it. A ruling derived through *qiyās*, on the other hand, will not be universally applicable. When a jurist reasoned out a ruling of *fiqh* through *qiyās*, however, he often relied on the fact that this ruling would promote the same goal as the ruling from which it was derived. Naturally, this *qiyās*-based ruling was binding only so long as it continued to serve the end that had led the jurist to select it as a ruling in the first place. The distinction between universal rulings and contingent rulings was an important one, because it influenced the way that jurists could perform the second method of interpretation (*taqlīd*) and it affected their belief that a state could develop a single enforceable law.

[56] Hallaq, *History*, 153.

III. *Using* taqlīd *to interpret the sharīʿa*

Although later jurists in the four Sunnī guilds of law spent considerable time discussing and debating *ijtihād*, they rarely used this method themselves when interpreting God's law. Instead, jurists used methods of deriving law by extrapolating from the interpretations of God's law that had already been developed by leading jurists within their guild. To put it differently, the jurists moved away from deriving law directly from the primary texts of Qurʾān and *ḥadīth* and instead began to reason from the precedents of their predecessors in the guild. The requirement that each jurist defer, in some way, to the precedents of his guild is generally referred to as a requirement that he practice *taqlīd*. The jurist whose discretion was bound by *taqlīd* was referred to as a *muqallid* vis à vis the jurist(s) whom he followed. As scholars have recently begun to stress, *muqallids* were not a homogenous group. Different *muqallids* had different levels of training, and they used a variety of methods of precedential reasoning.[57] In the interest of convenience, this discussion will subsume all these types of reasoning under the general rubric of *taqlīd*—but it will note some differences between the types of reasoning available to an advanced scholar and those available to less advanced scholars.

Because *ijtihād* was the ideal method of determining God's law, jurists had to justify their decision to abandon this method and to derive law through *taqlīd*. The guilds thus developed a legal fiction that there were no longer any "independent" *mujtahids*—that is to say, jurists sufficiently skilled in textual scholarship to derive rulings in every case through *ijtihād*.[58] As there were no more "independent"

[57] See, e.g., Sherman Jackson, *Islamic Law and the State: The Constitutional Jurisprudence of Shihāb al-Dīn al-Qarāfī* (Leiden: E.J. Brill, 1996); Sherman Jackson, "*Taqlīd*, Legal Scaffolding and the Scope of Legal Injunctions in Post-formative Theory: Muṭlaq and ʿĀmm in the Jurisprudence of Shihāb al-Dīn al-Qarāfī," *Islamic Law and Society* 4 (1996): 165–92; Brannon Wheeler, *Applying the Canon in Islam: The Authorization and Maintenance of Interpretive Reasoning in Ḥanafī Scholarship* (Albany: State University of New York Press, 1996); Wael Hallaq, *Authority, Continuity and Change in Islamic Law* (Cambridge: Cambridge University Press, 2001); Wael Hallaq, "*Takhrīj* and the Construction of Juristic Authority," in *Studies in Islamic Legal Theory*, ed. Bernard G. Weiss (Leiden: E.J. Brill, 2002): 317–336; Mohammad Fadel, *Adjudication in the Mālikī Madhhab: A Study of Legal Process in Medieval Islamic Law* (Ph.D. diss., University of Chicago, 1995), 215–36.

[58] The trend towards *taqlīd* is reflected in the biographical and legal literature by the decreasing references to *mujtahids* and the increase in references to *muqallids*. By

mujtahids capable of deriving laws directly from the text, jurists were, by necessity, forced to work from the established precedents laid down by earlier *mujtahids*.[59] Several scholars have recently studied this legal fiction, and they have tentatively proposed reasons why jurists were willing to assert, implausibly, that they could not develop law through their own *ijtihād*. First, some point out that the move to *taqlīd* helped augment the authority of the jurists as legal interpreters of the *sharīʿa* against possible competitors.[60] Others note that an insistence that law be developed through *taqlīd*, rather than *ijtihād*, made the law more evolutionary, predictable, and stable, and thus created a situation in which *fiqh* could more feasibly be applied as the law of a state.[61]

With respect to this second point, Mohammad Fadel has pointed out that the move to *taqlīd* did not eliminate debate or legal development, but instead gave legal reasoning more structure. That is to say, *taqlīd* tended to narrow the interpretive discretion of jurists. Rulers who appointed jurists trained in the *madhhabs* to serve as

---

the twelfth century, almost all members of the guilds (and thus all authoritative legal scholars) were thought to be adopting a posture of *taqlīd*—meaning that even the most qualified of them could not derive law by *ijtihād* in areas where the early *mujtahids* of the guild had already spoken. For a survey of the literature, see Wael Hallaq, "On the Origins of the Debate about the Existence of Mujtahids and Gate of Ijtihād," *Studia Islamica* 63 (1986): 129–41; Wael Hallaq, "Was the Gate of *Ijtihād* Closed?," *International Journal of Middle East Studies* 16 (1984): 3–41; Wael Hallaq, *Authority, Continuity, and Change*, 86–120. In reading these, please note that the *mujtahid* within a guild is, to some degree, in a posture of *taqlīd*. On this point, see the discussion in Jackson, *Islamic Law and the State*, 73–79.

[59] The idea that later scholars were less talented than their forbearers was certainly a legal fiction. In fact, the most qualified *muqallids* were said to be jurists who understood completely the method that their exemplars had used to derive law through *ijtihād*—meaning that theoretically they should have been able to perform *ijtihād* themselves. For a discussion of this point, see Jackson, *Islamic Law and the State*, 94–96.

[60] So long as *ijtihād* was a possibility, jurists in the four guilds could not claim that their legal interpretation had any unique authority. The doctrine of *taqlīd* solved this problem by asserting that only a handful of jurists in the past (the early stages of the four guilds) had ever been able to practice *ijtihād*. If this were true, then proper interpretation of Islamic law henceforth rested with the jurists in the *four* Sunnī *madhhabs* who alone understood the legal implications of these past jurists' doctrines. For books exploring the role of *taqlīd* in establishing juristic authority, see Wheeler, *Applying the Legal Canon*; Hallaq, *Authority, Continuity and Change*. See also Jackson, *Islamic Law and the State*, 79–83.

[61] On this point, see Fadel, *Adjudication*, particularly the discussions on 255–56, 283–84.

judges could trust them to interpret God's law in a manner similar to other jurists of their guild. If governments wished to limit judges' discretion further, they could require judges to rule based upon the preponderant opinion within their guild or upon the government's preferred version of *fiqh*. In short, Fadel argues, the development of *taqlīd* enabled the *fiqh* of the classical Sunnī jurists to become something more than an ongoing exercise in moral speculation—it permitted *fiqh* to be used as a source of unwritten state law in much the same way that the common law is a source of law in Great Britain or the United States.[62]

For many decades, both Muslim and Western scholars seemed to assume that precedential reasoning in Islam was rigid and that the move from *ijtihād* to *taqlīd* had led to a fossilization of Islamic law.[63] Over the last ten years, however, scholars have begun to study more closely the types of precedential reasoning used by *muqallid* jurists, and this body of research has made clear that reasoning in the age of *taqlīd* was quite subtle and creative.[64] As these recent studies demonstrate, the most skilled *muqallids* were expected to study the methodology of *ijtihād* and, as far as possible, to acquire the skills needed to perform *ijtihād*.[65] This is because the practice of more

[62] *Ibid.*

[63] See, e.g., Joseph Schacht, *An Introduction to Islamic Law* (Oxford: Oxford University Press, 1964), 70–71; Noel Coulson, *A History of Islamic Law* (Edinburgh: University of Edinburgh Press, 1964), 81–84. Critiques of *taqlīd* by modern Muslims are implicit in the desire of some modern scholars to revive the practice of deriving law by *ijtihād*. Explicit Muslim criticism of *taqlīd* often sounds remarkably like European criticism and may, indeed, have been influenced by it. For a sensitive discussion see Fadel, *Adjudication*, 202–05.

[64] *Muqallids* in the age of *taqlīd* were not equally restrained by the precedents of their guild. For a period, some jurists were considered to have the ability to reason by *ijtihād* in questions where the early *mujtahids* had not spoken. Such a jurist was referred to as an "affiliated *mujtahid*" (*mujtahid muntasib*) or as a "*mujtahid*" within the guild (*mujtahid fī al-madhhab*). See Hallaq, "Was the Gate of *Ijtihād* Closed?," 3–41. Over time, however, fewer and fewer jurists were recognized as being qualified to perform affiliated *ijtihād*. Thus, in cases where the great *mujtahids* of the guild had not spoken, even the greatest jurists in a *madhhab* would have to derive law by logically extrapolating from the laws that the great jurists had already laid down—much as a *mujtahid* would extrapolate upon laws that had been laid down in the Qur'ān and *ḥadīths*. Jurists who were not of the top rank were even more restricted. The lowest only issued rulings in cases where the great early *mujtahids* of the *madhhab* had settled upon a clear answer. When faced with an issue with no established answer, such jurists would have to seek guidance from the better-trained jurists who were able to extrapolate from the precedents. Idem; see also Weiss, *The Search for God's Law*, 135–36.

[65] Indeed, although later jurists did not feel themselves free to perform *ijtihād*,

sophisticated forms of *taqlīd* required jurists to understand not only what decisions the early jurists had reached, but how, at least in theory, they had reached these decisions. Such knowledge allowed later jurists in a particular *madhhab* to critique and expand upon their inherited tradition in a more sophisticated way. For example, jurists who studied the precedents left by the early *mujtahids* of the guild occasionally found inconsistent opinions on a particular legal question. Those who had studied the process of reasoning by *ijtihād* could review the competing opinions and consider for themselves which opinions represented the more convincing solution.[66] Similarly, jurists who understood the legal principles underlying earlier decisions could develop laws that seemed different from those laid down by the earlier *mujtahids*. The later jurists were able to argue that these later opinions reflected the rulings that the idealized earlier jurists would have reached if they were faced with the same question today. Consider, for example, a case in which a great *mujtahid* of the past had decided to prohibit "x." Would the later jurists of this *mujtahid's* guild continue to prohibit "x"? The answer depends on the reasons that the *mujtahid* had prohibited "x." To the extent that utilitarian reasoning had influenced a *mujtahid* when he derived the initial ruling, the *muqallids* would have to consider the consequences before applying that ruling in the future. For example, a *mujtahid* may have concluded that "x" was prohibited in part because the *mujtahid* believed that it led to results that the texts (or his own reason) told him were strongly disfavored. People's scientific knowledge might have developed, however, or circumstances might simply have changed. In either case, it might no longer be reasonable to believe that act "x" actually led to the disfavored results that had caused the *mujtahid* to prohibit "x" in the past. In such a case, the ruling could be abandoned on the grounds that the earlier *mujtahid* would himself have abandoned his earlier ruling. Thus, as Ibn al-Qayyim (d. 751 A.H./1350 C.E.) put it, a jurist deciding whether to apply past rulings of *fiqh* in the present day would have to consider whether the rulings were "universal legal rulings which do not change with the change of time

---

they continued to write ever more sophisticated works on *uṣūl al-fiqh*—books that were, for the most part, ruminations on the best methods of performing *ijtihād*.

[66] For a survey of this type of reasoning in Islamic legal literature before the nineteenth century, see Hallaq, *Authority, Continuity and Change*, 126–33.

or particular [acts of] *siyāsa* that are dependent upon [considerations of] human interests, thus being limited by time and place."[67]

In sum, precedential reasoning was sufficiently flexible that jurists who were recognized as talented were permitted to reason creatively within their *madhhab* and there was, in fact, considerable evolution in the law.[68] Indeed, substantive law in the age of *taqlīd* continued to develop in response to changing circumstances.[69]

IV. *Recapitulation: Classical methods of interpreting the* sharīʿa

Classical Sunnī jurists discussed two methods by which scholars could produce *fiqh: ijtihād* and *taqlīd.* Competence in the ideal method, *ijtihād*, was considered to have largely died out with the early jurists of the *madhhabs.* Later jurists turned increasingly to precedential forms of reasoning that I have subsumed under the title *taqlīd.* An understanding of *ijtihād* was considered essential for later jurists to fully reason out the subtleties of the law from the precedents of the early jurists. The most sophisticated jurists in the age of *taqlīd*, when they sought to derive a ruling for a new case, would study the rulings laid down in the past by eminent jurists of their own *madhhab.* They would determine why those jurists reached the decision they did and, working from this, how the earlier jurists would have ruled in the case at hand. *Taqlīd*, like *ijtihād*, allowed highly qualified jurists considerable interpretive discretion. Although each *madhhab* developed on most legal questions a preponderant interpretation of *fiqh*, which would be duly noted in *madhhab* textbooks, eminent jurists in the *madhhab* were free to challenge the preponderant view—to disregard it when giving legal advice and to try to convince the majority of jurists of their alternative position.[70] Even after the rise of *taqlīd*, there

[67] See Fadel, *Adjudication*, 65, n. 74, citing Ibn al-Qayyim al-Jawziyya, *al-Ṭuruq al-Ḥukmiyya*, ed. Muḥammad Jamīl Ghāzī (Cairo: al-Maṭbaʿat al-Madanī, 1977), 26.

[68] See the works cited in note 60.

[69] See, e.g., Baber Johansen, *The Islamic Law on Land Tax and Rent: The Peasants' Loss of Property Rights as Interpreted in the Ḥanafite Legal Literature of the Mamlūk and Ottoman Periods* (New York: Croon Helm, 1988); Baber Johansen, "Legal Literature and the Problem of Change: the Case of Land Rent," *Islam and Public Law*, ed. Chibli Mallat (London: Graham & Trotman, 1993), 29–47.

[70] For a discussion of the concept of preponderance, see Hallaq, *Authority, Continuity and Change*, 121–65; Fadel, *Adjudication*, 242–84.

were at least four different views on most legal issues—a predominant view within each *madhhab* and a number of dissenting views within that *madhhab*.

In speaking of *fiqh*, therefore, it often makes sense to refer to the *fiqh* of a particular jurist or of a group of jurists. One can, of course, speak of *fiqh* in the abstract, disassociating it from any particular jurist or guild. In such a sense, it refers to the aggregate interpretation of God's law developed over the years by the Sunnī jurists. If one uses *fiqh* in this second sense, however, one must remember that *fiqh* is not a monolithic, consistent body of norms. With respect to those few matters that are governed by rulings that are *qaṭʿī*, the *fiqh* of the jurists is fairly, if not completely, consistent. Outside of these matters, however, there were possible interpretations of the *sharīʿa*. Accordingly, *fiqh*, in this second sense, is a collection of competing, often inconsistent interpretations of God's will, each of which must in some larger sense be considered equally valid.

The presence of competing, mutually orthodox interpretations of God's law raised intriguing questions about state law. If there were a range of equally valid views concerning the rulings that God wants men to follow, could a ruler who is not trained in law select freely from among them and impose his own preferred view as law? Could a ruler distill from these competing views a single body of norms to be applied as law? The answers with which jurists came up will be the subject of the next chapter.

CHAPTER THREE

WHEN WAS A RULER'S LAW LEGITIMATE? THE CLASSICAL THEORY OF *SIYĀSA SHAR'IYYA*

Classical Sunnī legal theorists accepted that there might be at any one time a large number of competing, equally valid interpretations of God's law. This situation raised difficult questions about the way in which an Islamic ruler could legitimately establish a single body of state law. Most jurists accepted that Muslims should, if they were under compulsion, obey state law. But what if Muslims disagreed in good faith about the "Islamic" rule of behavior in a certain matter, and they could escape punishment? Jurists struggled to articulate theories that would explain when (and why) Muslims might have to defer to a ruler's law in preference to their own understanding of Islamic law.[1]

Prior to the thirteenth century, Sunnī-political thinkers developed theories asserting that the legitimacy of a law depended in some fashion upon the legitimacy of the ruler who imposed it. Certain

---

[1] Some elements of classical Islamic legal theory that might at first glance seem wholly abstract seem to have important consequences for political theory. For example, Ghazālī's doctrine of necessity states that a situation of necessity only arises when cases are "universal"—meaning as a practical matter that the doctrine only applies when the consequences of an action affect a whole society. Few actions reach this level. The doctrine is not, however, wholly abstract. One area that arguably does create a situation of necessity is rebellion against a strong ruler. Thus, Ghazālī suggested in places that the doctrine of necessity requires Muslims to obey an unjust state law whenever disobedience would cause grave harm to an entire society (as if for example, it led to a repression or war). See, for example, the discussion in Ghazālī, *al-Iqtiṣād fi al-I'tiqād* (Beirut: Dār al-Amānāt, 1969), Book IV, Chapter III. It is thus possible that Ghazālī's doctrine of necessity was not important in the *mujtahid*'s day-to-day attempt to identify the proper course of action and that its function was largely to explain the Muslim's obligation to obey rulers (even unjust rulers) whom one could not easily overthrow. To tie the duty of obedience to necessity, however, was an imperfect solution to the problem. People might disagree about whether they were under "compulsion" or about whether their rebellion would really cause grave social harm. This meant that there could be rebellion at times of political weakness. Thus, the challenge was to identify the circumstances under which Muslims would have an absolute obligation to obey their rulers' command—even if rebellion was feasible.

types of ruler had the authority to impose their understanding of God's law as the law of their realm—and their subjects would be obliged to obey this understanding of the law. Such a ruler was generally called the *imām* or *khalīfa.* The latter term has entered the English language as 'caliph,' which is the term I shall use in this book. Because a caliph had the right to delegate his authority, he could appoint jurists associated with one of the four Sunnī-guilds to serve as judges. He could also limit his appointees' discretion by instructing them to decide cases based on the appointees' own *fiqh* or the preponderant interpretation within the guild to which the appointee belongs. Laws imposed by rulers other than caliphs were of suspect legitimacy.[2]

By the late eleventh century, the shortcomings of caliphal political theories had begun to reveal themselves. It was becoming obvious that that the rulers of Muslim societies did not have (and for the foreseeable future would not have) the qualities demanded of a caliph. As a result, some jurists suggested that the legitimacy of a government should not depend on the personal qualities of the ruler who imposed it. Rather, they suggested, individual jurists could identify objective qualities that a law must have to be considered "just." In essence, this type of theory turned the assumptions of classical caliphal political theory on its head. It was not that the presence of a just ruler legitimized the law of the state. Rather, the presence of just laws legitimized the rule of a particular leader.

[2] It is beyond the scope of this book to discuss the many variations on caliphal political theory. For a survey and analysis of such theories, see, e.g., W. Madelung, "Imāma," in EI2, vol. III, 1163–69; Ann Lambton, *State and Government in Medieval Islam* (Oxford: Oxford University Press, 1991); Erwin J. Rosenthal, *Political Thought in Medieval Islam* (Cambridge: Cambridge University Press, 1958); H.A.R. Gibb, "Constitutional Organization," *Law in the Middle East*, eds. Majid Khadduri and Herbert Liebesny (Washington D.C.: The Middle East Institute, 1955); Malcolm Kerr, *Islamic Reform: The Political and Legal Theories of Muḥammad 'Abduh and Rashīd Riḍā* (Berkeley: University of California Press, 1966), 19–54. Most theorists concluded, however, that among his other qualifications, the caliph/*imām* would have to be from the family of the Prophet, must have the power to exercise *ijtihād*, and must have to be publicly recognized by a quorum of leading Muslims.

I. *The theory of* siyāsa sharʿiyya

For the purposes of this book, the most important theory articulating this position was the theory of *siyāsa sharʿiyya* (literally "statecraft in accordance with the *sharīʿa*"), which was developed by the fourteenth-century Ḥanbalī jurist Ibn Taymiyya (d. 728 A.H./1328 C.E.) and further elaborated by his pupil Ibn Qayyim al-Jawziyya (d. 751 A.H./1350 C.E.). The theory had a great impact on Ottoman legal and political theory and was the starting point for Islamic legal and political thinkers in the waning years of the empire.[3] Ultimately, many Islamic legal thinkers in twentieth-century Egypt adopted the vocabulary and conceptual framework of this theory, and they used it as the starting point for their reconceptualization of the Islamic state. As will become clear in later chapters, the decision to constitutionalize Islamic law in late twentieth-century Egypt represents a commitment to the idea that state law must be a modern analogue of *siyāsa sharʿiyya.*

Siyāsa literally means 'statecraft' or 'governance.' The promulgation of rules, the selection of rules of decision for courts and the decision to enforce a particular legal norm all fall under the rubric of *siyāsa.* A ruler's policies and governmental actions (his *siyāsa*) might naturally be based on non-Islamic considerations. *Sharʿiyya* is the adjectival form of *sharīʿa*—and describes something that is related to or consistent with the *sharīʿa.*[4] *Siyāsa sharʿiyya* thus means 'governance (including legislation and adjudication) in conformity with the *sharīʿa.*' Ibn Taymiyya and Ibn Qayyim al-Jawziyya argued that a ruler's law must always be presumed to be consistent with the *sharīʿa* and legitimate so long as the ruler had cooperated with the classical jurists in order to ensure that this law met two criteria: (1) it did not command people to sin' and (2) it advanced the public welfare.[5] Under

[3] Frank Vogel, "Siyāsa: (3) In the sense of *siyāsa sharʿiyya,*" in EI2, vol. IX, 694–696.

[4] See C.E. Bosworth, "Siyasa: (1) In the sense of statecraft, the management of affairs of state and, eventually, politics and political policy," in EI2, vol. IX, 693–94; Bernard Lewis, "Siyâsa," in *In Quest of an Islamic Humanism: Arabic and Islamic Studies in Honor of Mohamed El-Nowaihi,* ed. A.H. Green (Cairo: AUC Press, 1984); Vogel, "Siyasa: (3) In the sense of *siyāsa sharʿiyya.*" As many of these non-*fiqh* based rules appeared in the context of penal law, the term *siyāsa* came to be associated specifically with penal law in many medieval texts.

[5] See Ibn Taymiyya, *al-Siyāsa al-Sharʿiyya fī Iṣlāh al-Rāʾīwa al-Raʿiyya* (Beirut: Dār

this theory, legitimate state law could take two different forms: what I will call *qāḍī's fiqh*; and what I will call 'Islamic statutes.'

A. *The* Qāḍīs' fiqh

Under the theory of *siyāsa sharʿiyya,* a ruler can require his courts to find their rules of decision in a body of *fiqh.* (A jurist's *fiqh* will always be consistent with the universal rulings of the *sharīʿa* and will, presumably, be beneficial for society.) When a dispute arose, a Muslim's right to follow whichever version of *fiqh* he or she preferred ended. A qualified Islamic jurist who had been properly appointed as a judge (*qāḍī*) then issued a binding interpretation of God's law that resolved the dispute.[6] At this point, the parties were obliged to accept the *qāḍī*'s opinion and to conform their behavior to it—even if their preferred interpretation of *fiqh* would lead to a different result.[7] When referring to a rule of *fiqh* that has been selected and applied by a classical jurist serving as a judge and that binds the parties before the court, I will use the term "*qāḍī's fiqh.*"

A ruler could place limits on the interpretative discretion of his *qāḍī*s by demanding, for example, that they take their rules of decision from the *fiqh* developed by the jurists in one of the competing Sunnī-law guilds.[8] Rulers might even demand that they follow one

---

al Kutub al-ʿIlmiyya, 1988), 135–37. For a detailed analysis of Ibn Taymiyya's thought, see Henri Laoust, *Essai sur les doctrines sociales et politiques de Taḳī-d-dīn Aḥmad b. Taimiya* (Cairo: Imprimerie de l'Institut Français d'Archéologie Orientale, 1939), 278–318; Rosenthal, *Political Thought in Medieval Islam,* 43–61; Lambton, *State and Government,* 143–51.

[6] Classical jurists discussed in detail the question of how *qāḍī*s should be appointed and of how far the *qāḍī*s jurisdiction should extend. An analysis of their discussions is beyond the scope of this book.

[7] See, e.g., Ann I. Lambton, "Maḥkama: (3) Iran," in EI2, vol. VI, 11–12; Halil Inalcik, "Ḳānūn: (iii) Financial and Public Administration: (3) In the sense of non-religious legal prescription," in EI2, vol. IV, 559–61; Emile Tyan, *Histoire d'organization judiciare en pays d'Islam* (Leiden: E.J. Brill, 1960) vol. I, 258; Mohammad Fadel, *Adjudication in the Maliki Madhhab: A Study of Legal Process in Medieval Islamic Law* (Ph.D. diss., University of Chicago, 1995), 104–17.

[8] As noted above, in the age of *taqlīd,* each of the Sunnī guilds of law permitted its most qualified jurists to espouse his own version of guild doctrine. Nevertheless, on many disputed issues, the guild would recognize one opinion as "preponderant." Although the issue was debated, many jurists believed that a ruler could instruct jurists from a single guild to rule according to the predominant opinion of their guild.

line of thought within the guild. For example, to ensure that all jurists' understanding of their guild doctrine was consistent, the Ottomans began to appoint jurists from the Ḥanafī guild as the government's official *muftī* (an advisor on questions of Islamic law) and eventually required all *qāḍīs* to refer to this jurisconsult in legal questions.[9]

B. *"Islamic" statutes*

The doctrine of *siyāsa sharʿiyya* could be used to justify more, however, than the practice of appointing jurists to serve as *qāḍīs* applying *fiqh* as rules of decision. It could also be used to justify the promulgation and enforcement of statutes. In fact, the presence of statutory law—and of theories justifying it—existed prior to Ibn Taymiyya. As early as the eleventh century C.E., jurists such as al-Māwardī asserted that a caliph or his properly appointed political delegates could legitimately order his subjects to follow statutes applying rules that had not been developed by classical jurists applying their traditional methods of *ijtihād* or *taqlīd*. The caliph's subjects would be obliged to obey this positive law rather than juristic *fiqh*.[10] Some jurists suggested that this was permissible, only insofar as these statutes could be conceptualized as administrative regulations that clarified and supplemented rules of *fiqh*.[11] In practice, however, the line between an administrative regulation and a new law was difficult to draw. Some jurists tried to elaborate more concretely the types of statutory law that a ruler could legitimately promulgate and ask judges to apply.[12] After Ibn Taymiyya, the legitimacy of statutes could be discussed in terms of *siyāsa sharʿiyya*.

According to jurists such as Ibn Qayyim al-Jawziyya, any interpretation of God's law (his *fiqh*) necessarily included both "universal"

---

[9] See discussion of the Ottomans below.

[10] See Vogel, "Siyāsa: (3) In the sense of *siyāsa sharʿiyya*," 695, citing Māwardī, *Al-Aḥkām al-Sulṭāniyya* (Beirūt: 1410/1990), 148–70, 160, 361–63. This theory assumed, however, that the nominal head of the government enacting Islamic legislation would be a caliph.

[11] Bernard Lewis, *The Political Language of Islam* (Chicago: University of Chicago Press, 1988), 31.

[12] See Fadel, *Adjudication*, 103–04, who comments, "Whether or not we wish to consider the power to make legally binding decisions based on considerations of public welfare to be legislation or administration may be more a semantic issue than a substantive one."

rulings and "particular" rulings. "Universal" rulings were found through textual analysis of the Qur'ān or *ḥadīth* literature and rules ratified by *ijmāʿ*. They were absolutely certain to be rulings of the *sharīʿa*, and they were applicable at all times and places. "Particular" rulings, on the other hand, were to be applied only in cases where they would promote certain social results. These might be textual commands that by their very terms ordered people to act in a particular way only so long as it promoted a particular result. More commonly, these rulings had been derived by analogy in a way that took account of appropriateness. (As discussed in the last chapter, a jurist using appropriateness would conclude that an act fell in the category of "prohibited" only if both (a) the ruling seemed to be analogous to another act that was forbidden *and* (b) prohibiting this act would advance the same divinely favored social benefits as the prohibition from which it was derived.) In either case, the ruling was applicable only when certain beneficial results would be achieved. The command or prohibition would cease to apply in cases where it would not serve the relevant social benefits.

Often *fiqh* (the product of juristic examination of revealed texts) is contrasted with *siyāsa* (the product of the ruler's policy-oriented rule-making.) Ibn Qayyim al-Jawziyya, however, suggested that the particular rulings of *fiqh* could be conceptualized as "particular [acts of] *siyāsa* that are dependent upon [considerations of] welfare, thus being limited by time and place."[13] In so doing, he was saying that the particular rulings are the product of human attempts to understand what actions would best promote a divinely favored end. By referring to these rules as *siyāsa*, he seemed also to imply that the development of particular rules required the political and social knowledge possessed by rulers. Only trained Islamic jurists could identify the universal legal rules and the goals of the law. Once these universal rules and goals of the law were identified, however, the process of reasoning out which new rules would advance the aggregate public welfare necessarily involved policy judgments that fell within the province of *siyāsa*. Once jurists had determined what acts were sinful and what social benefits certain types of behavior (such as mar-

[13] Ibn Qayyim al-Jawziyya, *Al-Ṭuruq al-Ḥukmiyya fī al-Siyāsa al-Sharʿiyya* ed. Muḥammad Jamīl Ghāzī (Cairo: Maṭbaʿa al-Madanī, 1977), 26 as cited and translated in Fadel, *Adjudication*, 83.

riage) were supposed to promote, an experienced ruler would be competent to determine which of the permissible laws was most likely to lead to the appropriate results. As a practical matter, then, the theory of *siyāsa sharʿiyya* justified the idea that a ruler, within bounds set by the jurists, could enact and enforce statutory rules and to order judges to apply these rules instead of rules of *fiqh*.[14]

Writing in the 1960s, historians such as Joseph Schacht and Noel Coulson characterized the theory of *siyāsa sharʿiyya* as a capitulation by the jurists. It was, they suggested, an admission by the jurists that their incrementally evolving interpretation of God's law could not practically be applied as state law in a rapidly changing world.[15] More recently, scholars have begun to challenge this reading. Frank Vogel, for example, has suggested that the doctrine of *siyāsa sharʿiyya* was intellectually coherent as well as pragmatic:

> By this doctrine, Ibn Taymiyya advances both a more expansive vision for *fiqh* (among other things, embracing disputed doctrines by which *fiqh* draws on utility) . . . and also a constitutional theory by which the excesses of rulers may be curtailed and *Sharīʿa* legitimacy extended to actual states. In effect, his doctrine offers rulers *Sharīʿa* legitimation in return for a greater share of power for *ʿulamāʾ*;[16] it offers *ʿulamāʾ* greater *Sharīʿa* efficacy at the cost of their being implicated further in affairs of state.[17]

From this perspective, the jurists' acceptance of statutes constituting *siyāsa sharʿiyya* changed the role that juristic *fiqh* played in shaping state law. Although *fiqh* would no longer be the sole source of positive legal norms in an Islamic state, it remained a crucial source of negative restrictions on the state's legislative power. The ruler could only

[14] It is important to emphasize that neither Ibn Taymiyya, Ibn al-Qayyim, nor other proponents of *siyāsa sharʿiyya* thought that rulers should invariably apply statutes rather than *qāḍī's fiqh*. They merely accepted that the law of the legitimate Islamic state did not have to be *qāḍī's fiqh*.

[15] See, e.g., Joseph Schacht, *An Introduction to Islamic Law* (Oxford: Clarendon Press, 1964), 53–54; Noel Coulson, *A History of Islamic Law* (Edinburgh: Edinburgh University Press, 1964) 132–34; Noel Coulson, "The State and the Individual in Islamic Law," *The Traditional Near East*, ed. J. Stewart Robinson (Englewood, N.J.: Prentice Hall, 1966), 123–25. See also Jorgen S. Nielson, "Maẓālim and Dār al-ʿAdl under the Early Mamluks," *The Muslim World*, 66.2 (1976): 123. For a critique of these views, see Fadel, *Adjudication*, 61–65.

[16] The term *ʿulamāʾ* here being used to refer to the classical jurists.

[17] Vogel, "Siyāsa: (3) In the sense of *siyāsa sharʿiyya*," 695.

legislate within the limits set by (1) the precepts and principles that the jurists had identified as universally applicable and (2) the requirement that laws advanced the social benefits that the jurists had recognized as goals of the *sharīʿa.* In this way, the doctrine of *siyāsa sharʿiyya* was able to establish an Islamic "rule of law" that helped legitimate the Ottoman Empire, one of the most stable of the later Muslim empires.[18] Later, the doctrine fascinated Egyptian modernist Islamic legal and political thinkers—many of whom tried to re-imagine the theory in a modern form.

II. Siyāsa sharʿiyya *in the Ottoman empire*

Although the theory of *siyāsa sharʿiyya* did not sweep away entirely alternative political theories or alternative views of Islamic legislation, the theory is crucial to this book because of its impact on Ottoman legal and political theory.[19] Prior to the Ottomans, Sunnī regimes in the Mediterranean Middle East often established judicial systems with at least two types of courts: (1) *qāḍī* courts presided over by Sunnī jurists (*qāḍīs*) who were appointed to rule on the basis of *fiqh*; and (2) courts staffed by non-jurists who were appointed to rule on the basis of the king's edicts (*siyāsa*).[20] The Ottomans, however, were deeply concerned with questions of Islamic legitimacy and made a concerted effort to assert the legitimacy of their law in terms that drew heavily on the idea of *siyāsa sharʿiyya.*[21] This led them to develop a distinctive system of law-making and judicial administration.

The Ottoman courts of general jurisdiction were staffed by trained Islamic jurists. These *qāḍīs* were instructed to decide some types of case, on the basis of governmental edicts that laid down rules for

[18] My thanks to Bernard Weiss for suggesting that the provocative idea that the concept of *siyāsa sharʿiyya* might be seen as an analogue of the modern Western notion of the "rule of law."

[19] Vogel, "Siyāsa: (3) In the sense of *siyāsa sharʿiyya*," 695, 696. For examples of alternate approaches presented by fourteenth-century thinkers, see Ibn Khaldūn, *The Muqaddima*, ed. and trans. by Franz Rosenthal, 3 vols. (New York: Pantheon Books, 1958), particularly vol. 1. See also the description of Ibn Khaldūn's thought in Lambton, *State and Government*, 152–77, and the description of Ibn Farhūn's thought in Fadel, *Adjudication*, 84–89.

[20] See Schacht, "Maḥkama; (1) General," in EI2, vol. VI, 1–3.

[21] Inalcik, "State and Ideology under Sultan Suleyman I," 70.

that particular type of case. In all other cases, the rules of decision were to come from *fiqh*. To ensure that their imperial edicts (*qānūns*) could plausibly be characterized as *siyāsa sharʿiyya*, the Sultan appointed a jurist from the Ḥanafī guild to serve in a post known as the *Shaykh al-Islām*. His role was to be chief *muftī* to the imperial government.[22] Before any important or controversial undertaking, including the issuance of empire-wide *qānūn* law, "a Sultan would seek a *fatwā* [an advisory legal opinion given by a *muftī*] from the Mufti to legitimize his action."[23] Local officials had their own local Islamic jurists who could advise on issues of local concern. As a result of these steps, Ottoman statutes came increasingly to incorporate principles of *fiqh*, as understood by leading Ḥanafī jurists.[24] Ultimately, Ottoman officials, clearly vested in a vision of state edicts as *siyāsa sharʿiyya*, asserted that the imperial *qānūns* could not be conceptually differentiated from *fiqh*.[25]

---

[22] See R.W. Bulliet, "The Shaikh al-Islam and the Evolution of Islamic Society," *Studia Islamica* 35 (1971): 53–67; R.W. Bulliet, "Shaykh al-Islām: (2) In the Ottoman Empire," in EI2, vol. IX, 399–400.

[23] Colin Imber, *Ebu's Suʿud: The Islamic Legal Tradition* (Stanford: Stanford University Press, 1997), 7.

[24] In some cases, statutes seem to have been carefully drafted to be consistent with the *fiqh* tradition. Ottoman *qānūns* from the seventeenth and eighteenth centuries C.E. often codify contemporary generally accepted rules of Ḥanafī *fiqh*. Imber identifies petitions where the *Shaykh al-Islām* asks the Sultan to issue a regulation instructing judges to adopt one of a number of competing positions on a question of law. See, e.g., petitions "H" and "D," cited and trans. in Imber, *Ebu's Suʿud*, 262–63. In other cases, *qānūn*s lay down laws that have not been addressed by the existing *fiqh* tradition, but which are clearly based on principles adduced therein. See, e.g., petition "H," trans. in Imber, *Ebu's Suʿud*, 107–8. Gerber thus asserts that *qānūn*s, such as the penal *qānūn* of Sulayman I, are essentially digests of the existing *fiqh* tradition combined with laws that expand upon the tradition. See Haim Gerber, *State, Society and Law in Islam: Ottoman Society in Comparative Perspective* (Albany: State University of New York Press, 1994), 60–66. In others, cases, edicts were accompanied by elaborate, occasionally casuistic, justifications penned by leading jurists—designed to show that the law at issue was consistent with essential principles of *fiqh* and necessary to serve the goals of the *sharīʿa*. The work of Abū al-Suʿūd, in this area has received the bulk of scholarly analysis. See, e.g., Imber, *Ebu's Suʿud*, 115–37, 145–46; Gerber, *State, Society and Law in Islam*, 100–10; John Mandeville, "Usurious Piety: The Cash Waqf Controversy in the Ottoman Empire," *International Journal of Middle East Studies* 10 (1979): 289–308. The process of harmonizing Ottoman law with Ḥanafī jurists' evolving understanding of God's law continued over several generations, but Ottoman jurists ultimately claimed that they had "succeeded in bringing the *ḳānūn*, the administrative law of the Ottoman Empire, into agreement with the *Sharīʿa*—the sacred law of Islam." Joseph Schacht, "Abu'l Suʿūd," in EI2, vol. I, 152; see also Y. Linant de Bellefonds, "Ḳānūn: (i) law," in EI2, vol. IV, 556–57, cf. Imber, *Ebu's Suʿud*, p. x.

[25] See Uriel Heyd, *Studies in Old Ottoman Criminal Law*, ed. V.L. Menage (Oxford: Clarendon Press, 1973), 150.

Recently, some historians have challenged the claim that the Ottomans harmonized their state law with Ḥanafī *fiqh*.[26] In evaluating these claims, one should ask whether these historians implicitly reflect the view of scholars like Schacht who thought that jurists in a posture of *taqlīd* (which would mean nearly all Ottoman jurists) were theoretically required to follow rigidly the rulings of the great early jurists of their guild. This is not a view to which all later Muslims subscribed. As noted in the previous chapter, Muslim jurists in the age of *taqlīd* seem to have had a more dynamic and flexible understanding of precedent than was once thought to be the case. From at least the time of Ibn Taymiyya, many Sunnī jurists saw the established *fiqh* of their guilds as a bodies of law that obeyed certain essential and universally applicable precepts and principles of Islamic law. Many of the rules that had been derived by analogy were contingent, and they must be applied differently in different settings in order to meet social needs.[27] This explains why, notwithstanding the fact that the law applied in the Ottoman courts often differed from the law that was recorded in the oldest *fiqh* manuals, jurists (even those who were not serving as official legal advisors or judges) seemed to accept the Ottomans' claim that their law was consistent with *fiqh* and thus legitimate.[28] As Thomas Naff notes,

> The most distinguishing mark of Ottoman society emerging from the vast flux of Ottoman history is its profoundly religious core, which shaped attitudes and was the personal activating principle for the

[26] See, e.g., Imber, *Ebu's Suʿud*, 270–71.

[27] For evidence that Ottoman jurists shared this more flexible view, see, e.g., Baber Johansen, *The Islamic Law on Land Tax and Rent: The Peasants' Loss of Property Rights as Interpreted in the Ḥanafite Legal Literature of the Mamlūk and Ottoman Periods* (New York: Croon Helm, 1988); Baber Johansen, "Legal Literature and the Problem of Change: the Case of Land Rent," *Islam and Public Law*, ed. Chibli Mallat (London: Graham & Trotman, 1993), 29–47. Sunnī jurists seem to have accepted that Ottoman *qānūns* were consistent with evolving interpretations of *fiqh*. Many leading jurists were willing to serve in judicial posts that required them to apply, in many cases, a rule set forth in the *qānūns* rather than the rule that they might on their own have derived through their own *ijtihād* or *taqlīd*.

[28] Sunnī-jurists serving as private jurisconsults were not shy about criticizing Ottoman law or governmental policy when they felt it was unjust or inconsistent with the *sharīʿa*. In his study of two leading Ottoman jurists, for example, Gerber shows that both were perfectly willing to criticize Ottoman actions and regulations in their *fatwās* as contrary to Islamic law; he also finds that they seem to have accepted most Ottoman laws as consistent with Islamic law. Haim Gerber, *Islamic Law and Culture: 1600–1840* (Leiden: E.J. Brill, 1999), 58–60.

> Muslim citizen and his rulers. . . . Islam provided the Ottoman ruling house with two essentials for authority and stability without which its longevity and success would have been impossible: a moral link with its Muslim subjects and legitimacy for the government. The remarkable consistency with which Ottoman governments espoused and maintained a traditional order of Islamic society, reaffirmed and interpreted by each succeeding generation of religious authorities, and the extraordinary degree to which the civil laws of Islam infused its political fabric attest to the fundamental Muslim character of the Ottoman state.[29]

In a study of an influential Ottoman jurist, Haim Gerber agrees with this assessment. He concludes "there is hardly any doubt that the level of legitimacy of the Ottoman government, either in the eyes of most jurists or of the populace at large, was far reaching."[30]

By the time the Ottomans conquered Egypt, they were asserting their legitimacy in part upon the claim that the law applied in their courts was "Islamic" insofar as it was *siyāsa sharʿiyya.* Thus, after the conquest of Egypt in 1517, they reorganized the Egyptian legal system.[31] As in other parts of the Ottoman Empire, the new courts of general jurisdiction were staffed by Islamic jurists, and the law applied in these courts was either *qāḍīs' fiqh* or statutory law that had been examined and approved by jurists serving as official legal advisers.[32]

---

[29] Thomas Naff, "The Linkage of History and Reform in Islam: an Ottoman Model," *In Quest of an Islamic Humanism: Arabic and Islamic Studies in Memory of Mohamed el-Nowaihi,* ed. A.H. Green (Cairo: American University in Cairo Press, 1984), 123.

[30] Gerber, *Islamic Law and Culture: 1600–1840,* 49. As Baber Johansen recently noted, "the historical research of the last twenty-five years has amply confirmed the fact that the *fiqh* cannot be understood unless one takes into account the fact that it is the main normative reference for the judiciary systems of the Muslim world until the nineteenth century." Baber Johansen, "The Muslim *Fiqh* as a Sacred Law" in Baber Johansen, *Contingency in a Sacred Law: Legal and Ethical Norms in the Muslim* Fiqh (Leiden: E.J. Brill, 1998), 61.

[31] For details of the Ottoman reforms, see Galal H. El-Nahall, *The Judicial Administration of Ottoman Egypt in the Seventeenth Century* (Minneapolis: Biblioteca Islamica, 1979), 7–9.

[32] As El-Nahall has noted, "The courts of Ottoman Egypt made that 'ideal doctrine for an ideal society,' the Shariʿah, a vital part of every citizen's life. The Shariʿah provided a solid theoretical foundation for the practical application of law to legal problems. And because the Shariʿah regulated so many areas of men's relations to each other, the courts were deeply involved in the day to day life of everyday Egyptians. . . . The Shariʿah was not the only law applied in Ottoman Egypt, but it was central, and the existence of different philosophical approaches to the Shariʿah gave the qadis some options in applying the law flexibly to the peculiar needs of particular cases. The *qānūns* of the sultan which were also applied in the

This system remained in place until the second half of the nineteenth century, and it deeply affected the expectations that Egyptians had with respect to state law. Though the Sultans' control over their provinces, particularly the province of Egypt, was not always firm, the behavior of those who challenged the authority of the central government was apparently shaped by the Ottomans' commitment to a legal theory that equated legitimate state law with *siyāsa sharʿiyya.* When, in the nineteenth century, Egyptian rulers began to seek autonomy, they were initially committed to governing in a manner that could be characterized as legitimate in traditional Ottoman terms. Social, intellectual, and political developments in modern Egypt ultimately led people to rethink some of the epistemological axioms that underlay classical Islamic legal theory. Even then, however, many Egyptians remained wedded to a reconceptualized notion of *siyāsa sharʿiyya.* As a result, many modern Egyptian Islamic thinkers proposed a number of new methods of identifying the universally applicable rules and goals of the *sharīʿa*, and they asserted that state law would be legitimate only so long as it (1) did not violate any of the rulings that their new methods established as universally applicable and (2) advanced the aggregate enjoyment of the benefits that they, using their new methods, determined to be goals of the *sharīʿa.*

Ottoman Egyptian courts, similarly grew from the Shariʿah, but expanded upon it, as in the extension of the interest ceiling to 10%." El-Nahall, *The Judicial Administration of Ottoman Egypt*, 72.

CHAPTER FOUR

POLITICAL, SOCIAL, AND INTELLECTUAL DEVELOPMENTS IN NINETEENTH-CENTURY EGYPT

As discussed in the previous three chapters, Islamic thinkers in the classical era reached consensus on some important points about theology, epistemology and hermeneutics. Working from these, they reached consensus about legal authority—about who could interpret the revealed texts and legal tradition in order to develop an interpretation of the *sharīʿa*. These authoritative jurists in turn developed a common approach to Islamic legal interpretation. Many came to embrace the theory of *siyāsa sharʿiyya*, which held that a state could legitimately impose laws that were consistent with (1) the universally applicable rulings of classical Islamic law and (2) the "goals" of the *sharīʿa*. The classical consensus on questions of legal interpretation and the broad acceptance of the doctrine of *siyāsa sharʿiyya* allowed the Ottoman government (and the provincial government of Egypt) effectively to establish its legitimacy.

As the following chapters will describe, the classical consensus on questions of Islamic legal theory and political legitimacy began to break down in the nineteenth century. In Egypt, some "secularist" thinkers began to question whether the legitimacy of state law depended upon its consistency with Islamic law. Many continued to believe that state law *should* be consistent with the universally applicable rulings and goals of Islamic law. However, they questioned the traditional methods of identifying these rulings and goals and proposed a number of modern alternatives. This chapter outlines some social, cultural and intellectual developments that led Egyptians to question old assumptions about Islamic legal theory—leading some to embrace secularism and others to embrace modernist Islam. Subsequent chapters will discuss some of the most important new theories of Islamic law and will describe how different Islamist political factions embraced different Islamic legal theories. With this background, Part II will describe the challenges facing the government of Egypt as it tried to establish a new, consensus theory of Islamic law that could legitimize the law of modern Egypt, and will explore the judiciary's approach to meeting these challenges in the course of its Article 2 jurisprudence.

I. *Social and political developments in nineteenth-century Egypt*

To understand the development of secularism and of Islamic modernism in nineteenth-century Egypt, it helps to consider several developments. First, in the nineteenth and twentieth centuries, an independent Egyptian nation-state emerged, and this new nation had to develop a legal system and establish its legitimacy. Second, as Egypt gradually established its new legal system, its government tried to adopt policies that had proved effective in modernizing European states. Third, among these was the ideal of legal positivization—meaning that courts were required to find their rules of decision not in unwritten bodies of law, but rather in codes of statutory law. Finally, as Egypt moved towards independence and positivized its legal system, the Sunnī legal guilds, which had long enforced the boundaries of Islamic legal orthodoxy, began to decline. Thus, as Egypt began to codify a new body of Egyptian law, Egyptians found themselves free to study, teach and promote untraditional, arguably unorthodox ideas about the relationship of state law to the *sharīʿa*, and those who were interested in maintaining a close linkage between *sharīʿa* norms and state law were able to explore radical new ideas about Islamic legal interpretation. Together these developments had profound effects on Egyptian attitudes towards law and governance. They led some Egyptians to embrace secularism—the ideas that state law did not have to comply with the classical doctrine of *siyāsa sharʿiyya*. They also led Islamists to develop new methods of identifying the rulings and goals of the *sharīʿa*. Many of these Islamists reimagined the classical doctrine of *siyāsa sharʿiyya*, arguing that the state must apply a code of law that was drafted in accordance with some re-imagined modern version of *siyāsa sharʿiyya*.

A. *The emergence of independent Egypt*

From the sixteenth until the nineteenth century, Egypt remained part of the Ottoman Empire.[1] Over the course of the nineteenth century,

[1] Though Egyptian military figures would occasionally rebel against the Ottoman

however, Egypt began to drift out of the Ottoman political orbit. Egypt's path to independence began in 1798, when Napoleon invaded and briefly occupied the Ottoman province. After Napoleon's departure and the restoration of Ottoman rule in 1802, the ambitious new governor, Muḥammad ʿAlī, had no intention of being a subservient Ottoman vassal. He began to centralize Egyptian governmental administration, reform the economy, strengthen the local Egyptian military, and turn Egypt into a regional power, with the goal of achieving autonomy and/or independence from the Ottoman empire. After the Ottoman emperor granted Muḥammad ʿAlī the right to appoint his children as his successors, his descendants pursued further reform and sought further concessions from the Ottoman Sultans. Eventually, they ruled semi-autonomously with the title of Khedive (Vice-Regent).[2]

In the last quarter of the nineteenth century, Khedival Egypt achieved a more decisive break with the Ottoman Empire—though not in the manner that its rulers wanted. In the late nineteenth century, the Egyptian Khedive fell deeply into debt. Although Egypt remained part of the Ottoman Empire, European governments began seriously to meddle in Egyptian affairs. In 1882, the British, claiming, disingenuously, to act with the best interests of the Ottoman Sultan in mind, invaded the quasi-independent state of Egypt. For the greater part of the next forty years, Egypt remained *de jure* a part of the Ottoman Empire. It was, however, a *de facto* British colony. In 1922, after the rise of a vigorous nationalist movement and the collapse of the Ottoman Empire, Egypt finally emerged as an independent nation state.[3]

Sultan, Ottoman political philosophy seems not to have been questioned. For a history of some of these rebellions, see Afaf Lutfi al-Sayyid Marsot, *A Short History of Modern Egypt* (Cambridge: Cambridge University Press, 1985), 40–53. Nevertheless, Egypt remained formally a part of the Empire and was administered by leaders who were steeped in the Ottoman traditions of government. For an analysis of the ruling elites of the early nineteenth century, see Juan R.I. Cole, *Colonialism and Revolution in the Middle East: Social and Cultural Origins of Egypt's ʿUrabi Movement* (Princeton, Princeton University Press, 1993).

[2] For the career and policies of Muḥammad ʿAlī, see Afaf Lutfi al-Sayyid Marsot, *Egypt in the Reign of Muhammad ʿAli* (Cambridge: Cambridge University Press, 1984); Khaled Fahmy, *All the Pasha's Men: Mehmed Ali, His Army and the Making of Modern Egypt* (Cambridge: Cambridge University Press, 1997); and F. Robert Hunter, *Egypt under the Khedives 1805–1879: From Household Government to Modern Bureaucracy* (Pittsburgh: University of Pittsburgh Press, 1984), 9–33.

[3] For the reigns of Muḥammad ʿAlī's descendants. See generally P.J. Vatikiotis, *The History of Modern Egypt*, 4th ed. (Baltimore: Johns Hopkins University Press, 1991), 70–178; Hunter, *Egypt under the Khedives*, 35–178.

B. *The study of European models of governance*

Muḥammad ʿAlī's reforms not only led to Egyptian independence, but they changed the way that Egyptians thought about the nature of legitimate law and government. As part of his attempt to reform Egypt, Muḥammad ʿAlī encouraged the study of European nations—many of which seemed to provide a useful model for effective top-down political, legal and social reform. He sent Egyptians to observe European governments and societies, and sponsored a movement to translate European texts.[4] Shortly thereafter, he imposed major reforms of the administration, legal system, economy, and educational system. The program of Europeanization had unintended consequences. Muḥammad ʿAlī seemed to have accepted traditional Ottoman ideas about legitimacy, and he and his advisors initially tried to justify his reforms in traditional terms as *siyāsa sharʿiyya.* Yet the study of Europe and the experience of modernity led later generations to rethink classical assumptions about governance.

By the end of the nineteenth century, Egypt enacted codes of law borrowed from Europe, which could not easily be justified as *siyāsa sharʿiyya.* More intriguing still, by the early twentieth century, Egyptians who wished to scrap these "European" codes in favor of "Islamic codes" had ceased to call uniformly for the introduction of codes consistent with the classical doctrine of *siyāsa sharʿiyya.* Rather, they were calling for the adoption of codes that were Islamic according to new, distinctly unclassical theories of Islamic law. The history of twentieth-century politics would thus be marked by struggle between secularism, neo-traditional Islamism and several different modernist visions of Islamism.

[4] After the First World War, the Ottoman Empire collapsed, and the British naturally found it impossible to keep up the pretense that they were ruling Egypt with Ottoman permission. Other European powers, however, pressured Britain not to annex Egypt into its colonial empire. As a result, in 1922 the British government unilaterally declared Egypt a sovereign state. For an overview of the events leading up to Britain's grant of independence, see Vatikiotis, *History*, 252–272. In discussing "independence," it is important to note that Britain worked hard to shape the new Egyptian national government, and the British (and some other foreign powers) retained significant, intrusive privileges in matters of Egyptian foreign policy and in matters involving the legal treatment of foreigners. The Egyptian government gained full sovereignty only after the Second World War.

C. *The embrace of legal positivism*

As Egyptians began to think about the type of law that should govern them, one sees remarkable consensus that the legal system should be positivized. That is to say, Egyptians began to agree that state courts should not draw rules of decision from unwritten bodies of law, but should, instead, draw it from statutes that had been published in codes.

The embrace of positivism seems to be a direct result of Muḥammad ʿAlī's attempt to identify and import useful continental European approaches to government. The classical doctrine of *siyāsa sharʿiyya* permitted a state to apply in its courts either judge-made law (in the form of *qāḍī fiqh*) or statutory law (in the form of Islamic legislation). Historically, most governments in the Muslim Mediterranean had applied both types of law. In the nineteenth century, however, many continental European states embraced a very different model of law in which courts employed only statutory law.[5] When resolving a case, judges in civil law countries, such as France, looked to codes of law which would ideally contain a definitive answer to every legal question. Appellate courts were established to ensure that courts provided consistent interpretation. In such a system, the task of creative judicial "interpretation" was, at least theoretically, kept to a minimum, meaning that the government's statutes would be applied consistently. One scholar has described the nineteenth-century conception of a civil law judge as follows:

> The judge becomes a kind of expert clerk. He is presented with a fact situation to which a ready legislative response will be readily found in all except the extraordinary case. His function is merely to find the right legislative provision, couple it with the fact situation, and bless the solution that is more or less automatically produced from the

[5] For a history of Arab contact with Europeans, see Bernard Lewis, *The Muslim Discovery of Europe* (New York: W.W. Norton, 1982). For a discussion of the political events that led to this contact and some of the social and intellectual developments that resulted, see Albert Hourani, *A History of the Arab Peoples* (London: Faber & Faber, 1991), 253–315. See also Ibrahim Abu Lughod, *The Arab Rediscovery of Europe* (Princeton: Princeton University Press, 1963); Albert Hourani, *Arabic Thought in the Liberal Age* (Oxford: Oxford University Press, 1970), 51–54, 69–72. By the early nineteenth century, students in Muḥammad ʿAlī's secular schools were taught first in Italian, and then in French, and in 1816 one could already find works by Voltaire, Rousseau, and Montesquieu in the libraries of these schools. See Hourani, *Arabic Thought in the Liberal Age*, 54.

> union.... The net image is of the judge as an operator of a machine designed and built by legislators.[6]

The experience of some nineteenth-century European nation states suggested that embracing this ideal could increase the efficiency of government and improve its ability quickly to impose top-down reform on a society. Thus, many Egyptians (and many others in the Ottoman empire as well) came to believe that if a state was effectively to govern, it must eliminate the uncertainty and inefficiency that allegedly arose when judges decided legal disputes on the basis of their own interpretation of unwritten jurists' law.[7]

The move towards codified law promised seriously to alter the role that Islamic jurists played in Egypt.[8] In the traditional Ottoman system, some areas of law were governed by unwritten *fiqh*. That is to say, judges would often have to reason out a rule of *fiqh* for themselves—meaning in turn that judges needed to have intensive training in classical Islamic legal interpretation. This would not be true, however, in the idealized type of civil law system. Even if Islamic training was needed to draft a code, the judges who applied the code would simply apply the rule as written, and would not need to have any knowledge of how the law had been derived. Thus, moving to a system of codified law meant that people without a classical legal training could serve as judges. Leading jurists seem to have been comfortable with the move to codification so long as a code was drafted, in consultation with Islamic jurists, in accordance

[6] On the French civil law system that impressed elites in the nineteenth-century Ottoman Mediterranean, see John Henry Merryman, *The Civil Law Tradition*, 2nd ed. (Stanford: Stanford University Press, 1985), 26–47; and Alec Stone, *The Birth of Judicial Politics in France: The Constitutional Council in Comparative Perspective* (Oxford: Oxford University Press, 1992), 23–27.

[7] Merryman, *The Civil Law Tradition*, 36. Although it proved impossible as a practical matter to remove interpretation entirely from the process of judicial decision-making, this remained the ideal of the civil law tradition through the nineteenth century.

[8] Not only were Egyptians becoming enamored of positivism, but leading Ottoman legal thinkers were too, and they supported postivization of law as a method of centralizing and strengthening the application of imperial law in the provinces. Imperial reforms as well as state reforms combined to promote the rapid systematization, centralization, and positivization of the legal system in Egypt.

with the classical doctrine of *siyāsa sharʿiyya.*[9] Initially, positivization took place with an eye to that classical doctrine.

Administrative and legal reforms in Egypt initially focused on tweaking the existing legal system in which courts of general jurisdiction heard a wide range of cases—applying *qāḍī fiqh* to resolve some types of dispute and *siyāsā sharʿiyya* to resolve others. When it came to disputes in areas governed by the *qāḍī*'s *fiqh*, reformers worked with leading jurists to control and systematize the *qāḍīs*' interpretation and application of *fiqh.*[10] Official *muftīs* were appointed to whom difficult questions of *fiqh* had to be referred and to whose opinions judges would have to defer. Appeals courts were also established to ensure that Islamic law was interpreted consistently.[11]

In a second stage of positivization, the Egyptian government began to promulgate statutory law to govern areas that had once been governed by *qāḍī*'s *fiqh.*[12] In doing so, they acted with an eye on the theory of *siyāsa sharʿiyya* and took pains to ensure that the new statutes could plausibly be described as Islamic legislation.[13] In their studies

[9] For insightful explorations of the way in which codification changes both the conceptualization of the *sharīʿa*, the way in which law is developed and the way in which it is experienced by citizens subject to it, see Ann Mayer, "The Sharīʿah: A Methodology or a Body of Substantive Rules?," in *Islamic Law and Jurisprudence*, N. Heer, ed. (Seattle: University of Washington Press, 1990), 177–198; Brinkley Messick, *The Calligraphic State: Textual Domination and History in a Muslim Society* (Berkeley: University of California, 1992).

[10] Many Egyptians, including many members of the *ʿulamāʾ*, apparently welcomed the codification of Islamic law, or at least accepted it as inevitable. Some enthusiastically supported the codification of law in areas that had traditionally been governed by *qāḍī fiqh.* When the government adopted a secular code of law in 1882, the *ʿulamāʾ* asked that it be replaced by an Islamic code. There seems to have been tolerance for the government's plans to codify the law in the few areas still governed by *qāḍī fiqh.* In 1899, the classically trained scholar, Muḥammad ʿAbduh, was hired by the government to study the *sharīʿa* courts' system and to issue proposals for improvements. In his report, he decried the inefficiencies of judge-made law in modern courts and proposed codification of the personal status law. In his report to the government, *Taqrīr Iṣlāḥ al-Maḥākim al-Sharʿiyya*, he apparently argued forcefully that the government should codify the law of personal status. See the discussion in A. Chris Eccel, *Egypt, Islam and Social Change* (Islamkundliche Untersuchungen 81; Berlin: Klaus Schwartz, 1984), 81–93, particularly 92–93, and Malcolm Kerr, *Islamic Reform* (Berkeley: University of California Press, 1966), 199–202.

[11] Nathan Brown, *The Rule of Law in the Arab World: Courts in Egypt and the Gulf* (Cambridge: Cambridge University Press, 1997), 59.

[12] See, e.g., the provisions of the *Sharīʿa* Courts Ordinances of 1856 and 1880 described in Rudolph Peters, "Murder on the Nile: Homicide Trials in Nineteenth-Century Egyptian Shariʿa Courts," *Die Welt des Islams* 30 (1990): 99, n. 3.

[13] At first, the Egyptian government's "legislation" consisted in large part of

of Egyptian law, Nathan Brown and Rudolph Peters have both argued that the rules laid down by the governmental councils were, in fact, consistent with *fiqh*.[14] Peters concludes that:

> In spite of the increasing modernization of the country [in the early nineteenth century], one does not observe a tendency to abandon the Sharia. To the contrary, with the better organization of the Egyptian state apparatus, Sharia justice during the second half of the nineteenth century, became better organized too by means of clearer legislation, the regulation of the function of the mufti, and the creation of procedures to watch over the qadis' decisions.[15]

Finally, in a third and final stage of positivization, the government decided to move to a system of pure statutory law. In the 1870s, the Egyptian government, now fully autonomous, decided to abrogate the existing Ottoman and Egyptian laws in most areas of the legal system, replacing them with comprehensive codes of Egyptian law.[16] In 1882, the Egyptian government promulgated new codes—including a new civil and commercial code.[17] Thereafter, in Egypt, only a very few areas of law were governed by unwritten *fiqh*. (By the 1930s, the government had codified Egyptian law in many of these areas as well.[18])

What is most striking about the third phase of positivization is that the Egyptian government decided not just to codify the law, but to codify a body of law that could not easily be characterized

---

modifications to the Ottoman *qānūns*. See, e.g., Gabriel Baer, *Studies in the Social History of Egypt* (Chicago: University of Chicago Press, 1969), 111–30.

[14] Thus, jurists were regularly appointed to sit on the councils, presumably to ensure that their work was consistent with their understanding of *sharīʿa* norms. For example, Ziadeh reports that four jurists, one from each of the four Sunnī guilds, sat on the Governor's Council, the most important of these bodies, and jurists sat on other judicial-administrative bodies as well. See Farhat Ziadeh, *Lawyers, the Rule of Law, and Liberalism in Modern Egypt* (Stanford: Hoover Institution, 1968), 11, 14.

[15] See Brown, *The Rule of Law*, 25; Rudolph Peters, "Sharia and the State: Criminal Law in Nineteenth Century Egypt," in *State and Islam* eds. C. Van Dijk and A.H. de Groot (Leiden: Research School CNWS, 1995), 152–57.

[16] Peters, "*Sharīʿa* and the State," 174.

[17] Codification was at this time very much a trend among reforming states in the Muslim Mediterranean. In the 1870s, the Ottomans began to codify much of their law, and in 1876, they unveiled a new civil code for Ottoman areas that, unlike Egypt, remained under their effective control. See R.H. Davison in "Tanẓīmāt" in EI2, vol. X, 205–206; C.V. Findley, "Medjelle" in EI2, vol. VI, 971–72.

[18] On the reorganization of new courts and promulgation of new national codes, see Brown, *The Rule of Law*, 29–31.

as consistent with classical Sunnī Islamic norms—and that thus could not be considered legitimate according to the doctrine of *siyāsa sharʿiyya*. Before discussing this development, however, it is important to explore a third development.

D. *The decline of the Sunnī law guilds*

At the time that Muḥammad ʿAlī began his program of reform, classical Sunnī jurists associated with the Sunnī law guilds controlled the important educational institutions in the country, the most important of which was the venerable mosque-university of al-Azhar in Cairo.[19] They also staffed most of the courts in the country and provided advisors to the government. Finally, they played a valuable role in mediating between the government and the masses.[20] Thus, when Muḥammad ʿAlī first began to plan his program of reform, he tried to cooperate with the jurists, and he apparently expected that they would continue to be a leading role in his modern state. In order to prepare the jurists to work in his modernizing state, Muḥammad ʿAlī suggested that the leading jurists implement educational reforms at al-Azhar. In particular, he proposed that the curriculum be altered so that the next generation of jurists could be trained in new subjects such as foreign languages, mathematics, and science—disciplines that he thought the next generation of legislators, judges, and governmental advisors should know. However, for complex reasons of economic self-interest as well as ideology, the leaders of al-Azhar refused to accept Muḥammad ʿAlī's proposed curricular changes. This alienated both the government and the more progressive members of the Sunnī law guilds. As their relationship with the government began to deteriorate, the guilds and the jurists who were associated with them incrementally lost both influence with the government and popular prestige.

[19] See Joseph Schacht and Aaron Layyish, "Maḥkama: (4) The Arab Lands and Israel in the Modern Period: (i) Egypt" in EI2, vol. VI, 22–25.

[20] For an informative discussion of both the organization of the *ʿulamāʾ* in Ottoman Egypt and the role that they played in Egyptian society, see Afaf Lutfi al-Ayyid Marsot, "The Ulama of Cairo in the Eighteenth and Nineteenth Centuries," *Scholars, Saints, and Sufis: Muslim Religious Institutions in the Middle East since 1500*, ed. Nikki R. Keddie (Berkeley: University of California Press, 1973).

Rebuffed by conservative leadership of the Sunnī law guilds, the Egyptian government turned to progressive Sunnī jurists, such as Rifāʿa Rāfiʿ al-Ṭahṭāwī for guidance on how to reform Egypt,[21] and it looked to Europeans as well.[22] The government established new "national schools" that were unaffiliated with the traditional Sunnī guilds of law and taught a European-style curriculum.[23] As these new national schools flourished and multiplied at the expense of more traditional institutions, their graduates came to rival and, eventually, to supplant the classically-trained jurists as the intellectual elite of the country. Not surprisingly, when hiring civil servants or seeking advisors, the government looked to graduates of the new national schools.

In the new courts (which were increasingly applying statutes, rather than *qāḍīs*' *fiqh*) judges did not necessarily need to be classically trained. After all, they did not need to come up with rules of decision themselves. Rather, they were applying rules of decision that had been written down in clear language in the official law codes. Thus, intellectually gifted Egyptian Muslims seeking a role in Egyptian government or law increasingly chose to attend the prestigious and practical national educational institutions, rather than seek a classical religious education. By the second half of the nineteenth century, many of the most important administrators, judges, and teachers

[21] See Daniel Crecelius, "Non-Ideological Responses of the Ulama to Modernization," *Scholars, Saints, and Sufis: Muslim Religious Institutions in the Middle East since 1500*, Nikkie R. Keddie, ed. (Berkeley: University of California Press, 1973), 167–90; Afaf Lutfi Al-Sayyid Marsot, "The Beginnings of Modernization among the Rectors of al-Azhar," *Beginnings of Modernization in the Middle East*, eds. William R. Polk and Richard L. Chambers (Chicago: University of Chicago Press, 1968), 267–80, particularly 270–76. Ṭahṭāwī, a trained Ottoman jurist, made an extensive tour of France in the 1820s. Upon his return to Egypt, he began supervising the translation of European works into Arabic, and he established an elite school of translation that taught European languages to a new generation of elite Egyptians. For Ṭahṭāwī's legal and political thought and his influence in the new Egyptian school system, see Hourani, *Arabic Thought in the Liberal Age*, 68–83. For a discussion of the translation movement under the supervision of Ṭahṭāwī and a list of some of the works translated, see Ibrahim Abu Lughod, *The Arab Rediscovery of Europe* (Princeton: Princeton University Press, 1963), 28–65.

[22] For example, with the blessing of the Egyptian government, French followers of Saint Simon established an institution of higher learning modeled on the French Institut Polytechnique, which was intended to help train Egyptians who could then systematically begin the process of planning the course of state development. Timothy Mitchell, *Colonizing Egypt* (Cambridge: Cambridge University Press, 1988), 33.

[23] For an overview of the the educational reforms, see Crecelius, "Non-Ideological

in Egypt were disaffected Islamic scholars, alienated from the leadership of the guilds, or else they were graduates of the new government schools.[24] Ultimately, the guilds became so marginalized that the Egyptian government was able to wrest control of al-Azhar from them—controlling appointments and discipline and imposing curricular reforms.[25]

Thus, over the course of the nineteenth and twentieth centuries, the Sunnī guilds of law ceased to have any major role as autonomous, self-governing institutions controlling the evolution of law in Egypt. Indeed, by the middle of the twentieth century, religious scholars graduating from al-Azhar were no longer scholars licensed by an independent non-governmental guild of jurists. Rather, they were scholars with government-granted diplomas certifying that they had studied, among other things, classical Islamic legal theory and the substantive doctrines of various guilds. It is probably not appropriate to refer to any modern Egyptian Islamic thinkers—even those who had received classical training—as "jurists" in the narrow sense that was used in previous chapters. Scholars were no longer trained by independent *madhhabs*, licensed by these *madhhabs*, or subject to the discipline of a *madhhab*. To emphasize this point, I will from this point on refer to classically-trained Islamic thinkers of the modern era as Islamic scholars, or "*ʿulamāʾ*" rather than "jurists."

II. *The secularization of Egyptian state law*

When Egypt began to plan for more or less complete codification of its laws, a debate arose between Islamists and secularists. As I will use these term repeatedly in this book, it is important that they be defined carefully. By "Islamists," I mean people who embrace the traditional Sunnī Islamic idea that when legislating, a government must take steps to ensure that its legislation is consistent with Islamic norms. Islamists may, however, have any number of different

Responses of the Ulama to Modernization," 180–84; Marsot, *Egypt in the Reign of Muhammad Ali*, 66–70; Vatikiotis, *History*, 58–59, 90–123. For a slightly different perspective, see Fritz Steppat, "National Education Projects in Egypt before British Occupation," *Beginnings of Modernization in the Middle East*, 281–97.

[24] Crecelius, "Non-Ideological Responses of the Ulama to Modernization," 182–90.

[25] For a history of al-Azhar, see generally Eccel, *Egypt, Islam and Social Change*.

ideas about how Islamic norms should be identified or about the precise nature of the relationship between *sharīʿa* norms and state law. By "secularists," I mean people who believe that when legislating, a government should not be required to check its statutes against any type of "Islamic" norms.

As noted already, legal postivization was a novel development in the Islamic Mediterranean, but it was not, by itself, incompatible with an Islamist viewpoint. One could even justify some types of codification under the classical doctrine of *siyāsa sharʿiyya*. Under traditional Ottoman understanding of Islamic legal theory, a ruler could enact statutory legislation so long as he consulted with jurists to ensure that it was consistent with both the established rules and overarching "goals" of the *sharīʿa*. Theoretically, this could support the total codification of law—with the caveat that *sharīʿa* norms provided a negative restriction on the government's legislative discretion. Working from this premise, the Ottomans in the 1870s, promulgated an "Islamic" civil code, known as the *Mecelle*, that was applied in provinces that, unlike Egypt, were still under effective Ottoman control.[26]

In Egypt, however, codification was accompanied by secularization of the law. As the Egyptian government began to move towards a codification of Egyptian law, its advisors were increasingly drawn from the graduates of the national schools, whose commitment to the classical Ottoman Islamic ideal was wavering. When the Egyptian government in the 1870s decided to codify Egyptian law, secularists and Islamists debated whether the law should reflect classical Islamic norms and, eventually, the secularists won.

Islamists in the top ranks of the government wanted the new code to be consistent with classical Islamic legal norms, and the government was initially inclined to their position. It instructed the Minister of Justice, Muḥammad Qadrī, to draft a code that would be, for the most part, a digest of existing rules of *fiqh*. A new generation of secularists countered that, as a practical matter, it would be unwise to draft and apply such a code. Egypt was an autonomous province prized by colonial powers such as France and Egypt. If Egypt wanted

For further material on the modern reforms, see J. Jomier, "Al-Azhar" in EI2, vol. I, 817–21.

[26] The Ottoman government had also considered the possibility of translating and adopting the French Civil Code, but decided instead to draft a new code based on

to avoid being colonized, it would have to modernize rapidly, and secularists argued that this required the province to adopt a code modeled on European codes.[27] If Egypt wanted to evolve into a European-style nation state, it was not enough merely to adopt the structure of a European legal system. It should adopt the substantive law of Europe as well. The British invasion of Egypt in 1882 and the establishment of a de facto British protectorate in Egypt provided secularists with ammunition, and caused the Egyptian government to reconsider the wisdom of adopting an Islamic code. Although the British had not explicitly demanded that the new Egyptian legal system be modeled on a European system, many important members of the Egyptian government became convinced that the adoption of such a code would give Egypt leverage in its dealings with the occupying power.[28]

In 1883, the Egyptian government pragmatically abandoned Qadrī Pasha's draft Islamic code. Instead, it hastily drafted and promulgated codes based closely on European models.[29] The government also established a new centralized court system modeled on the French system that would apply these codes throughout the country.

Ḥanafī *fiqh*. The code, the *Mecelle-yi Aḥkām-i ʿAdliyye*, or *Mecelle*, was finished in 1876. See R.H. Davison in "Tanẓīmāt" in EI2 and C.V. Findley, "Medjelle" in EI2.

[27] The following paragraph draws heavily on Brown, *The Rule of Law*, 29–31.

[28] The adoption of a modified French Code had several benefits for Egypt. First, it helped take away one of the potential justifications that the colonialists might use to annex Egypt completely into the British Empire. Second, the adoption of a French Code would mean that more or less the same law was applied in both the national courts and the mixed courts. The mixed courts were a special body of courts that the Egyptian government had agreed to set up to try cases involving a European. These courts applied French law, were staffed by panels of European and Egyptian judges, and heard cases in French. The Egyptian government despised the mixed courts and hoped that the European powers would allow the Egyptians to start trying Europeans in the national courts. They were well aware, however, that such a concession was unlikely unless the national court system was modeled on the mixed court system and applied a similar law. On this point, see Ziadeh, *Lawyers, the Rule of Law and Liberalism*, 34. Finally, the adoption of the French code allowed the Egyptian government to stymie their British masters. The British, who were completely unfamiliar with the system, were hampered in their attempt to govern Egypt behind the scenes by their unfamiliarity with the system, and complained bitterly about it. Nevertheless, the British, who enjoyed a delicate detente with the French at this time, found it impolitic to dismantle it. See Brown, *Rule of Law*, 38–39 and accompanying citations.

[29] Ziadeh notes that the codes were actually drafted in French and then translated into Arabic. *Lawyers, the Rule of Law and Liberalism*, 35. Other scholars, however,

The decision to adopt European codes of law was a watershed event. It represented an official endorsement of the secularist position that governments in modern states did not need to (and often should not) use laws that were checked against classical Islamic norms. Significantly, the Egyptian public, with the exception of the *ʿulamāʾ* were comfortable with the government's decision to embrace secularism and to apply a body of law that was not drafted with an eye to conformity with classical *sharīʿa* norms. Although the leading *ʿulamāʾ* refused to give their blessing to the new secular codes,[30] there was no groundswell of elite or popular protest against the adoption of the 1882 civil code; nor was there, for several decades, a popular political organization that was willing to take up the *ʿulamāʾ*'s call for the adoption of an Islamic code.[31] It was not until the early twentieth century that a powerful Islamist opposition appeared. Even then, it struggled against regimes, some of them quite popular, that refused to accept any absolute obligation (implicit or explicit) that they conform their laws to the *sharīʿa.* Until the amendment of Article 2 in 1980, the Egyptian government would never recognize such an obligation.

The adoption of "secular" legal codes in the 1880s made clear that changes in Egyptian society had loosened the grip of classical Islamic legal theory on the hearts and minds of Egyptians—particularly those in the elite. Further evidence was provided by the rise

have pointed out that there were some modifications from the French Code. See Brown, *The Rule of Law*, 30–31.

[30] By the end of the nineteenth century, the chief Ḥanafī *muftī* at al-Azhar had become the *primus inter pares* of the traditional *ʿulamāʾ*. When the government asked him for a *fatwā* approving the new codes, he refused. See Jakob Skovgaard-Petersen, *Defining Islam for the Egyptian State* (Leiden: E.J. Brill, 1997), 100–3. Ziadeh reports that all questions that touched upon Islamic law were ultimately referred to a less prestigious *muftī* at the Ministry of Justice whose allegiance to the government apparently outweighed his allegiance to his guild and who provided favorable opinions. (Ziadeh, *Lawyers, the Rule of Law and Liberalism*, 35 n. 29.) The leading *ʿulamāʾ* were opposed not to the idea of codifying Egyptian law—but rather to the idea that the code would have been drafted without reference to Islamic legal norms. Over the next decade, they called publicly for the government to replace the 1883 Code either with Muḥammad Qadrī's discarded code of Islamic law or some other codified form of Islamic law. For example, in 1893, the Chief *Muftī* of Egypt explicitly called for the adoption of Qadrī's codification of Ḥanafi law in place of the national code. See Skovgaard-Petersen, *Defining Islam*, 101.

[31] See Brown, *The Rule of Law*, 33. Why this should be is not entirely clear. Nathan Brown has suggested, plausibly, that popular discontent was forestalled in

of Islamic modernism. Islamists opposing the secularization of Egyptian law tended to embrace modernist Islamic legal theories rather than classical ones.

III. *The emergence of Islamic modernism in Egypt*

Subsequent chapters will demonstrate that in the twentieth century, Islamists did not all call for the re-establishment of a classical Islamic state. At most, some groups embraced a neo-traditional view of Islamic political legitimacy. The most effective members of the Islamist opposition were inspired by radical new theories of Islamic law. They favored new methods of interpreting Islamic law and of drafting Islamic legal codes. Where did Islamic modernist thought come from and why were diverse forms of modernist Islam able to flourish side by side in Egyptian society?

As noted already, the *ʿulamāʾ* over the course of the nineteenth century lost their ability to police the boundaries of acceptable Islamic legal and political thought. With the rise of the national schools, the Sunnī law guilds no longer set the curriculum for educated Egyptians. Furthermore, people whom the guilds had not certified as expert in Islamic law (or who espoused unorthodox ideas) increasingly served as government advisors or judges.[32] The *ʿulamāʾ* thus watched helplessly as Muslims educated in the national schools and even some of the younger *ʿulamāʾ* began to question old assumptions about Islamic legal interpretation and the role of Islamic law in the state. That freedom was evident not only in the rise of secularism, but in the rise of Islamic modernism.

That iconoclastic Islamic legal thinkers had new freedom to operate is clear from the career of Muḥammad ʿAbduh (d. 1905)—a

---

part by the decision not to force people to have disputes settled in the new national courts according to the new civil law. The government allowed *sharīʿa* courts to hear all civil cases that were brought before them. See Brown, *The Rule of Law*, 33 n. 20. It is also possible that at a time of considerable turmoil and foreign occupation, the theoretical illegitimacy of state law was not, for most Egyptians, a matter of pressing concern. One wonders if the lack of protest may also reflect a decline in the prestige of the *ʿulamāʾ* among the masses.

[32] In this regard, see, e.g., the discussion of Taḥṭāwī above and of ʿAbduh, below.

member of the *ʿulamāʾ* who is often considered the father of Egyptian modernist legal thought.[33] At al-Azhar, the young Muḥammad ʿAbduh's unorthodox theological ideas led quickly to problems with his professors, and he received mediocre grades.[34] ʿAbduh's career was not harmed, however, by his professors' disapproval. The Egyptian government saw in ʿAbduh a model of the kind of jurist that they now wanted, someone eager to rethink traditional Islamic assumptions and willing to engage with Western ideas and institutions. At the suggestion of the prime minister, ʿAbduh was hired in 1878 to teach at a newly formed national school.[35] Although ʿAbduh's involvement with nationalist political movements eventually caused him to be exiled for six years, he returned to Egypt in 1888 and served in a series of high posts in education and the judiciary. He was eventually appointed to be the Chief *Muftī* of Egypt—the government's official advisor on questions of Islamic law.[36]

Throughout his career, ʿAbduh championed iconoclastic ideas about epistemology and Islamic legal interpretation. For example, he asserted that elite jurists should not reason from the precedents of their guild, but should return to the practice of interpreting *sharīʿa* through direct interpretation of the scriptures—the process of reasoning known as *ijtihād* that had fallen out of use.[37] More radical still, ʿAbduh departed

[33] There have been many biographies of ʿAbduh both in Arabic and in Western languages. See, e.g., Rashīd Riḍā, *Tārīkh al-Ustādh al-Imām al-Shaykh Muḥammad ʿAbduh* (Cairo: Maṭbaʿat al-Manār, 1933); Charles C. Adams, *Islam and Modernism in Egypt: A Study of the Modern Reform Movement Inaugurated by Muḥammad ʿAbduh* (1933; repr. New York: Russell and Russell, 1968); Kerr, *Islamic Reform.*

[34] Among his controversial notions was the idea that unaided human reason could, in many cases, distinguish on its own between right and wrong. This notion, long associated with heretical Muʿtazilite theologians, had potentially serious implications for the way in which jurists should interpret God's law. ʿAbduh later reported that he had been denounced as a Muʿtazilite by some of his fellow students at al-Azhar apparently on the ground that he had established reading groups that discussed texts that explained Muʿtazilite views. See Adams, *Islam and Modernism*, 42–43, citing *al-Manār*, vol. VIII: 391–93. For an analysis of ʿAbduh's thought in light of Muʿtazilite thought, see Robert Caspar, "Le renouveau du Moʿtazilism," *Mélanges de l'Institut Dominicain d'Études Orientales du Caire* 4 (1957): 57–72.

[35] See Adams, *Islam and Modernism*, 44–45.

[36] On ʿAbduh's later career, see, e.g., Adams, *Islam and Modernism*, 68–103. On the contributions he made during his later life to Islamic educational reform in Egypt, see, e.g., Eccel, *Egypt, Islam and Social Change*, 145–95; for more details on his career as Chief Muftī, see Skovgaard-Petersen, *Defining Islam for the Egyptian State*, 119–33.

[37] The assertion that contemporary jurists could interpret law through *ijtihād* was

from traditional Sunnī orthodoxy, asserting that in many cases, reasoned observation of the natural world could provide trustworthy knowledge about the goodness or badness of an act.[38] This idea revived some of the ideas of the Muʿtazilite school of theology (which in the classical period had come to be considered unorthodox), and it had important implications for legal theory.[39] As was noted in previous chapters, classical legal theory accepted axiomatically that good acts bring well-being to humans, and bad acts bring harm. This did not push thinkers to utilitarianism, however, because information derived directly from revealed texts was considered superior to knowledge that arises from the exercise of reason, and vastly superior to the knowledge that arises from the rational study of the natural world. Thus, classical jurists felt they could not say with confidence what was "good" for humans without confirming that God's textual commands tended to promote that good. By calling for *ijtihād* and asserting that humans could distinguish the helpful from the harmful through their reason alone, ʿAbduh's position implied provocatively that a jurist could come up with Islamic legal rulings through utilitarian reasoning—by rationally determining whether or not the act would benefit society.[40]

---

not unprecedented but it was not common. For a discussion of later Sunnī thinkers who claimed the right to practice *ijtihād* or whose followers described them as *mujtahids*, see two articles by Wael Hallaq, "On the Origins of the Debate about the Existence of Mujtahids and Gate of Ijtihād," *Studia Islamica* 63 (1986): 129–41; and "Was the Gate of Ijtihād Closed?," *International Journal of Middle East Studies* 16.1 (1994): 3–41. An insistence that modern Muslims could and should interpret Islamic law through *ijtihād* was to become a staple feature of modernist thought.

[38] See, e.g., Muḥammad ʿAbduh, *Risālat al-Tawḥīd*, ed. Rashīd Riḍā (Cairo: Maṭbaʿat al-Manār, 1346 A.H.), 52–54, trans. in Kerr, *Islamic Reform*, 125: "The human mind has known these things for a long time. It has divided them into harmful and useful, and has called the former bad actions and the latter good actions. It is on this division that the distinction rests between virtue and vice.... Man's reason, together with his senses, can distinguish beautiful actions from ugly ones according to the different significations we ascribed to them above, without need to find support in revelation."

[39] For a study of the relationship between the thought of ʿAbduh and other modernist theologians and the Muʿtazilite school, see Caspar, "Le Renouveau du Mo'tazilism," 57–72.

[40] "In Islam, life takes precedence over religion" and thus in Islamic law "the health of bodies takes precedence over the health of religions." *Al-Islām wa al-Naṣrāniyya* (Cairo: n.d.), 74–76, trans. and cited in Kerr, *Islamic Reform*, 117.

It is possible that ʿAbduh did not fully appreciate (or was not fully comfortable with) the utilitarian ramifications of his thought. This would explain why, in issuing Islamic legal opinions, his reasoning seems fairly traditional.[41] Nevertheless, without explicitly espousing it, he opened the door to a type of nakedly utilitarian reasoning from which the traditional Sunnī jurists had shied.[42] And as will become clear in the next chapter, a number of Islamic thinkers in the early twentieth century saw the open door and walked in.

ʿAbduh thus laid the groundwork for those who would develop new methods of interpreting Islamic law—and particularly those who would develop utilitarian methods of deriving Islamic law. And as education spread in Egypt, a new class of educated middle class Muslims appeared—one that had been trained in western sciences as well as (and in some cases instead of) classical Islamic sciences. This class produced a wide range of iconoclastic thinkers. Ultimately many members of this class who remained wedded to Islamist ideals were attracted to modernist ideas about the way in which Islamic law should be interpreted and the nature of law in an Islamic state. According to such scholars, Egyptian law should not take classical Islamic legal norms into account, because classical methodology as practiced by the classical jurists was deeply flawed. Nevertheless it could (and indeed it was required to) take into account Islamic rulings and Islamic goals as derived by interpreters using modern methods of Islamic legal interpretation. In other words, they called for the state to embrace a radically re-imagined version of the doctrine of *siyāsa sharʿiyya.*

At the end of the century, on the heels of an English invasion, when the Egyptian government embraced a secularist legal philoso-

---

[41] In a recent study of *fatwās* dealing with *waqf* (charitable institutions) produced by the chief *Muftīs* of Egypt, Andreas Kemke notes that ʿAbduh's *fatwās* generally follow traditional Ḥanafī *fiqh* on the subject. *Stiftungen im muslimischen Rechtsleben des neuzeitlichen Ägypten*, ed. A. Schall (Frankfurt: Peter Lang, 1991), 109–17. Whether he took a more radical line in his *fatwās* has been debated. Compare Kerr, *Islamic Reform*, 145, and Charles C. Adams, "Muhammad ʿAbduh and the Transvaal Fatwa," *The Macdonald Presentation Volume* (London: Oxford University Press, 1933), 17–20, with Oussama Arabi, *Studies in Islamic Law and Jurisprudence* (The Hague: Kluwer, 2001), 35–38.

[42] See the discussion of Rashīd Riḍā in Chapter 6.

phy, there was no groundswell of support for a return to the classical model of *siyāsa sharʿiyya* on the Ottoman model. As the next chapters will demonstrate, the most effective Islamist movements proved to be those that embraced unclassical methods of Islamic legal interpretation. The next chapter will discuss three particularly important types of "modern" Islamic legal theory, each of which was embraced by an important faction of Islamists. The lack of consensus on basic questions of Islamic legal theory would weaken Islamist political movements and complicate the lives of politicians who wanted to create some generally acceptable compromise between a modern Egyptian legal system, built up under secularist regimes, and the demands of Islamism.

CHAPTER FIVE

MODERNIST EGYPTIAN LEGAL THEORIES AND MODERNIST APPROACHES TO DRAFTING ISLAMIC LEGISLATION

As the last chapter discussed, social and political changes in the nineteenth century led to Egyptian independence, an embrace by Egyptians of legal positivism, and a radical decline in the power of the Sunnī guilds that had long controlled Islamic legal thought. By the last quarter of the nineteenth century, a crucial portion of the Egyptian elite embraced a secularist legal ideology and convinced the government to promulgate legal codes whose rules were taken from European models. There was, at first, little popular resistance to the codification and secularization of Egyptian law. The lack of public outrage over secularization did not necessarily mean that Egyptians had despaired of measuring Egyptian law against some interpretation of Islamic law. It merely revealed widespread doubts among the politically active classes about the degree to which a modern state could be governed by classical Islamic law—as this law was understood by the *ʿulamāʾ*. Yet, when new theories of Islamic law appeared articulating plausible methods for developing "Islamic" codes of law, such theories were rapidly embraced by significant numbers of Egyptians. Thus, the twentieth century saw the rise of powerful Islamist opposition movements. These movements tended to embrace radically reconceived versions of the doctrine of *siyāsa sharʿiyya.* That is to say, they believed that Egyptian law needed to be consistent with the universally applicable rulings of the *sharīʿa* and the goals of the *sharīʿa*—but also argued for new methods of interpretation to identify and apply these rulings and goals.

This chapter will describe three important Egyptian modernist Islamic legal theories which impacted this movement. The theories developed in the twentieth century each began with different assumptions about who could interpret Islamic law and where interpreters should look for information about God's commands. This resulted in very different approaches to Islamic legal interpretation and to the drafting of state legislation. Although the theories differ radically, each of them came to enjoy support among important segments of the Egyptian public. Before delving into the contrasts between the theories, it is important to identify the aspects they shared.

First, each theory accepted the basic premise of the classical theory of *siyāsa sharʿiyya*, which informed Ottoman political ideology and the actions of the Egyptian government until the 1880s. That is to say, each theory assumed that Muslims can identify (1) some universally applicable rulings of *sharīʿa* and (2) some divinely-favored social results—principles corresponding to the classical "goals" of the *sharīʿa*.

Second, the first half of the twentieth century was a period of strident anti-colonialism, and many of the thinkers in Egypt who articulated modernist Islamic legal theories during this period were affected by the anti-colonial mood of the time. Thus, although modernist Islamic legal theories generally reflect an awareness of European enlightenment philosophy and trends in modern European legal and political theory, the thinkers who advocated these theories wished to demonstrate that their theories grew organically out of classical Islamic theory. Rhetorically, then, the modernist Islamic theorists discussed here utilized many traditional Islamic words and concepts, such as "*ijtihād*," "*ijmāʿ*" or "*maṣlaḥa*." As a result, Egyptian modernist legal theories often "sound" classical at first. Only closer inspection reveals how most modernist theorists subtly redefined these terms.

Finally, each of the theories discussed in this book approved of the codification of national law. Each of the thinkers assumed that the age of judge-made law was past and that their theory would be applied by thinkers to develop codes of law. This may explain why Egyptian Islamic modernists did not share the classical jurists' concern with limiting interpretive discretion. Classical Islamic legal theorists seem to have assumed that judges would often be required to develop rules of decision on a case-by-case basis to resolve the particular matter before them. To ensure the predictability of judicial rules of decision, legal theorists had to limit interpretive discretion and, in particular, the degree to which subjective considerations could influence an interpretation of the *sharīʿa*. Modern Islamic legal theorists in Egypt, however, could safely assume that judges would not use their method every time a case came before them. Rather, legislators would use their theory to develop codes that would be consistently applied. Perhaps as a result, modern legal thinkers seemed to be far less concerned than classical jurists with setting limits on interpretive discretion and on the use of inherently subjective criteria. No matter how much discretion had existed at the rule-making stage, the law of the state would be clear and the outcome of cases predictable. Under their methods, the range of permissible interpretation grew wider. Indeed, in many cases, a Muslim's opinion about whether a state law was consistent with Islamic rulings and goals came to depend, in large part, upon the interpreter's subjective beliefs about the nature of human welfare.

In sum, the modernist legal theories examined in this chapter all represent attempts to re-imagine the classical theory of *siyāsa sharʿiyya*, with an eye to creating modern codes of Islamic law. This chapter will begin by describing a type of theory that, for want of a better term, I will describe as "neo-traditional." It will then proceed to two influential modernist theories developed respectively by Rashīd Riḍā (d. 1971 C.E.) and Abd al-Razzāq Aḥmad al-Sanhūrī (d. 1935 C.E.). Riḍā's theory urged Muslims to interpret the universal Islamic rulings and goals and to draft Islamic codes through a method that can reasonably be conceptualized as a utilitarian form of neo-*ijtihād*. Sanhūrī's theory called for Muslims to interpret the universal Islamic rulings and goals and to draft Islamic codes through a method that I will conceptualize as a form of "comparative neo-*taqlīd*." It is important to focus on these three types of theories because, as later chapters will describe, they have influenced the SCC's Article 2 jurisprudence. The Court implicitly has rejected the fundamental tenets of neo-traditional theory, and instead has tried to synthesize aspects of theories espousing utilitarian neo-*ijtihād* with theories advocating comparative neo-*taqlīd*.

I. *"Neo-traditional" theories of Islamic law*

As a practical matter, classical Islamic legal interpretation was carried out exclusively by jurists trained in and licensed by the Sunnī law guilds. These classical jurists were bound by the traditional methodological and substantive legal doctrines of their guilds—doctrines described in Chapters 1 through 3. As defined in this book, "neo-traditional" theories attribute to modern classically-trained scholars (*ʿulamāʾ*) a unique ability to interpret Islamic law. Or, to put it differently, neo-traditional theories assert that an interpretation of Islamic law can only be trusted if it was developed by a member of the *ʿulamāʾ*. Neo-traditional theories differ from classical theories, however, because the thinkers who qualify as *ʿulamāʾ* in the modern world have very different training and institutional affiliations than the classical jurists, and use slightly different methods of interpreting the *sharīʿa.*

As mentioned in the previous chapter, changes during the nineteenth century in Egypt destroyed the Egyptian branches of the Sunnī *madhhabs*, the transnational Sunnī guilds of law that had for centuries trained jurists and had controlled the educational institutions, licensed jurists, and set the bounds of orthodoxy. By the middle of the twentieth century, successful students of Islamic law at al-Azhar no longer received from a jurist a "license" authorizing them to issue opinions according to the doctrines of that jurist's particular guild. Instead, they received a government-issued diploma in Islamic legal studies from al-Azhar. They were not indoctrinated into a system that assumed they should follow a particular guild's method of interpreting Islamic law. In the twentieth century, *ʿulamāʾ* thus came to embrace methods of interpreting Islamic law or of drafting Islamic legislation that did not require an interpreter to interpret Islamic law in light of the doctrines of any particular guild of law.

For example, many neo-traditionalists argued that national codes should be drafted with the assistance of the *ʿulamāʾ* using methods of Islamic legal reasoning known as *talfīq.*[1] One who derives law through *talfīq* comes up with an "Islamic" rule applicable to modern times by surveying the rules that the four competing guilds of law had laid down in the past and selecting the rule that seems most likely to advance the public welfare. It is instructive to compare this to the very different classical methods of precedential reasoning described in Chapter 2—the methods that I subsumed under the rubric *taqlīd. Talfīq* can paradoxically be characterized both as more flexible and more rigid than traditional methods of *taqlīd.* It is more flexible insofar as it expands the range of rulings that a member of the *ʿulamāʾ* can accept as precedential. A member of the modern *ʿulamāʾ* is not limited to respecting the precedents associated with one guild. Rather, he is permitted to look to the early *mujtahids* of all guilds. In fact, in the twentieth century, some came to argue that

[1] See, e.g., J.N.D. Anderson, *Law Reform in the Muslim World* (London; Athalone Press, 1976), 51–58, A. Chris Eccel, *Egypt, Islam and Social Change: al-Azhar in Change and Accommodation* (Islamkundliche Untersuchungen 81; Berlin: Klaus Schwartz, 1984), 452; Wael B. Hallaq and Aharon Layish, "Talfīḳ" in EI2, Vol. X, 137.

he could even look to the opinions promulgated in guilds other than the surviving Sunnī guilds, such as the Ẓāhirī guild, or even by Shīʿī jurists.[2] At the same time, the process of deriving a rule of Islamic law through *talfīq* did not permit jurists to come up with unprecedented solutions to legal questions. The contemporary jurist practicing *talfīq* had to select from among the rules established by the classical jurists and did not have the flexibility to abandon precedents entirely and create a new rule (unless he could argue that such a departure was required under some analogue of the classical doctrine of necessity).[3]

Some neo-traditionalists recognized that a code developed by *talfīq* obeyed the letter of the classical Islamic interpretations of law (*fiqh*) at the expense of their spirit. Accordingly, some neo-traditionalists followed Muḥammad ʿAbduh in asserting that members of the Egyptian *ʿulamāʾ* should return to the practice of *ijtihād*.[4] Neo-traditionalists debated, however, the skills that a Muslim needed in order to perform *ijtihād*.[5] Furthermore, the type of *ijtihād* championed by neo-traditionalists did not always mirror the type of *ijtihād* that had been elaborated by the classical Sunnī jurists.[6] Rather, some inclined towards some of the utilitarian methods of neo-*ijtihād* that will be described below.

[2] In 1959 the Rector of al-Azhar, Maḥmūd Shaltūt, not only concluded that modern circumstances justified the adoption of legal positions traditionally associated with Shiʿism, but also published a *fatwā* in the university's official journal declaring, in effect, that Shiʿite legal opinions were as valid as Sunnī opinions. Therafter, Al-Azhar established initiatives that would facilitate the study of competing opinions and the practice of *talfīq*. See Hamid Enayat, *Modern Islamic Political Thought* (Austin: University of Texas Press, 1982), 49–50. On Shaltūt generally, see Kate Zebiri, *Maḥmūd Shaltūt and Islamic Modernism* (Oxford: Clarendon Press, 1993). On al-Azhar's attempt to train jurists systematically in the practice of *talfīq*, see Eccel, *Egypt, Islam and Social Change*, 452.

[3] As discussed in Chapter 2, classical legal theory assumed that rulings derived by analogy were generally valid only so long as they continued to serve the results that they had been established to advance. Jurists who practiced *taqlīd* were permitted, under some circumstances, to reject rules of decision that had been applied in the past and, instead to develop new rules that they felt better served the appropriate "goals of the *sharīʿa*."

[4] See the discussion of *ijtihād* in Chapter 2.

[5] Some thinkers claimed that there were no living *mujtahids*; others identified one or more alive in their time; and still others argued that any Muslim, whether or not he was a member of the *ʿulamāʾ*, was qualified to practice *ijtihād*. For a discussion of this debate, see Eccel, *Egypt, Islam and Social Change*, 422–23 and accompanying citations.

[6] Among the differences is an increased reliance on utilitarian reasoning. Indeed,

Because neo-traditional theories start from the assumption that state law must be consistent with the *ʿulamāʾ*'s interpretation of Islamic law,[7] it is hardly surprising that the *ʿulamāʾ* have proved to be the leading partisans of neo-traditionalism in Egypt. From the adoption of the 1882 civil code, they agitated for a state that "would allow [for] secular legislation to exist, but in a constant state of review by the *ʿulamāʾ* in light of their ongoing derivation of sacred law for modern times."[8] As the next chapter will point out, the *ʿulamāʾ* have also found political partners in the public at large. Nevertheless, many modern Egyptians were skeptical of the assumptions that neo-traditionalists made about the nature of their authority. As a new class of educated Muslims appeared, trained in national schools both at home and often in Europe as well, Islamic legal thinkers began to challenge the notion that the *ʿulamāʾ* had a unique ability to interpret a scriptural text or to reason from precedent. According to some modernist thinkers, any educated Muslim has the ability to interpret Islamic law. Different modernist theories have emerged, each proposing a different approach that interpreters should take when looking for the rulings and goals of God's law. In the rest of this chapter, I will focus on two other important modern theories. One theory proposes that Islamic law be derived in the modern world through a new method of scriptural exegesis and rationalist analysis, which I call "utilitarian neo-*ijtihād*." The second, competing theory urges that modern Islamic laws be developed through a form of precedential and rationalist reasoning that I will call "comparative neo-*taqlīd*."

II. *Modernist theories calling for Muslims to interpret the* sharīʿa *and develop state law through utilitarian neo-*ijtihād

In the early years of the twentieth century, Rashīd Riḍā proposed a revolutionary theory that applied an essentially utilitarian method to interpret Islamic law. Riḍā was a protégé of Muḥammad ʿAbduh,

there can be an area of overlap between theories that permit states to measure state law against norms derived by neo-traditional *ijtihād* and theories insisting that states develop legislation using the distinctly modern types of reasoning that I describe as utilitarian neo-*ijtihād*.

[7] Ideally, they would be administered in consultation with the *ʿulamāʾ* as well.

[8] Eccel, *Egypt, Islam and Social Change*, 83, referring to al-Azhar's *Mashrūʿ al-dustūr al-Islāmī*, articles 46–50.

and his theory explored the most radical utilitarian implications of ʿAbduh's thought and put them to use in a systematic utilitarian method of interpreting *sharīʿa* and developing a body of state law that was consistent with both the universal rulings and overarching goals of the *sharīʿa*.[9]

Riḍā entirely rejected the central premise of *taqlīd*—the premise that Muslims' understanding of God's law should be constrained by interpretations of law promulgated by great jurists in the past. Rather, he believed Muslims should seek to uncover the universal rulings and goals of the *sharīʿa* through direct engagement with the Qur'ān and *ḥadīth* literature.[10] Riḍā urged states to derive Islamic laws by something that he called *ijtihād*. This *ijtihād* can sound, at first glance, like classical *ijtihād*. On close inspection, however, it becomes clear that Riḍā modified many of the classical concepts that he had appropriated and subtly redefined many of the classical terms that he used. Ultimately, Riḍā created a novel, essentially utilitarian, method of interpreting Islamic law and creating codes of Islamic state law.

Riḍā's new form of "*ijtihād*" was a two-step method of identifying Islamic rules that could be codified and applied by the government of a Muslim state. In the first step, a religio-legal specialist looked to Islamic scriptures (and the records of communal consensus) to find a body of "universal" rulings and goals of *sharīʿa*. The rulings require some acts and prohibit others. The goals tell Muslims the results to which their actions should lead. In developing state laws, a state should try to identify the rules that will be consistent with the universal rulings and that will also maximize the achievement

[9] Riḍā's theory has been analyzed by a number of scholars over the years. My own reading has been informed by the discussions found in Enayat, *Modern Islamic Political Thought*; Wael Hallaq, *A History of Islamic Legal Theories: An Introduction to Sunnī Uṣūl al-Fiqh* (Cambridge: Cambridge University Press, 1997); Malcolm Kerr, *Islamic Reform: The Political and Legal Theories of Muhammad Abduh and Rashid Rida* (Berkeley: University of California Press, 1966); Henri Laoust, "Le Reformisme orthodoxe des 'Salafiyya,' et les caractères généraux de son organization actuelle," *Revue des Études Islamiques* 6 (1932): 175–224; and also by Laoust's introduction and notes to Rashīd Riḍā, *al-Khilāfa aw al-Imāma al-Uẓmā* (Cairo: Maṭbaʿat al-Manār, 1341 A.H./1923 C.E.), also published in *al-Manār*, 23–24, Henri Laoust, trans., *Le califat dans la doctrine de Rasid Rida* (Beirut: Institut Français de Damas, 1938). The discussion in the following pages draws upon these works, and particularly on Kerr.

[10] Riḍā, *al-Khilāfa*, 90–91, and see discussion in Enayat, *Islamic Political Thought*, 78–81.

of the *sharīʿa*'s goals.[11] While this mirrors, in its broadest outlines, the classical method of *ijtihād*, Riḍā proposed an untraditional method of identifying textual commands and of determining to what they might apply in the modern era.

First, departing dramatically from the assumptions underlying classical methods of *ijtihād*, Riḍā insisted that a person interpreting the Qur'ān and *ḥadīth* can accept as "universal," and thus legally probative, only those rules that (1) are found in religious texts of indubitable authenticity and (2) are absolutely "certain *both* in their transmission and meaning" (*qaṭʿī al-dalāla wa-'l-riwāya*) (emphasis added).[12] This was radical. Classical jurists had thought that Muslims should obey any *sharīʿa* ruling that was found in a text that was certain (*qaṭʿī*) with respect to either the authenticity or its meaning (so long as that text was at least "presumptive" (*ẓannī*) with respect to the other). Riḍā's more restrictive approach caused him to reject the authority of many rules the classical jurists would have accepted. As discussed in Chapter 3, classical legal theory held that only *ḥadīth*s meeting the strict standards of *tawātur* could be considered indubitably authentic (*qaṭʿī bi-'l-thubūt*). Classical theorists believed, however, that people were bound to obey clear rules that were found in *ḥadīth*s that were "sound" even if they were not absolutely certain to be authentic.[13] Indeed, the vast majority of scriptural rules that jurists derived from *ḥadīth*s were rooted in less-than-certain *ḥadīth*s. Riḍā's insistence that scriptural rules needed to be certain with respect

[11] Riḍā, *Al-Khilāfa aw al-Imāma al-ʿUẓmā* (Maṭbaʿat al-Manār, 1341 A.H./1923 C.E.), 90–91, and see discussion in Enayat, *Islamic Political Thought*, 78–81.

[12] See, e.g., Riḍā, *Yusr al-Islām wa Uṣūl al-Tashrīʿ al-ʿĀmm* (Cairo: Maṭbaʿat Nahḍat Miṣr, 1375 A.H./1956 C.E.), 77; and the discussion in Wael Hallaq, *A History of Islamic Legal Theories* (Cambridge: Cambridge University Press, 1997), 219. In this, Riḍā was extending a point that had been made by Muḥammad ʿAbduh in his *Risālat al-Tawḥīd*. ʿAbduh had expressed some doubts about whether one was really obliged blindly to accept the authenticity of a non-*mutawātir ḥadīth* that seemed inconsistent with the Qur'ān or with what our reason told us was plausible. Muḥammad ʿAbduh, *Risālat al-Tawḥīd*, ed. Rashīd Riḍā (Cairo: Maṭbaʿat al-Manār, 1346 A.H.), 223. See also the discussions in Daniel Brown, *Rethinking Tradition in Modern Islamic Legal Thought* (Cambridge: Cambridge University Press, 1996), 37, and G.H.A. Juynboll, *The Authenticity of the Tradition Literature: Discussion in Modern Egypt* (Leiden: E.J. Brill, 1969) 1923 C.E., 15–18.

[13] The following discussion draws heavily on the analysis in Juynboll, *The Authenticity of the Tradition Literature*, 21–63, 114–21, 139–52; and Brown, *Rethinking Tradition*, 32–38, 97–98, 116–22, 129–41.

to both authenticity and meaning meant that he would find fewer universally applicable scriptural rulings than the classical jurists had found.[14]

Riḍā's method of determining scholarly consensus (*ijmāʿ*) was also untraditional. Classical theory held that an interpretation of *sharīʿa* which would otherwise be considered "probable" should be accepted as certain if it was ratified by scholarly consensus. Riḍā accepted this point, with one crucial distinction. While the majority of classical jurists held that scholarly consensus consisted of the agreement of all the scholars of a generation, Riḍā followed the minority view of Ibn Taymiyya, arguing that only those points of law on which the companions of the Prophet reached a consensus are absolutely certain.[15] The companions were not known to have agreed on many points of law. Thus, if a ruling was not absolutely certain with respect to both its authenticity and meaning, consensus was unlikely to reveal that it was universal.

An interpreter using Riḍā's method was unlikely to find many universal rulings of *sharīʿa*. Accordingly, a Muslim's understanding of correct conduct would be guided not by rulings about the legality

[14] Riḍā tried to soften the impact of his principle of absolute certainty somewhat by suggesting that Muslims could accept the authenticity of a non-*mutawātir ḥadīth* so long as the text was consistent with unequivocal Qur'ānic precepts and/or the jurists' own sense of utility. But the importance of this should not be overstated. The importance of the classical acceptance of sound *hadīths* was that it provided knowledge that the Qur'ān and reason could not provide us—and the rulings that one found did not have to be measured against the jurist's sense of utility. Quite to the contrary, the jurist's understanding of utility should be informed by the assumption that anything commanded by a sound *ḥadīth* was beneficial to humans. He also downplayed the radical nature of this step by asserting that earlier jurists, including Ibn al-Qayyim, had at times rejected the authenticity of *ḥadīths* that most considered sound and thus, of probable (and binding) authenticity.

The pillar of faith is the Qur'ān and the customs of the Prophet which are transmitted through *mutawātir* traditions . . . The remaining traditions with one or only a few *isnāds* (*āḥād*), the transmission of which is doubtful or do not specifically indicate anything, are subject to independent judgment (*ijtihād*). We see that some *imāms* [eminent jurists] using their independent judgment have rejected many sound traditions . . . The learned Ibn al-Qayyim has produced more than a hundred examples of those sound traditions with which the Hanafiyya are at variance.

Muḥammad ʿAbduh and Rashid Riḍā, *Tafsīr al-Manār*, 12 vols. (Cairo: Maṭbaʿat al-Manār, 1346–1353 A.H.), repr. from *al-Manār*, 27, 616ff., trans. Juynboll, *Authenticity*, 22–23.

[15] For Riḍā's position, see Hallaq, *History*, 216, citing Riḍā, *Yusr*, 24–28. For the position of Ibn Taymiyya, see discussion in Chapter 3 and accompanying citations.

of certain types of action. Rather, he would be guided by his answer to the question, "What would advance the goals of the *sharīʿa?*". To put it differently, Riḍā's method of interpretation, by its very nature, suggested that interpreters (and thus Islamic states) could ignore rulings that classical legal theorists considered universally binding. Under Riḍā's approach, there were few rulings that a modern Islamic state must adopt wholesale into its codes. In many legal areas, the state was simply required to apply laws that its rulers believed would advance the goals of the *sharīʿa*.

Not only did Riḍā increase the importance of goals analysis as a component of Islamic legal analysis, but he departed from classical Sunnī assumptions about the goals of the *sharīʿa* and turned the analysis of these goals into a largely utilitarian exercise. Riḍā agreed that God clearly explained that some commands were revealed in the interest of promoting certain social outcomes and that one could use induction to identify some social results (including al-Ghazālī's five necessaries) that God wanted societies always to promote.[16] Nevertheless, he insisted, revelation is not the only source of knowledge about these goals. From observation of the natural world and the exercise of their unaided reason, Muslims can distinguish beneficial outcomes from harmful ones. Thus, where there is no ruling on point, an interpreter can determine laws a state should promulgate simply by determining what laws will best advance the welfare of Muslims.

In his discussions on the proper method of deriving rules in cases when there is no universal ruling on point, Riḍā characterized this

[16] As discussed in Chapter 2, the classical Sunnī tradition generally insisted that knowledge of the benefits be achieved in the first instance from scriptural analysis. By working inductively from the universally-applicable laws, classical jurists believed they could, through a study of the textual rulings of the *sharīʿa*, identify a number of social results that God wanted humans to enjoy. Sometimes a text would explicitly state what result a law was supposed to reach. In that case, the result was known for certain to be a "benefit" (*maṣlaḥa*), and its achievement would be a "goal" of the law. Using induction, jurists could also find patterns in the law which suggested that God wanted to advance certain other benefits. These were "textually-unregulated" benefits (*maṣāliḥ mursala*). These textually unregulated benefits were arranged in a hierarchy, at the top of which sat the so-called "necessaries." All classical jurists agreed that these included preservation of religion, life, property, reason, and children. Some classical jurists included a sixth, honor (*ʿirḍ*), as well. There were also subsidiary benefits.

method as a form of "*qiyās*."[17] This method, however, was very different from the method approved by most classical jurists, following instead the method proposed by the idiosyncratic (and long-neglected) jurist Ṭūfī. As described in Chapter 2, most classical jurists held that *qiyās* was a process of reasoning by analogy to rules that they discovered in scripture or *ijmāʿ*. In drawing analogies, jurists gave only limited consideration to the benefits that the law was supposed to provide. According to the classical jurists, every rule of *sharīʿa* advanced some benefit. Insofar as a Muslim could identify the benefit that the original rule was designed to advance, he could be sure that any rule derived by a correct analogy would serve the same goal. When Riḍā performed *qiyās*, however, the method of reasoning he used did not look anything like this carefully circumscribed classical form of analogical reasoning.[18]

Invoking the writings of the idiosyncratic and long-neglected thinker Ṭūfī, Riḍā placed great weight on the *ḥadīth* "no harm and no retribution" (*lā ḍarar wa lā ḍirār*). Following Ṭūfī, Riḍā asserted that this *ḥadīth* revealed a supreme utilitarian principle commanding people to act in the service of public good.[19] This was his principle of "benefit" (*maṣlaḥa*) or "necessity" (*ḍarūra*).[20] More revolutionary still, Riḍā incorporated the most radical implications of ʿAbduh's theology. He asserted that, as a general rule, reason and observation could reveal whether an act constitutes a harm (*ḍarār*) or benefit

[17] Riḍā, *Yusr*, 70ff.

[18] One wonders whether his departure was not inevitable, given the rigorous criteria that he applied before recognizing a rule as universal. Riḍā recognized very few textual rulings—far fewer than the classical jurists. The sample seems to have been sufficiently small, that one could not effectively identify patterns and thus induce "goals of the *sharīʿa*."

[19] Riḍā, *Al-Khilāfa*, 124–25. For Ṭūfī's thought and the controversy surrounding it, see discussion in Chapter 3. Riḍā published Ṭūfī's treatise on *maṣlaḥa* in *al-Manār*, the magazine that he edited: *al-Manār*, vol. 9: 745–70.

[20] Riḍā, *Al-Khilāfa*, 124–25. Given his skepticism about the *ḥadīth* literature, there was a certain irony in his reliance on this *ḥadīth* because as noted in Chapter 2, this was a *ḥadīth* that the classical jurists would not have considered to be of certain authenticity. He is no more successful than his predecessor in answering two questions: why this principle should be considered certain; and why, if it were accepted as a certain principle, it would take precedence over other certain principles. Like Ṭūfī, he glossed over the fact that (1) this *ḥadīth* was not *mutawātir* and (2) even if it were *mutawātir*, there is no reason to give it precedence over other "certain" commands.

(*maṣlaḥa*): "Islam is the religion of natural disposition and cannot possibly contradict the laws of creation nor can its customs contradict those of nature, for everything is from God."[21] Working from this premise, Riḍā was able to argue that an interpreter can determine the legality of an action largely on the basis of subjective value judgments or policy preferences. Riḍā argued that a Muslim could reason from the supreme utilitarian principle that people should never do what reason tells them is "harmful." Because unaided reason can distinguish benefit from harm, the legality of an action can be determined simply by asking whether reason suggests that the action will lead to net benefit or harm.[22] Even where there was a textual ruling on point, Riḍā believed it could be ignored whenever it would undoubtedly cause significant general harm to society. Because the "no harm" principle was for him paramount, scriptural rules could be set aside in the interest of advancing welfare (*maṣlaḥa*): "*maṣlaḥa* takes precedence over a textual source [i.e. the Qur'ān, authoritative *ḥadīth* or rule ratified by consensus]."[23] And because reason reveals what is beneficial, a reasoned conclusion that an allegedly "universal" rule is counterproductive was sufficient grounds to set that rule aside. In other words, Riḍā asserted that a jurist could choose not to apply a textual precept whenever he felt that application of the precept would cause net harm to society. In Riḍā's own words:

> Beyond decreeing the elements of virtue such as the necessity for justice in laws and equality in rights and forbidding rebelliousness, aggression, deceit and treachery and establishing penalties for certain crimes and beyond imposing the principle of consultation, the Lawgiver [God] delegated the affair in its detailed applications to the leading *'ulamā'* and rulers . . . to decide by consulting one another what is most beneficial for the community according to the circumstances of the times. . . . [Thus the companions of the Prophet] saw that the correct principle was to adopt whatever course was beneficial rather than to cling to the details and subsidiary rules of laws.[24]

---

[21] Riḍā, ed., *Al-Manār*, vol. 4: 216, trans. in Kerr, *Islamic Reform*, 157.

[22] Working on what seems to a be a grossly misleading oversimplification of the fourteenth-century Mālikī jurist Shāṭibī, he asserts that utilitarian reasoning leads inevitably to the same result as reasoning by classical Sunnī *qiyās*. See the discussion in Hallaq, *History*, 218, and Kerr, *Islamic Reform*, 194–95, each citing Riḍā, *Yusr*, 72–77. I have not checked Kerr's translations.

[23] Riḍā, ed. *Al-Manār*, vol. 9: 745–46, trans. in Kerr, *Islamic Reform*, 207.

[24] Riḍā, ed. *Al-Manār*, vol. 4: 209–10, trans. in Kerr, *Islamic Reform*, 190.

In understanding how such a theory was supposed to work in practice, it is helpful to remember that Riḍā's utilitarian neo-*ijtihād* was not supposed to be used by judges developing rules on a case-by-case basis. Rather, it was to be employed by government officials in charge of developing codes of legislation. It might be thought of as an analogue not of classical *ijtihād* per se, but rather of a two-step classical method of identifying the rulings and goals of Islamic law through *ijtihād* and then developing Islamic legislation that was consistent with these rulings and goals.

Critics have suggested that, compared to the classical methods of identifying Islamic legal rulings and goals, Riḍā's approach is problematic. Because it allows decisions about God's command to rest largely on rational calculations of utility, it empties Islamic law of anything uniquely "Islamic." Wael Hallaq has suggested that:

> Riḍā's doctrine amounts to a total negation of classical legal theory. . . . What is interesting is that he draws extensively on a highly limited and minor concept in that theory in order to suppress the rest of it[25]. . . . To accept, on the one hand, the revealed text's affirmation of the cause of welfare, interest and necessity, and, on the other hand, to reject nearly all other stipulations of rules and precepts without proper theoretical justification, amounts to nothing less than sheer arbitrariness.[26]

Arguably, another problem with Riḍā's method is that it fails to provide any real check on a state's legislative freedom. Whatever the state's hand-selected interpreters believe to be in the best interest of the people must be accepted as "Islamic." Riḍā recognized this potential problem, and he argued that, in modern times, the Muslim community could develop constitutional safeguards to prevent manipulation of Islamic law.[27] He suggested that Muslim states could form a new

---

[25] Hallaq, *History*, 219.

[26] Hallaq, *History*, 224. Similarly, shortly before his death, Fazlur Rahman said that Islamic legal reasoning that permit states to derive law largely through utilitarian analysis must always "guard against undue subjectivity. . . . Simply to talk of public interest can be an unconstrained, dangerously relativistic activity." Fazlur Rahman, "Towards Reformulating the Methodology of Islamic Law," *New York University Law Journal* 12.2 (1979): 223.

[27] "Most of the *'ulamā'* of the community avoided explicit reference to the principle [of *maṣlaḥa*] because of the fear—as Qarāfī says—that tyrannical leaders would take it as an excuse for following their own desires and imposing their absolute

type of caliphate in which a cadre of pious men trained in the nuances of utilitarian neo-*ijtihād* would help rulers prepare proper codes of Islamic laws.[28] These men would be able to depose any ruler who passed laws of which they did not approve.[29] As some have pointed out, however, Riḍā's proposals for a constitutional structure are underdeveloped and, perhaps, impractical.[30]

Notwithstanding these theoretical and pragmatic criticisms of Riḍā's theory, his ideas proved attractive to many later Islamic legal thinkers in Egypt and elsewhere. There was nothing to prevent *'ulamā'* from using Riḍā's method (and some embraced an analogue of it). Some neo-traditionalists, such as Maḥmūd Shaltūt, found aspects of the theory attractive, arguing that if they are sufficiently skilled in neo-*ijtihād*, the modern *'ulamā'* may use this approach to vet legislation.[31] At the same time, however, this theory did not seem to require a full classical education. It would seem that it could be performed by anyone with a knowledge of the Qur'ān and the *ḥadīth* literature, even if they were not steeped in the classical tradition of textual criticism, hermeneutics and logic. Thus, Riḍā's method of Islamic legal reasoning appealed to a new generation of Muslim intellectuals who were educated, but did not have classical religious training. Analogues of Riḍā's method took root in the academy, where thinkers such as

power on the property and persons of the population. The *'ulamā'* therefore thought to guard against this by tracing all laws back to revealed sources. . . . They converted the notion of *maṣāliḥ mursala* into one of the most technical forms of the *'illa* in *qiyās* so that it was not subject to the interpretation of princes and governors. This fear was justified at the time." Riḍā, *Yusr*, 75–76, trans. in Kerr, *Islamic Reform*, 195.

[28] For Riḍā's major political treatise see *al-Khilāfa*, also published in *al-Manār* 23–24. See also the introduction to the French translation by Henri Laoust, *Le califat dans la doctrine de Rasid Rida* (Beirut: Institut Français de Damas, 1938). For further analysis, see Henri Laoust, *Essai sur les doctrines sociales et politiques de Taḳī-d-Dīn Aḥmad b. Taimiyya* (Cairo: Institut Français d'Archéologie Orientale, 1949), 573ff.; Enayat, *Modern Islamic Political Thought*, 69–83, particularly 77–81; Kerr, *Islamic Reform*, 153ff.

[29] See the discussion in Kerr, *Islamic Reform*, 183.

[30] See, e.g., Albert Hourani, *Arabic Thought in the Liberal Age: 1798–1939* (Cambridge: Cambridge University Press, 1970), 239–40; Kerr, *Islamic Reform*, 220–21.

[31] Although Shaltūt's methodology differs from Riḍā's in some ways, his theory bears a number of resemblances. He held that only the consensus of the companions is infallible, that legal interpretation must be based largely on a consideration of *maṣlaḥa*, and that any Muslim can use his method. Shaltūt's thought can comfortably be described as a form of utilitarian neo-*ijtihād*. See Zebiri, *Maḥmūd Shaltūt and Islamic Modernism* (Oxford: Clarendon Press, 1993).

ʿAbd al-Wahhāb Khallāf proposed slightly modified methods of utilitarian neo-*ijtihād*.[32] More important, perhaps, the approach appealed to the new urban middle classes.

III. *Modernist theories calling for Muslims to interpret the* sharīʿa *and develop state law through comparative neo-*taqlīd

Shortly after Rashīd Riḍā began to argue publicly for his theory of utilitarian neo-*ijtihād*, ʿAbd al-Razzāq Aḥmad al-Sanhūrī proposed a very different method of Islamic legal interpretation. Modern states could use this alternate method to identify "universal" principles of law and, working from these principles, to develop Islamic codes of law.[33] If Riḍā's method of legal interpretation represents a radically new type of *ijtihād*, Sanhūrī's represents a radically new type of *taqlīd*.

Sanhūri's Islamic legal theory reflected his sophisticated understanding of important contemporary trends in European legal thought. After studying at the University of Cairo, Sanhūrī pursued graduate legal study in France. There his legal thinking came to be shaped by two movements. The first was the comparative legal studies movement which influenced European nationalist movements. The second was the rising movement espousing an anti-formalist, sociological jurisprudence. Eventually, he wrote and published two well-received doctoral dissertations.[34] In the first, he engaged in a formal comparative study of legal institutions. In the second, he considered

[32] See the summary of Khallāf's thought in Hallaq, *History*, 220–24.

[33] For Sanhūrī's biography and thought, the work of Enid Hill is indispensable. Like all writers after her, I have drawn heavily upon the insights in her work: *Al-Sanhuri and Islamic Law: The Place and Significance of Islamic Law in the Life and Work of ʿAbd al-Razzaq Ahmad al-Sanhuri, Egyptian Jurist and Scholar 1895–1971* (Cairo: American University in Cairo Press, 1987), and the following section will reflect her conclusions. For further enlightening analyses of Sanhūrī's life and work, see Amr Shalakany, "Between Identity and Redistribution: Sanhuri, Genealogy and the Will to Islamize," *Islamic Law and Society*, 8.2 (2001): 201–44.

[34] ʿAbd al-Razzāq al-Sanhūrī, *Les restrictions contractuelles à la liberté individuelle de travail* (Paris: Marcel Giard, 1925) and ʿAbd al-Razzāq al-Sanhūrī, *Le califat: son évolution vers une societé des nations orientales* (Lyons: Librairie Orientaliste Paul Geuthner, 1926). On the reception of these works, see Shalakany, "Between Identity," 207–14; Hill, *Al-Sanhuri and Islamic Law*, 24–26, 40.

whether comparative law and sociological jurisprudence might fruitfully be put to use in the Muslim world. He concluded in this dissertation that Muslim nations should consider establishing a supra-national organization that would supervise the drafting of codes of "Islamic" legislation. Going farther, he proposed in skeletal form, the method that member states should use to draft "Islamic" codes regulating non-ritual issues that corresponded roughly to the so-called *muʿāmalāt.*[35] The method drew upon the modern techniques of European comparative legal studies and of sociological legal studies. I shall describe it in more detail below. After publishing this work, al-Sanhūrī discussed and refined his proposal. Over the course of his life, he also carried out a number of legal drafting projects that employed his methodology to create civil laws for Muslim countries.

Like the process of developing classical *siyāsa sharʿiyya* (and Riḍā's proposed method of identifying codifiable Islamic norms through utilitarian neo-*ijtihād*), Sanhūrī's method was a two-part process designed to be used to draw up codes of Islamic law. In the first stage, legal specialists derive a body of universally applicable rules and a set of goals that the law of a Muslim state should serve. In the second stage, the government, in consultation with the legal specialists, drafts laws that are consistent with these universally applicable rules and social goals.

How did Sanhūrī propose to identify the Islamic rulings and goals that states must respect? Like Rashīd Riḍā, Sanhūrī was eager to come up with a method of interpretation to free Muslim states from the obligation to impose and enforce traditional rules of *fiqh.* Like his older contemporary, Sanhūrī proposed a new method of identifying universal rulings and goals of *sharīʿa.* His method was, however, strikingly different from that of his older contemporary. I will characterize Sanhūrī's interpretive approach as one of comparative neo-*taqlīd.*

---

[35] See, e.g., Sanhūrī, *Le califat,* 571. Initially, Sanhūrī envisioned his method as being employed in a caliphate. Ultimately, however, Sanhūrī argued, it could be used to develop a code for a state without a caliph. Furthermore, Sanhūrī believed the methodology could also be used to resolve legal questions when judges found a legal question that needed to be addressed and that was not dealt with explicitly in the code. As Shalakany points out, his later writings reflect an anti-formalist assumption that codes contain gaps, that judges must legislate within these gaps and that such judicial legislation could and should be informed by the same Islamic impulse as the initial process of drafting. See Shalakany, "Between Identity," 228–35.

Sanhūrī thought it would be unproductive for Muslims of his day to return to scriptures that had been exhaustively interpreted by great jurists in the past. He thought that, if the universal principles of Islamic law were to be fully understood, such knowledge should grow from the exegetical tradition that represented the accumulated wisdom of the Muslim peoples. In his view, one should apply to one's study of the *fiqh* literature comparative and sociological tools similar to those that Europeans had used to study German or French law in order to draw up national codes.

Sanhūrī called the first step in his process of drafting Islamic legislation the scientific phase ("*phase scientifique*"). In this phase, a legal scholar would look to the competing interpretations of Islamic law that had been proposed over the years. The major source would be the *fiqh* literature produced by the classical jurists. According to Sanhūrī, a legislator could compare and contrast all the rules of *fiqh* proposed by *'ulamā'* over the years and consider the specific conditions of the society in which particular rules were proposed. With this information, he or she would be able to identify principles of law that are valid at all times and places. These may be rules that have been explicitly followed at all times and places, or they may be overarching principles that can be induced from the Islamic tradition.[36] Sanhūrī referred to these as "fixed rules" ("*règles stables*") and described them as "universal and permanent" principles. These rules were identified by the fact that they had been respected and applied at all times in all places ("*[Le règle stable est] le principe qui est fondé sur des raisons d'êtres permanentes de nature à se réproduire dans tous les temps et dans tous les lieux . . . la règle stable et permanente et universelle.*")[37] States were required to ensure that they did not promulgate or enforce laws that were inconsistent with these fixed rules.

According to Sanhūrī, Muslims were not bound by "variable rulings" proposed by one classical Sunnī jurist but rejected (implicitly or explicitly) by others. Since a variable ruling was not accepted

[36] Sanhūrī, *Le califat*, 580–81. See also the discussion in Hill, *Al-Sanhuri and Islamic Law*, 5, 38–39.

[37] See, e.g., Sanhūrī, *Le califat*, 580 and n. 7. See also his "Le droit musulman comme élément de refonte du code civil égyptien," in *Introduction à l'étude du droit comparé: Receuil d'études en l'honneur d'Édouard Lambert* (Paris: Librairie Générale de Droit et de Jurisprudence/Librairie de la Société Anonyme du Recueil Sirey, 1938), 623.

at all places and at all times, it represented, at most, an attempt to apply a universal legal principle in the context of a particular society at a particular point in time. Even assuming that the ruling was correct for the society in which it was first developed, it might cease to be the most appropriate method of applying the principle. Variable rules will thus regularly be replaced by new variable rules.[38] Thus, although states were required to ensure that their laws were consistent with all the fixed rules, they were free to ignore variable rules.

Before continuing, it is important to make two points. First, although it does not explicitly characterize itself as an analogue of the classical doctrine of *siyāsa sharʿiyya*, Sanhūrī's theory can be described as one. Among the principles that might be induced from the Islamic legal tradition are principles stating that certain types of behavior are always required or prohibited—principles which correspond to classical interpretations of the "rulings" of *sharīʿa*.[39] They might also contain consequentialist principles stating that particular actions are always supposed to promote certain types of result. For example, a modern thinker who had compared the different rules of marriage set forth in different books of classical *fiqh* might conclude that laws, although they differ in details, all tended to promote result "x." Knowledge of the systematically-favored results correspond to what the classical jurist and Rashīd Riḍā each would have conceptualized as knowledge of the goals of the *sharīʿa*. Seen through the paradigm of a theory of *siyāsa sharʿiyya*, the fixed rules that Sanhūrī abstracted from the tradition contain analogues both of the "universal rulings" of the *sharīʿa* and the goals of the *sharīʿa*.

---

[38] "La règle variable est une règle qui s'est inspire de l'état d'un milieu et d'une époque déterminés. Tandis que la règle stable est permanente et universelle, la règle variable est temporaire et particulaire." Sanhūrī, *Le califat*, 580 and n. 7. Compare with Sanhūrī, "Le droit musulman comme élément de refonte du code civil égyptien," 623.

[39] Sanhūrī's abstracted, universally applicable rulings, which I will call "universal" rules of the *sharīʿa*, should not be confused with the rulings that classical jurists would have recognized as universal by virtue of the fact that they had been ratified by scholarly consensus (*ijmāʿ*). The classical doctrine of consensus said that the agreement of a single generation on a point of law demonstrated the correctness of that law. According to most classical Sunnī jurists, juristic consensus (*ijmāʿ*) of the companions, or of a later generation of jurists, concerning the validity of a certain rule of behavior was incontrovertible evidence that the rule was absolutely certain and universally binding. Rashīd Riḍā had espoused a more limited version of *ijmāʿ*, accepting the consensus of the Prophet's companions as an indication of certainty.

Second, Sanhūrī's approach to developing positive Islamic rules to include in codes differed from that of neo-traditional scholars practicing *talfīq*. The *ʿulamāʾ* practicing *talfīq* had to select a rule from the rules which jurists in the past had proposed. Sanhūrī, on the other hand, tried to induce an overarching principle that reconciled all the competing rulings of the past. He then came up with a rule (perhaps unprecedented) that was consistent with this overarching principle. Joseph Schacht contrasted the method of *talfīq* practiced by the *ʿulamāʾ* and comparative neo-*taqlīd* advocated by Sanhūrī by saying that a person developing a code of Islamic law through comparative neo-*taqlīd* will start with "not the positive solutions of strict Islamic law [i.e., rules of *fiqh* that had been elaborated over the years by a particular group of Sunnī jurists] but the general formal principles which were elaborated by the early scholars and . . . [would derive] from them a new, modern law."[40] Baber Johansen has noted that, unlike the neo-traditionalists who insisted on literal fidelity to one of the classical *fiqh* texts (although they were free to choose from whichever text they preferred), al-Sanhūrī argued that an interpreter should "apply the methods of comparative private law to *fiqh* texts in order to disengage from their casuistry the principles which govern the *fiqh*'s legal reasoning and which can be translated into a sufficiently abstract and general form to be applied in the codification of modern national law."[41]

In Sanhūrī's second stage, governments would develop legislation that is consistent with the fixed rules. This is a direct analogue of both the process by which rulers such as the Ottomans worked with classical jurists to develop statutes meeting the criteria of *siyāsa sharʿiyya*

Sanhūri rejected the idea that a single generation (even that of the Prophet's companions) could come up with rulings that bound all later generations. Consensus revealed the indubitable correctness of a ruling for the time that the jurists agreed upon the ruling. It could not, however, be taken as evidence that the same ruling inevitably applied to later generations. Accordingly, in Sanhūrī's thought, juristic "consensus" is not a hermeneutic tool but rather a principle establishing the "Islamic" roots of democratic lawmaking in areas where there is no "universal" Islamic principle that explains exactly how people should behave. See, e.g., Sanhūrī, *Le califat*, 6–7. See also "Le droit musulman comme élément de refonte du code civil égyptien," 621–23.

[40] Schacht, *Introduction to Islamic Law*, 107.

[41] Baber Johansen, *Contingency in a Sacred Law: Legal and Ethical Norms in the Muslim Fiqh* (Leiden: E.J. Brill, 1999), 58.

and also of the process by which Rashīd Riḍā thought states should develop law through utilitarian neo-*ijtihād*.

From the description so far, one can understand why people have had trouble coming up with a name for Sanhūrī's approach. (Joseph Schacht tried to avoid the problem of characterizing it, and described it simply as a "modernist reshaping of Islamic law.")[42] Some observers over the years have even questioned whether al-Sanhūrī's strongly historical and sociological theory of Islamic law can be considered Islamic in the same sense as the *'ulamā''*s neo-traditional methods or the methods of utilitarian neo-*ijtihād*. For example, neo-traditionalist Islamists and the champions of utilitarian neo-*ijtihād* in modern Egypt have each criticized Sanhūrī for denying that the essential principles of Sunnī Islamic law were revealed to the Muslim community in the words of the Qur'ān or the prophetic example as recorded in the *ḥadīth* literature.[43] Sanhūrī's critics contended that no body of law can be called Islamic if it did not accept as primary those principles

---

[42] Joseph Schacht, *An Introduction to Islamic Law* (Oxford: Oxford University Press, 1964), 107. Noel Coulson actually described Sanhūrī's method of developing statutes as a form of neo-*ijtihād*. See, e.g., Noel Coulson, *A History of Islamic Law* (Edinburgh: Edinburgh University Press, 1964), 203–04. Coulson's characterization, while theoretically defensible, can be misleading. Like the jurists who argued for the classical regime of *taqlīd*, Sanhūrī believed that jurists could not productively search for universal "Islamic" principles in the texts of the Qur'ān or *ḥadīth*. This Sanhūrī method did not try to extrapolate from rules that are set forth in these scriptures—the approach classical *mujtahids* and the practitioners of utilitarian neo-*ijtihād* applied. Rather, Sanhūrī, like the classical champions of *taqlīd*, assumed that God's command should be sought in the secondary texts written by eminent jurists of the past. However, Sanhūrī's approach to developing codifiable Islamic rules is clearly not *taqlīd* or *talfīq*. The process of drafting laws through Sanhūrī's method differs in a subtle but significant way from the neo-traditional method of developing law through *talfīq* that I described earlier. In *talfīq* the rules proposed by a classical jurist must be applied. Under Sanhūrī's theory, the interpreter is not obliged to continue enforcing any classical rules of *fiqh*. He need only come up with rules that respect the overarching principles that caused classical jurists to come up with the rules that they had. Thus, the drafter is free to adopt whatever new rules are necessary, so long as these respect the general principles that all Islamic jurists have respected and advanced the results that classical jurists tried to promote. Sanhhūri's method of drafting Islamic rules requires Islamic legal interpreters to draft codes with an eye on the *fiqh* tradition. But it also allows them to draft rules that are entirely unprecedented. Hence, my decision to call the approach comparative neo-*taqlīd*.

[43] For a discussion of criticisms made during the debates over ratification of Sanhūrī's Egyptian Code, see Farhat Ziadeh, *Lawyers, the Rule of Law and Liberalism in Modern Egypt* (Stanford: Hoover Institution, 1968), 143, citing *al-Muḥāmāh*, March, 1948, 4–7 and insert before 3; see also the discussion in Chapter 6.

that had been announced clearly in the Qur'ān and the *ḥadīths*. More interestingly, some eminent historians of Islamic thought seem implicitly to have taken the critics' position as their own. Two important recent surveys of Islamic legal theory include substantial discussions of Rashīd Riḍā's attempt to find the universally applicable principles of Islamic law through utilitarian neo-*ijtihād*, but do not mention Sanhūrī's attempt to identify them through comparative neo-*taqlīd*.[44] Criticism of Sanhūrī has been exacerbated by the fact that Sanhūrī unapologetically included in his Islamic codes many laws taken from European sources. Since such laws were included only where they could be reconciled with the universal Islamic legal principles, Sanhūrī thought they were simultaneously "European" and "Islamic."[45] In an era of impassioned post-colonial politics, such subtlety was not always appreciated. As Enid Hill, an admirer of Sanhūrī, points out, "If the *sharī'a* rulings become embedded in the modern, abstract language of codes so that they lose their identity except to the legally erudite, Islamization has not, for all practical purposes, taken place. The verdict on the popular and fundamentalist level as to whether Sanhuri's civil code is Islamic—or sufficiently so—must clearly be in the negative."[46]

Although many Islamists rejected Sanhūrī's codes as insufficiently Islamic, his views about legal interpretation have nevertheless had a powerful impact on Egyptians' understanding of what it means to live their lives in an "Islamic" fashion, and what it means for state legislation to be "Islamic legislation." In the 1930s, Sanhūrī published a series of studies that began to identify some of the underlying principles of law that would be used to draft a code.[47] In the

[44] See Hallaq, *History*; Bernard Weiss, *The Spirit of Islamic Law* (Athens: University of Georgia Press, 1988). Although there is apparently a reluctance to characterize Sanhūrī as a legal theorist, histories of substantive Islamic law do discuss him as a thinker who integrated classical *fiqh* into modern legal systems. See, e.g., Baber Johansen, *Contingency in a Sacred Law*; Schacht, *An Introduction to Islamic Law*; Coulson, *A History of Islamic Law*.

[45] Sanhūrī's own characterization of them tended to shift with the political winds. He would sometimes stress their European-ness and at other times, their Islamic-ness. On this point, see generally Shalakany, "Between Identity and Redistribution."

[46] Hill, *Al-Sanhuri and Islamic Law*, 72

[47] Hill, *Al-Sanhuri and Islamic Law*, 40–42, citing 'Abd al-Razzāq al-Sanhūrī, *'Aqd al-Ijāra* (The Contract of Leasing) (Beirut: n.d.) and *Naẓariyyāt al-'Aqd* (The Theory of Contract) (Cairo: 1934).

1930s and 40s, he successfully convinced the Egyptian government to revise its laws by adopting laws drafted, in part, through comparative neo-*taqlīd*.[48] Furthermore, academics, lawyers, and politicians in Egypt and throughout the Islamic world have implicitly come to accept Sanhūrī's essential premise that the historical interpretations of Islamic law can provide valuable information about God's law. As Baber Johansen has pointed out:

> Even the Islamist movements of the late eighties and nineties who often criticize Sanhūrī or Cheheta's conceptions do apply their methods, mostly with much less skill, when they produce projects of new codes. Successful or failing attempts to draw up civil codes with a strengthened reference to the heritage of the *fiqh* have been numerous over the last twenty years. But what is important is that in all these attempts to bring *fiqh* back into law, those who want to do so act as jurists who refer to legal texts [i.e., works of *fiqh* as opposed to the Qur'ān, *ḥadīth*s, and consensus of the companions].[49]

IV. *Conclusion: Competing methods of Islamic legal interpretation and of drafting Islamic codes*

By the early twentieth century, many members of the Egyptian elite had come to be convinced both that Egypt should become an independent state and that Egyptian law should be codified. The question that taxed Egyptians was whether the statutory law in the new state should be measured against "Islamic" legal norms. Some Egyptians embraced secularism and answered in the negative. Many, however, clung to the belief that Egypt should be an Islamic state in which all statutory legislation would respect the universally applicable rulings and "goals" of the *sharīʿa*. Modern Egyptians who continued to maintain this "Islamist" outlook did not embrace a purely classical approach to identifying and interpreting the rulings and goals of

[48] Al-Sanhūrī, "Le droit Musulman comme élément de refonte du code civile égyptien," 621–42. See also Hill, *Al-Sanhuri and Islamic Law*, 50–64, citing al-Sanhūrī, "Wujūb Tanqīḥ al-Qānūn al-Madanī al-Miṣrī wa ʿalā Ayy Asās Yakūn Hādhā al-Tanqīḥ," *Majallat al-Qānūn wa-'l-Iqtiṣād* 6 (1936): 1–142; al-Sanhūrī, "ʿalā Ayy Asās Yakūn Tanqīḥ al-Qānūn al-Madanī al-Miṣrī," *al-Kitāb al-Dhahabī li-'l-Maḥākim al-Ahliyya* (Cairo: al-Maṭbaʿa al-Amīriyya bi-Būlāq, 1938), vol. 2, 106–43.

[49] Baber Johansen, *Contingency in a Sacred Law*, 59.

sharīʿa. Indeed, few did. Rather, in the late nineteenth and early twentieth centuries, thinkers in Egypt, as elsewhere in the Muslim world, began to develop and popularize new approaches to Islamic legal interpretation. Neo-traditional theories included a range of theories each ascribing to the contemporary *ʿulamāʾ* a unique ability to interpret *sharīʿa.* Alongside (and sometimes overlaping with) neo-traditional theories were theories arguing that *sharīʿa* should be interpreted (and Islamic legislation drafted) through utilitarian neo-*ijtihād.* Finally, scholars trained in European legal theory developed a method of interpreting *sharīʿa* through a process of comparative neo-*taqlīd.* The breakdown of consensus on questions of Islamic legal theory had an impact on Egyptian politics. Once Egypt finally gained independence from the Ottoman Empire and from the British, different Islamic political factions in modern Egypt embraced different methods of interpreting *sharīʿa* and thus came to propose very different types of Islamic code.

CHAPTER SIX

POLITICAL ISLAMISM IN TWENTIETH-CENTURY EGYPT AND THE COMPETING MODERNIST THEORIES OF ISLAMIC LAW

When popular Egyptian nationalist movements arose in the twentieth century, they proposed reforms of Egyptian law. Many of these nationalists, inspired by modernist Islamic thought, argued that, when Egypt became independent, its law should be an analogue of *siyāsa sharʿiyya.* Since positivism had come to hold sway, they assumed that Egyptian law would have to be codified. Nevertheless, the codes should respect the universally applicable rulings of the *sharīʿa* and must promote the goals of the *sharīʿa.* These new movements generally did not call, however, for the adoption of traditional *siyāsa sharʿiyya.* Rather, each embraced one of the various new methods of developing "Islamic" legislation and pressed for the Egyptian state to reform its legal system and apply only laws that were "Islamic" according to one or another of the new approaches to Islamic interpretation.

I. *Islamist factions during Egypt's Liberal Period, 1922–1952*

At the beginning of the twentieth century, Egypt was officially a province of the Ottoman Empire. For all practical purposes, however, it was a British colony. After the Ottoman Empire's collapse in 1922, the British could no longer pretend that they were merely assisting with the administration of an Ottoman province. Political realities made it impossible for Britain to absorb Egypt into its global empire. Thus, it unilaterally declared Egypt to be an independent state. To smooth the transition and to ensure that the government of the new state remained friendly to Britain, the British "advised" the Egyptian elites who had governed the nation during the British occupation as they drafted a constitution and took power.[1] The

[1] See Afaf Lutfi al-Sayyid Marsot, *Egypt's Liberal Experiment: 1922–1936* (Berkeley:

former Ottoman Khedive (Vice-Regent) of Egypt was now recognized as a king, and headed a state modeled on continental European constitutional monarchies. The Egyptian constitutional monarchy lasted from 1922 until the Second World War, a period that Afaf Lutfi al-Sayyid Marsot has referred to as Egypt's "liberal experiment."[2] Although the chaotic period during and immediately after the Second World War does not fit neatly into this period, I will, for the sake of convenience, consider it to be the tail end of the liberal period. I will refer to the entire period from independence up to the military coup in 1952 as the "liberal period."

At the time of independence, the ruling Egyptian elites did not wish to limit their power by committing to rule in accordance with "Islamic legal norms." The 1922 Constitution did not contain any provision requiring Islamization. Although Article 149 of the Constitution asserted that "Islam is the religion of the state," it was unclear what this meant in practice. The Constitution required the king to obey only the Constitution and "the laws of the Egyptian people," not the commands of the *shari'a*. It did not explicitly require the government to ensure that the laws that it enforced were "Islamic."[3] In short, the government was permitted but not required to ensure that the law of Egypt was consistent with Islamic law. And, in fact, neither the king nor the Parliament in the 1920s or 1930s seems to have made any serious effort to ensure that law was "Islamic." Most controversially, the government continued to use its old civil code—which had been drafted as a response to the British invasion without consistent reference to Islamic legal norms.

Increasingly, however, Egyptians were challenging the implicit secularism of the government. A number of new popular political organizations with Islamist platforms sprang up, alongside class-based parties and other political groupings, and the new Islamist groups called for a new government that would govern in accordance with

University of California Press, 1977), 43–73; P.J. Vatikiotis, *The History of Modern Egypt*, 4th ed. (Baltimore: Johns Hopkins Press, 1991), 260–86.

[2] Hence the title of al-Marsot's *Egypt's Liberal Experiment*. Vatikiotis refers to the period from 1922 to 1939 as Egypt's "experiment in constitutional government." Vatikiotis, *The History of Modern Egypt*, 273–97.

[3] Art. 149. See Nadav Safran, "The Abolition of the Shari'a Courts in Egypt: Part II," *The Muslim World* 48 (1958): 132.

God's commands. Inspired by these groups, middle-class Islamists in the government and in professional organizations began to press for some kind of Islamization. As popular criticism of the government became phrased in Islamic terms, intellectuals and nationalist politicians who were once associated with secular nationalist theories began to explore Islamist nationalism.[4] Islamism thus came to be integrated generally into Egyptian nationalism and pan-Arab nationalism. In this environment, the failure of the newly independent government to revise the national legal codes in order to "Islamize" them proved to be an issue with enormous emotional resonance.

Those who called for Islamization of the law were hardly a homogenous group. Demand for reform of the civil code had come to be heavily influenced by modernist Islamic thinkers. As these thinkers disagreed about the proper method of interpreting Islamic law and identifying the norms against which state law must be measured, Egyptian Islamists found themselves deeply divided.

During the liberal period, neo-traditionalism was politically stronger than it would be later in the century. Neo-traditionalism, as discussed in the previous chapter, was a movement asserting that the state legislation must conform to *sharʿī* norms derived by the *ʿulamāʾ*. The *ʿulamāʾ* had support in the palace and in the countryside, and in the 1930s a form of neo-traditionalism even began to make some inroads into the urban middle class, which was becoming increasingly active politically. The *ʿulamāʾ*, for example, used every opportunity to call for the Egyptian government to adopt a sort of neo-traditional code which they themselves would draft and apply in the *sharīʿa* courts. By allying themselves loosely with the king, who was continually squabbling with the Parliament, and by championing the king's attempt to be recognized as a new caliph, the *ʿulamāʾ* were able to insert themselves into the national debate about codes.[5] In

---

[4] See the analysis in Israel Gershoni and James Jankowski, *Redefining the Egyptian Nation: 1930–1945* (Cambridge: Cambridge University Press, 1995), 65–78; Vatikiotis, *The History of Modern Egypt*, 326–27.

[5] See, e.g., Gabriel Baer, "Islamic Political Activity in Modern Egyptian History: A Comparative Analysis," *Islam, Nationalism and Radicalism*, eds. Gabriel R. Warburg and Uri M. Kupferschmidt (New York: Praeger, 1983), 44–46; Vatikiotis, *The History of Modern Egypt*, 327–28. For an analysis of al-Azhar's role in the debates about whether King Fuʾad should be recognized as Caliph, see Eli Kedourie, *The Chatham House Version and other Middle Eastern Studies*, new ed. (Hanover: Brandeis University Press, 1984), 177–212.

the 1930s, the government finally began flirting with the possibility of drafting new codes of legislation, and the Azharite *ʿulamāʾ* enthusiastically proposed that Egypt adopt a neo-traditional code that they would vet for consistency with Islamic law. This proposal was widely discussed in the press.[6] The *ʿulamāʾ* found allies in a political organization called Young Egypt. Inspired by the contemporary fascist movements in Europe, Young Egypt called for a monarchy that would purge Egypt of all foreign influence and would impose legislation that was consistent with an interpretation of the *sharīʿa* developed by the *ʿulamāʾ* of al-Azhar.[7]

Neo-traditional Islamist movements were eclipsed both in passion and effectiveness by a mass political organization inspired by the writings of Rashīd Riḍā. The Society of the Muslim Brothers (the "Muslim Brotherhood") was founded in 1928 by Ḥasan al-Bannā (d. 1949 C.E.).[8] Under Bannā's leadership, the Muslim Brotherhood called for spiritual and political renewal and advocated the imposition of a form of Islamic law drafted through utilitarian neo-*ijtihād*.[9]

A political activist rather than a systematic political thinker, Bannā described his program only very generally. His writings, however, clearly draw from those of Riḍā. First, Bannā and the Brothers adopted and amplified Riḍā's call for Muslims to identify the universally applicable principles of the *sharīʿa* by analysis primarily of the Qurʾān and of the "purified" *hadīths* taken from trustworthy authorities.[10] Like Riḍā, Bannā and the early Brothers accepted that

---

[6] Farhat Ziadeh, *Lawyers, the Rule of Law and Liberalism in Modern Egypt* (Stanford: Hoover Institution, 1968), 139. The judges of the *sharīʿa* courts had first insisted that Egypt should centralize the administration of justice, not by increasing the jurisdiction of the National Courts, but rather by increasing the jurisdiction of the *sharīʿa* courts. For these facts, see Nathan Brown, *The Rule of Law in the Arab World: Courts in Egypt and the Gulf* (Cambridge: Cambridge University Press, 1997), 64.

[7] On Young Egypt, see Vatikiotis, *The History of Modern Egypt*, 330–34.

[8] Upon Riḍā's death in 1935, Bannā temporarily took over the publication of Riḍā's magazine, *al-Manār*. Jacob Skovgaard-Petersen, *Defining Islam for the Egyptian State: Muftīs and Fatwās of the Dar al-Iftā* (Leiden: E.J. Brill, 1997), 156.

[9] A spiritual and political activist rather than a theological or legal theorist, Bannā never published a detailed explanation of what Islamic law was or how it was derived. For a sample of his thought, see, e.g., Ḥasan al-Bannāʾ, *Five Tracts of Hasan al-Bannaʾ: A Selection from the Majmuʿat Rasaʾil al-Imam al-Shahid Hasan al-Bannaʾ*, trans. Charles Wendell (Berkeley: University of California Press, 1975), 19–20. See also the discussion in Ibrahim Abu-Rabiʾ, *Intellectual Origins of Islamic Resurgence in the Modern Arab World* (Albany: State University of New York Press, 1996), 79.

[10] As the reference to purification suggests, the Brothers, like Riḍā, refused to

the Qur'ān and authoritative *hadīths* provided the contemporary Muslim only with generally applicable principles that he would have to apply in light of contemporary circumstances, rather than specific precepts that he should apply at all times. They believed that the state should identify these general principles, and then draft codes of legislation to conform to them.[11] Like Riḍā, the Brothers accepted that a state had vast discretion to interpret and apply Islamic principles so as to advance social welfare. As Branjar Lia puts it, Bannā "stressed that interpretations of the meanings of the Glorious Qur'an must be linked 'scientifically, socially and morally' to aspects of modern life, and 'modern theories and ways of thinking' should be employed'" in order to understand the correct course of action.[12] Bannā and the Brothers stressed that, when a government established new codes of state legislation, it could base them on existing codes.[13] Similarly, a handbook given to the Brothers in 1938 says that they should "explain Islamic laws to foreigners and ignorants and teach them that Islamic legislation is compatible with the most modern systems of legislation."[14]

---

accept the traditional determinations of authenticity, insisting that they would not accept the validity of a *ḥadīth* if it proved inconsistent with their understanding of the Qur'ān or of the natural world. Although Bannā himself would cite *ḥadīths* taken from the canonical collections of al-Bukhārī (d. 256/870) and Muslim (d. 261/875), some of the Brothers believed that a critical re-examination of the *ḥadīths* would demonstrate that most were not authoritative. Some went so far as to suggest that a person seeking law would have to ignore all *hadīth* and rely entirely on the Qur'ān. See Richard P. Mitchell, *The Society of the Muslim Brothers,* reprint with new intro. (New York: Oxford University Press, 1993), 238, citing oral sources and Muḥammad 'Abd Allāh al-Sammān, *al-Islām al-Muṣaffā* (Cairo: 1954), 94–96.

[11] See the official publication *Dustūruna* (Cairo: n.d.), 4–5, cited in Mitchell, *The Society of the Muslim Brothers,* 237. A similar sentiment was apparently expressed by Muḥammad 'Awda. See Muḥammad 'Awda, *Al-Islām wa 'Awdatuna al-Siyāsiyya,* (Cairo: 1951), 170–80, translated by Michael Pallis in Anouar Abdel-Malek, ed. *Contemporary Arab Political Thought* (London: Zed Press, 1983), 49–50. ("The general judgments and principles mentioned by the *Sharī'a* must be taken as the general rules of Islamic legislation; they provide the basic armature which determines the characteristics and forms of control of Islamic legislation. The *Sharī'a* leaves it to the wise and to public opinion to complete the edifice of legislation, to elaborate its details and interconnections within the framework of principles and fundamental rules laid down in the *Sharī'a.*") I have not been able to check the original.

[12] Branjar Lia, *The Society of the Muslim Brothers in Egypt: The Rise of an Islamic Mass Movement, 1928–1942* (Reading: Ithaca Press, 1998), 76.

[13] See Mitchell, *The Society of the Muslim Brothers,* 260.

[14] Lia, *Society of Muslim Brothers in Egypt,* 213. Lia does not provide a citation for the handbook.

This message proved attractive to a large number of civil servants, students, urban laborers, and members of the lower middle classes—people who were able to read the Qur'ān and *hadīths* for themselves and who tended to see the *ʿulamāʾ* as obscurantists who had helped to create and justify a socially and economically unjust society.[15] Spreading quickly into all segments of society, the Brothers became "the first organized Islamic political movement of the middle class."[16] The Brothers were not only able to mobilize this important segment of the polity, but also willing to use any means, including violence, to achieve their goals.[17]

Though the Brothers were always opposed to the atheism of communism, their social program shared some of the idealistic qualities of socialist thought. While this trend is apparent in the writings of Bannā, it was to flourish more fully in the work in the next generation, and particularly in the work of Sayyid Quṭb, who, after Bannā's assassination by the Egyptian government in 1949, rose to a prominent position within the Muslim Brotherhood.[18] Quṭb's book, *Social Justice in Islam* (*al-ʿAdāla al-Ijtimāʿiyya fī al-Islām*), published in several, quite different, editions, was not a book of legal theory.[19] Nevertheless,

---

[15] See Mitchell, *The Society of the Muslim Brothers*, 9–34; Ahmed M. Gomaa, "Islamic Fundamentalism in Egypt during the 1930s and 1970s: Comparative Notes," *Islam, Nationalism and Radicalism*, 143–46; al-Marsot, *Egypt's Liberal Experiment*, 235–37; Vatikiotis, *The History of Modern Egypt*, 326–33.

[16] Baer, "Islamic Political Activity in Modern Egyptian History," 44–46. The standard history of the Muslim Brothers is Mitchell, *The Society of the Muslim Brothers*.

[17] This is a point in some dispute: cf. Hamid Enayat, *Modern Islamic Political Thought* (Austin: University of Texas Press, 1982), 87–88; Mitchell, *The Society of the Muslim Brothers*, 234–35; A. Chris Eccel, "ʿĀlim and Mujāhid in Egypt: Orthodoxy v. Subculture, or Division of Labor?," *The Muslim World* 68 (1988): 201–04; and Olivier Caré, "From Bannā to Qutb to 'Qutbism': The Radicalization of Fundamentalist Thought under Three Regimes," *Egypt from Monarchy to Republic*, ed. Shimon Shamir (Boulder: Westview Press, 1995), 181–94.

[18] Although scholars such as Mitchell have traditionally traced the rise of a concern with social justice to the works of Sayyid Quṭb, Lia argues that the concern appears far earlier in the works of Bannā. Compare Mitchell, *The Society of the Muslim Brothers*, 239 n. 20 with Lia, *Society of Muslim Brothers in Egypt*, 81–82.

[19] On the importance of the differences between the editions, see William Shepherd, "The Development of the Thought of Sayyid Quṭb as Reflected in Earlier and Later Editions of *Social Justice in Islam*," *Die Welt des Islams* 32 (1992): 196–236. The analysis in the following pages will rely on the first edition, trans. Sayyid Quṭb, *al-ʿAdāla al-Ijtimāʿiyya fī al-Islām* (Cairo: Lajnat al-Nashr li al-Jāmiʿiyyīn, 1949); and on the annotated translation by Hardie and Algar, Sayyid Quṭb, *Social Justice in Islam* trans. John B. Hardie, rev. trans. Hamid Algar (Oneonta, New York: Islamic Publications International, 2000). In this book, I will follow the Hardie-Algar translation and all references will be to this translation.

it assumes that Islamic law should be interpreted through an implicitly utilitarian method, and it explores some of the implications of applying Islamic law. According to Quṭb, God has revealed in the Qur'ān and a few authentic *ḥadīth*

> general, universal rules and principles . . . leaving their application in detail to be determined by the processes of time and by the emergence of individual problems. But Islam does not deal with the incidental related issues of the principle, except insofar as such are expressions of an unchanging principle whose impact is felt universally.[20]

Among these principles is a supreme utilitarian principle requiring the maximization of human welfare, which he equated with "social justice."[21] Therefore, once "general, universal principles" have been identified, society is "still confronted by that [issue of] of the specific legal enactments that will ensure a sound form of Islamic life and which will guarantee social justice to all." Quṭb then added:

> *In this question, it is not possible to take a stand purely on the form of the original Islamic life.* Rather, we must utilize all possible and permissible means that fall within the general principles and the broad foundations of Islam. Nor must we be afraid to use all the discoveries that man has made in the way of social legislation and systems, so long as they do not run counter to the principles of Islam. . . . We must include these in our legislation so long as they conduce to the true welfare of society, or so long as they ward off any impending evil. In the two principles of "public interest" [*maṣlaḥa*] and "blocking of means" we have two clear Islamic principles which give wide powers to the temporary ruler to ensure the general welfare at all times and in all places. [Italics added.][22]

---

[20] Quṭb, *Social Justice*, 33–34.

[21] Quṭb is explicit that the validity of a state law depended ultimately on the degree to which it maximized the aggregate social justice in the world. When discussing predatory pricing, for example, Quṭb asserts that acts that are carried out for malicious reasons and that do hurt a few Muslims should be encouraged so long as they benefit a larger number of Muslims. A Muslim can legally drive his competitors out of business, even if he does so out of spite: "His action from the point of view of intention is a means to evil, but externally it is a means to public and private benefit. Undoubtedly the seller benefits by selling, by the circulation of his goods, and by the good-will which he gains; equally certainly the public benefits by the cut in price, by which a general lowering of prices is encouraged." Quṭb, *Social Justice*, 300–01.

[22] Quṭb, *Social Justice*, 295–96.

Such a passage suggests that Muslims today are bound only by a few broad principles found in the Qur'ān and, perhaps, a few *ḥadīths*. Among these, principles of general welfare (which overlap with social justice) held a special position. Quṭb's writing, like Riḍā's, implied a tolerance for authoritarianism. Because one person's idea of social justice might differ from another's, Quṭb believed that a ruler must be given great discretion in areas where good Muslims could reasonably disagree. Quṭb called this "the statutory aspect of political theory in Islam."[23] Towards the end of the book, he admitted that the advancement of Islamic society would depend upon the ruler's ability wisely to "set up the Islamic legislation to regulate life."[24]

Eventually imprisoned and killed by the Egyptian government, Quṭb's writings provided inspiration to many youth who joined armed radical Islamist groups in the 1970s and 1980s.[25] Although these extremist Islamist groups often lacked a coherent legal ideology, their writings suggest that they were influenced by theories of utilitarian neo-*ijtihād*.[26]

As the Brothers in the 1920s and 30s were creating a political movement calling for the promulgation of codes drafted through utilitarian neo-*ijtihād*, Sanhūrī was rallying support for his proposal to Islamize Egyptian law by adopting a new civil code drafted, at least in part, through comparative neo-*taqlīd*. Although his scheme did not have the mass appeal of the Brothers' program, it proved attractive to members of the new legal profession and, more generally, to members of the elite.

Although Sanhūrī's ideas never seemed to gain a popular audience in the way that neo-traditional ideas or the ideas of Rashīd Riḍā did, Sanhūrī's connections with the rising elites served him well. After World War II, when the Egyptian government began seriously to prepare for legal reform, it asked Sanhūrī to chair the

---

[23] Quṭb, *Social Justice*, 124–25.

[24] Ibid., 285.

[25] During the 1970s and 1980s, Islamic student groups inspired by the writings of Quṭb and Bannā were gaining strength at Egyptian universities. See Gilles Kepel, *Le Prophete et Pharaon*, trans. Jon Rothschild as *Muslim Extremism in Egypt: The Prophet and Pharaoh* (Berkeley: University of California Press, 1985).

[26] Skovgaard-Petersen, *Defining Islam*, 214; John L. Esposito, *The Islamic Threat* (New York: Oxford University Press, 1992), 133–39; Abu-Rabi', *Intellectual Origins*, 94.

committee that would draft an Egyptian civil code.[27] Sanhūrī used a number of methods, including comparative neo-*taqlīd*, to find the precepts and principles that were included in his code.[28] Sanhūrī believed that his new code was a giant step towards Islamization.[29] He hoped that, if an independent and properly-trained judiciary interpreted and applied this code, Egyptian law would become increasingly "Islamic."

As might be expected, the political factions associated with neo-traditionalism or with utilitarian neo-*ijtihād* disagreed with Sanhūrī's assessment. Their antipathy to Sanhūrī's method of Islamic legal interpretation became apparrent in 1948, when Sanhūrī's draft code was debated in Parliament. When the draft was unveiled, secularists predictably denounced it as too Islamic. Ironically, neo-traditionalists, including leading members of the *ʿulamāʾ*, teamed up with the champions of utilitarian neo-*ijtihād*, including leading Muslim Brothers, to declare that it was not "Islamic" enough.[30] As the Islamist opponents articulated their concerns, it became clear that they did not object to the substance of the rules that the draft code would require Egyptians to obey. Nor were they necessarily upset that many of these rules were taken from European codes of law. That became apparent when the *ʿulamāʾ* and the Brothers presented the Parliament

[27] The Code drew law from a number of sources: the rulings of traditional Islamic law, the law codes of European countries and the jurisprudence that had developed in the national courts and mixed courts. See Ziadeh, *Lawyers, the Rule of Law and Liberalism*, 138–39.

[28] For a description of al-Sanhūrī's methodology in drafting the Egyptian code, see Enid Hill, *Al-Sanhuri and Islamic Law* (Cairo Papers in Social Sciences 10; Cairo: American University in Cairo Press, 1987), 50–64. For a description of the slightly different method he used to draft the Iraqi code, see Ibid., 43–49.

[29] In 1948, when he finished his draft code, al-Sanhūrī did not claim that his draft code, in its current form, was as fully "Islamic" as it ideally would be in the future. Egypt's economy and society had developed around laws that did not meet his criteria of an "Islamic law." To remove suddenly the laws that people had assumed when they made long-term economic or social plans would be, he argued, enormously disruptive. Nevertheless, al-Sanhūrī suggested that his code could be a bridge between the existing codes that were then in force and a purely Islamic code for the future. He had carefully drafted the code, he explained, so that non-Islamic elements would be reduced organically through the process of interpretation. Any lingering non-Islamic laws should be replaced through later amendment. Al-Sanhūrī, "al-Qānūn al-Madanī al-ʿArabī," *Al-Qaḍaʾ* XX, 1–2 (1962): 13, trans. in Hill, *Al-Sanhuri and Islamic Law*, 81. See also the discussion in Ziadeh, *Lawyers, the Rule of Law and Liberalism*, 143ff.; Amr Shalakany, "Between Identity and Redistribution," *Islamic Law and Society* 8(2) (2001): 228–35, particularly 224–25 and 233–35.

[30] See Ziadeh, *Lawyers, the Rule of Law and Liberalism*, 145–46; 135–47; Hill, *Al-Sanhuri and Islamic Law*, 65–70.

with an alternative draft code of "Islamic law," which proved to contain provisions that were also adopted from European codes and that were, in many cases, similar to Sanhūrī's code. Rather, the champions of neo-traditionalism and utilitarian neo-*ijtihād* rejected the legitimacy of Sanhūrī's method of selecting his rules. They worried that adopting Sanhūrī's code would represent an official endorsement of his approach to Islamic interpretation—and that this might have terrible effects when other codes were drafted.[31] Sanhūrī, outraged by the attacks on his code, enumerated the similarities between his draft and the alternative Islamic draft, point by point, and argued that these proved that his code was as "Islamic" as that proposed by al-Azhar and the Brothers.[32] Apparently convinced, the Parliament adopted the draft code.[33]

II. *Islamist factions under Nāṣir, 1952–1970*

In the years following the adoption of Sanhūrī's civil code, serious political strife erupted between secularists and a variety of compet-

[31] The concern that this raised among the *'ulamā'* is easy to understand. If Islamic law was defined as law that was consistent with precepts uncovered by lawyers using comparative neo-*taqlīd*, then the *'ulamā'* would be denied their traditional role as the authoritative interpreters of Islam. From that time on, members of the bar rather than members of the traditional Sunnī guilds of law would be the authoritative voices on questions of Islamic law and they would coordinate the harmonization of state and Islamic law. The Brothers' concerns seem to have been more abstract. The embrace of Sanhūrī's vision of Islamic legislation meant that the state would not define Islam by reference to principles derived from divine revelation (as found in the Qur'ān and a few authoritative *ḥadīth*), but would rather define it by reference to historical interpretations of those principles. Thus, during the debates over ratification, the judge Ḥasan Ismā'īl al-Huḍaybī, who was later to be a leader of the Muslim Brotherhood, argued that Sanhūrī's code was unacceptable because Egyptian law must be based on Islamic law based on the commands of the Qur'ān. In other words, Islamic law cannot be derived by analyzing legal opinions (which is a form of *taqlīd*). Rather, it has to be an interpretation of the Islamic religious texts through some form of *ijtihād* or neo-*ijtihād*. Ziadeh, *Lawyers, the Rule of Law and Liberalism*, 143, citing *Al-Muḥāmāh*, March, 1948, 4–7 and insert before 3. See also J.N.D. Anderson, "The Shari'a and Civil Law," *Islamic Quarterly* 1 (1954): 45.

[32] See Egyptian Ministry of Justice, *al-Qānūn al-Madanī*: Majmū'at al-'Amal al-Taḥḍīriyya, 7 vols. (Cairo: 1949), 85–90, cited in Shalakany, "Between Identity and Redistribution," 227.

[33] *al-Qānūn al-Madanī* (Egypt), Law No. 131 (1948). For an English translation of the Code as adopted, see Perrot, Farner, and Marshall, *The Egyptian Civil Code* (Cairo: Tipografia dell'Instituto Don Bosco, 1952).

ing Islamist groups. Political order was only restored in 1952, when a group of military officers led by Jamāl ʿAbd al-Nāṣir seized power. The new regime had a troubled relationship with the Islamist groups discussed earlier.

The leaders of the 1952 coup had initially courted the support of Islamist groups, and they had responded favorably. Once Nāṣir had firmly taken control of the government, however, he came to consider Islamism problematic. Embracing an explicitly secular, Arab nationalist, and socialist ideology, Nāṣir set out to establish a homogenous political arena controlled by his party, the Arab Socialist Union. The government was supposed to control all the areas of Egyptian life that might lead to friction between Egyptians, including politics and the economy, and all forms of Islamism constituted a threat to Nāṣir's supposedly apolitical state. He thus tried to subdue or destroy each of the various Islamist factions in Egypt. The divisions between the factions made his task considerably easier—at least for a time.

To control the *ʿulamāʾ*, Nāṣir imposed radical "reforms" on al-Azhar, culminating in the nationalization of the university and the imposition of central control.[34] Through the further selective use of pressure, Nāṣir "brought the *ʿulamāʾ* to heel without completely annihilating them."[35] The leading *ʿulamāʾ* put up little resistance, a reaction that brought scorn from less accommodating Islamist groups like the Muslim Brotherhood and even some younger members of the *ʿulamāʾ*.[36] (The breadth and depth of many Egyptians' disrespect for

---

[34] See Tamir Moustafa, "Conflict and Cooperation between the State and Religious Institutions in Contemporary Egypt," *International Journal of Middle East Studies* 32 (2000): 4–7; Malika Zeghal, "Religion and Politics in Egypt: The Ulema of Al-Azhar, Radical Islam, and the State," *International Journal of Middle East Studies* 31 (1999): 371–75.

[35] Zeghal, "Religion and Politics in Egypt," 374. Nāṣir co-opted members of the *ʿulamāʾ* at al-Azhar, and asked them to issue legal opinions that supported all of his policies in an attempt to provide Islamic cover for policies that many Egyptians recognized as un-Islamic. The willingness of the *ʿulamāʾ* to give these opinions was widely considered by the Egyptian public at large, and even among some members of the *ʿulamā*, as a sign of weakness and capitulation. See, e.g., Moustafa, "Conflict and Co-operation," 9–10; Barry Rubin, *Islamic Fundamentalism in Egyptian Politics* (New York: St. Martin's Press, 1990), 80.

[36] Some members of the *ʿulamāʾ* seem to have become disgusted with their leaders' policy of toadying to the regime, and began to align themselves with some of the *jamāʿāt*. Some scholars believe that this movement began as early as the 1960s. Eccel, "ʿĀlim and Mujāhid," 204–8. Others seem to believe that it developed primarily in the 1980s. See, e.g., Zeghal, "Religion and Politics in Egypt," 386–89.

the quietism of the *ʿulamāʾ* became apparent in the 1970s and had important and often violent ramifications.)

The Muslim Brothers were less pliant than the *ʿulamāʾ*, and they suffered greviously for their resistance. From time to time, Nāṣir banned the whole organization.[37] He also regularly singled out Brothers hostile to the regime for persecution and imprisoned many of the leading Brothers. Sayyid Quṭb was executed and came to be seen as a martyr to the cause of Islamism. Supporters of the Muslim Brothers reacted by splitting into moderate and radical camps. Moderates and radicals both continued to call for the establishment of an Islamic state whose legislation would be systematically checked for conformity with universal principles of *sharīʿa*. Moderates differed from radicals primarily in the tactics that they believed were appropriate in the battle to establish such a state. Moderates rejected violence and believed in working to the extent possible within existing constitutional structures. Radicals, on the other hand, embraced violence wholeheartedly. Contemporary radical Islamic ideology is usually said to have developed out of the later writings of Sayyid Quṭb. In Quṭb's later works, he implied that society was so corrupt as to be non-Muslim, and that Muslims might have to use violence to bring about a truly Muslim state.[38] This position was extraordinary because it implied that the leading *ʿulamāʾ*, or even the more moderate Muslim Brothers, might actually be non-Muslim enemies of Islam and thus legitimate targets of violence.

In the late 1960s and the early 1970s, radical Islamists inspired by the late writings of Sayyid Quṭb began to establish shadowy organizations dedicated to the establishment by force of an Islamic state. These revolutionary cells became part of a growing body of informal Muslim organizations that were known popularly as the *jamāʿāt*. These *jamāʿāt* rarely had a clear political or legal program, but to

[37] For Nāṣir's Machiavellian policy towards the Brothers during the first years of his reign, see, e.g., Kirk J. Beattie, *Egypt during the Nasser Years: Ideology, Politics and Civil Society* (Boulder: Westview Press, 1994), 81–85, 94–97. See also P.J. Vatikiotis, *Nasser and his Generation* (New York: St. Martin's Press, 1978), 95–96, 134–37; Vatikiotis, *The History of Modern Egypt*, 381–88.

[38] Eccel has suggested that there had always been a radical wing of the Muslim Brotherhood that was willing to use violence. Eccel, "ʿĀlim and Mujāhid in Egypt," 201–4. For a more cautious view, see Olivier Caré, "From Bannā to Quṭb to 'Quṭbism,'" in *Egypt from Monarchy to Republic*, Shiman Shamir, ed. (Boulder: Westview Press, 1995), 181–94.

the extent that they did, they called for the Islamization of the state in terms like those of the Muslim Brotherhood.[39] It soon became apparent that the radicals' embrace of violence was not merely theoretical.

Nāṣir's regime had a more ambivalent relationship with those who embraced comparative neo-*taqlīd*. It would have been extremely difficult to scrap Sanhūrī's recently enacted Civil Code, which had been drafted, in part, using comparative neo-*taqlīd*. Thus, the government had to tolerate the teaching of Sanhūrī's ideas. Nevertheless, Nāṣir rejected the idea that legal professionals should continue to try to identify supra-legislative norms that the executive and legislature would have to respect. He sought to control the legal profession and all independent legal institutions that might propose the existence of such norms, explore their nature, or, worse yet, apply them against the executive and legislative branches.[40] He consistently pursued policies designed to emasculate independent legal institutions such as the bar association, the law faculties, and the independent judiciary.[41] Accordingly, the government tried to ensure that the 1948 Civil

[39] For the ideology of the members of one of the most radical *jamāʿāt*, see the discussion of the 1977 trial of its leader, Shukri Mustafa, in Kepel, *Le prophète et pharaon*, 70–83. Altman has argued that the Islamic ideology of the Islamic student groups and radical organizations can be distinguished from the Muslim Brotherhood. Despite the ambivalent feelings of leading Brothers about the *ḥadīth*, Altman points out that Muslim Brothers who proposed concrete legislative reforms in the 1970s actually tended to derive a number of laws from the *ḥadīth*. In other words, they had come to use utilitarian calculations only sparingly, when following prophetic practice would clearly be inappropriate to modern times. The radical groups, on the other hand, usually looked only to the Qur'ān for legal guidance, and, given the dearth of Qur'ānic legislation, were forced to rely more heavily on utilitarian analysis to derive "Islamic" laws. Israel Altman, "Islamic Legislation in Egypt in the Early 1970's," *Asian and African Studies* 13 (1979): 202–6. The potential drift towards textualism among the Brothers is a point that bears further study. The discussions which Altman studied, however, often occurred in the context of a debate about concrete reform in a few areas of law, often involving family law, or banking. These issues seem to have had a unique emotional resonance.

[40] See Beattie, *Egypt during the Nasser Years*, 97.

[41] In a deeply symbolic action, supporters of Nāṣir in 1954 physically attacked al-Sanhūrī, who was then acting as the president of the Council of State. More important he imposed "reforms" of the Bar Association and Judiciary, which culminated in the mid-1960s with an all-out push to promote an ideology of "socialist legality" that required judges, in interpreting and applying the law, to respect the values of "the socialist order" as defined by the President. Brown, *The Rule of Law*, 85. He also arranged for several constitutions to be enacted, none of which mandated that state legislation be checked against an evolving understanding of Islamic

Code was not interpreted, amended, or supplemented, as Sanhūrī had hoped, to reflect an evolving understanding of Islamic norms. Rather, the government strove to ensure that it was interpreted and applied through a paradigm that favored the explicitly secular, socialist goals of the regime.[42]

Nevertheless, Sanhūrī and some other members of the legal community continued quietly to explore the idea of drafting new legislation or interpreting existing legislation with an eye to principles derived through comparative neo-*taqlīd.* Because legal education at this time naturally focused on Egyptian civil law, judges were deeply familiar with Sanhūrī's vision of Islamic legal principles as an authentic and powerful check on executive and legislature. At the same time, Sanhūrī and other academics such as Chafic Cheheta continued to carry out academic studies of the classical Islamic legal tradition and to induce principles of the *sharīʿa* that had been universally respected in the tradition. To this day, a great number of juristic monographs and doctoral dissertations take the form of comparative studies of traditional *fiqh.*[43] Such studies represented the first phase—what Sanhūrī had called the scientific phase—of Islamic legislative drafting.[44] The appeal of Sanhūrī's vision may be seen, for instance, in the thought of Ṣūfī Abū Ṭālib, a department chair at the University of Cairo Law School. Abū Ṭālib, who studied law when Sanhūrī was the dominant Egyptian legal academic, wrote a dissertation demonstrating a facility with the comparative methodology that lay at the heart of comparative neo-*taqlīd.*[45] In his controversial mono-

norms but rather required the judiciary to promote "secular democratic socialism"—a concept whose contours were defined by official idealogues. See Vatikiotis, *The History of Modern Egypt*, 404.

[42] See Shalakany, "Between Identity and Redistribution," 241–42, citing Muḥammad al-ʿAṭṭār, *Naḥw Qānūn Madanī ʿArabī fī Ḍaw' al-Idiyyūllūjiyya al-ʿArabiyya al-Thawriyya* (Baghdad: 1978).

[43] Baber Johansen, *Contingency in a Sacred Law: Legal and Ethical Norms in the Muslim Fiqh* (Leiden: E.J. Brill, 1999), 59.

[44] Johansen, *Contingency in a Sacred Law*, 58. See, e.g., Sanhūrī, *Maṣādir al-Ḥaqq fī al-Fiqh al-Islāmī*, 3 vols. (Cairo: Arab League Publications, 1956); Chafik Chehata, *Théorie générale de l'obligation en droit musulman* (Paris: Sirey, 1969).

[45] See Soufy Hossain Abou-Talib (Ṣūfī Ḥusayn Abū Ṭālib), *Le periculum rei venditae en droit roman et en droit Musulman* (Cairo: Imprimerie Université du Caire, 1958). This work compared the Islamic and Roman laws of bills of sale, and was the type of study that al-Sanhūrī had explicitly called for as a preliminary step in the formation of fully Islamic codes. Furthermore, like al-Sanhūrī, Abū Ṭālib argued that the essential principles of Islamic law were found through comparative study of the

graph, *The Arab Society* (*al-Mujtamaʿ al-ʿArabī*), Abū Ṭālib suggested that modern socialist ideologies could be tempered by (and harmonized with) "Islamic" values—values that, it seemed, would be identified through some type of comparative neo-*taqlīd*.[46]

Furthermore, the judiciary as a whole was also quietly steadfast in defying Nāṣir's repeated assaults on their freedom.[47] They exercised their independence in the service of an incremental Islamization of the sort that Sanhūrī had advocated. In a recent study, Maurits Berger has argued that that incremental judge-driven Islamization of the law continued, albeit haltingly, when judges interpreted and applied the doctrine of "public policy."[48] Important judges, apparently inspired by al-Sanhūrī's writings, co-opted this principle and used it as a tool of incremental Islamization.[49] Islamists in the academy and the judiciary did not always embrace al-Sanhūrī's theory

substantive legal doctrines laid down by the great Islamic jurists of the past. He also held that Muslim scholars could advance the cause of comparative law and develop an effective, modern code of laws from such principles. See, e.g., Ibid., 1–11, 409–11.

[46] On Abū Ṭālib and his own characterization of the book, see Kirk Beattie, *Egypt during the Sadat Years* (New York: Plagrave, 2000), 168, citing Ṣūfī Abū Ṭalib, *Al-Mujtamaʿ al-ʿArabī* (Cairo: publisher unknown, 1965). Beattie reports that Abū Ṭālib's ideas were sufficiently controversial among the socialist faithful that he felt pressure to leave his prestigious post in Cairo and stayed in self-imposed exile at the University of Beirut until 1972. See Beattie, *Egypt during the Sadat Years*, 168–69.

[47] Judges' attempts to maintain their independence generated considerable respect among Egyptians. See Brown, *The Rule of Law*, 84–92.

[48] Sanhūrī had defined public policy as "those principles that aim at realizing the public interest, from a political, social, as well as economic perspective, which are related to the highest order of society and which supersede the interests of individuals." ʿAbd al-Razzāq al-Sanhūrī, *al-Wasīṭ fī Sharḥ al-Qānūn al-Madani: (I) Maṣādir al-Iltizām* (Cairo: Dār al-Nahda al-ʿArabiyya, 1964), 399, trans. Maurits Berger, "Public Policy and Islamic Law: the Modern Dhimmī in Contemporary Egyptian Family Law," *Islamic Law and Society* 8 (2001): 106 n. 70.

[49] In a number of cases, the Court of Cassation (al-Maḥkamat al-Naqd), Egypt's highest appellate court, argued that Islamic principles of historical importance to the Egyptian people should be considered rules of "public policy." The doctrine thus became a back door to permit an Islamist evolution in certain sectors of Egyptian law along the lines that al-Sanhūrī had proposed. For example, the principle that inheritance in Islamic families should follow the rulings elaborated in the Qur'ān and further elaborated in traditional *fiqh* was held to be a principle of public policy because these "rules are based on the absolutely certain textual rules of Islamic law . . . [and thus] have a strong link to the legal and social foundations which are deep-rooted in the conscience of society." See Case No. 17; year 32 (27 May, 1964), cited and translated in Berger, "Public Policy," 110–11. Cf. Court of Cassation Case No. 9, year 44, 14 December 1975.

of "Islamic law." Some espoused a neo-traditional vision of Islamic law, whereas others interpreted Islamic law through the use of utilitarian neo-*ijtihād*. Some developed extremely progressive theories of Islamic law that cannot easily be placed in any of the three "types" described earlier.[50] Nevertheless, the legal community continued to produce people who continued to support al-Sanhūrī's vision of Islamic law and who had the skills necessary to interpret Islamic law in the method that al-Sanhūrī proposed. Al-Sanhūrī's theory thus continued to be subtly influential throughout the period in which Nāṣir governed Egypt.

III. *The fractured state of Islamism at the dawn of the Article 2 era*

As the failures of the regime began to mount, Islamism took on a new life. Islamists continued, however, to be deeply divided. Although they agreed at some broad level that state law should be revised to be consistent with the rulings of the *sharīʿa* and with its overarching goals, Islamists continued to disagree about who could identify these rulings and goals and about the method that should be used. Immediately after the death of Nāṣir in 1970, President Sādāt called for public discussion about whether the constitution should require Egyptian legislation to conform to Islamic law. For over a month that year the semi-official newspaper *al-Ahrām* devoted considerable space to essays and letters discussing whether the constitution should require the laws of the state to be Islamic.[51] As J.P. O'Kane has shown, the letters revealed widespread support, in the abstract, for

[50] For an example of innovative legal thinking on the part of a judge in the 1970s and thereafter, one can look at the work of Muḥammad Saʿīd al-Ashmāwī. On Ashmāwī, see Johannes Jansen, *The Dual Nature of Islamic Fundamentalism* (Ithaca: Cornell University Press, 1997), 106–9; Muḥammad Saʿīd al-Ashmāwī, *Uṣūl al-Sharīʿa*, (Beirut: Dār Iqra', 1983). For a sample of writings in English, see also Muḥammad Saʿīd al-Ashmāwī, ed. Carolyn Fluehr-Lobban, *Against Islamic Extremism: The Writings of Muḥammad Saʿīd al-Ashmāwī* (Gainesville: University Press of Florida, 1998). See also Wael Hallaq's critique of his thought in Wael Hallaq, *A History of Islamic Legal Theories: An Introduction to Sunnī Uṣūl al-Fiqh* (Cambridge: Cambridge University Press, 1997), 231–41.

[51] J.P. O'Kane, "Islam in the New Egyptian Constitution," *The Middle East Journal* 26 (1972): 137–48.

a constitutional provision that would require Egyptian laws to be, at the very least, consistent with the norms of Islamic law. Many called for the constitution to make the *sharīʿa* the "chief source" (*al-maṣdar al-raʾīsī*) of Egyptian legislation.[52] This is striking because the term that I have translated as "chief" (*raʾīsī*) has connotations of supremacy, and a provision that made the *sharīʿa* the chief source of Egyptian law would apparently require Egyptian law to be consistent with the principles of *sharīʿa*.[53] At the same time, however, the letters revealed the divisions between Islamists who supported different Islamic legal theories. A substantial number of the contributors appeared not to have considered how to identify the norms of "Islamic law."[54] Among those who had, however, there was evidence of disagreement about

[52] See, e.g., Muḥammad al-Fakhkhām, Rector of al-Azhar, in a telegram to the preparatory committee for the drafting of the constitution in the National Assembly, reported in *al-Ahrām*, June 2, 1971, trans. in O'Kane, "Islam in the New Egyptian Constitution," 138; Ibrahīm Muḥsin, letter printed in *al-Ahrām*, June 8, 1971, trans. in O'Kane, Ibid., 139; comments of Dr. Jamāl al-ʿUṭayfī, member of the preparatory committee for the drafting of the constitution in the National Assembly, reported in *al-Ahrām*, July 21, 1971, 7, discussed in O'Kane, Ibid., 142ff.; the response to ʿUṭayfī's letter by Shaykh Muḥammad al-Ghazālī, printed in *al-Ahrām*, July 21, 1971, 7, summarized in O'Kane, Ibid., 142–43; Letter by Justice Ḥasan Muḥammad, cited in *al-Ahrām*, July 21, 1971, 7, discussed in O'Kane, Ibid., 145–46.

[53] The word *raʾīsī* defies easy translation. It is a word that carries connotations of primacy. The Egyptian government's "official translation" of the 1970 constitution opted to translate the word *raʾīsī* as "principal" and there was some reason to do so. The provision in Arabic suggested that the principles of the *sharīʿa* should be one of a number of important sources of legislation, and one can reasonably refer to these important sources as "principal" sources. Once the legislation was amended, however, to give the *sharīʿa* precedence over all other sources of law, one has to refer to it as the "chief" source. Although the official Egyptian translation of the constitution continues to translate the term *raʾīsī* as "principal," I have opted to translate it instead as "chief."

[54] The arguments in the letters are sometimes difficult to follow, because the writers in *al-Ahrām* are sometimes sloppy in their terminology—a point noted bitterly by some of the more sophisticated contributors to the debate. Many contributors conflated the terms *sharīʿa* and *fiqh*, a tendency that was decried by one of the more precise contributors to the debate. This conflation reflects the degree to which discussions of Islamic legal and political theory had devolved into sloganeering. Groups like the Brothers had come to use the term *sharīʿa* to refer to God's law, to human understanding of God's law, and even to state laws that were not inconsistent with human interpretations of God's law. On this point and on European and Egyptian works which discuss this phenomenon, see Skovgaard-Petersen, *Defining Islam*, 200. See also Bernard Botiveau, "Islamiser le droit?: l'éxample égyptien," *Maghreb-Mashrek* 126 (1989): 10–11.

how to interpret Islamic law and draft Islamic legislation. The letters are not long, but they make clear that the different contributors were committed to very different visions of the Islamic legislation: some supported a neo-traditionalist theory;[55] others envisioned Islamic codes developed through some form of neo-*ijtihād* (presumably utilitarian neo-*ijtihād*);[56] and a distinct minority apparently saw Islamic legislation developed through some form of neo-*taqlīd* (presumably comparative neo-*taqlīd*).[57]

IV. *Conclusion*

From the moment that Egypt became an independent state in the 1920s, powerful Islamist factions made their presence felt. By this time, however, the classical consensus on questions of Islamic legal authority and theory had collapsed, and Islamists embraced a range of modernist Islamic legal theories. As an earlier chapter described, three general "types" of Islamist theory became most successful. Neo-traditional theories held that the *sharīʿa* should be interpreted by the contemporary *ʿulamāʾ* and they should determine whether state law was consistent with the principles and goals of the *sharīʿa*. At the same time, modernists such as Rashīd Riḍā argued that codes of Islamic legislation should be drafted through a form of utilitarian neo-*ijtihād*. Finally, a number of legal professionals such as al-Sanhūrī argued that the universally applicable *sharīʿa* rulings and goals should be identified through a form of comparative neo-*taqlīd*, and codes drafted to be consistent with them. Various Islamist factions embraced different Islamic legal theories. Despite suppression by Nāṣir, the

[55] Some proposed that the constitution should require Egyptian legislation to be consistent with Islamic norms as defined by traditionally-trained *ʿulamāʾ* using traditional Sunnī methods of legal interpretation. See, e.g., the response of Shaykh Muḥammad al-Ghazālī, printed in *al-Ahrām*, July 21, 1971, 7, summarized in O'Kane, "Islam in the New Egyptian Constitution," 142–43.

[56] One contributor cited Rashīd Riḍā to bolster his argument that only laws derived through some vaguely-articulated form of utilitarian neo-*ijtihād* are authentically Islamic laws. Dr. Muḥammad Aḥmad Khalaf Allāh, representative of the Ministry of Culture, citing *al-Manār* 9 (1906): 705, discussed in O'Kane, "Islam in the New Egyptian Constitution," 145.

[57] Not surprisingly, the one clear example of this reasoning comes in a letter from a legal professional. See, e.g., the letter by ʿUṭayfī, discussed in O'Kane, "Islam in the New Egyptian Constitution," 142ff.

competing factions continued to agitate for law to respect Islamic legal norms—each championing a different vision of Islamic legal norms.

With this background, this book will turn to the history of Article 2. After Nāṣir's death in 1970, his successor, Anwār al-Sādāt, recognized the power of Islamism and decided to reach out to Islamists. Article 2 of the new constitution of 1970 made the *sharīʿa* "*a* chief source of Egyptian legislation" [emphasis added]. Shortly thereafter, the political branches of the government tried develop an Islamization policy that would satisfy a diverse body of Islamists, while still permitting the government to pursue cherished policies. After the assassination of President Sādāt, the government abandoned its dream of developing such a policy. By this time, however, Article 2 had been amended to make the principles of the *sharīʿa* "*the* chief source" of legislation (emphasis added), and Islamists had begun to bring suits challenging any number of laws as un-Islamic and thus unconstitutional. The justices of the Supreme Constitutional Court were thus left with the task of developing a convincing interpretation of a provision requiring Egyptian legislation to conform to the principles of the *sharīʿa*.

PART TWO

ARTICLE 2 OF THE EGYPTIAN CONSTITUTION

CHAPTER SEVEN

ARTICLE 2 AND THE ATTEMPT AT EXECUTIVE-SPONSORED ISLAMIZATION, 1970–1985

Part I of this book described classical Islamic legal theory, the breakdown of consensus in modern Egypt over questions of Islamic legal theory, and the rise of competing Islamist factions in twentieth-century Egypt. As we noted in the last chapter, the fracturing of the Islamist opposition made it easier for secularists to control Egypt. Nevertheless, Islamism retained sufficient strength that Egyptian regimes were wary of it.

Article 2 of the Egyptian constitution is the product of an unusual period in recent Egyptian history—a period in which the Egyptian government, then suffering a crisis of legitimacy, reached out to Islamists in the hope of forging a consensus theory of Islamic law that would allow it to legitimize its law in Islamic terms. By 1970, the Egyptian government was forced to pursue policies that were unpopular with its traditional supporters on the left. To gain support for these policies, President Sādāt and some of his advisors thought the government should seek to curry favor with Islamists. Thus, when the regime enacted a new constitution in 1971, Article 2 of that constitution suggested that Egyptian legislation should respect Islamic legal norms. Shortly thereafter, the government began to explore the possibility of an executive-sponsored program of moderate Islamization. Confident that such a program would be successful, the regime began to draft codes and hubristically decided in 1980 to amend and strengthen Article 2. The Article as amended suggested that Egyptian legislation must be revised to conform to Islamic legal norms. Roughly one year later, President Sādāt was assassinated by Islamists, and his successor decided to shelve the draft Islamic codes and abandon the program of Islamization.

This chapter will focus on the birth and amendment of Article 2 and on the events that caused the government to renounce its commitment to Islamization. Subsequent chapters will discuss the history of Article 2 after the renunciation of Islamization. Unfortunately for the Mubārak regime, the decision to renounce Islamization took place at a time when the Egyptian judiciary was regaining some of its independence from the executive branch and beginning to assert this independence in its exercise of constitutional review. When Islamists brought suits asking the courts to challenge laws as un-Islamic (and therefore unconstitutional under Article 2), the judiciary, after some delay, decided that it would have to accept the cases. It thus began to issue opinions determining whether Egyptian law conformed to Islamic norms.

I. *The adoption of Article 2 in 1971*

By the end of the 1960s, Jamāl Abd al-Nāṣir's regime was already showing signs of serious weakness. The Arab nations had suffered a humiliating defeat in the 1967 war with Israel, and Egypt was suffering from a lingering economic malaise. Nāṣir's personal charisma helped to maintain popular support for his government. After his death in 1970, his successor, Anwar al-Sādāt, examined the state of his nation and concluded that if it were to survive, the regime would have to engage in painful political and economic reform. The proposed reforms were deeply unpopular with the regime's traditional socialist "base"—particularly the program of privatization and economic liberalization.[1] Anticipating resistance from his traditional supporters, he reached out to groups that had been marginalized by Nāṣir, including the judiciary and Islamist political factions.[2]

In 1970, the government made an important gesture toward Islamists. In that year, a new constitution was drafted. Among those who supported the adoption of a constitutional Islamization provision, significant disagreement existed about the way in which Islamic legal principles should be interpreted and applied as a supra-

[1] On Sādāt's program of economic liberalization (the so-called "Open Door" policy), see P.J. Vatikiotis, *The History of Modern Egypt*, 4th ed. (Baltimore: Johns Hopkins University Press, 1991), 424–38; Raymond William Baker, *Egypt's Uncertain Revolution under Nasser and Sadat* (Cambridge: Harvard University Press, 1978), 132ff.

[2] On the anti-Nāsirist component of the Sādāt government's Islamic policies in the 1970s, see, e.g., Kirk Beattie, *Egypt During the Sadat Years* (New York: Palgrave, 2000), 200–10, 260–63; Nazih N. Ayubi, *The State and Public Policies in Egypt since Sadat* (Reading: Ithaca Press, 1991), 221–24.

legislative check on the political branches' legislative authority. The fact that Islamic legal issues were contested meant that the government might be able to shape public opinion on some of these questions and to help promote a vision of Islamic law that would be consistent with the economic and social policies that it wished to impose. The new Egyptian constitution, adopted in 1971, thus made a tentative move toward Islamism. Article 2 of the 1971 constitution contained the following phrase: "Islam is the religion of the state, Arabic is the official language, the principles of the Islamic *sharīʿa* shall be *a* chief source of legislation (*mabādiʾ al-sharīʿa al-Islāmiyya maṣdar*[un] *raʾīsī*[un] *li-ʾl tashrīʿ*)" (case endings and emphasis added).[3]

In its original form, Article 2 did not (as some Islamists had hoped) make the principles of the *sharīʿa* supreme over all other sources of legislation. Thus, it seemed, a law would not be invalid if it were inconsistent with the principles of *sharīʿa*. Furthermore, Article 2 was vague about what the principles of the *sharīʿa* were. It did not specify how these principles were to be identified and interpreted and thus left unanswered the question as to what these principles might require. In short, Article 2 as adopted in 1971 seemed to be a signal that the government wanted to negotiate with Islamists to see whether a public consensus could be reached both about the role that Islamic norms should play in shaping Egyptian legislation and about the way in which Islamic norms should be identified. After the adoption of the 1971 constitution, the executive branch and legislature, each controlled by the ruling party, began a dialogue with Islamists on these important questions.

[3] Arab Republic of Egypt, *Dustūr Jumhūriyyat Miṣr al-ʿArabiyya* (Constitution of the Arabic Republic of Egypt) (1971), Article 2. Future references to this constitution will be referred to as *Egyptian Constitution.* For a discussion of the nuances in this language, see Israel Altman, "Islamic Legislation in Egypt in the Early 1970's," *Asian and African Studies* 13 (1979): 202–6; Clark Lombardi, "Islamic Law as a Source of Constitutional Law in Egypt: the Constitutionalization of the Sharia in a Modern Arab State," *Columbia Journal of Transnational Law* 37.1 (1988): 86–88. Article 9 gave Islamic law a further role in shaping legislation dealing with women's issues. It asserted that the state would not give women any rights that they had not had under Islamic law. *Egyptian Constitution*, Article 9.

II. *The spread of Islamism after the adoption of Article 2*

After the adoption of the constitution, Sādāt allowed Islamists back into the public sphere. His government released members of the Muslim Brotherhood who had been jailed under Nāṣir, and he allowed the Muslim Brotherhood to publish journals again.[4] Although the government continued to conduct surveillance on Islamist organizations in order to monitor and, if necessary, suppress violent militant movements, it tolerated non-violent Islamist activities.[5] Given new freedom to organize, publish, and criticize (within limits) the government, Islamists of every type became increasingly vocal, and amassed new followers. Islamists did not, however, unite behind a single vision of Islamism. Competing factions saw an opportunity to influence the path of state legislation, and this brought latent tensions into the open.

Seeing an opportunity to re-establish their traditional Islamic role as the religious check on executive authority, the *ʿulamāʾ* of al-Azhar became more assertive in the early 1970s. In an interesting exercise in neo-traditionalism, al-Azhar apparently developed a draft code of *fiqh*.[6] In 1976, it set up a committee to propose legislative reforms, and shortly thereafter, it began to call openly for the government to revise its codes to ensure that they were consistent with (what they took to be) the principles of the Islamic *sharīʿa*.[7] During this same

---

[4] See Gilles Kepel, *Le prophète et pharaon*, trans. Jon Rothschild as *Muslim Extremism in Egypt: The Prophet and Pharaoh* (Berkeley: University of California Press, 1985), 74; Emmanuel Sivan, *Radical Islam: Medieval Theology and Modern Politics* (New Haven: Yale University Press, 1985), 120.

[5] On the continuing governmental repression of radical Islamic organizations, see Shimon Shamir and Ran Segev, "The Arab Republic of Egypt," in MECS I (1977–78), 296–97 and accompanying citations; see also Sa'ad Eddin Ibrahim, "Islamic Activism and Political Opposition in Egypt," *Egypt, Islam and Democracy: Twelve Critical Essays* (Cairo: American University in Cairo Press, 1996), 55–56. On Islamists' appreciation of the government's new policies, see Sivan, *Radical Islam*, 120.

[6] The codes were prepared by the Academy of Islamic Studies (*Majmaʿ al-Buḥūth al-Islāmiyya*), which was the think tank set up within al-Azhar to discuss issues of the age from an Islamic perspective. On the institution, see Jacob Skovgaard-Petersen, *Defining Islam for the Egyptian State: Muftīs and Fatwās of the Dār al-Iftā* (Leiden: E.J. Brill, 1997), 186–88. For their proposed codes, see ibid., 201.

[7] See Malika Zeghal, "Religion and Politics in Egypt: The Ulema of Al-Azhar, Radical Islam, and the State," *International Journal of Middle East Studies* 31 (1999): 380–83; see also Rudolph Peters, "Divine Law or Man-Made Law?," *Arab Law Quarterly* 3 (1988): 238. A draft of one proposal is found in Ghali Shoukri, *Egypt:*

period, the lay Muslim political organizations, which had long had an ambivalent relationship with the *ʿulamāʾ*, began to demand a role in shaping any Islamic reforms. The leaders of the Muslim Brotherhood were apparently reaching a détente with the *ʿulamāʾ* during these years, and often supported the *ʿulamāʾ*'s proposals. Nevertheless, they had their own agenda. Working through sympathetic members of parliament, they began to push for their own legislative reforms.[8] Furthermore, more radical lay organizations (groups referred to in the aggregate as the *jamāʿāt*) began to make significant inroads at universities and in cities.[9] As discussed earlier, these disparate groups, each apparently drawing inspiration from the later writings of Sayyid Quṭb, were deeply skeptical about the competence and integrity of the *ʿulamāʾ*.[10]

The Portrait of a President, 1971–1981 (London: Zed Press, 1981), 443–47. This translation should be used with caution; Peters, who has checked it, asserts that it is "not entirely trustworthy."

[8] Members of the People's Assembly who were sympathetic to the Muslim Brotherhood began to introduce bills proposing their own amendments to laws that they considered to be repugnant to the principles of the *sharīʿa*. See generally Peters, "Divine Law or Man-Made Law?," 233–40; and Altman, "Islamic Legislation," 199–219. Utilitarian neo-*ijtihād*, the method to which these figures was drawn, was an enormously flexible method of interpreting Islamic law and developing Islamic legislation and left considerable discretion to an interpreter. The proposed amendments reflected the fact that the Brothers were drawing from socially conservative sectors of society. Some bills sought to have the government start enforcing religious obligations such as the obligation to pay an alms tax (*zakāh*) or to fast during Ramadan. See Peters, "Divine Law or Man-Made Law?," 235, citing *al-Daʿwa*, vol. 26, no. 18 (Nov. 1977). Another bill proposed reinstating the traditional Islamic penalty for theft, amputation of the right hand. Another sought to bar men from serving as women's hairdressers because, it was argued, the *sharīʿa* bars men from touching women other than their wives and close relatives. For both of these bills, see Peters, "Divine Law or Man-Made Law?," 234, citing *al-Daʿwa*, vol. 25, no. 2 (Aug. 1976); Altman, "Islamic Legislation," 209–12, citing *al-Ahrām*, Feb. 12, 1975. A number of other proposed bills sought to ban the practice of charging interest on loans. See Altman, "Islamic Legislation," 212–13. These bills did not exemplify the progressive type of Islamic legal reform that Sādāt's ruling party had hoped to make the centerpiece of their turn to Islam. The leaders of the People's Assembly thus used parliamentary procedures to quash these bills without debate. Peters, "Divine Law or Man-Made Law?," 233, 235; Altman, "Islamic Legislation," 212–13.

[9] On the spread of *jamāʿāt* on university campuses and elsewhere, see Kepel, *Le prophète et pharaon*, 132–41. For the way in which Islamist service organizations associated with either the Brothers or the *jamāʿāt* became important providers of basic services in urban centers, see Ibrahim, "Islamic Activism," 58–61.

[10] For discussions of the *jamāʿāt* during this period, and the way in which their ideology derives from that of the Muslim Brotherhood, see, e.g., Olivier Carré, "From Banna to Qutb to 'Qutbism': The Radicalization of Fundamentalist Thought

In 1977, simmering tensions between the *ʿulamāʾ* and the *jamāʿāt* broke dramatically into the open when a radical Islamic organization abducted and murdered Shaykh Muḥammad al-Dhahabī, a prominent member of the Egyptian *ʿulamāʾ*.[11] The murderers justified their actions by asserting the radical position that *ʿulamāʾ* who allied themselves with an un-Islamic leader were non-Muslims, and thus were legitimate targets of violence.[12] When they were put on trial, the killers took the opportunity to criticize publicly the toadying of the *ʿulamāʾ* to the government, and the inability of the *ʿulamāʾ* to properly interpret Islamic law.[13]

While the *ʿulamāʾ* and lay Islamists argued publicly for their respective visions of Islamic legislation, Islamists in the legal community were also growing restless. Legal and judicial reforms of the Sādāt era had empowered the judiciary and the legal academy. During the 1970s, Islamist judges began to draw more overtly on Islamic legal principles. For example, in 1979, the Court of Cassation for the first time asserted not only that the principle of public policy would be used to interpret and supplement Egyptian law, but that in Egypt it would necessarily be informed by Islamic legal principles.

> Public policy represents the principles that aim at realizing the public interest of a country, from a political, social and economic perspective. The concept is based on a purely secular doctrine that is to be applied as a general doctrine. . . . However, this does not exclude that [public principle] is sometimes based on a principle related to religious doctrine in the case when such a doctrine has become intimately linked with the legal and social order, deeply rooted in the conscience

---

under Three Regimes," *Egypt from Monarchy to Republic*, ed. Shimon Shamir (Boulder: Westview Press, 1995), 181–94; Chris A. Eccel, "Ālim and Mujāhid in Egypt: Orthodoxy vs. Subculture, or Division of Labor?," *The Muslim World* 68 (1988): 201–4; Saad Eddin Ibrahim, "Anatomy of Egypt's Militant Islamic Groups: Methodological Notes and Preliminary Findings," *Egypt, Islam and Democracy: Twelve Critical Essays* (Cairo: American University in Cairo Press, 1996), 8–14.

[11] For some of Dhahabī's history and the implications of the hostility that some Islamist groups felt toward him, see Skovgaard-Petersen, *Defining Islam*, 218. For a more detailed analysis of the abduction and murder, see Kepel, *Le prophete et pharaon*, 94–102.

[12] See Kepel, *Le prophète et pharaon*, 94–102.

[13] See Shukrī Aḥmad Muṣṭafā, "Al-Naṣṣ al-Kāmil lī Aqwāl wa-Iʿtirāfāt Shukrī Aḥmad Muṣṭafā, Amīr Takfīr wa-'l-Hijra, amām Maḥkamat Amn al-Dawla al-ʿAskariyya al-ʿUlyā 1977," in Rifʿat Sayyid Aḥmad, *Al-Nabiyy al-Musallaḥ* (London: Riyāḍ Al Rayyis, 1991), Part I *Al-Rāfiḍūn*, 53–109, analyzed in J. Jansen, *The Dual Nature of Islamic Fundamentalism* (Ithaca: Cornell University Press, 1997).

> of society. . . . The definition [of public policy] is characterized by objectivity, in accordance with what the general majority of individuals of the community believe.[14]

More striking still was a decision by the Supreme Court, an institution that was soon to be reorganized and reestablished as the Supreme Constitutional Court.[15] In April 1976, the Supreme Court issued an opinion suggesting that Article 2, as vague as it was, might require all Egyptian law to be consistent with the essential principles of *sharīʿa*.[16] The Supreme Court decision was particularly striking because the Supreme Court was widely considered to be weak and generally susceptible to executive interference. That the Supreme Court would interpret Article 2 to require Islamization of the law suggested not only that there were Islamists in the upper reaches of the judiciary, but that the government was permitting them to speak out.

III. *Sādāt's Islamization policy and the amendment of Article 2 in 1980*

As Islamism (and its internal divisions) became more visible, Sādāt did not seem to lose enthusiasm for his plan to Islamize Egyptian law. If anything, he seems to have become more committed. Sādāt's optimism may have been driven, in part, by a latent sympathy for Islamism.[17] Pragmatic considerations also probably played a role. The

---

[14] Court of Cassation, Nos. 16 and 26, Year 48 (14 January 1979), trans. Maurits Berger, "Public Policy and Islamic Law: the Modern *Dhimmī* in Contemporary Egyptian Family Law," *Islamic Law and Society*, 8 (2001): 88–122.

[15] On the Supreme Court, see Baudouin Dupret and Nathalie Bernard-Maugiron, "Introduction: A General Presentation of Law and Judicial Bodies," *Egypt and its Laws*, eds. Nathalie Bernard-Maugiron and Baudouin Dupret (Arab and Islamic Law 22; London/The Hague/New York: Kluwer Law International, 2002), xxxiii–xxxv.

[16] A petitioner had asked that a law be struck down as contrary to Article 2 because it was inconsistent with Islamic law. Although the Court refused to strike down the law at issue, it did so on the grounds that the law at issue was, in fact, consistent with the essential principles of the *sharīʿa*. Implicitly, the reasoning suggested that the Court would strike down in the future laws that it believed to be inconsistent. Peters, "Divine Law or Man-Made Law?," 241 and n. 32.

[17] Before Nāṣir took power in the 1950s, Sādāt had been in regular contact with the Muslim Brothers. For his contacts with the Brothers, see, e.g., Ishak Musa Husaini, *The Moslem Brethren: The greatest of modern Islamic movements* (Beirut: Khayat, 1956), 125–26; Richard P. Mitchell, *The Society of the Muslim Brothers*, reprint with new intro. (New York: Oxford University Press, 1993), 89.

disputes among Islamists meant that the government would have some flexibility to negotiate with various parties in order to come up with a plan that met its needs. And ultimately, the Sādāt regime had little choice. As the 1970s progressed, the government's policies were becoming increasingly controversial among some of Nāṣir's traditional supporters. Although Egypt's modest victories during the 1973 war with Israel had improved the popular standing of Sādāt and his government, lingering economic and social problems continued to haunt the regime. By January 1977, a decision to stop subsidizing food commodities led to serious rioting.[18] Furthermore, over the course of 1977 and 1978, Sādāt concluded a controversial peace treaty with Israel. The government desperately needed a new source of support, and "Sadat's response to the growing opposition to his economic and foreign policies was to intensify his pursuit of Islamic legitimacy."[19]

Kirk Beattie's interviews with officials in the Sādāt regime revealed that, notwithstanding the doubts of some advisors, Sādāt had become convinced by the mid-1970s that his regime could negotiate successfully a plan for Islamization that would appeal to a broad cross-section of Islamists and would create significant Islamic support for the regime.[20] He thus initiated a series of public gestures, signaling to the members of the ruling party and the public at large that there might be a move toward Islamism—or, more precisely, toward a vision of Islamization that would be accepted by a critical mass of Islamists but would not interfere with the regime's economic, political and social initiatives.

In 1975, the Ministry of Justice announced the formation of a "Supreme Committee for Introducing Legislation According to the Islamic *sharīʿa*."[21] The government's continuing commitment to exploring Islamization was also reflected in its plans for reform of the rul-

[18] Vatikiotis, *The History of Modern Egypt*, 422.

[19] H. Hrair Dekmejian, *Islam in Revolution* (Syracuse: Syracuse University Press, 1985), 87.

[20] See Beattie, *Egypt During the Sadat Years*, 257–59.

[21] Its achievements remained minimal. Although this Committee was headed by a senior judge, it did not progress far with its reports. Peters, "Divine Law or Man-Made Law?," 236; Shamir and Segev, "The Arab Republic of Egypt," in *MECS* I (1977–78), 297. For citations to the entire list of proposed revisions, see Peters, "Divine Law or Man-Made Law?," 236 n. 17.

ing party. From an early date, Sādāt had planned to disband Nāṣir's ruling party, the Arab Socialist Union and to establish in its place a new ruling party, the National Democratic Party (NDP). The party was to have its own new ideology, one that was considerably less hostile to Islamist groups and the general ideals of Islamism than Nāṣir's regime had been. "Ever since his election to the presidency in 1970, Sadat ha[d] been aware of the lack of an ideological framework within which his political goals could be presented and which would fill the vacuum created by the decline of Nasserism, crystallize the identity of his own regime and counterbalance radical ideologies of the Left or the Right."[22] To clarify its new ideology of "Democratic Socialism," the government turned to Ṣūfī Abū Ṭālib. Some have questioned Abū Ṭālib's *bona fides* when it came to questions of Islamic legal reform.[23] Nevertheless, as Chapter 6 suggested, Abū Ṭālib had a history of advocating harmonization of Egyptian law with Islamic legal principles, and when the opportunity arose, he seemed to work diligently to achieve it.[24]

In 1975, Sādāt asked Abū Ṭālib to write a book outlining a political philosophy for the new regime. In response, he published a manifesto in 1978.[25] Combining socialist language with Islamist language,

[22] Jacques Reinich, "Arab Republic of Egypt," in MECS II (1977–78), 376–77.

[23] For example, Gilles Kepel described Abū Ṭālib as "an astute jurist trained in the law schools of Paris" who "defused" the calls for Islamization of the law by pretending to favor the drafting and promulgation of new Islamic codes. Kepel, *Le prophète et pharaon*, 126–27. Michael Winter makes similar claims in "Islam in the State: Pragmatism and Growing Commitment," *Egypt from Monarchy to Republic*, ed. Shimon Shamir (Boulder: Westview Press, 1995), 52.

[24] Kepel and Winter do not explain why they reach their conclusion that Abū Ṭālib's Islamism was affected. There seems to be scant evidence to support this view. As a law student, he wrote a dissertation that reflects the influence of Sanhūrī. His Islamist sympathies were sufficiently unpopular with some Nāṣirists in the 1960s that he felt compelled to leave Egypt. Reviewing his work as a legislator in the 1970s, Altman concluded: "As speaker, he directed *sharīʿa*-related activity in the PA [Peoples Assembly] and displayed personal interest and commitment to the application of the *sharīʿa* according to that view." Altman, "Islamic Legislation," 207. Beattie's interviews with Abū Ṭālib in 1994 similarly left him convinced that the speaker had pursued in good faith a plan to forge and implement a widely popular program of Islamization. See Beattie, *Egypt During the Sadat Years*, 170–72. The critics may be reading back into the Sādāt era the Mubārak regime's policy of espousing Islamism while attempting at all costs to forestall it. They may also be equating true "Islamization" with Islamization of the sort espoused by either al-Azhar or the Muslim Brothers.

[25] Ṣūfī Abū Ṭālib, "*Ishtirākiyyatūna al-Dīmūqrātiyya Īdiyūlūjīyāt Thawra at Māyū Sana*

this work espoused a vision "of a gradual transition to multi-party democracy, with a strong role for state activity and ownership in economic matters and underpinned by a strong commitment to religious values."[26] More striking still, it echoed the 1976 opinion of the Supreme Court, which had asserted that Article 2 required the government to ensure that all laws conform to Islamic norms: "According to constitutional stipulation, the legislator is committed in enacting new legislation after 1971, to go back to the *sharīʿa* and shun any regulation that appears contradictory to a given Islamic principle or source."[27]

Publication of Abū Ṭālib's manifesto was followed by concrete public steps toward implementing executive-sponsored Islamic reform of the legal system. Shortly after his manifesto was published, the NDP elected Abū Ṭālib as Speaker of the People's Assembly,[28] and created parliamentary committees charged with the task of preparing draft Islamic revisions to the codes of Egyptian law then in force.[29] The government apparently planned to negotiate the terms of Islamization so as to achieve maximum possible support, without giving up ultimate control over the process. Judging from his doctoral dissertation, Abū Ṭālib had at one time been impressed by the type of comparative legal scholarship that Sanhūrī exemplified.[30] The divisive debates in 1948 about the Islamic character of Sanhūrī's civil code, however, made clear that neo-traditionalists and champions of utilitarian neo-*ijtihād* were unwilling to accept as legitimately "Islamic" a new code that was checked only against principles identified through comparative neo-*taqlīd*. As the drafting committees drafted new codes, they consulted with various Islamist constituencies, including the judiciary and al-Azhar.[31] President Sādāt, around this time, is

---

1971," *al-Iqtiṣādī*, July 16, 1978; also published separately (Cairo: Publisher unknown, 1978), according to Beattie, *Egypt During the Sadat Years*, 169.

[26] Beattie, *Egypt During the Sadat Years*, 171; Jacques Reinich, "The Arab Republic of Egypt," in MECS II (1977–78), 391–92.

[27] See Abū Ṭālib, *Ishtirākiyyatūna al-Dīmuqrātiyya*, 13–14, as translated in Beattie, *Egypt During the Sadat Years*, 169.

[28] See Israel Altman, "The Arab Republic of Egypt," in MECS III (1978–79), 393.

[29] See Kepel, *Le prophète et pharaon*, 184.

[30] Soufy Hossain Abou-Talib (Ṣūfī Ḥusayn Abū Ṭālib), *Le periculum rei venditae en droit roman et en droit Musulman* (Cairo: Imprimerie Université du Caire, 1958).

[31] Peters, "Divine Law or Man-Made Law?," 236; Kepel, *Le prophète et pharaon*, 184, n. 13; see also Bernard Botiveau, "Islamiser le Droit?: l'éxample égyptien," *Maghreb-Mashrek* 126 (1989): 10–25 nn. 16–17; and Skovgaard-Petersen, *Defining Islam*, 201.

also reported to have arranged weekly meetings with Islamist figures who could help advise on Islamist youths' understandings of Islamic law.[32]

The most dramatic evidence that the government was committed to proceeding with negotiated Islamization was the decision to amend Article 2. On July 17, 1979, one-third of the members of the People's Assembly together proposed that the constitution be amended. According to the proposal, Article 2 would no longer provide that Islamic law was merely "a" chief source of Egyptian legislation. Rather it would provide that ". . . the principles of Islamic *sharīʿa* are *the* chief source of legislation" [italics added] (*mabādiʾ al-sharīʿa al-Islāmiyya al-maṣdar al-raʾīsī li-ʾl-tashrīʿ*).[33] On July 19, the People's Assembly approved the change in principle and, following normal procedures, sent the draft to a committee to be chaired by Ṣūfi Abū Ṭālib, which was to prepare an official report describing the effect of the proposed amendment. On April 30, 1980, the People's Assembly, dominated by the government party, overwhelmingly approved the amendment, and on May 22, 1980, the amendment was ratified by a popular vote and became law.[34]

What did the legislature think that it was accomplishing by this amendment? The official committee report concluded that the change would require the government to take steps to ensure that all Egyptian legislation was consistent with the principles of the Islamic *sharīʿa*:

> [The amendment] means that it is imperative to review the laws which were in effect before the Constitution of 1971 and to amend these laws in such a manner as to make them conform to the principles of Islamic law. . . .[35]

The report was deeply ambiguous, however, as to both the timing of the reforms and the type of "Islamic" legal norm that the state

---

[32] Beattie, *Egypt During the Sadat Years*, 259.

[33] Israel Altman, "The Arab Republic of Egypt," in MECS III (1978–79), 408, summarizing the reports in *al-Ahrām* of July 3, 16, 18, and 19, 1979; Israel Altman, "The Arab Republic of Egypt," in MECS IV (1979–80), 344. See also Peters, "Divine Law or Man-Made Law?," 236 n. 19.

[34] On the parliamentary vote, see Altman, "The Arab Republic of Egypt," in MECS IV (1979–80), 344. Although the official vote-count seemed to show overwhelming support for the amendment, a surprisingly low turnout seemed to reflect serious reservations among non-Muslims about the amendment of Article 2.

[35] Excerpt from the Report of the Drafting Committee, trans. in Hatem Laly Gabr, "Interpretation of Article Two of the Constitution," *Human Rights and Democracy*, eds. Kevin Boyle and Adel Omar Sherif (London: Graham and Trotman, 1996), 219.

would be obliged to respect. With respect to timing, the committee indicated that the legislature should be given some time to Islamize the laws, although it did not give any specific timetable: "[T]he change of the entire legal system should not be contemplated without giving the lawmakers an opportunity *and a reasonable period of time* within which to collect all legal materials and amalgamate them into a complete system within the framework of the Qur'ān, the Sunna,[36] and the opinions of learned Muslim jurists and Imams" (emphasis added).[37] The ambiguity about timing did not attract much notice at the time that Article 2 was adopted, because the government was already in the process of drafting Islamic reforms, and people expected them to be issued long before a "reasonable" period of time had elapsed. The next chapter will describe, however, how the government unexpectedly abandoned its plans for proposing Islamic reforms, and the ambiguity about timing would later become a major problem for the courts trying to interpret Article 2.

With respect to the types of Islamic norms to which the state would defer, there was further uncertainty. If all Egyptian legislation had to be consistent with the principles of the Islamic *sharīʿa*, it would have been helpful if the constitution had given the legislature and courts some guidance as to how these principles were to be identified and interpreted. On this point, however, the drafting committee was extraordinarily vague, noting nebulously that, when the legislature decides what "the principles of the Islamic *sharīʿa*" require, it must consider the "Qur'an, the *Sunna*, and the opinions of learned jurists and *imams*."[38] Other passages did not shed more light on the matter. The committee stated elsewhere only that a legislator drafting laws would be required to

> . . . have recourse to the rules of the *sharīʿa* in its quest for the rule of law which it is seeking to the exclusion of any other system of law;

[36] The *sunna* is the example of the Prophet as described in the *ḥadīth* literature.

[37] Report of the Drafting Committee. I have adopted here and elsewhere in this book the translation by Hatem Gabr in "Interpretation of Article 2 of the Constitution," in *Human Rights and Democracy: The Role of the Supreme Constitutional Court of Egypt*, Kevin Boyle and Adel Omar Sherif, eds. (CIMEL Book Series No. 3; London: Kluwer, 1996), 219. There was apparently a lack of consensus about how much time the parliament should be given to enact its reforms. See, e.g., the discussion in Peters, "Divine Law or Man-Made Law?," 236 n. 20, citing, *inter alia*, the comments of Dr. Muḥammad ʿAlī Maḥjūb, Chairman of the Parliamentary Committee for Religious Affairs in *al-Ahrām*, May 25, 1980.

[38] Excerpt from the Report of the Drafting Committee, trans. in Gabr, "Interpretation of Article 2 of the Constitution," 219.

> and in case it does not find the *sharīʿa*'s clear ruling, then it should apply the approved methods of deducting legal rules from the authorized sources of endeavor in Islamic jurisprudence. These may help the Legislator in reaching a ruling which does not contradict the principles and general framework of the *sharīʿa*.[39]

Sādāt presumably left Article 2 ambiguous about how the government would interpret *sharīʿa*, because he needed to maintain flexibility to negotiate a broadly popular form of Islamization. That he was willing to enact such a potentially explosive clause in such an ambiguous fashion suggests that he believed the political branches would remain actively involved in shaping Islamic reform and further that he expected the ruling party to retain control over the judiciary—which would ultimately be responsible for vetting the law for consistency with Article 2. As it turned out, neither of these assumptions was accurate.

IV. *The political branches' retreat from their policy of top-down Islamization, 1980–1985*

Immediately after the amendment of Article 2, the People's Assembly proceeded with its plans to negotiate and enact Islamic codes. In the second half of 1980, the Islamic codification committees completed preliminary drafts of six new codes: civil law, procedure, evidence, penal law, commerce, and maritime commerce.[40] They submitted these codes to the University of al-Azhar for review, and in January 1981 the university formally approved these drafts. (This approval seems not to have been a rubber stamp, since al-Azhar apparently rejected draft amendments to the laws governing, among others, banking and social insurance. The committees thus had to

[39] Ibid.

[40] The codes were published as appendices to the transcripts of the daily proceedings of the People's Assembly: Majlis al-Shaʿb, *Maḍbaṭat Majlis al-Shaʿb*, July 1, 1982. They were also summarized in *al-Ahrām* on July 12, 1982, Nov. 11, 1982, Nov. 14, 1982, and Dec. 6, 1982. The legislative history is discussed in Majlis al-Shaʿb, *Maḍbaṭat Majlis al-Shaʿb*, July 1, 1982, and May 4, 1985. See Enid Hill, "Law and Courts in Egypt. Recent Issues and Events Concerning Islamic Law," *The Political Economy of Contemporary Egypt*, ed. Ibrahim Oweiss (Washington D.C.: Center for Contemporary Arab Studies, 1990), 263 n. 44; and Peters, "Divine Law or Man-Made Law?," 237–38.

redraft sections of these codes.)[41] After approval by al-Azhar, Abū Ṭālib sent the draft codes to legislative committees that, pursuant to normal Egyptian legislative practice, would prepare reports that would be used to debate the codes prior to final adoption.

Shortly after the amendment of Article 2, Sādāt's dream of negotiating a program of quick Islamization began to sour. As it grew closer to publicly unveiling the codes that had been drafted by Abū Tālib and approved by the leading neo-traditionalists at al-Azhar, the regime apparently grew concerned about the criticisms that other Islamist factions might level at the code. Making clear that it would not tolerate criticism of the codes that it had produced, the government in 1981 banned the Muslim Brothers' publications and imprisoned its leaders (along with the known leaders of radical *jamāʿāt*).[42] Not surprisingly, the lay Islamist groups and their sympathizers grew increasingly suspicious of the regime's commitment to Islamization—or at least they worried that the government's vision of Islamization would be very different from their own. After the amendment of Article 2, these groups became more confrontational.[43] The escalating tensions exploded on October 6, 1981, when an extremist Islamic cell within the army assassinated Sādāt during a military parade.

After the assassination, executive power transferred smoothly to Ḥusnī al-Mubārak, but the transition led to a dramatic change in the ruling regime's attitude toward Islamization.[44] Mubārak quickly reestablished a state of emergency, and the new regime began incre-

[41] Peters, "Divine Law or Man-Made Law?," 237 n. 21, citing articles in *al-Ahrām*, April 22, 1979, December 3, 1980, and June 24, 1982.

[42] Observers were unsure whether the crackdown symbolized a permanent reversal of the government's liberalization policies or whether it was simply a tactical retreat—a warning that radical elements must continue to work within the bounds permitted by the government. *The International Herald Tribune* and *Ha'aretz* took the former view on September 8, 1981. The *Manchester Guardian* and *Ma'ariv* took the latter. For a digest of contemporary Egyptian and foreign news accounts and an analysis, see Ami Ayalon, "The Arab Republic of Egypt," in MECS V (1980–81), 427–33 and accompanying endnotes.

[43] For a list of the most serious riots and terrorist attacks and extensive references to contemporary newspaper accounts of the tensions, see Ami Ayalon, "The Arab Republic of Egypt," in MECS V (1980–81), 427–28 and its extensive citations to Egyptian newspaper reports.

[44] See Eccel, "ʿĀlim and Mujāhid in Egypt," 190–95; Kepel, *Le prophète et pharaon*, 191–222.

mentally to dismantle the Islamization initiatives that Sādāt had established. The regime's new policy revealed itself only gradually. Even as the regime suppressed radical Islamists in the aftermath of the assassination, it reached out to moderate Muslim leaders.[45] A few months after Sādāt's assassination, Mubārak released many of the figures arrested during Sādāt's final crackdown, including several leading Muslim Brothers.[46] For a time, the government also made a point to be seen moving forward with its preparation of the Islamic codes. On July 1, 1982, Ṣufī Abū Ṭālib distributed the six draft Islamic codes to the floor of the People's Assembly and sent them to committee for a report to be prepared for the eventual debates on the codes. Abū Ṭālib described the decision to enter this apparent legislative endgame as the realization of the government's promise to engage in Islamization: ". . . [T]his venerable House has fulfilled its pledge in record time. In forty months, this venerable house has carried out this work which God willing will be everlasting."[47]

Abū Ṭālib's celebration was premature. As time went on, it became increasingly clear that the new regime had decided to renounce its predecessor's Islamic policies. Shortly before the 1984 election, Ṣūfī Abū Ṭālib's term as Speaker of the People's Assembly ended.[48] Over the protests of the opposition, the government ran the 1984 elections in an irregular manner that guaranteed a comfortable majority for the ruling party.[49] Thereafter, the speaker of the new People's

---

[45] For a digest of contemporary Egyptian and foreign newspaper accounts and an analysis of the crackdown, see Ami Ayalon, "The Arab Republic of Egypt," in MECS VI (1981–82), 449–51; Vatikiotis, *A History of Modern Islam*, 439.

[46] Upon his release, a leading Muslim Brother, ʿUmar al-Tilimsānī, was quoted as saying that Egypt was in crisis and that all true Muslims should work with the government. He himself would "support the Government as long as it adhered to a policy of reforms." His speech was reported in *al-Jumhūriyya*, December 25, 1981 and trans. in Ayalon, "The Arab Republic of Egypt," in MECS VI (1981–82), 449–51. See also the newspaper reports of al-Tilimsānī's speeches in *al-Muṣawwar*, January 1, 1982 and *al-Sharq al-Awsaṭ*, January 6, 1982, trans. in the same article.

[47] *Maḍbaṭat Majlis al-Shaʿb*, session 70, 1–7, 1982, as trans. in Peters, "Divine Law or Man-Made Law?," 239.

[48] See Ami Ayalon, "The Arab Republic of Egypt," in MECS VIII (1983–84), 362, 383 n. 50.

[49] Although 58 members of the New Wafd party had been elected, eight of whom were known to be affiliated with the Muslim Brothers, the irregularities allowed the NDP to retain an overwhelming majority. See Ayalon, "The Arab Republic of Egypt," in MECS VIII (1983–84), 362. The opposition complained credibly of widespread unfairness in the election rules and of irregularities in the balloting. The complaints were sufficiently serious and plausible that in 1987, the Supreme

Assembly, Rifʿat Maḥjūb, used parliamentary procedures to shelve all plans to Islamize the law.[50] No plans were announced to draft new ones. With that, the executive and legislature, each controlled by the president's ruling party, simultaneously abandoned their attempts to negotiate some form of Islamization.

It is unclear when or why the government had decided to renounce its public commitment to Islamization of the law. But by 1985, there could no longer be any doubt that such a decision had been made.[51] To quiet protest, the government in 1985 initiated a two-pronged program to limit the public fallout. To forestall criticism that it was anti-Islamic, the regime actively promoted Islamic culture and allowed al-Azhar to censor the arts. Furthermore, even as it was celebrating Islam's influence on Egyptian culture, it clamped down on public discussion of the now-abandoned plan for Islamization of the civil law. The ruling party squelched any discussion of law in the parliament, and many contemporary observers suggested that it suppressed debate in the press as well. In a nation in which the government exercises considerable control over the media, one observer found that discussion of the Islamization issue dried up almost entirely after 1985.[52] Not surprisingly, what reporting the government permitted seems to have been designed to refute any suggestions that Egyptians were dissatisfied with government policy. In 1985, one of

Constitutional Court overturned the results of this election and ordered a new election. In the new election, candidates associated with the Muslim Brothers had far greater success.

[50] Maḥjūb scheduled parliamentary "debate" on Abū Ṭālib's six Islamic codes, which had by this time been languishing in committee for almost three years. Debate was to take place on May 4, 1985. But there was no debate. Maḥjūb used parliamentary procedures to call a vote before any Islamist members of parliament could speak, and then supervised a vote in which the members of the government party exercised their overwhelming majority to reject the idea of adopting the codes in their current form. Kepel, *Le prophète et pharaon*, 247. See also Hill, "Law and Courts in Egypt," 251–52; Skovgaard-Petersen, *Defining Islam*, 211–12.

[51] Enid Hill suggests that the government never really believed that Abū Ṭālib would succeed in preparing Islamic codes and was forced to squelch them when they appeared. See "Law and Courts in Egypt, 250–51. Rudolph Peters, on the other hand, has suggested three reasons for what he calls the government's "*volte-face*": a "hardening" of attitudes toward Islamists in the wake of the assassination of Sādāt, a fear of sectarian clashes, and concern about relationships with foreign donors (particularly the U.S.) on whom the Egyptian economy increasingly relied. See Peters, "Divine Law or Man-Made Law?," 239.

[52] Skovgaard-Petersen, *Defining Islam*, 212 n. 26.

the few reported comments on the government's policy consisted of implicit approvals by statements made by members of the *ʿulamāʾ* with close ties to the government, who declared either that the laws of Egypt were consistent with Islamic norms or that there was no sin in delaying Islamization.[53]

Islamist factions (and the public at large) were not nearly so sanguine about government policy as the selective reporting would imply. After people rallied during the 1987 elections in support of opposition parties calling for the immediate application of the *sharīʿa*, the government felt it was impossible not to respond in some way. The government party, the NDP, pledged to "adhere to religious values and to the *sharīʿa* as the chief source of legislation."[54] Nevertheless, what mention there was of Islamization was invariably vague. The government made no attempt to set a timetable for Islamization, nor to define the principles of the Islamic *sharīʿa*. By this time, the regime enjoyed sufficient control over society that it could not be forced through normal political channels to do more.[55] The closure of the political arena led some disgruntled Islamists to violent resistance.

V. *Article 2 litigation and the evolving judicial role in shaping Islamization*

As the political process closed, some Islamists decided that their best chance to effect Islamization was through litigation. Islamization was arguably more than a discretionary policy. Arguably, it was a policy required by the constitution. Article 2 as revised made the principles of the *sharīʿa* "the chief source of legislation," and a parliamentary

---

[53] For example, the acting Muftī of the Republic, ʿAbd al-Laṭīf Ḥamza, granted an interview in which he optimistically suggested that both he and the Shaykh al-Azhar agreed they must not take stands on any political questions. (In fact, the Shaykh al-Azhar could only have agreed with this proposition if he had had a sudden change of heart. A few months earlier he had explicitly called upon the parliament to adopt immediately new laws that were consistent with the principles of the *sharīʿa*.) Skovgaard-Petersen, *Defining Islam*, 247, citing an interview with ʿAbd al-Laṭīf Ḥamza in *Rūz al-Yūsuf*, May 6, 1985, 30–32. Similarly, in 1988, the newly appointed Muftī of the Republic, Sayyid Ṭanṭāwī, appeared in a trial of radical Islamists and stated that it was the duty of the People's Assembly alone to decide whether Egyptian law should be Islamized.

[54] See Ami Ayalon, "The Arab Republic of Egypt," in MECS XI (1987), 334.

[55] See, e.g., the comment of Kepel, *Le prophète et pharaon*, 247.

report had suggested that Article 2, as amended, obliged the political branches within a reasonable period to ensure that Egyptian law conformed to the principles of *sharī'a*. Even if the political branches failed in this responsibility, then the increasingly independent courts might be willing to take it on. Islamists thus began to bring lawsuits against numerous pieces of legislation that were arguably contrary to Islamic principles. Ultimately, albeit perhaps with some reluctance, the courts accepted the challenge that the political branches had declined. As the confrontations between Islamists and the government became increasingly violent, the courts, led by the Supreme Constitutional Court, began to develop an official theory of Islamic law and to measure state law for consistency with norms derived through its official method of interpretation. The following chapter will describe the judicial institutions that were entrusted with the responsibility to interpret Article 2. Later chapters will discuss the interpretation of Article 2 that the SCC developed and the reception of that theory by the public.

CHAPTER EIGHT

THE INTERPRETERS OF ARTICLE 2: THE EGYPTIAN COURTS AND THE SCC

In 1980, when Article 2 was amended, a new constitutional tribunal, the Supreme Constitutional Court of Egypt had recently been established as the highest authority on questions of constitutional interpretation. Ultimately, the SCC was responsible for giving an authoritative interpretation of Article 2. When the Court was first confronted with Article 2 cases, it was a young and fairly weak institution seeking to establish itself as a respected, independent court. It could not afford to offend either the secularists who controlled the executive branch, nor the various Islamist factions in Egypt. The SCC was also trying against difficult odds to impose a liberal constitutional rule of law in Egypt. This chapter will discuss the Court, its role in the Egyptian legal system, and the institutional concerns of the justices on the Court in the 1980s and 1990s. Subsequent chapters will explore the SCC's Article 2 opinions and the way in which the SCC's institutional concerns and its commitment to liberal democratic norms have helped to shape its interpretation and application of Article 2.

I. *The structure of the Egyptian court system and the role of the SCC*

The modern Egyptian legal system developed out of reforms in the late nineteenth century. These reforms accompanied the adoption of a national civil code and reflected an embrace of a positivist legal system modeled on the French legal system. As Enid Hill has noted, however, "French" institutions in Egypt have sometimes evolved in a way slightly differently than they did in France.[1] Furthermore, the

[1] See, e.g., Enid Hill, "Majlis al-Dawla: The Administrative Courts of Egypt and Administrative Law," *Islam and Public Law: Classical and Contemporary Studies*, ed. Chibli Mallat (CIMEL Arab and Islamic Laws Series 8; London: Graham & Trotman,

Egyptian legal system has since developed institutions that are found not in France, but in other civil law legal systems—such as the special constitutional court.[2]

The courts of general jurisdiction for private actions and criminal law are the national courts. Legal actions in this system are brought initially in courts of first instance, and can be appealed to appeals courts. The final appellate authority within the regular court system is the Court of Cassation (*al-Maḥkamat al-Naqḍ*), and there is no appeal from this court.[3] Alongside the regular courts sits a parallel "administrative" court system with jurisdiction over challenges to executive actions.[4] The administrative courts also hear disputes between branches of the government. If a person wishes to challenge an executive action (or certain types of administrative decrees) on the grounds that it is inconsistent with the powers granted to the executive (or a particular administrative department) or with laws passed by the legislature, he must bring a legal action in the administrative court system.[5] There is a hierarchy of administrative courts, beginning with the courts of first instance (*al-maḥākim al-idāriyya*) and moving to the appeals courts (*maḥākim al-qaḍā' al-idārī*). The final authority within the administrative court system is the High Administrative Court (*Al-Maḥkama al-Idāriyya al-ʿUlyā*). There is no appeal from a decision of the High Administrative Court. Alongside the national court system and the administrative court system, there are courts with more spe-

1993), 212–18; Enid Hill, "Change and Continuity in an Egyptian Judicial Institution: The *Niyāba*," *Law and Social Change: Problems and Challenges in Contemporary Egypt*, 2nd ed., eds. Cynthia Nelson and Klaus-Friedrich Koch (Cairo Papers in Social Science 2.4; Cairo: University of Cairo Press, 1983), 117–37.

[2] The most important of these is the Supreme Constitutional Court, discussed in detail below.

[3] See Baudouin Dupręt and Nathalie Bernard-Maugiron, "Introduction: A General Presentation of Law and Judicial Bodies," in *Egypt and its Laws*, Nathalie Bernard-Maugiron and Baudouin Dupret, eds. (Arab and Islamic Law Series 22; London/The Hague/New York: Kluwer Law International, 2002), xxviii–xxxi; Enid Hill, *Mahkama!: Studies in the Egyptian Legal System* (London: Ithaca Press, 1979).

[4] See Dupret and Bernard-Maugiron, "Introduction," xxxi–xxxiii; Hill, "Majlis al-Dawla," 207–28; Adel Omar Sherif, "An Overview of the Egyptian Court System," *Yearbook of Islamic and Middle Eastern Law* 5 (1998–99): 15–16, 20–25.

[5] For a general explanation of administrative courts in civil law systems, and particularly of the theoretical reasons why administrative cases could not be heard in the regular courts of a civil law nation, see John Henry Merryman, *The Civil Law Tradition: An Introduction to the Legal Systems of Western Europe and Latin America*, 2nd ed. (Stanford, CA: Stanford University Press, 1985), 85–89.

cialized jurisdictions which occasionally overlap with the jurisdiction of the national and administrative courts. For instance, the state security courts hear cases involving crimes against public security—meaning, for all practical purposes, political crimes and terrorism.[6] The so-called military courts have a vaguely defined jurisdiction that encompasses crimes by military personnel and crimes that involve the state.[7] The jurisdiction of these military courts overlaps to some extent with the jurisdiction of both the regular courts and the state security courts, and the executive has occasionally turned to them when other sectors of the judiciary have proven less pliant than it wishes.[8]

Since 1969, however, none of the courts described above has been given jurisdiction over constitutional disputes. The right to exercise constitutional review of legislation has been vested in special constitutional tribunals—first in a transitional Supreme Court and then in the Supreme Constitutional Court of Egypt.

II. *Constitutional review in the Egyptian legal system*

For many decades, all Egyptian courts were authorized to consider the constitutionality of legislation and could choose not to apply laws that they held to be unconstitutional—a practice called "abstention control."[9] Although courts generally did not exercise this in an

[6] See Sherif, "An Overview of the Egyptian Judicial System," 25–26; Adel Omar Sherif, "The Origins and Development of the Egyptian Judicial System," *Human Rights and Democracy: The Role of the Supreme Constitutional Court of Egypt*, eds. Kevin Boyle and Adel Omar Sherif (CIMEL Book Series 3; London: Kluwer, 1996), 24–27.

[7] Because these are tribunals staffed largely by military officers rather than judges, it is not clear whether these should properly be described as judicial courts.

[8] For example, in the 1970s and 1980s, the judiciary, including the judges on the State Security Courts, began to exercise increased independence from the executive, and to tie the hands of the government as it tried to suppress Islamists. As a result, the government decided to move many of the more controversial cases involving Islamists to the military courts, which are still very much under the control of the executive. For a discussion of this development, see Michael Farhang, "Terrorism and Military Trials in Egypt: Presidential Decree No. 375 and the Consequences for Judicial Autonomy," *Harvard International Law Journal* 35 (1994): 225–36.

[9] See Enid Hill, "Establishing the Doctrine of Judicial Review in Egypt and the United States," *The Role of the Judiciary in the Protection of Human Rights*, eds. Eugene

aggressive manner, President Nāṣir did not like the idea of judges retaining the theoretical power to overturn laws that the ruling party had enacted. In 1969, therefore, Nāṣir's captive legislature enacted Law No. 81 of 1969, which stripped the existing courts of the right to determine which laws were unconstitutional. It then issued Law No. 66 of 1970, which established a new Supreme Court to which courts could refer cases when they had doubts about constitutionality.[10] The new 1970 Constitution incorporated the idea of a special constitutional tribunal, but left the details of its operation to be settled in the future by the legislature. While the legislature developed implementing legislation, the Supreme Court served as a transitional organ vested with the power of constitutional review.[11]

The process of developing implementing legislation for the new constitutional court proved controversial and time-consuming. To understand the delay, it is necessary to know that the regime had established a new constitutional tribunal, in part, because it believed that the regular courts and administrative courts were too independent.[12] It expected to create a tribunal whose justices would be subject to executive control. Reasserting themselves after years of executive interference, the judiciary fought vigorously for a more independent constitutional court. They vociferously insisted in public that the new constitutional court, at the very least, should retain robust protections of judicial independence.[13] The regime compromised. Law 48

Cotran and Adel Omar Sherif (CIMEL Book Series 5; London: Kluwer, 1997). On abstention control specifically, see Awad Mohammed El-Morr, Abd El-Rahman Nosseir, and Adel Omar Sherif, "The Supreme Constitutional Court and Its Role in the Egyptian Judicial System," *Human Rights and Democracy: The Role of the Supreme Constitutional Court of Egypt*, eds. Kevin Boyle and Adel Omar Sherif (CIMEL Book Series 3; London: Kluwer, 1996), 38–39.

[10] Adel Omar Sherif, *Al-Qaḍā' al-Dustūrī fī Miṣr* [*Constitutional Justice in Egypt*], (Cairo: Dār al-Fikr al'Arabī, 1995), 88.

[11] Arab Republic of Egypt, *Dustūr Jumhūriyyat Miṣr al-'Arabiyya* (Constitution of the Arabic Republic of Egypt) (1971), Articles 174–78. Future references to this constitution will be to *Egyptian Constitution.*

[12] See Dupret and Maugiron, "Introduction," xxxv.

[13] On the reemergence of an aggressively independent judiciary, see, *inter alia*, Nathan Brown, *The Rule of Law in the Arab World: Courts in Egypt and the Gulf* (Cambridge: Cambridge University Press, 1997), 94–107; Hill, "Majlis al-Dawla," 220–225. James Rosberg, *Roads to the Rule of Law: The Emergence of an Independent Judiciary in Contemporary Egypt.* (Ph.D. diss., Massachusetts Institute of Technology, 1995); James Rosberg, "Information and Liberty: The Development of the Rule of Law in Authoritarian Regimes" available on-line at http://web.mit.edu/web~rjames/www/ruleoflaw.pdf. Their success can be seen in the fact that the Mubārak regime

of 1979 established a Supreme Constitutional Court, which had considerable independence.[14] Although some judges of the SCC were initially concerned that the protections for their independence were insufficient, their fears were not realized—at least for the first twenty years of the Court's existence.[15] The SCC strove in the 1980s and 90s to check executive abuses of power and defend citizens' rights.

Under Law 48 of 1979, the SCC was entrusted with three main duties. First, it was to serve as the final authority in case of a jurisdictional dispute between two Egyptian courts. Second, at the request of the government, it could issue authoritative interpretations of legislative texts. Finally, and most important, it had the right to perform constitutional review in certain cases.[16] The SCC's jurisdiction over constitutional cases raised in lower courts is complex. The SCC does not have jurisdiction over every court case that raises a constitutional challenge. According to laws governing the operation of the Court, lower courts determine which constitutional claims can be brought before the SCC—a function that is often referred to as their "gate-keeping function." As a result, all suits, including suits that raise a constitutional claim, must be brought initially to one of the other courts (national, administrative, security, and so forth). If this court, as gatekeeper, decides that a legitimate constitutional issue has been raised, it must refer the case to the SCC or, in the alternative, authorize the challenger to raise the constitutional issue before the SCC.[17] Once a case over which it has jurisdiction has been

---

was forced to make significant further concessions to the judiciary and to suffer a series of embarrassing setbacks in the courts. For example, national and security courts quashed convictions; administrative courts held that executive actions banning political activity or publications were inconsistent with the applicable laws. See Rosberg, "Information and Liberty"; Brown, *Rule of Law*, 126–28; Hill, "Majlis al-Dawla," 223–27.

[14] Law No. 48 (1979) (hereinafter, "SCC Law of 1979"). For a discussion of the politics surrounding the laws establishing working procedures for the Court, and an analysis of the safeguards designed to protect the Court's independence, see Brown, *The Rule of Law*, 102–3. For a complete discussion of the structure of the Court and the way in which its judges are appointed and monitored, see Sherif, "An Overview of the Egyptian Judicial System," 17.

[15] Brown, *The Rule of Law*, 103. Since 1998 and particularly since 2001, the Egyptian government has worked with some success to stifle the SCC's independence. See Tamir Moustafa, "Law versus the State: The Judicialization of Egyptian Politics," *Law and Social Inquiry* 28 (2003), 924ff."

[16] SCC Law of 1979, Art. 25.

[17] SCC Law of 1979, Art. 29.

properly referred, the Court must hear it. A symbiotic relationship exists between the regular courts (or administrative courts) and the SCC. The SCC relies largely on judges in these other courts to refer cases to it; and the judges in these other courts themselves rely entirely on the SCC to strike down legislation that they believe unconstitutional.[18]

When formed, the Supreme Constitutional Court was headed by a chief justice and staffed with a number of other justices. Law does not set the exact number of justices, but from 1979 through 2000, the period during which the SCC established its basic approach to Islamic legal interpretation, nine justices served on the Court.[19] A judgment was final after seven justices signed it.[20] A member of the Court's Commissioners' Body in 1996 drew attention to the importance of the fact that, although decisions do not have to be unanimous, dissents are not published.[21] Whether or not he is in the majority, the chief justice will either write the opinion or will assign it to a judge of his choosing. When the opinion is issued, it will not reveal the votes of the justices. Indeed, such information must, by law, be kept secret.[22] How such a system may affect judicial politics

[18] For a discussion of the way that the process works, see, e.g., Adel Omar Sherif, "Constitutional Adjudication," *Egypt and its Laws*, eds. Nathalie Bernard-Maugiron and Baudouin Dupret (*Arab and Islamic Law Series* 22; London/The Hague/New York: Kluwer Law International, 2002), 329–38; Sherif, "An Overview of the Egyptian Judicial System," 19–20.

[19] El-Morr, Nosseir, and Sherif, "The Supreme Constitutional Court and Its Role in the Egyptian Judicial System," 42–43. In 2001, in an attempt to tame the liberal activist judges then on the SCC, the government arranged for the number of judges to be increased. See Moustafa, "Law versus the State," 924–25.

[20] El-Morr, Nosseir, and Sherif, "The Supreme Constitutional Court and Its Role in the Egyptian Judicial System," 42–43; Adel Omar Sherif, "The Freedom of Judicial Expression," *Human Rights and Democracy: The Role of the Supreme Constitutional Court of Egypt*, eds. Kevin Boyle and Adel Omar Sherif (CIMEL Book Series 3; London: Kluwer, 1996), 142.

[21] If the seven justices on the Court cannot agree about the proper outcome, the Court will simply issue one opinion, and the dissenting justices will not be permitted to explain their contrary position. If there are three or more conflicting positions, the chief justice counts the number of votes for each position and identifies the two positions that have the most support, and drops all the others. The justices are then required to cast their votes again, and are only permitted to vote for one of the two remaining opinions. For a complete discussion of the process, see Sherif, "The Freedom of Judicial Expression," 137–58.

[22] Sherif, "The Freedom of Judicial Expression," 144–45.

is not entirely clear, but the power to write or assign opinions combined with the absence of dissents could give the chief justice extraordinary power to shape the Court's jurisprudence.[23]

III. *Institutional and ideological concerns of the SCC*

The SCC is a relatively new institution that has, since 1979, served as the final authority on questions of constitutional interpretation. To what end has the SCC exercised its power? First, the justices of the SCC through the 1990s showed a marked, occasionally self-serving, concern with defining and enforcing the separation of powers among the branches of the Egyptian government. In practice, this meant curbing executive abuses of power,[24] guaranteeing the integrity of national elections,[25] and promoting the rights of speech and association with the explicit goal of empowering civil society to check executive power.[26]

[23] One might suspect that this type of system means that, so long as the chief justice is in the majority, the justices have little incentive to compromise in their opinions. One jurist seems to have suggested that this is a serious problem. See the veiled comments in Sherif, "The Freedom of Judicial Expression," 153. Over time, the SCC's jurisprudence might be subject to somewhat unpredictable swings as the personnel on the Court change.

[24] For example, in Case No. 22, Judicial Year 2 (May 4, 1985), the Supreme Constitutional Court limited the President's power to define his own emergency powers. It struck down a decree law enacted by the President on the grounds that it was not, in fact, necessary to deal with any real emergency. For a chief justice's summary of the Court's philosophy and the jurisprudence to date in this area, see Dr. Awad El-Morr and Adel Omar Sherif, "The Separation and Powers and Limits on Presidential Powers under the Egyptian Constitution," *Human Rights and Democracy*, 63–73.

[25] The Court has several times struck down laws governing the administration of national elections. See Case No. 131, Judicial Year 6 (May 16, 1987); Case No. 23, Judicial Year 8 (April 15, 1989); Case No. 14, Judicial Year 8 (April 15, 1989); Case No. 37, Judicial Year 9 (May 19, 1990).

[26] For example, the Supreme Constitutional Court has struck down a law banning any political party opposed to peace with Israel. Case No. 44, Judicial Year 7 (May 7, 1998). It has also overturned laws interfering in the structure of workers' syndicates. See, e.g., Case No. 6, Judicial Year 15 (April 15, 1995). For a chief justice's summary of the Court's philosophy and the jurisprudence through 1997, see Dr. Awad El-Morr and Adel Omar Sherif, "Democratic Participation," *Human*

Not surprisingly, the SCC also acted to protect the courts' power to check legal or administrative abuses and its own specialized power to exercise constitutional review over most government action.[27] In short, during the 1980s and 90s the courts and the SCC in particular tried to ensure what Americans would think of as procedural due process. That is to say, they tried to protect individuals from executive and legislative abuse of power by (1) requiring the political branches to act only through the mechanisms permitted them by the Constitution, and (2) ensuring that the political branches remain subject to criticism for offensive actions. Historically in Egypt, the "rule of law, as envisioned by judges, focuses on achieving fairness and equity in application of the law much more than it focuses on making good law."[28]

Starting in the early 1990s, however, the SCC also began to go beyond the traditional focus on procedural safeguards of rights, to define for itself the scope of substantive individual rights, and to strike down laws that impose on them. It also started to identify certain constitutional principles that the executive branch or private citizens may never violate. Even if the political branches, acting through legitimate democratic means, explicitly create laws that permit certain types of behavior, these laws will have no effect if they lead to violations of essential rights. Thus, as Nathan Brown puts it, since the early 1990s the Court

> has departed from th[e] traditional judicial focus to advance a substantive, and not simply procedural, view of the rule of law. When its decisions over its first decade and a half are taken together, a vision emerges of an admittedly political jurisprudence . . . [T]he mandate of the court to render authoritative rulings on constitutional issues compels a more adventurous interpretive role than is usual for Egyptian courts, because of the vagueness (which often seems intentional) and contradictions contained in the 1971 constitution. (As mentioned above,

Rights and Democracy: The Role of the Supreme Constitutional Court of Egypt, eds. Kevin Boyle and Adel Omar Sherif (CIMEL Book Series 3; London: Kluwer, 1996), 76–84, and Yakoot Alashmawy and Adel Omar Sherif, "Freedom of Expression," *Human Rights and Democracy*, 129–36. For a more recent summary by one of the Court's counselors, and an explicit statement regarding the connection between free expression and a functioning civil society, see Adel Omar Sherif, "Constitutional Adjudication," 340.

[27] For examples, see Sherif, "Constitutional Adjudication," 339–400.

[28] Brown, *The Rule of Law*, 118.

one of the chief characteristics of the constitution is to combine vague liberal language on rights and freedoms with specific, often authoritarian language empowering the executive.) Working with such a text, it becomes virtually impossible to claim that the Court is simply mechanically applying a self-evident text.[29]

The Supreme Constitutional Court's move to define and protect individual rights in the 1990s is of great interest here because, as later chapters will show, it may have helped to shape the Court's interpretation of Article 2.

In an important comparative article, Baber Johansen pointed out that like some recently created European constitutional courts, the Supreme Constitutional Court has consistently held that the constitution must be interpreted as an organic whole.[30] In reading the constitution holistically, the Court has tried to ensure that it will interpret constitutional provisions guaranteeing individual rights in such a way that there are no inconsistencies with other constitutional provisions. The SCC's constitutional jurisprudence is thus not supposed to be an agglomeration of different jurisprudences, such as "free speech jurisprudence," "voting rights jurisprudence," "equal rights jurisprudence," and so on. Rather, it is supposed to be an internally consistent whole in which the various clauses are interpreted simultaneously and underlying principles elucidated. The third chief justice of the Court once described the Court's job as one of developing

> . . . a homogenous understanding [of constitutional norms] that transforms these norms into a coherent texture between whose parts, there is no discord. The straight completion of the constitutional building will rise through this organic unity, which characterizes the order of the constitutional norms. This unity will realize the congruity of the texts of the constitutions, and it will remove the obscurity that may be mixed with it and the contradictions with which people may think it to be afflicted. . . .[31]

To the extent that constitutional principles are ambiguous, they are to be interpreted by reference to other principles that the SCC has

---

[29] Brown, *The Rule of Law*, 119.

[30] Baber Johansen, "Supra-legislative Norms and Constitutional Courts: The Case of France and Egypt," *The Role of the Judiciary in the Protection of Human Rights*, eds. Eugene Cotran, Adel Omar Sherif (CIMEL Book Series No. 5: London: Kluwer, 1997), 347–76.

[31] Muḥammad 'Alī Balīj, in *SCC* vol. III, 4, cited and translated in Johansen, "Supra-legislative Norms," 365–66.

already identified. Through this mechanism, the SCC has tried to ensure that the principles remain consistent with each other. That is to say, of the many possible meanings that an ambiguous textual passage may have, the correct one is most consistent with constitutional principles that the Court has already elucidated. The gaps in the Court's understanding of a constitutional text are constantly to be filled in by triangulation against established constitutional principles. Starting with its second volume, the SCC's official Court Reporter began to list in an appendix some of the most important principles that the Court had, to date, identified.[32]

To assist in the process of organic interpretation, the Court has identified a handful of meta-principles that implicitly provide the unifying thread for all constitutional principles. Among these the Court has singled out four that are of particular importance. The first three are the following: (1) an overarching principle requiring Egypt to remain "democratic" and to respect the separation of powers; (2) a commitment to equitable social and economic policy that balances between the right to enjoy private property with the need for some economic redistribution or regulation; and (3) a commitment to ensuring that Egyptian law respects the "rule of law."[33] The Court has interpreted this last principle as requiring the government to respect human rights, including ones widely recognized as fundamental human rights in international agreements and by constitutional courts around the world.[34] More recently, the Court has argued that Article 2 creates a fourth meta-principle—namely, that Egyptian law must respect the principles of the *sharīʿa*. The following pages will discuss the first three principles. In subsequent chapters, I will address the Court's interpretation and application of the fourth principle.

---

[32] My thanks to Baber Johansen for pointing out the importance of this point.

[33] See, e.g., SCC Justice Adel Omar Sherif's article, "Constitutional Law," *Egypt and its Laws*, eds. Nathalie Bernard-Maugiron and Baudouin Dupret (*Arab and Islamic Law Series* 22; London/The Hague/New York: Kluwer Law International, 2002), 318–19. The Court's meta-commitments to democracy and human rights are certainly reflected in the conferences that were held with the active cooperation of the Court. The proceedings have been published and co-edited by one of the Court's commissioners: *Human Rights and Democracy* and *The Role of the Judiciary in the Protection of Human Rights*.

[34] See discussion below.

A. *The commitment to democracy and separation of powers*

As noted already, the SCC was during its first twenty years committed to ensuring that executive power was checked and that the separation of powers respected. To explain its evolving jurisprudence and to tie it in with aspects of its substantive rights jurisprudence, the Court has identified the protection of democracy and separation of powers as one of the overarching goals of the Egyptian constitution.[35]

B. *The commitment to equitable social and economic policies*

Early in its history, the SCC developed a jurisprudence of economic rights. The SCC apparently moved aggressively in this area of constitutional law because economic policy-making in Egypt had been hampered by political battles over the role of the private sector in the economy—battles that were exacerbated by insecurity arising from mixed signals in the constitution regarding property rights.[36] When the regime of Jamāl ʿAbd al-Nāṣir held power in the 1950s and 1960s, it was heavily influenced by communist regimes. The government moved quickly to redistribute wealth from the private sector to the public sector, where, supposedly, it would be managed for the common weal. When Anwār Sādāt took power in 1970 and prepared the 1971 Constitution, he wished to reinvigorate the private sector. Articles 29–36 of the constitution, which deal with property rights, represent a curious mixture of provisions. The echoes of communism are heard in several provisions which provide for central planning and limits on private ownership.[37] On the other hand,

[35] See, e.g., Sherif, "Constitutional Law," 318–19. Also of interest is a summary of the SCC's jurisprudence written in English by chief justice ʿAwad El-Morr and published in a special section (paginated in English numerals) at the back of *SCC*, vol. VII. See Human Rights as Perceived by the Supreme Constitutional Court of Egypt," *SCC*, vol. VII, 2ff., particularly the discussion at 2–14. Of interest too is Dr. El-Morr's article, "Towards a Universal Declaration of Democracy," *SCC* vol. VII, 122–132. For recent SCC moves away from its commitment to checking executive power, see Moustafa, "Law versus the State," 294ff.

[36] This argument has been made most persuasively by Enid Hill in "The Supreme Constitutional Court of Egypt on Property," *Le prince et son juge: droit et politique dans l'Égypte contemporaine*, eds. Nathalie Bernard Maugiron and Baudouin Dupret, a special issue of *Egypte/Monde Arabe* 2 (1999): 55–92. My discussion draws in many ways upon her analysis in that article.

[37] Article 30 calls the public sector "the vanguard of progress in all spheres." Article 32 requires the state to establish laws regulating private capital, "in the

several provisions require the protection of private property and reimbursement for expropriation.[38]

All in all, the property provisions represent a cautious attempt to reorient the regime away from the statist model of the Nāṣir years, without repudiating popular socialist rhetoric about property. Not only is the 1971 constitution schizophrenic on the subject of property rights, but, during the 1970s, the government was inconsistent in its policies. The government tried to implement liberal reforms that assumed protection of private property rights. Nevertheless, powerful vested interests were in favor of the status quo, and laws providing for privatization or desequestration (returning seized properties) were hamstrung by laws on the books or by misguided reforms. In the confusion, a number of property owners turned to the courts and filed claims for property that had been seized by the state or sought to overturn regulations that limited their right to use or dispose of property. When the Supreme Constitutional Court began to hear cases in 1979, it quickly focused its attention on these property cases as ones particularly in need of resolution.[39]

Early on, the SCC identified in Articles 29–36 conflicting principles requiring the protection for private property but also the protection of "a balance of income, of protecting legitimate earnings and of realizing an equitable sharing of public expenses and responsibilities."[40] From these, it concluded that legislation must strike a pragmatic balance between the competing principles. The Court thus

service of the national economy within the framework of the development plan without abuse or exploitation. The ways of its utilization shall not contradict the welfare of the people." Article 37 states that the law shall set a maximum limit on land ownership for the purpose of preventing exploitation of farmers. On the other hand, there are hints that ownership provides rights.

[38] Article 32's command not to establish abusive laws could be construed as protecting private owners from unfair seizure. Articles 34 and 35, which provide protections for those whose land is expropriated, reinforce such a suggestion.

[39] See generally the article and digests of cases by Chief Justice Awad El Morr, "The Status and Protection of Property in the Constitution," *Human Rights and Democracy: The Role of the Supreme Constitutional Court of Egypt*, eds. Kevin Boyle and Adel Omar Sherif (CIMEL Book Series 3; London: Kluwer, 1996), 115–27; and Enid Hill, "The Supreme Constitutional Court of Egypt on Property."

[40] See, e.g., Case No. 1, Judicial Year 1 (March 2, 1985). The quote is taken from Adel Omar Sherif's summary discussion of the Court's fundamental principle of "Overall Economic and Social Planning" in Sherif, "Constitutional Law," 318.

began to enforce the balance by striking down some property seizures (and some regulations of property rights) as indefensible violations of the right to private property and upholding others as violations that were tolerable because they were narrowly tailored to the need to promote the broader social welfare.

As Enid Hill points out, the SCC has provided invaluable support to the ruling party, in its attempts to move the nation away from a statist economy and towards economic liberalization—an attempt that has been carried out against the fervent opposition of many entrenched interests within the party. The Court was able to play the role it did because it was not controlled by the ruling party and was effectively outside the political process. It was insulated from leftist and nationalist political pressures that were making it impossible for the executive branch or legislature to establish a coherent and effective policy.[41]

At the same time, in the course of its decisions, it subtly bolstered its own prestige and power. The Court established its right to uphold and strike down legislation on the basis of judicial interpretation of very general principles. In the 1990s, it began to assert this right in new areas of jurisprudence—human rights and Islamization.

C. *The commitment to international human rights*

In the 1990s, the SCC's jurisprudence evolved in two notable ways. First, the Court identified a fundamental constitutional principle requiring the government to obey "the rule of law," which it has interpreted to require the protection of internationally recognized human rights. As the Court has put it, "the rule of law which restricts a 'legal state' and dominates its activities, ought to be outlined and demarcated in line with standards that are generally recognized and broadly applied in democratic countries."[42] Second, the SCC began to elaborate its theory that Article 2 imported into the constitution

[41] Enid Hill, "The Supreme Constitutional Court of Egypt on Property," 88.

[42] Case No. 2, Judicial Year 8 (January 4, 1992), *SCC*, vol. V, Part I, 89, cited and translated in Kevin Boyle, "Human Rights in Egypt: International Commitments," *Human Rights and Democracy: The Role of the Supreme Constitutional Court of Egypt*, eds. Kevin Boyle and Adel Omar Sherif eds. (CIMEL Book Series 3; London: Kluwer, 1996), 90.

a body of unwritten Islamic legal principles that were to be interpreted by the Court and imposed on the political branches. This chapter will discuss the first of these developments and leave to later chapters a discussion of the second.

The Egyptian constitution contains a number of provisions providing Egyptian citizens with vaguely defined individual rights—not only economic rights, but civil and political rights as well. To flesh out the meaning of these constitutional rights, the Court began to look to the interpretation of analogous rights found in the constitutions of other countries or in international human rights documents. In the preface to volume IV of the SCC's official reporter, the sixth president of the Court, Mamdūḥ Muṣṭafā Ḥasan, suggested the new direction that the Court's jurisprudence was taking. Individual rights, he said, "in their present development take an international character which transcends the various regional limits. Their tendencies find their clear expression in a number of international documents and in the institutions of the international judiciary which is in charge of these rights."[43]

In a seminal 1992 case, Ḥasan's court enshrined this principle in Egyptian law. In Case No. 22 of Judicial Year 8 (decided on January 4, 1992), the Court looked at the broad provisions in the Egyptian constitution guaranteeing the "rule of law" alongside the "democratic" and "socialist" concepts, and it asserted that such provisions required the Court to check Egyptian law against evolving international legal norms:

> Under Article 65 of the Constitution: "The State is subject to the rule of law . . ." Furthermore, under Article 1, 2 and 4 of the Constitution, "the regime of the State, including its economic system, lies within democratic and socialist concepts and that people are supreme and its sovereignty is to be exercised as specified by law." These provisions taken in conjunction with Article 65 inferred in the opinion of the Court that insofar as fundamental citizens' rights and freedoms are concerned, the content and scope of the rule of law which restricts a "legal state" and dominates its activities, ought to be outlined and demarcated in line with standards that are generally recognized and broadly applied in democratic countries.[44]

[43] Mamdūḥ Muṣṭafā Ḥasan, in *SCC*, vol. IV, 4–5. Here I have excerpted from the translation in Johansen, "Supra-legislative Norms," 367.

[44] Case No. 22, Judicial Year 8 (January 4, 1992), *SCC*, vol. V, Part I, 89ff. See

Kevin Boyle has summed up the import of this decision as follows: "the effect of this decision is, that what are considered generally recognized human rights principles by democratic states, including the Universal Declaration of Human Rights, are to be treated as constitutional norms and together with the written provisions of the constitution on rights and freedoms will be enforced by the Supreme Constitutional Court."[45] Although, at first glance, this might seem an unduly expansive interpretation of the opinion, his reading corresponds fully with the Court's own understanding of its decision. Since the 1992 decision, the SCC has regularly cited international human rights documents or the opinions of other constitutional courts in order to shed light on the rights that the Egyptian constitution guarantees to Egyptians.[46]

Furthermore, justices and members of the Court's commissioners' body have published a considerable amount of scholarship in the areas of comparative constitutional law and human rights law.[47] In public speeches and published writings, justices on the Court have embraced the broadest possible reading of the 1992 case. In 1997,

---

the analyses in Adel Omar Sherif, "Unshakeable Tendency in the Protection of Human Rights: Adherence to International Instruments by the Supreme Constitutional Court of Egypt," *The Role of the Judiciary in the Protection of Human Rights*, eds. Eugene Cotran and Adel Omar Sherif (CIMEL Book Series 5; London: Kluwer, 1997), 37–38; Boyle, "Human Rights," 89–90; Johansen, "Supra-legislative Norms," 367–68. I have used the translation in Boyle as it was published in conjunction with a book co-edited by a Counselor of the Court in close cooperation with the chief justice of the SCC and other members of the Court.

[45] Boyle, "Human Rights: International Commitments", 90.

[46] See, e.g., Case No. 13, Judicial Year 15 (December 17, 1994); Case No. 23, Judicial Year 16 (July 3, 1995); Case No. 8, Judicial Year 16 (August 5, 1995).

[47] See, e.g., articles by the chief justice of the SCC, Awad El-Morr: "Human Rights in the Constitutional Systems of Egypt and Other Islamic Countries, International and Comparative Studies," *Human Rights and Democracy: The Role of the Supreme Constitutional Court of Egypt*, eds. Kevin Boyle and Adel Omar Sherif eds., (CIMEL Book Series 3; London: Kluwer, 1996), 161–215; Awad El-Morr, "Enforcing the Universality of Human Rights," *Al-Ahrām Weekly*, July 18, 1996, 3; "Judicial Sources for Supporting the Protection of Human Rights," *The Role of the Judiciary in the Protection of Human Rights*, eds. Eugene Cotran and Adel Omar Sherif (CIMEL Book Series 5; London: Kluwer, 1997), 5–33. Of interest also is a paper by the late justice Abdel Rahman Nosseir, "The Supreme Constitutional Court of Egypt and the Protection of Human Rights." Chicago, 1992. Photocopy on file at AMIDEAST office in Cairo. For works by members of the Court's Commissioners' Body, see, e.g., Sherif and Alashmawy, "Freedom of Expression," 401–40; Adel Omar Sherif, "Unshakeable Tendency," 35–45; Sherif, "The Freedom of Judicial Expression, 137–58.

the chief justice of the Supreme Constitutional Court, Awad El-Morr (ʿAwaḍ al-Murr), decided to include in the Court's official reporter, a series of articles interpreting the evolution of the Court's jurisprudence and identifying areas that needed clarification. Most of these were written by members of the Court—giving them a peculiar status between academic commentary and an attempt at official clarification of the Court's decisions. In the first of the articles, the chief justice himself stressed the importance of the Court's decision to read internationally recognized rights into the Egyptian constitution:

> Reading Articles 1–3 of the Constitution, which declare the democratic regime as the basis of governance and vest sovereignty in the hands of the People, in conjunction with Article 65 which subjects the State to the rule of law, demonstrates that in the vindication of basic human rights and freedoms, the content of the rule of law by which the State shall abide is to be outlined in light of standards and patterns generally recognized by democratic countries and strictly applied as a systematic way of conduct.[48]

Similarly, in a contribution to a collection of essays on comparative constitutional jurisprudence co-edited by a colleague at the Court, chief justice El-Morr tried systematically to explain this decision to incorporate international legal norms into Egyptian constitutional law. He argued that it was an inevitable outgrowth of the Court's vision of the Egyptian constitution as an integrated, organic entity. For El-Morr, one can induce from the constitution an overriding concern with, among other things, the protection of human rights. Since international treaties, international scholarship, and courts outside Egypt have explored and illuminated the true nature of human rights, he asserted, it is only logical to look to these sources for guidance as to what courts should do to protect human rights in Egypt:

> Defining the judiciary's role in the protection of human rights raises a question about what sources a constitutional court uses in analyzing issues in human rights cases.
>
> ... Constitutional provisions are brought into existence through a collective popular will, superior in nature to that which underlies statutes ... These various kinds of provisions do not clash, but are a collectively integrated and interrelated, organic unity, tending to achieve

[48] El-Morr, "Human Rights as Perceived by the Supreme Constitutional Court of Egypt," 4.

coherent ends, and promoting an ordered, evolving society. These provisions are understood as a coherent body of rules, reconciled and brought together by methods of construction that are coordinated with reference to societal values. No single provision is viewed as standing in isolation from any other. Many provisions provide direct and specific protections for individual human rights.

... But there are sources for the protection of human rights beyond the direct meaning of specific constitutional provisions. Courts must look within and behind these specific provisions, to identify and enforce rights, which are found on in their penumbras or in the activities that are essential to the purpose and effective operation of the Constitution as a whole.

... So the Constitutional Court, through its power of judicial review, uses the Constitution in protecting human rights within the country. But the Court's sources should not be limited only to its own Constitution. The world has become too small and the universality of fundamental human rights and duties has become too well established for a nation's judiciary to look only inward.

... Only when the judiciary taps all these constitutional sources can they protect human rights fully and effectively for all their citizens and residents.[49]

Although El-Morr's discussion makes the Court's decision seem inevitable, it represented a serious move away from the traditional policy of judicial restraint exercised by the Egyptian judiciary, and from its traditional preference for protecting rights by insisting on fidelity to the larger principle of separation of powers and on respect for constitutionally mandated procedures. Taking a half-step away from the policy of judicial restraint and from the positivist orientation of the Egyptian judiciary, the SCC came to argue that written provisions of the constitution themselves direct judges to apply as "law" unwritten bodies of supra-legislative norms.[50]

[49] El-Morr, "Judicial Sources for Supporting the Protection of Human Rights," 5–10.

[50] One wonders what would happen if the government were to amend the Constitution to take out the "rule of law" provisions that are considered the textual door through which international norms enter the constitutional system. It is possible that the justices of the SCC, clearly steeped in the study of international human rights, might argue that such norms still bind the state.

IV. *Conclusion*

The SCC is a fairly new institution, and it is notable for its commitment to a holistic interpretation of the constitution. Because the Court incorporated international human rights norms into Egyptian law, its policy of developing a holistic interpretation of the constitution led it to demand that Egyptian constitutional law be harmonized with unwritten international human rights norms. Even as the Court was committing itself to international human rights norms, the Court was also grappling with the implications of Article 2 which made "the principles of the Islamic *sharīʿa*" the "chief source" of Egyptian law. How could the commitment to international human rights be reconciled with an apparent command to place Islamic legal norms above all other constitutional norms? As the next chapter will make clear the SCC was not, at first, sure. It was initially very cautious in its Article 2 jurisprudence, holding that it had jurisdiction over only a fraction of Article 2 cases. For some time thereafter, the Court did not establish any clear method of interpreting and applying Article 2. In the early 1990s, however, the Court began publicly to elaborate a more systematic theory of Islamic legal norms as a source of imported, supra-legislative constitutional norms. Chapter 10 will describe this theory and will show how the theory has been articulated in such a way that it (1) resonates with a number of different theories of Islamic law, (2) allows judges to act as authoritative interpreters of the *sharīʿa*, at least for the purpose of constitutional litigation, and (3) leaves these judges sufficient discretion in interpreting Islamic law that they can develop a jurisprudence of Islamic law that preserves (and even reinforces) the Court's existing jurisprudence—including its progressive property rights and women's rights jurisprudence.

CHAPTER NINE

DEBATES ABOUT THE SCC'S JURISDICTION OVER ARTICLE 2 CASES

As the Mubārak government began to distance itself from its predecessor's promises to enact Islamic reforms of Egyptian law, Islamists turned increasingly to the courts to try and compel the government to carry through with Islamization.[1] In a pair of 1985 cases, the SCC held that it had authority to perform Article 2 review in some, but not all, cases. (It could only exercise review over cases involving laws enacted after the amendment of Article 2 in 1980.) This decision allowed it to dispose of a number of particularly difficult cases and to postpone for a number of years the date on which it would have to issue Article 2 opinions.

I. *Why might Article 2 cases be non-justiciable?*

As Article 2 cases were multiplying in the Egyptian courts, some judges apparently wished to enter the Islamization debate at once.[2]

---

[1] Rudolph Peters describes six cases from the early to mid-1980s in which the defendants challenged the same provision—asking the courts to void Articles 226 and 227 of the Civil Code, which permitted Egyptians to lend money with interest and to write contracts including penalty clauses for late payments: "Divine Law or Man-Made Law? Egyptian Politics and the Application of the Sharīʿa," *Arab Law Quarterly* 3 (1998): 242–43 and accompanying footnotes. He and Enid Hill have found records as well of Islamist lawyers asking courts to void or to enjoin enforcement of various provisions of the penal law. Peters, "Divine Law or Man-Made Law," 242–43; and Enid Hill, "Law and Courts in Egypt: Recent Issues and Events Concerning Islamic Law," *The Political Economy of Contemporary Egypt*, ed. Ibrahim Oweiss (Washington D.C.: Center for Contemporary Arab Studies, 1990), 247. Islamists also notoriously brought challenges to 1979 amendments to Egypt's marriage and divorce laws—laws which increased the rights of women. See, e.g., the discussion below of Case No. 28, Judicial Year 2 (May 4, 1985).

[2] See generally the discussions of the judiciary and the quotes from judges in Bernard Botiveau, "Les juges égyptiens saisis par le doute," *Annuaire de l'Afrique du Nord* 28 (1989): 261–68; Bernard Botiveau, "Contemporary Re-interpretations of

Many in the judiciary, however, did not show any appetite for answering Article 2 questions. There were sound reasons for the courts to abstain from entering the debates about Islamization of Egyptian law. In most constitutional systems (including those of Egypt and, for that matter, the U.S.), constitutional courts are not thought to have jurisdiction over every constitutional question, or, in the alternative, may not be considered to have the authority to decide certain types of cases. The U.S. Supreme Court refuses to decide cases that turn on what it would characterize as "political questions."[3] Similarly, the Egyptian Supreme Constitutional Court believes it cannot or should not issue cases that challenge the constitutionality of acts that fall into the category of acts of sovereignty.[4] It could be plausibly argued that some, and maybe all, Article 2 cases fell into that special category of constitutional cases that the SCC might not have the power to decide.

The preparatory committee report for the amendment had stated that the legislature needed to be given an opportunity to define the nature of "the principles of the Islamic *sharī'a*." Furthermore, the political branches, through negotiation and experimentation, might be better able than courts to define "the principles of the Islamic *sharī'a*" in a politically acceptable way. It was not unreasonable to suggest that the political branches should be given the first opportunity to propose an approach to Islamization and that, if the approach selected by the political branches was reasonable, the courts should accept that approach.

Moreover, the courts might reasonably have worried that an overly aggressive policy of Article 2 review could destabilize the legal

Islamic Law in Egypt," *Islam and Public Law: Classical and Contemporary Studies*, ed. Chibli Mallat (London: Graham and Trotman, 1993), 277; and Hill, "Law and Courts in Egypt," 261 n. 32.

[3] See Erwin Chemerinsky, *Federal Jurisdiction*, 2nd ed., (Boston: Little Brown & Co., 1994), 142–45 and the sources cited therein.

[4] As the late justice Abdel Rahman Nosseir noted, "The general guidance given by the court in this concern is that such political questions (or acts of sovereignty) are closely interrelated with the sovereignty of the State, internally and externally, and encompass, by their nature, profound political considerations which justify giving the legislative or executive branches full discretionary power in order to realize the security and well-being of the country. As a result, this category of political questions (or acts of sovereignty) may not be subjected to legal control, neither on its constitutionality or its legality." Abdel Rahman Nosseir, "The Supreme Constitutional Court of Egypt and the Protection of Human Rights," Paper delivered at DePaul University Law School, 1992. Photocopy.

system. If the Court declared itself willing to review all existing laws governing important legal issues (such as the legality of bank interest), there would be a period of time during which the constitutionality of all Egyptian legislation would be in doubt.

Finally, the courts were at this time seeking to re-establish their historical independence from the executive branch and burnish their reputation with the public as an independent and trustworthy voice. If the Court entered the highly divisive discussions about Islamization, it would inevitably offend some important constituency.

So long as the government seemed to be working towards a voluntary program of Islamization, some highly placed judges thought it prudent to avoid the difficult and politically sensitive questions surrounding Islamization—both whether it should occur and, if so, how Islamic law should be interpreted. For example, a 1982 opinion issued by the Court of Cassation, Egypt's highest appeals court, suggests that some senior judges were inclined to allow the executive and legislative branches an indefinite period to develop a program of Islamization. In this case, the Court of Cassation was asked to void the conviction of two criminals who asserted that the evidence against them was insufficient as a matter of Islamic law to support a conviction.[5] In rejecting their claim, the Court of Cassation refused even to refer the constitutional issue to the SCC. The Court noted the disagreements about the proper methods of identifying and interpreting the universally applicable principles of the *sharīʿa*. It also pointed out that Article 2 did not give any guidance to the courts as to what method they should use. In so doing, the Court appeared to suggest that, given the diversity of opinion about questions of Islamic legal interpretation, the question of whether, when, and how to Islamize had to be left to the executive branch and legislature. To its mind, no court had the power to interpret and apply Article 2 until the legislature had enacted a new law clarifying the meaning of the phrase "principles of the Islamic *sharīʿa*":

[5] The Court considered an appeal from a lower court decision convicting two police officers of brutality. The only evidence of the alleged assault was the testimony of the alleged victim himself. According to the officers, it is a principle of Islamic law that a person cannot be convicted on the evidence of his alleged victim alone. Therefore, they asserted, the courts had violated Article 2 when they ordered a conviction. See Peters, "Divine Law or Man-Made Law?," 242, n. 33, citing the report in *al-Ahrām*, April 7, 1982.

> . . . The provision of Article 2 of the Constitution to the effect that the principles of the *sharīʿa* are the principal source of legislation has no legal force in and of itself. . . . [T]he *sharīʿa* can only be applied after the Legislator has obeyed this instruction and has formulated its [the *sharīʿa*'s] exalted principles in well-defined and precise enactments according to which the judiciary must pass judgment. . . . [T]he opposite view would lead to a blending of, on the one hand, the obligation of the judiciary to enforce the existing legal enactments and, on the other hand, the enactment of legal principles that are incompatible with a precise definition of its jurisdiction, not to mention the fact that the application of the *sharīʿa* requires that it should be determined which exactly of the manifold conflicting views of the founders of the law schools [*madhhabs*] . . . must be used as a basis for judgments. . . .[6]

There were clearly good reasons for the SCC to follow the Court of Cassation's lead and stay out of the debates about Islamization. On the other hand, there were increasingly good reasons for it to speak up in some way. For one, the argument that the political branches should be given an extended period of time to propose reforms, though plausible, was not indisputable. Some leading members of the People's Assembly who had voted for the amendment were on record as believing that citizens had the right to bring suits to void un-Islamic laws.[7] Egypt's chief prosecutor also publicly opined that the courts should decide Article 2 cases.[8]

The argument in favor of abstention became increasingly less compelling over the course of the 1980s. The best constitutional and prudential arguments for withholding judgment assumed that the political branches would use the time given them to develop a program of Islamization. When it became obvious that the executive branch and legislature were not using the time granted them to develop a plan for Islamization, the delay provoked a storm of protest. In 1983, the New Wafd Party was formed as a new political party with connections to the Muslim Brothers. During the campaigns for the 1984 election races, the New Wafd regularly raised the issue of

[6] Reported in *al-Ahrām*, April 7, 1982, cited and partially translated in Peters, "Divine Law or Man-Made Law?," 242, n. 33.

[7] See the discussion in Peters, "Divine Law or Man-Made Law?," 236, n. 20, citing, *inter alia*, the comments of Muḥammad ʿAlī Maḥjūb, Chairman of the Parliamentary Committee for Religious Affairs in *al-Ahrām*, May 25, 1980.

[8] See Peters, "Divine Law or Man-Made Law?," 242, citing the article by Muṣṭafā Farāghlī al-Shuqayrī in *al-Jumhūriyya*, September 3, 1983.

Islamization.[9] In December 1984, leaders of Islamist factions won majorities in student union elections at all major Egyptian universities and called for Islamic behavior at universities, including mandatory "Islamic dress" for women and separation of the sexes.[10] Islamist students also demonstrated a capacity for violence.[11] Not wishing to stand behind the Muslim Brothers in their zeal for Islamic law, the leading *ʿulamāʾ* of al-Azhar began also to complain publicly about the delays in obeying Article 2's command to Islamize. In 1985 the Shaykh of al-Azhar insisted that the "People's Assembly represents the people . . . and the people are eager to see the Holy Law applied," and added, "the country is perfectly prepared for the application of the *sharīʿa* . . . without delay."[12] Judges and legal academics also criticized the delay in proposing any plan for complying with Article 2's command to Islamize.[13]

The SCC, as a brand-new constitutional court, was still trying to establish itself as a prestigious and independent judicial body. At this early stage in its career, the Court could not afford to act in a way that might tarnish its growing reputation for integrity and independence. On the other hand, it could not act in a way that might be perceived by some as "winking" at the political branches' willful defiance of a constitutional obligation.

II. *The SCC's 1985 Article 2 decisions*

On May 4, 1985 the Court issued two opinions that used an ingenious, if somewhat casuistic, argument to compromise between the

---

[9] Ami Ayalon, "The Arab Republic of Egypt," in MECS VIII (1983–84), 359, citing, *inter alia*, *al-Wafd*, April 12, 1984, and *al-Shaʿb*, April 24, 1984.

[10] Ami Ayalon, "The Arab Republic of Egypt," in MECS IX (1984–85), 355. For a digest of contemporary news accounts and an analysis of other events, see Ayalon, "The Arab Republic of Egypt," in MECS VIII (1983–84), 355–57.

[11] In 1984 and 1985, violent Islamist demonstrations erupted in Cairo. For example, in November 1984, students at al-Azhar rioted after a student was run over by a police car. See Ayalon, "The Arab Republic of Egypt," in MECS IX (1984–85), 356.

[12] ʿAlī Jādd al-Ḥaqq, *Akhbār al-Yawm*, February 22, 1985, trans. in Ayalon, "The Arab Republic of Egypt," in MECS VIII (1983–84), 348.

[13] For example, see the complaint of a judge printed in *Al-Wafd*, January 17, 1985, trans. in Ayalon, "The Arab Republic of Egypt," in MECS IX (1984–85), 352. See also the examples in Bernard Botiveau, "Contemporary Re-interpretations of Islamic Law in Egypt," 277, and Hill, "Law and Courts in Egypt," 261 n. 32.

two camps arguing for total abstention from Article 2 cases on the one hand, or immediate active review, on the other.[14] While it did not approve the government's decision to halt the Islamization program, the SCC held that it was powerless to force wholesale Islamization. According to the Court, it had limited authority to exercise Article 2 review. It could not exercise review of laws that were in force at the time that Article 2 was amended in 1980. It could, however, review laws that entered into force thereafter. As explained in more detail below, this holding had the effect of postponing rather than eliminating Article 2 review of Egyptian legislation.

A. *Case 1: The enforceability of contracts requiring repayment with interest (ribā)*

The first of the May 4 opinions rejected a challenge brought by the university of al-Azhar to Article 226 of the Egyptian Civil Code, which permitted creditors to charge 4% interest on late payments of debt.[15] During the 1970s, Al-Azhar University had bought supplies for its medical school, but it failed to make its payments on time. As he was entitled to do under Article 226, the seller charged the university interest on the outstanding balance. The university refused to pay. According to the university, Article 2, as amended, required all Egyptian legislation to be consistent with Islamic law. Laws permitting creditors to charge a fixed rate of interest on delayed payments, it continued, were inconsistent with Islamic law and thus the courts could not enforce a contract that permitted such interest. The case began in a regular court. Viewing the constitutional challenge to Article 226 as plausible, this lower court referred the constitutional case to the SCC.[16] The case illustrated perfectly the problems

[14] This was the same day that the People's Assembly shelved Abū Ṭālib's draft revisions to Egyptian law. Given the nature of the opinions, the timing seems too convenient to have been coincidental.

[15] Case No. 20 Judicial Year 1 (May 4, 1985), *SCC*, vol. III, 209–224. It is also published in *al-Jarīda al-Rasmiyya* 28.20 (May 16, 1985), 992–1000, trans. Saba Habachy, "Supreme Constitutional Court (Egypt)—Sharīʿa and Riba: Decision in Case 20 of Judicial Year 1," *Arab Law Quarterly* 1 (1985–1986): 100–7. When translating the case, I have followed the Habachy translation.

[16] For a more detailed history of the case, see Hatem Aly Labib Gabr, "The Interpretation of Article 2 of the Constitution: Islamic Sharīʿa Principles as a Source of Law," *Human Rights and Democracy: The Role of the Supreme Constitutional Court of Egypt*, eds. Kevin Boyle and Adel Omar Sherif (CIMEL Book Series 3; London: Kluwer, 1996), 217–19.

the SCC could expect to face if it began to hear Article 2 challenges to existing legislation. There were no politically palatable decisions that a court could reach in this case.

On the one hand, it would be hard to convince the Egyptian public that Articles 226 and 227 were consistent with "the principles of the Islamic *sharīʿa*." Although hypothetically a plausible case might be made that laws permitting interest were consistent with Islamic law, few Islamists in Egypt were likely to accept this. During the classical period, Islamic jurists developed a complex series of regulations that precluded many types of interest bearing loan.[17] In the modern era, Islamic legal thinkers and Islamist political factions reevaluated the traditional restrictions. Initially, modernists were willing to consider the permissibility of interest. Over time, however, thinkers associated with each of the modernist methods of legal interpretation increasingly came to advocate a prohibition on interest.[18] In the contemporary period, most Islamic legal thinkers and Islamist political factions inclined, though not universally, to retain the classical prohibition on explicit interest-bearing contracts. Such thinkers included champions of neo-traditionalism,[19] utilitarian neo-*ijtihād*,[20]

---

[17] The Qurʾān and *ḥadīth* are not entirely clear about the permissibility of charging interest. *Qurʾān* 2:275 states that God "permitted sale and prohibited *ribā*." In the classical period, the precise meaning of the word *ribā* was hotly debated. For a succinct summary of the majority opinion within the classical Sunnī law guilds, and the opinions of some idiosyncratic scholars within each, see Nabil A. Saleh, *Unlawful Gain and Legitimate Profit in Islamic Law* (New York: Cambridge University Press, 1986), 24–35.

[18] For the evolving position of modern thinkers, see generally Sami Hassan Homoud, *Islamic Banking* (London: Arabian Information, 1985), 123–26, and Chibli Mallat, "The Debate on *Riba* and Interest in Twentieth-Century Jurisprudence," *Islamic Law and Finance* (London: Graham & Trotman, 1988), 75–85. The following discussion of modern attitudes towards interest draws heavily on these works.

[19] By the 1970s the *ʿulamāʾ* of al-Azhar had opined that Islamic law forbade interest-bearing contracts, and, thus, the case at bar had actually been brought by al-Azhar. See, e.g., the discussion in Jakob Skovgaard-Petersen, *Defining Islam for the Egyptian State: Muftīs and Fatwās of the Dār al-Iftā* (Leiden: E.J. Brill, 1997), 299–302; Jaques Jomier, "Les Congrès de l'Académie des Recherches Islamiques dépendant de l'Azhar," *Mélanges de l'Institut Dominicain des Études Orientales au Caire* 14 (1980): 106, 131.

[20] The early proponents of utilitarian neo-*ijtihād* such as Muḥammad ʿAbduh and Rashīd Riḍā maintained the traditional prohibition on interest, although they wavered on the question of interest-equivalents. Muḥammad ʿAbduh issued a *fatwā* in 1903 in which he declared that postal savings accounts which paid depositors a fixed rate of interest were prohibited. He pointed out, however, that a savings scheme could in fact be formally constructed as a *muḍāraba* contract, in which case it would be

and comparative neo-*taqlīd*.[21] If the Court had wanted to argue that interest bearing loans were permissible under the *sharīʿa*, it would have faced the further difficulty that the party challenging the law happened to be the University of al-Azhar. The legislature itself had recognized al-Azhar's expertise in questions of Islamic law when it asked the university to review the draft Islamic codes.[22] In short, a decision declaring interest-bearing contracts to be permissible under the *sharīʿa* was certain to be painted by critics as an implausible

legal. *Al-Manār* 6 (1903): 717–18. Riḍā similarly asserted that Muslims could not lawfully enter into money-lending contracts that paid a fixed interest rate, but they could open savings accounts that paid out a fixed percentage of any investment profits to which their money gave rise. *Al-Manār* 9 (1906): 335 discussed in Homoud, *Islamic Banking*, 123–26; Mallat, "The Debate on *Riba* and Interest," 75–76; Skovgaard-Petersen, *Defining Islam*, 298–99. As utilitarian neo-*ijtihād* took root among lay Muslims with populist leanings, groups like the Muslim Brotherhood and the Muslim *jamāʿāt* came adamantly to insist that the charging of interest was socially unjust and thus contrary to Islamic law. For a general analysis of the Brothers' evolving economic theory, see Richard Mitchell, *The Society of the Muslim Brothers*, reprint with new intro. (New York: Oxford University Press, 1993), 272–74, analyzing, *inter alia*, al-Bannā's tract, *Mushkilātuna* (n.d.), 83–92 and *Al-Rasā'il al-thalāth (Naḥwa al-Nūr)*, 119–20. See also Sayyid Quṭb, *Social Justice in Islam* (*al-ʿAdāla al-Ijtimāʿiyya fī al-Islām*) trans. John B. Hardie, rev. trans. Hamid Algar (Oneanta, New York, Islamic Publications International, 2000), 128–138.

[21] Although the writings of guild jurists suggested a principle that prohibited interest, the actual practice of Muslim societies painted a more ambiguous picture of the legality of interest. The early practitioners of comparative neo-*taqlīd* were thus conflicted about whether Muslims should be allowed to loan money at a fair, flat rate of interest. Apparently influenced by the writings of Ibrahīm Zakī al-Badawī, Sanhūrī concluded that interest-bearing contracts should be permitted, and thus included Articles 226 and 227 of the Egyptian Civil Code. See *al-Qānūn al-Madanī*, Articles 226–33. For Badawī's early opinion, see Mallat, "The Debate on *Riba* and Interest," 79. For the influence of Badawī on Sanhūrī, see generally Mallat, "The Debate on *Riba* and Interest," 79–80. Sanhūrī defended these provisions by building on Badawī's arguments. See ʿAbd al-Razzāq al-Sanhūrī, *Maṣādir al-Ḥaqq fī al-Fiqh al-Islāmī* (Cairo: Jāmiʿat al-Duwal al-ʿArabiyya, Maʿhad al-Buḥūth wa-'l-Dirāsat al-ʿArabiyya, 1956), vol. III, 222–237, analyzed in Nabil A. Saleh, *Unlawful Gain and Legitimate Profit in Islamic Law* (New York: Cambridge University Press, 1986), 36–37; Mallat, "The Debate on *Riba* and Interest," 83–85. In 1964, however, Badawī wrote a book renouncing his earlier belief in the permissibility of interest-bearing contracts. This added fuel to the arguments that Articles 226 and 227 violated the principles of the *sharīʿa*. Mallat, "The Debate on *Riba* and Interest," citing Badawī, *Naẓariyyat al-Ribā al-Muḥarram* (Cairo: al-Majlis al-Aʿla li-Riʿāyat al-Funūn, 1964), 254–57. It was thus possible for champions of comparative neo-*taqlīd* to believe that the *sharīʿa* actually barred the lending of money with interest—meaning that financial transactions would have to create "Islamic" financial instruments.

[22] See discussion in Chapter 7.

decision—one that could be explained as a capitulation to the executive branch, which had borrowed heavily on the international markets.

Although the Court could not uphold interest-bearing contracts without losing prestige, it would be nearly impossible, as a practical matter, to strike them down. The Egyptian economy, like all modern industrial economies, was financed largely through interest-bearing loans and investments. It would have been disastrous for the Egyptian economy simply to declare interest clauses unenforceable—particularly if the law provided no grandfather clause or substitute financial mechanism. In short, the SCC was faced with a situation in which it could not really afford either to uphold the law being challenged or, on the other hand, to strike it down. The case brought into view the types of problem that would inevitably arise if existing laws were regularly struck down before the political branches had replaced the unconstitutional laws with new laws.

The Court's solution to its dilemma was to announce a justiciability doctrine that has come to be known as the doctrine of "the non-retroactivity of Article 2." According to this doctrine, Article 2 imposed on the legislature an obligation to ensure that all Egyptian law (including previously enacted law) was consistent with "the principles of the Islamic *sharīʿa*." In the Court's words, the Article "imposes on the Legislator, from a political point of view, the duty of purifying the texts of such past legislation and clearing them from any trespass from the said principles."[23] When it came to the question of enforcing this obligation, however, the doctrine drew a distinction between (1) cases involving laws that had been enacted prior to the amendment of Article 2 in 1980 and (2) cases involving laws enacted thereafter. Cases of the first type were not justiciable. The SCC would not force the political branches to replace any existing laws—even if they were contrary to "the principles of the Islamic *sharīʿa*" (as the Court divined them). Since the preparatory report indicated that the legislature would be given an indeterminate period of time to amend laws to bring them into compliance with Article 2, the Court held that the legislature had meant to retain for itself

[23] Case No. 20, Judicial Year 1 (May 4, 1985), *SCC*, vol. III, 224; *al-Jarīda al-Rasmiyya*, 999–1000; Habachy, "Supreme Constitutional Court (Egypt)," 106.

plenary power to determine for itself whether an existing law needed to be replaced. Thus, the Court could not strike down laws that were already in force on the date that Article 2 was adopted. The Court stated that "[Article 2 as amended] cannot be made applicable to former legal enactments which were already in force before it was adopted."[24] Cases of the second type, however, were justiciable. Once the legislature had decided to amend a law or enact a brand-new law, it would be obliged to follow Article 2.

In short, even if the Court was unwilling to exercise Article 2 review over legislation enacted prior to the amendment of Article 2, it was willing to exercise Article 2 review over legislation enacted thereafter. Adopting this doctrine had the same practical effect as reading a grandfather clause into Article 2—as if Article 2 had been changed to read "the principles of the Islamic *sharīʿa* are the chief source of legislation *enacted after the amendment of Article 2*." For this reason, the doctrine is often called, as noted above, the doctrine of the "non-retroactivity of Article 2"—even by justices on the Court. To be precise, the SCC did not actually read this type of grandfather clause into Article 2. The Court simply asserted that the political branches can suffer only "political" punishment for violating Article 2 with respect to laws enacted prior to its amendment in 1980. Courts had the power to only sanction them for violating Article 2 with respect to laws enacted after that date.

It would be beyond the scope of this book to discuss the peculiarities of the Court's non-retroactivity decision. The Court was apparently aware, however, that as a formal matter, its proposed compromise might seem a bit strained to some. The opinion thus contained language suggesting that the adoption of this policy was driven by larger concerns about the separation of powers and the practical impact of over-broad Article 2 review. Addressing those who might not be convinced by its interpretation of Article 2, the SCC noted the consequences that would arise if the Court were to agree to review any and all Egyptian laws for consistency with the ill-defined "the principles of the Islamic *sharīʿa*." The Court warned that such a policy would "lead to contradiction and confusion in the judicial process, in a manner which would threaten stability."[25]

---

[24] Case No. 20, Judicial Year 1 (May 4, 1985), *SCC*, vol. III, 221; *al-Jarīda al-Rasmiyya*, 997; Habachy, "Supreme Constitutional Court (Egypt)," 104.

[25] Case No. 20, Judicial Year 1 (May 4, 1985), *SCC*, vol. III, 223; *al-Jarīda al-*

B. *Case 2: The constitutionality of "Jihān's law" (Law 44 of 1979)*

In declaring its doctrine of non-retroactivity, the SCC had implicitly threatened to perform Article 2 review of newly enacted legislation. But was this a real threat? One would have forgiven Islamists for asking themselves whether the new institution would have the independence and courage to defy the executive and legislative branches and actually strike down laws. A second opinion, handed down on May 4, 1985, suggested that the government would have to take seriously its threat to review and strike down legislation in the future.[26] This opinion involved a challenge to a law that changed the provisions of Egyptian family law, and, among other things, increased a woman's rights *vis à vis* her husband when the husband sought a divorce.

Through the 1970s, Islamic family law in Egypt had been governed by statutes that incorporated rules from traditional works of Sunnī *fiqh.* (Most of the rules were drawn from the preponderant doctrines of the Ḥanafī guild, but some provisions were drawn from the doctrines of other Sunnī guilds.) During the 1970s, the thinking of many Egyptians, particularly within the elite, had come to recognize women's right to equality—as that right was understood in the West. Some thus suggested that provisions of Egyptian family law were inappropriate to modern times. Among progressives, there was particular concern about provisions involving divorce and polygamy. Ultimately, President Sādāt, supposedly under pressure from his wife Jihān, sided with the critics and called for the reform of the Egyptian family laws.[27] Sādāt's proposed reform was deeply unpopular and widely derided by Islamists as anti-Islamic. This put Sādāt in an awkward position. Publicly emphasizing his commitment

Rasmiyya, 999–1000; Habachy, "Supreme Constitutional Court (Egypt)," 106. In a discussion with the author years later, a justice of the SCC specifically pointed to this language as a key to understanding the decision.

[26] Case No. 28 of Judicial Year 2 (May 4, 1985), printed in *SCC,* vol. III, 195–208. For a detailed discussion of the case, which was co-authored by the President of the SCC at the time of the decision, see Awad El-Morr and Adel Omar Sherif, "Separation of Powers and Limits on Presidential Powers," *Human Rights and Democracy: The Role of the Supreme Constitutional Court of Egypt,* eds. Kevin Boyle and Adel Omar Sherif (CIMEL Book Series 3; London: Kluwer, 1996), 68–71.

[27] For a discussion of the legislative reforms that led to this case, see Fauzi M. Najjar, "Egypt's Laws of Personal Status," *Arab Studies Quarterly* 10 (1988): 323ff.

to Islam, he did not want to suffer the embarrassment of rancorous parliamentary debates over the consistency of a proposed law with Islamic principles. Imperiously, therefore, he took a short cut. Egypt during these years was under a state of emergency declared by Sādāt himself, who, as a result, enjoyed extraordinary powers. Among these was the power to enact decree laws while the People's Assembly was in recess—whenever he was faced with a situation that required immediate attention. Such a decree law would be in force until the People's Assembly could review it, and it would take permanent effect if the People's Assembly ratified it.[28] Declaring the reform of the family laws an issue of national importance, Sādāt enacted by decree a law with the following provisions, *inter alia*: eliminating a husband's traditional right (recognized in Ḥanafī law) to prohibit his wife from leaving the house; requiring husbands to notify their wives of a divorce; permitting women to have a marriage dissolved whenever a husband took a second wife; and allowing a judge to order a man to pay his ex-wife a payment analogous to alimony so long as he was to blame for the break-up of the marriage.[29]

Several leading members of the *ʿulamāʾ*, including the Chief *Muftī* of Egypt, gave their imprimatur to the legislation by serving on the President's drafting committee and issuing *fatwās* certifying the consistency of the law with the *sharīʿa*.[30] Nevertheless, Islamists publicly savaged the new decree, which they sneeringly called "Jihān's law." They also mocked the *ʿulamāʾ* who had approved it.[31] Given Sādāt's personal interest in the decree and his control of both the executive and legislative branches, there was no doubt that the new law would be ratified. Jihān's law was approved by the People's Assembly and

---

[28] *Egyptian Constitution*, Article 147.

[29] See Najjar, "Egypt's Laws of Personal Status," 323ff.

[30] See, e.g., Dār al-Iftā, *al-Fatāwā al-Islāmiyya* (Cairo: Wizārat al-Awqāf, 1980–1993), vol. 8, nos. 1190, 1192; *ibid.*, vol. 9, no. 1197. See also the statement issued by the Office of the Muftī, published *ibid.*, vol. 8, 3028–41, as well as the analysis in Skovgaard-Petersen, *Defining Islam*, 232–233.

[31] For example, Islamists reminded the public that in the past, the Minister of *Awqāf*, who now eagerly supported the bill, had publicly opposed on Islamic grounds a draft bill that was almost identical. See column by Muḥammad al-Sammān in *al-Iʿtiṣām*, vol. 42, no. 9 (August 1979): 2–3, analyzed in Najjar, "Egypt's Laws of Personal Status," 324. This and other such attacks damaged the reputation of these scholars among Islamists and a large portion of the Egyptian populace. See Skovgaard-Petersen, *Defining Islam*, 232–33.

published as Law 44 of 1979.[32] Predictably, after Article 2 was amended, some Islamists began to bring constitutional challenges to Jihān's law.[33] A lower court referred one of these claims to the SCC, which issued an opinion on the same day that it decided the *ribā* case.

Because Jihān's law had been enacted before the amendment of Article 2, the SCC applied its doctrine of non-retroactivity and held that it could not decide the Article 2 issue. It did, however, strike down the law on alternate grounds. According to the Court, President Sādāt had exceeded his powers under the Emergency Laws when he promulgated Law 44. Under the Emergency Laws, the President can enact decree laws only when he is faced with a situation that requires immediate action. The SCC held that family law reform did not require urgent emergency action. Because ratification by the People's Assembly could not cure a constitutional defect, Jihān's law was void.

The decision was not an Article 2 decision, but it must have been heartening for Islamists. For one, the Court was clearly willing to overturn laws, even in cases where the executive branch would be embarrassed. Furthermore, the decision to overturn Jihān's law had a practical benefit for Islamists. If the government wished its new rules to take effect, it would have to re-enact Jihān's law. Because the re-enactment would take place after the promulgation of Article 2, the new law would be subject to Article 2 review. The significance of this became immediately apparent. When the government decided to re-enact Jihān's law, it removed two of the provisions that had been most offensive to Islamists. Even with the removal of these provisions, the newly-enacted law offended some Muslims. Various provisions were thus challenged in court, and these challenges led to a number of seminal Article 2 cases.

[32] See Najjar, "Egypt's Laws of Personal Status," 319–44. I refer to the law as "Jihān's law" only for the sake of convenience and not as a political position on the nature of the law.

[33] These challenges received a boost after two members of the *ʿulamāʾ* who had publicly supported Jihān's law (and whose support for the bill had been crucial to its passage) recanted their earlier support for the bill and asserted that it was, indeed, contrary to the principles of the *sharīʿa*. See Najjar, "Egypt's Laws of Personal Status," 337.

III. *The ramifications of the doctrine of Article 2's non-retroactivity*

Since most Egyptian laws in force predated the amendment of Article 2, the SCC's decision rendered most current laws immune to review. At the same time, the SCC implicitly asserted the right to review laws enacted after the amendment to ensure that they were consistent with "the principles of the Islamic *sharīʿa*." As a practical matter, this opinion gave the political branches the power to choose for themselves the pace of Islamization. If the political branches did not wish to Islamize, they could simply choose not to enact new laws. But when they acted, their legislation or administrative rules would be subject to Article 2 review.

Not all judges were happy with this compromise. Some lower-court judges with Islamist sympathies continued to refer Article 2 cases to the SCC, even though the SCC had held that it did not have the authority to decide them. In other words, a handful of lower-court judges were asking the Court to force immediate Islamization of the law by exercising review over legislation enacted before the amendment of Article 2.[34] The SCC, however, stood firm and consistently reaffirmed the doctrine that Article 2 challenges to such legislation were non-justiciable.[35] Watching from a distance, some European observers seemed to sympathize with the frustration of these lower-court judges. They concluded that the SCC's 1985 decisions represented a capitulation by the courts to the executive branch. Shortly after the decisions, Gilles Kepel, a scholar of radical Islamism, suggested that the SCC, in announcing the doctrine of Article 2's non-retroactivity, had decided not to take a major role in defining the course of Islamization in Egypt. "The workings of the political systems have remained out of bounds, and even the judicial system has been shielded from the constraining logic of the

---

[34] For a discussion of this phenomenon and a more general overview of Egyptian judges' occasional use of their power of judicial review to promote Islamist aims, see Bernard Botiveau, "Contemporary Reinterpretations of Islamic Law," 276–77.

[35] For examples of SCC opinions dismissing on non-retroactivity grounds cases docketed after the 1985 decision, see, *inter alia*, Case No. 32, Judicial Year 10 (November 4, 1989); Case No. 35, Judicial Year 10 (November 4, 1989); Case No. 12, Judicial Year 11 (November 4, 1989); Case No. 33, Judicial Year 10 (November 4, 1990); Case No. 34, Judicial Year 10 (January 5, 1991).

watchwords demanding the application of the *sharīʿa*," Kepel wrote in 1985.[36]

The SCC's approach, however, turned out to be more subtle than its critics had anticipated. Governments regularly amend laws, replace laws, or enact new laws to deal with new situations. Theoretically, every one of these new amendments would be subject to Article 2 review. As old laws were retired and new legislation was enacted, the SCC would have to review these laws for consistency with the principles of the Islamic *sharīʿa*, and would nullify laws that it considered to be inconsistent. Although the SCC took a more limited role than some wanted, it was a serious role nonetheless. The SCC would not require immediate action, but it suggested that it would supervise an incremental Islamization of the law. Before it could do so, it had to develop its own theory of Islamic legislation—and its own method of identifying and interpreting the Islamic principles against which state law would be measured.

[36] Gilles Kepel, *Le prophète et pharaon*, trans. Jon Rothschild as *Muslim Extremism in Egypt: The Prophet and Pharaoh* (Berkeley: University of California Press, 1985), 247.

CHAPTER TEN

THE SCC'S SUBSTANTIVE ARTICLE 2 JURISPRUDENCE: AN OVERVIEW

Over the course of the 1980s, the controversy over the government's stalled Islamization program became more heated. After issuing its 1985 decisions resolving jurisdiction over Article 2 cases, the SCC apparently tried to avoid becoming unnecessarily involved in the debates. For several years, the Court did not issue any substantive Article 2 opinions. When it first began to do so, it issued only cursory opinions, which did not give much insight into the method that it used to identify and interpret "the principles of the Islamic *sharī'a*." Only in 1993 did the Court begin to issue Article 2 opinions which dwelt in depth upon the SCC's reasoning.

This chapter will provide an overview of the SCC's post-1985 jurisprudence. First, it will discuss briefly the Court's jurisprudence prior to 1993, when the Court was apparently reluctant to articulate a systematic theory of Islamic legal interpretation. It will then give an overview of the Court's jurisprudence after 1993. In formulating an interpretation of Article 2, the SCC appropriated language and concepts drawn from a wide range of competing theories of Islamic law. Yet the Court has not adhered to any one theory, but instead has put these disparate concepts together in a novel fashion. The resulting theory has been ambiguous in places and thus, to some degree, embryonic. Like many other modernist theories of Islamic legal interpretation, the SCC's theory has permitted the justices to draw upon their reason (and arguably their subjective value judgments). As a practical matter, it allowed the justices to interpret the revealed texts and the historical traditions in light of their own liberal constitutional values. It thus represents a tentative attempt to articulate, in terms that would resonate with a wide range of Egyptian Islamists, a liberal interpretation of Islamic law. The theory, as applied to date by the Court, has actually reinforced the Court's jurisprudence in the area of property rights and fundamental human rights.

I. *The earliest substantive Article 2 opinions*

At the time that the SCC declared Article 2 to be non-retroactive in 1985, only two cases on the Court's docket involved laws that had been enacted after the amendment of Article 2 in 1980.[1] These were the only justiciable cases that could be heard, and the Court was apparently in no hurry to hear these two cases or the other justiciable cases that followed.[2] The SCC waited until 1989 to issue an opinion in the first of these cases.[3] In this, its first substantive Article 2 opinion, the Court was not very forthcoming about the method it had used to determine whether the law was consistent with "the principles of the Islamic *sharīʿa*." The Court was able to avoid substantial discussion of its reasoning because all of these cases involved two claims. That is to say, the appellant had argued that a law violated both a secular provision of the constitution and the provisions requiring Egyptian law to be consistent with "the principles of the Islamic *sharīʿa*." Once the Court had upheld or struck down the legislation at issue on secular grounds of property rights, it simply stated that the principles of the *sharīʿa* required the same result.

That the Court would take this approach was not entirely surprising. In this and other early cases, the "secular" provisions at issue were provisions to which the Court was then devoting considerable attention. In fact, most of these cases argued that the law at issue violated provisions guaranteeing the right to private property as well as Article 2.[4] The Court, at this time, was forcefully establishing a property rights jurisprudence which rejected the statist biases of the Nāṣir regime and towards the protection of private property.[5]

---

[1] Nathalie Bernard Maugiron has listed eighteen cases that the Court dismissed on non-retroactivity grounds between 1985 and 1992. Of these, eight (including the two 1985 cases) were already on the Court's docket at the time that the doctrine of non-retroactivity was announced. See Nathalie Bernard Maugiron, "La Haute Cour constitutionelle Égyptienne et la sharīʿa islamique," *Awrâq* (Madrid) 19 (1998): 110–11.

[2] Among the cases that could not be dismissed on non-retroactivity grounds were Case No. 68, Judicial Year 3 (March 4, 1989) (challenging Article 1, Para. 2 of Decree Law 141 of 1981) and Case No. 65, Judicial Year 4 (May 16, 1992) (challenging Articles 2 and 6 of Decree Law No. 141 of 1981 as well as Article 10 of Law No. 69 of 1974).

[3] Case No. 68, Judicial Year 3 (March 4, 1989). The second case was not decided until 1992.

[4] See the discussion of the SCC's liberal constitutional jurisprudence in Chapter 8.

[5] Drafted at a time when Egypt was first moving away from Nāṣirism, the Egyptian

The public was likely to believe that the principles of the Islamic *sharīʿa* required strong protections of private property.[6] Accordingly, in cases involving both property rights claims and Article 2 claims, the SCC was able to explain why the property rights provisions required the law at issue to be struck down and then to assert, without much explanation, that the principles of the *sharīʿa* required the same result. In two of these cases, the SCC upheld laws on property rights and Islamic grounds,[7] and in three of them it struck them down on both grounds.[8] The Court in 1992 upheld a law against

---

Constitution of 1971 was ambivalent about the question of property rights. Compare, e.g., Articles 29, 20, 31, 32, 34, and 35. The SCC had, almost from the time of its inception, tried to bring order to this area. To determine the constitutionality of a government taking of private property or of a regulation imposing on the right to use or transfer property, the Court employed a balancing test. But the test assumed that society had a strong interest in protecting private property rights and permitted taking or regulation only when the public's interest in the property was clear and substantial. As a practical matter, then, property owners came to enjoy greater rights against expropriations and onerous regulation than they had enjoyed under the Nāṣirist constitutions. For a description of the Court's early jurisprudence by a justice on the Supreme Court, see Awad El-Morr, "The Status and Protection of Property in the Constitution," *Human Rights and Democracy: The Role of the Supreme Constitutional Court of Egypt*, eds. Kevin Boyle and Adel Omar Sherif (CIMEL Book Series 3; London: Kluwer, 1996), 115–127. For a perceptive and thoughtful analysis by an academic, see Enid Hill, "The Supreme Constitutional Court of Egypt on Property," *Le prince et son juge: droit et politique dans l'Égypte contemporaine*, a special issue of *Egypte/Monde Arabe* vol. 2, no. 2, eds. Nathalie Bernard Maugiron and Baudouin Dupret (1999), 55–92.

[6] Classical jurists tended to live in cities in a mercantile environment, and as discussed in Chapter 2, they considered the promotion of moveable property to be one of the five "necessaries"—the overarching goals of the *sharīʿa*. As discussed in Chapter 6, modernist Islamist thinkers such as the Muslim Brotherhood's Sayyid Quṭb contrasted Islamic visions of social justice with communist visions—in part on the grounds that Islamic law provided more protection for private property. As also noted above, Ṣūfī Abu Ṭālib's controversial call to "Islamize" Nāṣirist ideology involved, among other things, a call to abandon the statist biases of traditonal Nāṣirism create more liberal private property protections. Thus, during the 1970s the Egyptian government reached out to Islamists in part because it assumed they would support the governments liberal economic policies.

[7] Case No. 23, Judicial Year 9 (decided May 4, 1991), *SCC*, vol. IV, 335–45 (upholding a law requiring landowners to obtain a governmental permit before building structures on agricultural land); Case No. 36, Judicial Year 9 (decided March 14, 1992), *SCC*, vol. V, Part 1, 274–91 (upholding Article 22, para. 2, of Law No. 136 (1981) which provided that if a person renting a dwelling, builds a house with more than three units, such person must either (1) abandon the rented dwelling or (2) offer his landlord a unit in his new building). For other analyses of these cases, see Bernard-Maugiron, "La Haute Cour," 124–25 and Hill, "The Supreme Constitutional Court," 73–75.

[8] Case No. 68 of Judicial Year 3 (decided March 4, 1989), *SCC*, vol. IV, 148–64

an equal protection challenge, rather than a property rights one, and included a short passage mentioning that the law did not violate Article 2 either—but this case was aberrant.[9] When the Court began to decide more cases that dealt with issues other than property, it began to focus more attention on the Article 2 claims and articulated a more systematic approach to Islamic legal interpretation.

Even if they did not contain much systematic discussion of Islamic legal theory, the SCC's earliest Article 2 opinions did suggest some underlying assumptions about Islamic law and Islamic legal interpretation. To begin, the Court's opinions did not inquire into the opinions of the contemporary *ʿulamāʾ*, implying that the Court had rejected the neo-traditionalist argument that the modern *ʿulamāʾ* had unique authority in questions of Islamic legal interpretation. The SCC seemed to be asserting that lay Muslims, including judges who had not received a traditional religious training, could interpret Islamic law for themselves. Second, the SCC seemed willing to strike down laws on the grounds that, the government's protestations notwithstanding, they were inconsistent with the *sharīʿa.* This implied that the Court would show little, if any deference, to executive or legislative conclusions about the *sharīʿa.* The SCC's interpretation of Islamic law also tended to coincide with its liberal constitutional values—implying that the Court's interpretation of Islamic texts and of

(striking down a government order interpreting and applying of Paragraph 2 of Article 1 of Decree Law 141 in order to expropriate the real property not only of a wealthy landowner but of all his adult children); Case No. 65 of Judicial Year 4 (decided May 16, 1992), *SCC,* vol. V, Part 1, 344–62 (striking down (a) Articles 2 and 6 of Decree Law No. 141 (1981) and (b) Article 10 of Law No. 69 (1974) which together provided for the desequestration of lands sequestered in 1964—provided that their value was not greater than 30,000 Egyptian pounds); Case No. 25 of Judicial Year 11, (decided on May 27, 1992), *SCC,* vol. V, Part 1, 408–28 (striking down Article 55, para. 2 of Law No. 17 (1983)). For other analyses of these cases, see Barnard-Maugiron, "La Haute Cour," 124–26 and Hill, "The Supreme Constitutional Court," 61.

[9] Case No. 37, Judicial Year 7 (decided March 7, 1992), *SCC,* vol. V, Part 1, 229–39. The legislative provision under attack in this case dealt with retirement pensions and treated pensioners differently depending on when they claimed their pension. Plaintiffs claimed first that the laws violated the rights of equal opportunity and equality before the law that were guaranteed in Article 8 and Article 40 of the Constitution. They then suggested that these provisions violated Article 2 as well. The Court disagreed on all counts. In keeping with the pattern established in the property rights claim, the court focused most of its attention on the equal rights claims—asserting that the law demanded equal treatment only for citizens who were similarly situated. It then mentioned, almost as an aside, that the law sought to achieve justice and thus did not violate the principles of the *sharīʿa.* For other analyses of this case, see Bernard-Maugiron, "La Haute Cour," 125.

Islamic precedents was being shaped by its normative commitment to constitutional liberalism. In later cases, similar patterns can be found. More interestingly, the Court began to articulate a more systematic theory of legal interpretation that explained these patterns and implicitly tried to justify them in terms that would be appealing to diverse groups of Islamists.

II. *Later Article 2 opinions: articulating a theory of Islamic law and legal interpretation*

By 1993, the Court seemed to feel a need to explain publicly the method that it was using to identify and interpret the principles of the *sharīʿa*. At this point, the battle between the secularist government and Islamist militant groups had become exceedingly violent, and Egypt seemed on the brink of civil war. The increasingly authoritarian government had largely closed the political process to political factions who were sympathetic to the Islamist cause. Islamist violence and the indiscriminate suppression of Islamists were together coming to threaten the liberal constitutional order that the Court had struggled to establish and that was slowly beginning to take root.[10] The judiciary was the branch capable of mediating between the warring sides and to propose some kind of acceptable compromise.

It is probably not coincidental that in 1993, the SCC began to articulate more fully its theory of Islamic legal interpretation and to

[10] Throughout the early 1990s, the attitudes between Islamists and the government hardened to the point where compromise seemed impossible. See Ami Ayalon, "Egypt," in MECS XIV (1990), 320–22. The Ibn Khaldun Center in Egypt has performed a quantitative analysis of incidents which indicate socio-political unrest. The numbers reveal an extraordinary increase in such events over the course of the Mubārak regime. See Saad Eddin Ibrahim, "The Changing Face of Egypt's Islamic Activism" (1995), repr. in Saad Eddin Ibrahim, *Egypt, Islam and Democracy: Twelve Critical Essays* (Cairo: America University of Cairo Press, 1996). The violence could be dramatic and deeply symbolic. Thus, Islamists assassinated Rifʿat Maḥjūb (the speaker of the People's Assembly who had formally shelved the Islamic codes) and targeted secularist intellectuals, and even began targeting the tourists on whom the Egyptian economy was coming increasingly to depend. Under these circumstances, the SCC may have felt pressure to open a dialogue—to demonstrate that it was taking Article 2 seriously and to offer the courts as a forum in which Islamists could get a real hearing for their concerns. For it to do this, the SCC had to demonstrate that it was committed to developing a theory of Article 2 that reflected a serious respect for (and facility with) the Islamic legal tradition.

apply it in high-profile cases.[11] The SCC's theory seems calculated to appeal rhetorically to diverse Islamist factions—drawing vocabulary and concepts from a range of classical and modernist Islamic legal theories, but leaving unclear its position on some particularly controversial matters. The method, as described, left considerable discretion to interpret Islamic law in light of reason and, arguably, intuitions about utility. It thus permitted the justices to interpret God's commands to be consistent with the liberal constitutional principles that the SCC has read into Egyptian constitutional law. Indeed, at a time when the nation tottered between secularism and Islamism, the SCC's opinions implicitly suggested that liberal constitutionalism could flourish under either ideology.

On May 15, 1993, the SCC issued its opinion in Case No. 7 of Judicial Year 8 (released on May 15, 1993).[12] The opinion embraced the general premises shared by the classical doctrine of *siyāsa sharʿiyya* and by most important modernist Islamic legal thinkers discussed in this book: God had revealed to the Prophet Muḥammad certain rulings about the lawfulness of behavior and revealed certain social benefits that he wanted people to enjoy. The government could enact whatever laws it felt to be useful so long as its laws were not inconsistent with these rulings or impeded the realization of these benefits. In the 1993 opinion and in opinions ever since, the Court has also elaborated a method of identifying the relevant Islamic rulings and goals. The Court's method draws from several modernist legal theories, and, interestingly, the Court has also left its approach ambiguous in certain controversial areas. In its Article 2 opinions since 1993, the Court has thus articulated a theory with broad rhetorical appeal, while retaining considerable discretion in the short term both to decide individual cases in keeping with its pre-existing normative commitments and, if necessary, to develop the theory in a manner that will attract more public support.

---

[11] There were reasons other than political reasons for the Court to begin at this time to articulate a more systematic theory. For one, the SCC was beginning hear constitutional challenges that were premised only on Article 2 claims. In a case where the constitutionality of a law depended entirely upon the Court's interpretation of Article 2, the public might expect a more elaborate discussion of the Court's reasoning.

[12] Case No. 7 of Judicial Year 8 (May 15, 1993), *SCC*, vol. V, Part 2, 265–90.

A. *Article 2 requires Egyptian legislation to be consistent with the universal rulings and goals of the* sharīʿa

At the start of its May 15, 1993 opinion, the SCC made clear that Article 2 commanded the Egyptian government to respect (1) the rulings of the *sharīʿa* which established the moral quality of particular actions, and (2) the goals of the *sharīʿa*.

> A legislative text is not permitted to contradict Islamic legal rulings that are absolutely certain in their authenticity and meaning (*al-aḥkām al-sharʿiyya al-qaṭʿiyya fī thubūtihā wa dalālatihā*). It is these rulings alone in which *ijtihād* is not permitted. They represent the Islamic *sharīʿa*, its universal principles and established roots which are not subject to interpretation or alteration (*mabādiʾuhā al-kulliyya wa-uṣūluhā al-thābita allatī lā taḥtamil taʾwīl*[an] *aw tabdīl*[an]); and it is inconceivable that the interpretation of them [the universally applicable principles] will change with a change of time or place. . . . [It may only contravene] the rulings that are probable whether with respect to their authenticity or their meaning or both (*al-aḥkām al-ẓanniyya sawāʾ fī thubūtihā aw dalālatihā aw fihimā*). The sphere of *ijtihād* is limited to them [the probable rulings of the *sharīʿa*] . . . And they [the rulings that are merely probable] change with the change of times and place in order to guarantee their malleability and vigor in order to face new circumstances and in order to organize the affairs of the people, with respect to their welfare from the consideration of law . . . It is necessary that *ijtihād* occur within the frame of the universal roots of the Islamic *sharīʿa* (*al-uṣūl al-kulliyya li-ʾl-sharīʿa al-Islāmiyya*) . . . building practical rulings and, in discovering them [these rulings], relying on the justice of the *sharīʿa*, [and] expecting the result of them [these rulings] to be a realization of the general goals of the *sharīʿa* (*al-maqāṣid al-ʿāmma li-ʾl-sharīʿa*), among which are the protection of religion, life, reason, honor, and property.[13]

The rulings that the state must respect are those rulings (*aḥkām*) unambiguously recorded in scriptures that are known to be authentic. Apparently, there are also two types of goals: "universal roots" (*al-uṣūl al-kulliyya*) of Islamic law; and the general goals of the *sharīʿa* (*al-maqāṣid al-ʿāmma li-ʾl-sharīʿa*). The Egyptian legislature has the right on its own in the first instance to enact legislation that it believes complies with the twin requirements of Article 2. The SCC has the authority and obligation to review the legislature's conclusions that the new law conforms to Islamic rulings and principles.

[13] Case No. 7 of Judicial Year 8 (May 15, 1993), 283.

This raises two questions. How does the Court identify the rulings of the *sharīʿa* that all Islamic states must respect? And how does the Court identify the social results that state laws must promote? The passage just cited gives some indication. This chapter will explain how the Court identifies the rulings of the *sharīʿa* that all Islamic states must respect, and the social goals that state laws must promote.

Before describing the Court's theory, some quirks should be noted in the Court's use of technical terms. These idiosyncrasies appear in the passage quoted above and, in fact, recur consistently in the Court's Article 2 opinions. The most obvious example involves the term *ijtihād*.[14] As discussed in Chapter 2, the majority of classical jurists used the term *ijtihād* to refer to the method by which classical jurists identified scriptural rules and expanded upon them to develop rulings of *fiqh* and to identify the goals of the *sharīʿa*. These rulings and goals could be used to resolve a dispute being tried in an Islamic court. In the alternative, once *ijtihād* had been performed, the ruler could use the rulings and goals that had been derived to help him understand the boundaries of permissible legislation. Then, in a second process of reasoning that the jurists did *not* call *ijtihād*, the government would come up with rules that it wished to enact—rules that did not violate any of the established Islamic rulings and goals that had been established by *ijtihād*.

As the passage above makes clear, the SCC uses the term *ijtihād* in a very different way. Like Rashīd Riḍā and the champions of utilitarian neo-*ijtihād*, it employs the term to describe the process that a *walī al-amr* should use to come up with regulations for behavior that is not governed by clear scriptural rulings. Thus, in its Article 2 jurisprudence, the SCC has regularly said that whenever a government regulates behavior that is not governed by clear scriptural rulings, it is operating in the sphere of *ijtihād*. This means that legislators must reason out, as best they can, what rules will best

[14] For a detailed discussion of the Court's idiosyncratic understanding of *ijtihād*, see Frank Vogel, "Conformity with Islamic Sharīʿa and Constitutionality under Article 2: Some Issues of Theory, Practice, and Comparison," *Democracy, the Rule of Law and Islam*, eds. Eugene Cotran, Adel Omar Sherif (CIMEL Book Series No. 6: London: Kluwer, 1999), 525–44.

advance the goals of the *sharīʿa*. Conversely, when the government regulates behavior that is governed by established rulings of the *sharīʿa*, it is operating in a sphere in which *ijtihād* is forbidden. In those areas governed by clear scriptural rulings, the government must adopt and enforce the known rulings of the *sharīʿa*. In many later Article 2 opinions, the SCC begins with a passage that repeats these ideas using very similar language.[15]

What method would the SCC employ to identify and interpret these rulings? The language in these passages is obviously dense, and it incorporates many technical terms. From this book's previous discussion of Islamic legal theories, however, many of these terms will be familiar, and it will be clear that the SCC is applying them in the service of an idea that is, in its broad outline, non-controversial. At the same time, this passage does not give any details about the Court's interpretive method. If the Egyptian government is constrained to respect certain rulings and certain goals of the *sharīʿa*, how can it determine what these rulings and principles are or how they are to be applied in modern times? When the Court reviews the legislature's laws for consistency with the principles of the *sharīʿa*, must it take the route suggested by neo-traditionalists and simply defer to the contemporary *ʿulamāʾ*'s understanding of God's law? Or can legislators and judges who are not classically trained try to reason out the rulings and principles on their own? If the latter, what method should the justices use? Should the justices use classical methods of Islamic legal interpretation, a method similar to that championed by Rashīd Riḍā and other proponents of utilitarian neo-*ijtihād*, or a method akin to that championed by Sanhūrī and other proponents of comparative neo-*taqlīd*? Should it perhaps develop some new method of its own? This passage does not answer any of these questions about interpretive method. The Court has never systematically provided an answer to all of them. To understand the Court's approach, an answer must be extrapolated from the Court's opinions.

[15] See, e.g., Case No. 29, Judicial Year 11 (March 26, 1994), *SCC*, vol. VI, 248–49; Case No. 8, Judicial Year 17 (May 18, 1996), (version printed in *al-Jarīda al-Rasmiyya* [The Official Gazette] No. 21, (May 20, 1996), 1032–33.

B. *In interpreting the* sharīʿa, *the SCC need not defer to the contemporary* ʿulamāʾ

If it had wished to do so, the Court could easily have interpreted Article 2 to require that Egyptian legislation respect the principles of the *sharīʿa* as interpreted by "the leading *ʿulamāʾ*." It could have made a good argument that the legislators who amended Article 2 had intended the term "the principles of the Islamic *sharīʿa*" to refer to the principles as interpreted by the leading *ʿulamāʾ*. As discussed in Chapter 7, Article 2 was enacted at a time when the Egyptian regime was voluntarily drafting Islamic codes of law, and submitting them to al-Azhar for approval. That fact suggests that the legislature, when it enacted Article 2, felt that the opinions of the *ʿulamāʾ* at al-Azhar were, at the very least, probative on the question of whether the law conformed to the principles of the *sharīʿa*. The SCC, however, clearly did not wish to look to the *ʿulamāʾ* for guidance. In developing its theory of Islamic law and legal interpretation, the SCC departs from the central assumption of what this book has been calling neo-traditional theory. It implicitly rejects the idea that only those with formal religious training can be trusted to interpret the *sharīʿa*.

In its first six Article 2 cases from 1989 through 1992, the SCC never tried to justify its interpretation of Islamic law by referring to interpretations put forth by a member of the *ʿulamāʾ*. This is also true of the lengthy discussions of its jurisprudence in decisions after 1993. In explaining why it reaches the conclusions it does about Islamic law and about the consistency of state legislation with the principles of the *sharīʿa*, the SCC has never deferred to the opinion of the *ʿulamāʾ* or even cited the *ʿulamāʾ* as additional evidence to support a conclusion that it had independently reached. When it comes to determining whether laws are consistent with Article 2, it is clear who the SCC believes should be ultimately responsible for interpreting "the principles of the *sharīʿa*: the justices of the SCC.

It should not be surprising that the justices of the SCC would perform *ijtihād* on their own. The Egyptian public was not shocked by the idea that judges would be capable of interpreting Islamic law. Many Egyptian modernists, including the members of the Muslim Brotherhood, believe that people who are not formally trained as *ʿulamāʾ* can interpret Islamic law. The attraction of this approach for the Court was obvious. It allowed the Court to maintain control over the evolution of Article 2 doctrine. It also enabled the Court to ensure that Article 2 was not used in bad faith by the political branches to weaken the liberal jurisprudence that the Court had imposed through the secular provisions of the constitution.

C. *Identifying the absolutely certain rulings of the* sharīʿa

Having asserted the authority to perform interpretation, how did the justices of the SCC determine whether a piece of legislation is consistent with principles of the *sharīʿa*? As the passage cited above makes clear, the Court believes that legislation cannot be considered to be consistent with the principles of the *sharīʿa* unless it can satisfy a two-prong test. First, the legislation in question cannot violate any universally-applicable scriptural ruling. Second, the legislation cannot impede the realization of the "goals of the *sharīʿa*." It cannot stand in the way of the larger ends that the Islamic law tries to attain. To understand the nuances of the Court's two-prong test, each prong must be examined separately.

To satisfy the first prong of its test, Egyptian legislation must be shown not to violate any universally applicable ruling of the *sharīʿa*. The Court repeatedly says in its opinion that these binding rulings can be identified because they are "absolutely certain with respect to their authenticity and meaning" (*al-aḥkām al-sharʿiyya al-qaṭʿiyya fī thubūtihā wa dalālatihā*). This book will henceforth refer to these rulings as "absolutely certain" rulings. In several opinions, the Court also states suggestively that "it is inconceivable that the interpretation of them [the absolutely certain rulings] will change with a change of time or place. . . ."[16] It is worth considering the juxtaposition of these two statements, because they suggest that a ruling will not bind the state unless it meets two criteria. First, the Court must be able to find evidence of this ruling in an unambiguous revealed text that is of indubitable authenticity—either the Qurʾān or one of the few *ḥadīths* that are known with absolute certainty to be accurate. Second, it must also have been consistently recognized as binding by jurists in different times and places. To understand how these two requirements fit together in the Court's theory, it is important to examine

[16] Case No. 7 of Judicial Year 8 (May 15, 1993), 283.

the steps that the Court generally goes through to identify the rulings that are "absolutely certain with respect to their authenticity and meaning" (*al-aḥkām al-sharʿiyya al-qaṭʿiyya fī thubūtihā wa dalālatihā*).

Like a classical jurist performing *ijtihād* or like Riḍā, the Court begins its search for absolutely certain rulings by looking to revealed texts. When it comes to the question of how to evaluate scriptural authenticity, the SCC has not described the method that it uses. From the opinions, it is clear that the Court assumes the authenticity and accuracy of the Qur'ānic text. It is not clear how the Court is evaluating the authenticity of *ḥadīth*s. In its first major Article 2 decision in 1993, the SCC never even discussed the *ḥadīth* literature. Some passages in that opinion even suggested that a jurist should look exclusively in the Qur'ān in order to find rulings absolutely certain with respect to both their authenticity and meaning. In later opinions, the SCC occasionally does cite *ḥadīth*s as sources of binding legal principles. It never explains, however, why it considers these particular *ḥadīth*s to be authentic.[17]

The Court's method of interpreting texts and of establishing clear meaning is better articulated than its method of establishing their authenticity. When it comes to interpreting texts, the SCC fuses methods of interpretation favored by different types of Islamic legal thinkers. As discussed in Chapter 4, the champions of utilitarian neo-*ijtihād* rejected the classical idea that modern Muslims are bound either to follow the interpretive method used by the classical *mujtahids* of one of the Sunnī law guilds or even to accept the correctness of the interpretations upon which the classical *mujtahids* were agreed. Rather, they asserted that modern Muslims must re-examine afresh the texts of certain meaning and identify any unambiguous legal principles that they seem to contain. Shunning the hyper-technical

[17] Though one cannot be certain, it seems that the Court is adopting a somewhat subjective approach to identifying authentic *ḥadīths* similar to that proposed by Rashīd Riḍā and some of the later champions of utilitarian neo-*ijtihād*. Such a conclusion would be supported by the fact that one of the few *ḥadīths* that the Court explicitly accepts as authentic (and which it cites regularly) is one dear to the champions of utilitarian neo-*ijtihād*: "*lā ḍarar wa lā ḍirār*." Private conversations with a justice in 2001 further confirmed that at least some justices' have followed Rashīd Riḍā's method insofar as these justices believe one can evaluate the authenticity of a *ḥadīth* by seeing whether the ruling announced therein to be consistent with the justices' interpretation of Qur'ānic commands or with the overarching utilitarian principle that lies at the heart of God's command.

methods of exegesis that mark classical interpretive technique, they looked for a plain meaning. If such a clear meaning could not be found, then the rule was not certain with respect to its meaning.

The champions of comparative neo-*taqlīd*, on the other hand, doubted the ability of people to discover the true meaning of God's command through personal interpretation of scriptures. To their mind, the most trustworthy method of discovering the essence of God's command was to study the evolving interpretations of God's law. To identify the universal rulings of Islamic law, they performed an inductive survey, looking for general principles implicitly accepted by the Muslim community over the years. The champions of comparative neo-*taqlīd* were not only looking for specific rules that all *mujtahids* over the years had articulated and held to be binding. They were also looking for overarching principles that seemed to be implicitly accepted by the *mujtahids* over the years and that unified the apparently conflicting rulings.

When the SCC determines whether a principle of Islamic law has an absolutely certain meaning, it has combined aspects of these two methods. To tell whether an authentic textual ruling is unambiguous, the Court looks first to see if the texts before it have an apparent meaning. But in most cases, it does not stop there. After describing the absolutely certain rulings in the 1993 opinion in textualist terms as rulings of the *sharīʿa* that are found in unambiguous and absolutely authentic texts, the Court added, "It is inconceivable that the interpretation of them [the absolutely certain rulings] will change with a change of time or place."[18] It is easy to overlook the significance of this sentence, because at first glance, this passage could be thought merely to say that absolutely certain rulings bind the ruler today just as they bound people in the past. On closer inspection, however, the SCC seems to be saying something more provocative—not just that people *should* recognize the rule as binding, but rather that they actually *have* recognized the rule as binding. Thus, a ruling of the *sharīʿa* is an "absolutely certain" ruling that the legislature must respect if (1) it seems explicitly to have been set forth in a scriptural text (a Qurʾānic passage or a *ḥadīth* that has been authenticated through some, as yet undefined method) and (2) it seems implicitly

[18] Case No. 7 of Judicial Year 8 (May 15, 1993), 283.

to have been respected by the classical jurists over the years. Accordingly, whenever the Court finds what it thinks is an unambiguous, indubitably authentic ruling, it often checks its interpretation of the text. That is to say, the justices try to interpret the textual command. They then check to see whether the classical jurists, at different times and places, all interpreted Islamic law in a fashion that was consistent with their understanding of the command.[19] In short, to confirm that a ruling is an absolutely certain ruling that Egyptian law must respect, the rulings must have the qualities not only of Riḍā's "universal" ruling (namely, the quality of being tied to a scriptural passage that is certain with respect to authenticity and meaning), but also, for all practical purposes, of Sanhūrī's "fixed rule" (namely, the quality of being "permanent and reproducing itself in all times and all places").[20]

The Court's hybrid approach to textual interpretation raises a number of interesting questions. For example, what is the relative importance of apparent linguistic clarity, on the one hand, and historical trends in interpretation, on the other? If the Court were to rely heavily on the interpretation of past scholars, one might ask which jurists the Court looks to when it wants to survey the range of *fiqh* opinions.[21] And how will the SCC comprehensively survey the

---

[19] For example, in the SCC's first 1993 opinion, and consistently thereafter, the SCC did not do a detailed exegesis of the religious texts that it identified as authentic. Rather, it reached an initial conclusion about the meaning of a text. Then, to determine whether that interpretation was indubitably correct, the Court asked whether Islamic jurists over the years had recognized and accepted this principle as binding and, accordingly, had issued rulings that were consistent with it. See, e.g., Case No. 29, Judicial Year 11 (decided March 26, 1994), 255; Case No. 8, Judicial Year 17 (decided May 18, 1996), at 1032. In subsequent cases it has followed a similar pattern.

[20] See, e.g., Abd al-Razzāq Aḥmad al-Sanhūrī, *Le califat* (Paris: Librairie Orientaliste Paul Geuthner, 1926), 580 and n. 7. See also his "Le droit musulman comme élément de refonte du code civil égyptien," in *Introduction à l'étude du droit comparé: Recueil d'études en l'honneur d'Édouard Lambert* (Paris: Librairie Générale de Droit et de Jurisprudence/Librairie de la Société Anonyme du Recueil Sirey, 1938), vol. 3, 623.

[21] The Court has made clear that it views the opinions of jurists in the Ẓāhirī guild, notwithstanding the fact that, from the twelfth to nineteenth century, they were not considered orthodox Sunnī thinkers. In looking to the Ẓāhirī jurists, the SCC is merely following in the path of thinkers as diverse as Sanhūrī, Rashīd Riḍā and even neo-traditional *'ulamā'* such as Maḥmūd Shaltūt. One wonders whether they will look, as some of these thinkers did, to Shi'ite thinkers. One also might

extensive *fiqh* literature? The justices of the SCC are civil law and constitutional judges who have not, for the most part, received a comprehensive training in *fiqh*.[22] The Court has yet to give full answers to these questions. It is certain, however, that the Court is imposing very high standards for both certainty of authenticity and for certainty of meaning, and this has important practical consequences. The SCC has identified very few rulings that are absolutely certain and that provide them with universally applicable precepts. Thus, most laws will pass the first prong of the Article 2 test: the Court will find that they do not violate any ruling that is absolutely certain with respect to its authenticity and meaning. Rather, the question of whether a law violates Article 2, depends, in most cases, on whether that law impedes the overarching goals of the *sharīʿa*.

D. *Identifying the goals of the* sharīʿa

If the SCC concludes that a piece of legislation does not violate any legally binding ruling of the *sharīʿa*, this does not mean that this piece of legislation is constitutional. It means that the Court can proceed to the second prong of its test and ask if the law is inconsistent with the goals of the *sharīʿa*. Like all the theories of Islamic legislation examined in this book, the SCC assumes that obedience to Islamic law, properly understood, will advance justice and human welfare. Thus, in areas where God's specific command is not clear, an Islamic government is nonetheless required to make a good faith effort to promote (or at least to not impede) human welfare. Accordingly, Article 2 requires the SCC to strike down any legislation that requires people to act in a way that seems to impede the realization of the goals of the *sharīʿa*. But how does the SCC identify these goals? And having done so, how does the Court determine whether a law will impede them?

ask whether they are limiting themselves to pre-modern jurists or will look to modern jurists as well and, if so, which ones.

[22] Will they rely on certain authoritative versions of guild doctrine, or particular secondary sources? Do secular trained judges have sufficient knowledge about the various bodies of *fiqh* developed over the years to perform this analysis with confidence?

1. *Overview of the goals of the* sharīʿa

The Court's discussions of the goals of the *sharīʿa* tend to be extremely confusing. Because the opinions use a considerable amount of technical language, it is useful to review briefly some of the competing approaches proposed over the years to understanding the goals of the *sharīʿa*. As discussed in Chapter 2 and Chapter 5, classical jurists, neo-traditionalists and the champions of utilitarian *ijtihād* have all hypothesized that Muslims can induce from the commands revealed in texts a number of goals of the *sharīʿa* (*maqāṣid al-sharīʿa*). According to this theory, the worldly results that God wants his people to enjoy must axiomatically be considered "benefits" (*maṣlaḥa*, sing; *maṣāliḥ*, pl.). These benefits/goals include the so-called "necessaries": the protection of religion, life, reason, progeny and property. (Some classical jurists argued that there was a sixth "necessary," which was honor (*ʿirḍ*).) Alongside the "necessary" goals were other subsidiary goals. Classical jurists and modernist thinkers often disagreed, however, about the method by which humans could come to understand the goals of the *sharīʿa*, and they disagreed also about how consideration of the goals should influence legal theory.

Classical jurists and modernist thinkers, even if they agreed on the overall concept of the goals of the *sharīʿa*, tended to disagree about how Muslims could determine whether a law was beneficial. The classical jurists suggested that the hierarchy of *sharīʿa* goals should be induced from the rulings that were known to be "certain" and thus universally applicable. By contrast, the champions of utilitarian neo-*ijtihād* simplified the process of determining whether a piece of legislation promotes the goals of the law.[23] They declared that the supreme principle of the *sharīʿa* was a utilitarian principle established clearly in the *ḥadīth* "*lā ḍarar wa-lā ḍirār*," "no harm and no retribution"). For the advocates of utilitarian neo-*ijtihād*, this *ḥadīth* required Muslims to act in the way that reason tells them maximizes human welfare. Believing that reason could distinguish what was beneficial to humans, the champions of utilitarian neo-*ijtihād* naturally sought

[23] As discussed in Chapter 5, their drive to simplify goals analysis was necessitated, in part, by their attitude towards scripture. To their mind, few scriptural rulings were sufficiently clear and authentic to be legally probative, and it would have been difficult to find patterns that would allow them to induce a hierarchy of benefits.

information about the benefits not only in revelation but in nature as well.

Furthermore, classical jurists and modernists disagreed about how to make use of their knowledge that God wanted humans to enjoy certain benefits. Except in rare cases of absolute necessity, classical jurists tended to believe that knowledge of the goals of the law should influence legal reasoning only indirectly by allowing jurists to draw tighter and more convincing analogies. Modernists like Riḍā, on the other hand, believed that humans could reason out with confidence the long-term results of a law. As a result, it was possible to determine the Islamic legal quality of an act by reasoning out whether the law led to more benefit than harm.

Although Sanhūrī and the champions of comparative neo-*taqlīd* did not formally adopt the conceptual framework and language of the classical theory of the "goals of the law," they recognized analogues of the goals. They required state legislation to respect the legal principles that were commonly followed (and thus implicitly accepted as binding) by Islamic jurists and Islamic rulers over the years. Such principles might be very specific rules of behavior. They might also, in some cases, be principles requiring certain types of activity to lead to certain types of benefit for certain types of people.[24]

How does the SCC conceptualize the notion that law should serve human welfare? The SCC in its 1993 opinion indicated that it was adopting the vocabulary and overarching conceptual framework of the "goals of the law":

> It is necessary that *ijtihād* occur within the frame of the universal roots of the Islamic *sharīʿa* (*al-uṣūl al-kulliyya li-'l-sharīʿa al-Islāmiyya*) . . . building practical rulings and, in discovering [these rulings], relying on the justice of the *sharīʿa*, [and] expecting the result of them [these rulings] to be a realization of the general goals of the *sharīʿa* (*al-maqāṣid al-ʿāmma li-'l-sharīʿa*), among which are the protection of religion, life, reason, honor, and property.[25]

---

[24] See discussion in Chapter 5. Take, for example, a case in which jurists writing at different times and places disagreed about the details of a certain law (say custody law). The rulings seem systematically designed to promote result "x." Proponents of comparative neo-*taqlīd* would suggest that there is a universally applicable principle that Islamic legislation must try to promote "result x," although it may choose whatever method it likes to reach that end. This is the same as saying that the promotion of result "x" is a goal of the *sharīʿa*—at least in the area of custody law.

[25] Case No. 7, Judicial Year 8 (May 15, 1993), 283.

In later cases, the SCC regularly included passages that make similar points. For example, in a 1996 opinion, it proclaimed:

> presumptive rulings (*al-aḥkām al-ẓanniyya*) are not absolutely certain with respect to their authenticity, their meaning, or both. They fall within the realm to which *ijtihād* is limited and beyond which *ijtihād* does not extend. They develop by their nature—changing according to time and place, in order to guarantee their [own] flexibility and vitality, and to confront different events. They organize the affairs of the people (*al-ʿibād*) with an eye to protecting those interests of [the people] that are legally appropriate (*maṣāliḥahum al-muʿtabara sharʿan*) and should not interfere with their activities in life. *Ijtihād* must always fall within the framework of the *sharīʿa's* universal "roots" (*al-uṣūl al-kulliyya li-'l-sharīʿa*) . . . adhering to [the *sharīʿa*'s] fixed controls (*ḍawābiṭihā al-thābita*). It [*ijtihād*] must pursue methods of reasoning out the rulings (*al-aḥkām*) and binding supports (*al-qawāʿid al-ḍābiṭa*) for the "branches" of *sharīʿā* (*furūʿiha*), guarding the general goals of the *sharīʿa* (*al-maqāṣid al-ʿāmma li-'l-sharīʿa*) so that religion, life, reason, honor, and worldly goods are protected.[26]

When it comes to identifying the goals of the law, the SCC fuses in an interesting way the approaches of classical jurists, modernists like Riḍā and even champions of comparative neo-*taqlīd* such as Sanhūrī. How does the SCC identify the goals and, having done so, how does it make use of this knowledge to evaluate the constitutionality of laws? In both of the opinions quoted above, the SCC's discussion of the goals raises a number of questions. For example, the Court includes among the goals of the law the promotion of five necessaries: the preservation of religion, self, reason, honor, and property.[27] This list recalls the classical list of "necessaries" that were taken axiomatically by classical jurists to represent the paramount goals of the *sharīʿa*. Nevertheless, it does not mirror them exactly. The list includes only four of the five necessaries recognized by al-Ghazālī and most subsequent jurists (it drops the preservation of progeny). Adopting a minority position, it accepts the preservation of "honor" as a "necessary" goal of the *sharīʿa*. Furthermore, the Court implies that the list is non-exclusive, which leaves open the question of how it identified these five goals and how it will identify

---

[26] Case No. 8, Judicial Year 17 (May 18, 1996), 1031.

[27] Case No. 29, Judicial Year 11 (March 26, 1994), 249; Case No. 8, Judicial Year 17 (May 18, 1996), 1031–32.

others. And if one tries to follow the Court as it actually identifies "goals," the SCC sometimes seems to use different methods of identifying and interpreting these goals.

Over the course of many opinions a pattern emerges. The Court generally recognizes two types of goals. The first are what I will call "specific goals." For the SCC, God has revealed that certain types of law are supposed to promote certain goals. These specific goals are identified through textual analysis of the rulings dealing with a certain area of law, as supplemented by a Sanhūrī like analysis of what goals the jurists seem to have thought certain types of law should promote. What I call the "general goals" of the *sharīʿa* are the results that God wants human behavior, in the aggregate, to promote.

Knowledge of the specific goals seems to help the SCC better understand the general goals, and vice versa. For example, the Court seems to assume that laws that promote the specific goals of the law will, in the aggregate, promote the general goals in society. Knowledge of the specific goals thus helps the Court better understand the broader nature of human welfare. Conversely, accumulated understanding of human welfare helps the Court identify with more specificity the goals that apply in a certain area. If scriptures and historical interpretation suggest several possible results that might be the specific goals that God's law wants to promote in a particular area, the Court will select the specific goal that will maximize the general welfare.

2. *Identifying the specific goals of the* sharīʿa

In a 1995 opinion, the SCC suggested that, in considering what is harmful, Muslims must always bear in mind that, "whatever God prohibits to us is likely to harm us, and what he requires of us or makes permissible is certainly beneficial."[28] This apparently means, to begin, that the holder of power, the *walī al-amr*, may not violate an absolutely certain scriptural ruling of *sharīʿa* on the grounds that he believes the violation will advance what reason tells him is the public benefit. It also implies more broadly that inductive analysis

[28] Case No. 35, Judicial Year 9 (August 14, 1994), *SCC*, vol. VI, 331–58 at 350–351.

of scriptural commands can help humans understand what is truly beneficial to them—with respect to both this world and the next. The SCC does not take this to mean, however, that it should simply induce the goals of the *sharīʿa* from textual rulings in the same systematic way as the classical jurists. Indeed, it is hard to see how the Court could reach this conclusion, since the justices recognize so few textual rulings as legally probative.[29] Rather, the Court takes this to mean that Muslims must use whatever tools are available to them to dig behind the rulings of the *sharīʿa*. It is significant that in looking for the goals the Court will look beyond the absolutely certain rulings and will consider as well what social results the presumptive rulings of the *sharīʿa* seem to promote.

For example, the Court sometimes finds an ambiguous Qurʾānic command that would seem to regulate behavior of the type that an Egyptian law regulates. Because this command is not absolutely certain with respect to both its authenticity and meaning, the SCC will not recognize the command as providing a ruling that the state must incorporate into its law. Such a command might, however, provide important information about the worldly results that God wants laws in this area to promote. An example might clarify how the Court works. In its first detailed Article 2 opinion, issued in 1993, the Court heard a challenge to a law requiring men to pay their divorced wives some form of compensation analogous to alimony.[30] It found Qurʾānic passages that discuss payments to wives, but it did not identify a clear ruling that expressly requires such payments or that expressly absolves men of the obligation to make such a payment. These passages mention, however, that women are to be treated "with kindness." The Court concludes from the Qurʾān that, in regulating men's behavior towards their divorced wives, God has established a goal that women be treated with generosity. An Egyptian statute

[29] From the discussion so far, it should be clear that the SCC would have trouble following the traditional method of inducing the goals of the law from Islamic legal rulings that it had identified as binding. This is for the same reason that the champions of utilitarian neo-*ijtihād* found it hard: the SCC applies such strict criteria when it looks for legally binding rulings, that it is likely to find very few of them. And if it does not have a sufficient number of rulings with which to work, it will not be able to use induction with any confidence.

[30] Case No. 7, Judicial Year 8 (May 15, 1993), 283.

permitting a judge to order separation payments (analogous to alimony in the American legal system) is thus consistent with the specific goal of the *sharīʿa* (namely, protection of divorced wives) that divorce laws are supposed to promote.

It is also notable that when looking for specific goals applicable to a certain type of law, the Court does not rely exclusively on direct textual analysis, but often supplements this with an analysis of the historical interpretation of the sacred texts. For example, the Court sometimes concludes that textual commands do not clearly explain what results God wants a certain type of law to promote. In such a case, the Court can sometimes perform a Sanhūrī-like analysis and determine that the jurists, despite their disagreement about whether certain acts are required, do seem to agree that God wants humans to act in ways that promote certain results. Thus, the SCC concluded in 1994 that the Qurʾānic passages requiring men to take care of their children do not state clearly whether a court can retroactively order a man to pay child support (meaning that he would be required to pay support for a period prior to the issuance of the order). Although classical jurists disagreed about this question, the Court found an implicit consensus among the jurists that, whatever rule was imposed, it must ensure the well-being of the child.[31]

> Where there is no [religious] text that is certain in its meaning and authenticity . . . it is not permissible for the holder of power (*walī al-amr*) to overstep them. He (the *walī al-amr*) must derive a rule that protects the welfare of the custodial children (*maṣlaḥat al-maḥḍūn*) as is required by the goals of the *sharīʿa*.[32]

Deciding that retroactive orders of support would tend to benefit children, the Court concluded that a law permitting such orders did not impede (and indeed promoted) the specific goals of support law.

Similarly, in 1996 the Court considered the constitutionality of a law prohibiting girls in public schools from wearing veils that covered the whole face.[33] It concluded that the Qurʾānic verses requiring women to veil themselves were ambiguous on the question of whether a woman had to cover up her face and hands. Reviewing

---

[31] Case No. 7, Judicial Year 8 (May 15, 1993), 287.
[32] Case No. 7, Judicial Year 8 (May 15, 1993), 285.
[33] Case No. 8, Judicial Year 17 (May 18, 1996).

the classical jurists' different rulings on the question, however, the Court concluded that there was general agreement that a woman must dress in a manner that will help her preserve her modesty and chastity, and that the differences arose simply because the jurists disagreed about what type of clothing was likely to tempt men to sin.[34] Thus, it found that the specific goal of the *sharīʿa* in the area of women's dress was the promotion of women's honor and the constitutionality of a state law regulating women's dress would depend on whether it impeded that goal. Based on this, the Court found that the law was consistent with that goal and thus constitutional.

Identifying "specific goals" can raise almost as many questions as it answers. By requiring Muslims to promote the "welfare" of a particular class of people, or to promote open-ended results such as "justice" or "modesty," the law commands them to promote values that have no universally agreed-upon meaning. To help resolve the ambiguities inherent in some of these "specific" goals, the Court considers what I will call the "general goals" of the *sharīʿa*.

3. *Identifying the "general goals" of the* sharīʿa

Alongside the "specific goals" of the *sharīʿa*—the results that particular types of law are supposed to promote—the Court asserts that there are aspects of social welfare that all rulings of the *sharīʿa* must serve. These are analogues of the "necessaries" in the classical theory of the goals of the *sharīʿa*. In its opinions, the SCC consistently asserts that these "general goals" of the *sharīʿa* include the promotion in society of religion, life, reason, property and honor. (As seen earlier, this list is similar, although not identical, to the traditional list of "necessaries.") The Court also implies, however, that this list is non-exclusive. In a 1994 opinion, the SCC seemed to adopt the principle that God simply wants humans to enjoy whatever reason tells them is beneficial. In a passage strongly reminiscent of Riḍā, the Court said that, even where there are no universal rulings that the state must incorporate when governing in a particular area of law, and even when the Court cannot identify a specific goal that laws in this area are supposed to apply in that area, the state's legislative discretion is still limited by "the universal rule (*al-qāʿida*

[34] Case No. 8, Judicial Year 17 (May 18, 1996), 1035–36.

al-kulliyya) that the Prophet, peace be upon him, formulated by saying, "no harm and no retribution," *lā ḍarar wa-lā ḍirār*.[35] This universal rule is, it says:

> a chief rule (*qāʿida raʾīsiyya*) from among the pillars of the Islamic *sharīʿa*. Its applications are many even if it is precise in its conciseness[36]. . . . And from this principle the jurists derived a number of rulings which are to be considered interpretations of it. Among these—and this is to be considered to be further an extension of the principle—is [the rule] that harm has to be pushed away as much as possible, and [the rule] that harm should be eliminated, and [that] harm must not endure through its likeness so that its extent will reach alarming proportions [in other words, one harm should not be repaid with another, thereby increasing the net harm]; and [that] the competition between two harms demands the choice of the lesser harm so as to push away the greater; and that one must bear the specific harm (*al-ḍarar al-khāṣṣ*) if it is necessary to ward off a general harm (*ḍarar ʿāmm*).[37]

As a general rule, absolutely certain rulings and specific precepts preclude the government from enacting some laws, but still leave open a range of possible regulations. When deciding which of the permissible regulations to enact, the SCC says the government may not regulate in a way that is likely to decrease the aggregate enjoyment of justice and human welfare in society. For example, in one case, the Court considered how much discretion the government has in establishing rules of child custody. The SCC determined that a specific goal of the *sharīʿa* in the area of child custody is the promotion of the welfare of the child. This begs the question: how does the SCC define "welfare"? According to the Court, Muslims must simply use their reason to determine whether a child is better or worse off. The rules of custody, the Court said, are:

> *ijtihādī* questions where views differ. Then, in each view, we must consider what is seen as most beneficial to determine what is most beneficial, each one [i.e., each practitioner of *ijtihād*] utilizing his own view to determine what is most likely to benefit the young child within the limits set by rights and justice.[38]

---

[35] Case No. 35, Judicial Year 9 (August 14, 1994), 354.

[36] The SCC goes on to note that "Qur'ānic texts of various provenance are discovered from it" and to quote Qur'ānic verses that advocate treating family members kindly.

[37] Case No. 35, Judicial Year 9 (August 14, 1994), 354–355.

[38] Case No. 7, Judicial Year 8 (May 15, 1993), 284.

Similarly, in the 1996 veil case, the Court could not find any absolutely clear scriptural ruling that required, prohibited or permitted face veils. Asking whether Islamic scriptures and the Islamic tradition seemed systematically to promote any particular social end, it concluded that Islamic laws of veiling always aimed to promote modesty among women. Thus, state laws that regulated women's clothing must not impede the greater goal of promoting female modesty. But this of course only raised the deeper question: what does "modesty" entail? (What is modest for one person may be lewd to another.) In determining what the divine command to promote "modesty" requires as a practical matter, the SCC concluded that modesty cannot require covering that is so complete as to impede the realization of the general goals in society. Working from this premise, the Court suggested that the specific goal of veiling legislation, namely to promote modesty, can never be interpreted to require behavior that makes it difficult for women to get an education or gainful employment.[39] The justices apparently believed that in modern Egypt, the practice of veiling the face harms women's self-esteem and imposes on their ability to function. Thus, they held that a state law prohibiting schoolgirls from covering their face is not inconsistent with "the principles of the *sharīʿa*."[40]

Finally, when the Court finds no universal ruling of the *sharīʿa* and no specific goal that the law wants to pursue, the utilitarian principle provides guidance as to what types of law will be appropriate.[41] Accordingly, in a 1995 case, the Court again said that in a case where there is no more specific guidance, the *walī al-amr* is required to act in a way that reason tells us will do more good than harm:

> the holder of power (*walī al-amr*) has a right to act so as to push away harm (*ḍarar*) as much as possible and also to prevent the causing of harm. . . . If two harms (*ḍararān*) compete, it is necessary to bear the lesser of them in order to ward off the greater. And included in this [principle] is the acceptance of the specific harm (*al-ḍarar al-khāṣṣ*) in order to repel the general harm (*al-ḍarar al-ʿāmm*).[42]

---

[39] Case No. 8, Judicial Year 17 (May 18, 1996), 1036.

[40] Ibid.

[41] In fact, it would seem to be a bit more complex. The Qurʾān explicitly commands people to spend their money in accordance with God's command, without explaining what God's command is.

[42] Case No. 6, Judicial Year 9 (March 18, 1995), *SCC*, VI, 542–66 at 561.

In determining whether a law advances the goals of the law, the Court must make judgments that seem inescapably subjective. First, identifying the specific goals of the law in a particular area seems more an art than a science. As for determining whether a law serves the general goals of the *sharīʿa*, this seems, ultimately, to be an exercise in utilitarian balancing. The indeterminate nature of the "goals" analysis means that the question of whether a law serves the goals of the *sharīʿa* can rest on a vague and potentially subjective determination. Thus, reasonable people might disagree about whether a particular law is consistent with the goals of the *sharīʿa* and is constitutional.

It would be plausible for the Court to hold that it should give some deference to the political branches when it comes to determinations about the impact that a law will have on society. It is unclear, however, what level of deference, if any, the Court is giving to the political branches. The Court has never, to date, explicitly suggested that it has any obligation to defer to the executive branch's judgment about whether a law will be beneficial or harmful. Furthermore, the Court has actually exercised review in an aggressive fashion. In the six substantive Article 2 cases decided prior to 1993, the SCC determined that half of the laws it reviewed were inconsistent with the principles of Article 2. After 1993, the Court has continued, occasionally, to find laws inconsistent with the principles of the *sharīʿa* and, thus, unconstitutional.[43]

Because the SCC's theory allows it to make judgments in part upon subjective value judgments and does not require the Court to defer to executive or legislative judgment, the SCC can interpret Islamic law in a way that is consistent with, and even reinforces, its liberal jurisprudence in the area of property rights and international human rights.

[43] In some of these cases, the SCC struck down the law on Article 2 grounds. See, e.g., Case No. 6, Judicial Year 9 (March 18, 1995) discussed above. In others, however, the law in question had been enacted prior to 1980 and thus not subject to Article 2 review. In striking down the law on other grounds, the SCC found that it was inconsistent with principles of the *sharīʿa*. This suggests that the law would be unconstitutional under Article 2 as well. See, e.g., Case No. 23, Judicial Year 16 (March 18, 1995), *SCC*, vol. VI, 567–96; Case No. 31, Judicial Year 16 (May 20, 1995), *SCC*, vol. VI, 716–39; Case No. 25, Judicial Year 16 (July 3, 1995), *SCC*, vol. VII, 45–94.

III. *Conclusion*

The SCC's Article 2 opinions issued prior to 1993 do not parse the words of Article 2 or systematically articulate a complete theory about the interpretation of the *sharīʿa* or about the qualities that a piece of legislation must have to be considered "Islamic." However, they suggest certain implicit conclusions about Islamic legal interpretation. The SCC's opinions from 1993 onwards articulate a more systematic theory of Islamic law and legal interpretation. In elaborating the criteria that a law must meet to be considered consistent with the "principles of the Islamic *sharīʿa*," the Court rhetorically pays homage to a range of theories dealing with the question of how to interpret the *sharīʿa* and draft Islamic legislation: neo-traditional theories; theories proposing that Islamic legislation be drafted using utilitarian neo-*ijtihād*; and those that suggest that it should be drafted using comparative neo-*taqlīd*. The Court combines the disparate elements in a novel fashion. When it comes to "the principles of the Islamic *sharīʿa*" that the Egyptian state must respect, there are, apparently two separate types of norm: *sharīʿa* rulings and goals of the *sharīʿa*. The rulings are identified through a method that fuses Riḍā's method of identifying absolutely certain norms of Islamic law with the very different method championed by al-Sanhūrī and the champions of comparative neo-*taqlīd*. The Court's criteria for finding absolutely certain rulings of the *sharīʿa* are extremely strict, and the Court has found few of them. When determining whether a law is consistent with the goals of the *sharīʿa*, the Court apparently looks to see whether the law serves the specific goals of the *sharīʿa*—meaning the results that a particular type of law is supposed to serve; and the general goals—meaning, for all practical purposes, the general welfare. The Court's analysis of the specific goals begins with an analysis of revealed texts (whether absolutely certain or merely probable) and of the classical jurists' interpretation of these texts. The analysis of texts is impressionistic, but whenever a comparative survey of the classical juristic literature reveals an overwhelming consensus on what results a certain type of law should promote, then the Court tends to accept that as the specific goals for that type of law. Usually, the Court will assume that a law advancing the appropriate, specific goals of the *sharīʿa* will also promote the public interest (and thus promote the general goals). If it is unclear, however, what the specific goals are, or whether the law advances them, then the Court seems to ask what rule would advance the general welfare. Furthermore, in some cases, there may be a case analogous to the classical situation of "necessity" in which the general social harm caused by the application of a law is so obvious and so grievous that God could not possibly approve. It is important always to bear in mind the importance of the general goals in the Court's scheme, and to note as well the way in which the theory permits (and perhaps requires) the justices to interpret the general goals in light of their existing normative assumptions. Goals analysis as the court performs it seems rationalist in outlook. It turns out to be the mechanism by which the Court harmonizes its interpretation of Islamic law with its liberal economic and human rights jurisprudence.

In the next chapter, I will examine five important cases in which the SCC has applied its theory between 1993 and 1996. We will see how the Court's theory of Islamic legal interpretation has been applied in a manner that reinforces the Court's liberal constitutional values and the liberal jurisprudence that it has already established to date in the areas of economic rights and human rights.

CHAPTER ELEVEN

THE SCC'S ARTICLE 2 JURISPRUDENCE AS APPLIED: CASE STUDIES

Since 1993, the SCC has incrementally developed a theory of Islamic law and a distinctive method of Islamic legal interpretation. Its theory, which combines elements of several modernist theories, permits the Court to uphold or strike down legislation based in large part upon extra-textual judgments about the utility of the law in question. The Court has explicitly set forth some elements of its interpretive method, but it has not made clear all the steps in its method of Islamic legal interpretation. Furthermore, there are lingering ambiguities about the way that the Court will carry out the steps that it has articulated thus far. In other words, the Court has formally described (and has thus bound other courts to follow) a general approach to Islamic legal interpretation, but has left later courts free to elaborate more fully some of the steps and thus to shape, in significant ways, the official judicial method of interpreting the *sharīʿa*. The last chapter also suggested that there are telling patterns in the Court's application of its theory. Based on these patterns, it seems the justices on the Court have a preferred, if unstated, approach to Islamic legal interpretation.

This chapter will provide close readings of five Article 2 cases that the SCC decided between 1993 and 1997, and a summary of some non-Article 2 cases. The Article 2 cases illustrate the Court's theory in action (as well as the lingering ambiguities in its preferred approach). They also show the interpretive choices that the Court makes in its opinions, and the assumptions that seem to inform the justices' utilitarian conclusions. They also make clear that the Court's theory as applied to date allows the Court to maintain and even reinforce its progressive interpretation of the Egyptian Constitution. The non-Article 2 cases are intriguing because they show how the court's Article 2 jurisprudence is being integrated with other areas of the Court's jurisprudence. In the next chapter, we will see how academics and lower courts have reacted to the SCC's evolving Article 2 jurisprudence.

I. *Five Article 2 cases*

A. *Case No. 7 of Judicial Year 8, decided on May 15, 1993*[1]

Case No. 7 of Judicial Year 8 (decided on May 15, 1993) arose in the aftermath of a divorce in which there were children. In setting the terms of the divorce, the judge who supervised the divorce was required to look to the provisions of Personal Status Law 25 of 1929, as amended by Law 100 of 1985.[2] Article 20 of Personal Status Law 25 granted special child custody rights to women who had been divorced by their husbands without cause (in other words, when the woman was not at fault). Article 18 of Personal Status Law Number 25 permitted a judge to order a man to pay his divorced wife a sum of money analogous to an alimony payment—a payment that it characterized as "*mutʿa*." Applying these provisions, the judge awarded the divorced mother permanent custody of the children of the marriage, and he ordered the husband to pay his ex-wife a *mutʿa* payment. Upset by the terms of the divorce, the father challenged Articles 20 and 18 as unconstitutional—arguing that they were inconsistent with Islamic law and thus impermissible under Article 2. The claim was referred to the SCC.

This was the first case in which the SCC had to decide a constitutional challenge that involved a challenge under Article 2 alone, rather than Article 2 and other provisions of the Constitution as well. The SCC resolved the case in a long opinion, in which it addressed each of the two challenges separately.[3]

---

[1] Case No. 7, Judicial Year 8 (May 15, 1993), printed in *SCC*, vol. V, part 2, 265–90. My copy of this case was kindly provided to me by justice Adel Omar Sherif of the SCC. Nathalie Bernard Maugiron has written about this case using a text that has a different pagination. I have not been able to explain the discrepancy. See Nathalie Bernard Maugiron, "La Haute Cour Constitutionelle Égyptienne et la sharîʿa islamique," *Awrâq* (Madrid) 19 (1998): 653–80.

[2] Law 100 of 1985 was a revised version of "Jihān's Law," discussed earlier in Chapter 9.

[3] A third claim was dismissed on procedural grounds.

Issue No. 1: Was a law inconsistent with the principles of the sharīʿa *if it permitted a judge to permanently award custody of a non-infant child to the mother?*

1. *Background*

The Qur'ān and the *ḥadīth* literature do not clearly establish detailed rules for custody of children after a divorce. The classical jurists in all of the four Sunnī guilds of law generally agreed, first, that there was a period during which the child needed the nurturing that only a mother could give, and, second, that older children generally needed the strict moral guidance that only a father (and his family) could provide. Accordingly, the jurists distinguished between two types of custody: custody of an infant who needs a mother's care (*ḥaḍāna*); and the guardianship of education (*wilāyat al-tarbiyya*), when the father's family would generally take custody and supervise the education of the child. The jurists of the traditional guilds disagreed, however, about the age at which *ḥaḍāna* ended and *wilāyat al-tarbiyya* began.[4] In broad strokes, the doctrines of the guilds went as follows. The jurists of the Ḥanafī guild generally held that *ḥaḍāna* of a son lasts until the son reaches the age of discretion (which most scholars believed was reached at the age of seven or nine) and of a daughter who reaches the age of pre-puberty (which most jurists said was nine).[5] The Shāfiʿī and Ḥanbalī guilds, on the other hand, came to hold that a woman must be given custody of children of either sex until the age of seven, at which point the child could choose which parent it wished to have as a custodian.[6] The Mālikīs, on the other

[4] For a detailed analysis of the classical jurist's understanding of the different needs of children at different ages and the different types of custody that was appropriate for children at these ages, see Yves Linant de Bellefonds, *Traité de Droit Musulman Comparé* (Paris: Mouton, 1973), vol. III, 139–248. See particularly 150–84. The discussion of classical doctrines will be based on this as well as the other sources cited below.

[5] See Yves Linant de Bellefonds, "Ḥaḍāna," in EI2, vol. III, 16–17; see also Joseph Schacht, *An Introduction to Islamic Law* (Oxford: Oxford University Press, 1964), 167; Jamal J. Nasir, *The Status of Women under Islamic Law* (London: Graham & Trotman, 1990), 135.

[6] For the Shāfiʿī position, see Linant de Bellefonds, "Ḥaḍāna," citing Shīrāzī, *Muhadhdhab* (Cairo: n.d.), 2.169ff. For the Ḥanafī position see *id.* citing Ibn Qudāma, *al-Mughnī*, 3rd ed. (Cairo: 1367 A.H.), 7.612ff.

hand, said that a divorced mother had the right to keep custody of a son until he reached puberty and of a daughter until she consummated her marriage.[7]

In pre-modern Egypt, the courts applied an un-codified version of Islamic law (the *qāḍī*'s *fiqh*), and, when seeking *fiqh* rulings, parties before the court were allowed to decide for themselves which guild's interpretation of Islamic law should apply to their case. The 1929 Code of Personal Status changed Egyptian law by requiring courts to apply the Ḥanafī rules in most areas of family law.[8] Accordingly, the 1929 Egyptian Code of Personal Status in its original form followed the Ḥanafī rule and allowed the judge, if "the interest of the child requires it," to extend the mother's custody (*ḥaḍāna*) over her son until he was ten and her daughter until she was twelve, at which point the period of *wilāyat al-tarbiyya* began and custody automatically reverted to the father.[9]

Ḥanafī rules of custody proved to be inconsistent with the values of colonial powers and with many of the emerging elites in the post-colonial Muslim Mediterranean. Over the course of the twentieth century, many Arab nations promulgated personal status law that abandoned the Ḥanafī rules of custody in favor of Mālikī rules, which gave judges discretion to extend a mother's period of custody past the ages of 10 or 12. In Egypt, the 1979 amendments to personal status law ("Jihān's law") took a step towards adoption of the Mālikī rule. Although Jihān's law was struck down on the ground that it had been enacted through an unconstitutional process, the government re-enacted the custody provisions as part of Law 100 of 1985.

---

[7] For the Mālikī position, see Linant de Bellefond, "Haḍāna," citing Ḥaṭṭāb, *Mawāhib al-Jalīl* (1929), 214ff.; Dardīr Daṣqī, *Sharḥ al-Kabīr*, II, 526ff.

[8] Prior to the Ottoman conquest of the southern Mediterranean, the rulers in this area had not followed the doctrine of the Ḥanafī guild. Even after the conquest, many Muslims in the Southern Mediterranean did not, when they had a choice, follow the doctrines of the Ḥanafī guild. As discussed in Chapter 4, however, the Egyptian government decided in the early twentieth century to codify many aspects of Egyptian personal status law. Because the elites throughout the Ottoman Empire had traditionally followed Ḥanafī doctrine, the Egyptian government decided to base most rules in the 1929 Code on Ḥanafī doctrines, and thereafter, these applied to all Egyptian citizens, even if their family had traditionally followed the doctrine of some other Sunnī guild of law.

[9] Egyptian Code of Personal Status (March 10, 1929), Article 20.

After 1985, Article 20 of Egypt's personal status law provided that a divorced woman automatically received custody of her male children of her marriage up to the age of ten and custody of her female children up to the age of twelve. If the judge believed it was in the best interest of a son, he or she could extend the mother's right of custody over that son until he reached the age of fifteen.[10] If the judge thought it was in the best interests of a daughter, he could extend the mother's custody of that daughter up to the consummation of her marriage and at the judge's discretion, the mother could be awarded child support.[11]

In Case No. 7, the appellant father argued that from 1929 until 1979, Egyptian personal status law had followed Ḥanafī doctrine. Accordingly, he argued, when the Egyptian legislature drafted Article 2 to require Egyptian law to conform to the principles of the *sharīʿa*, it must have intended that Egyptian law conform to the traditional Ḥanafī interpretation of the *sharīʿa*.[12] Because the personal status law, as amended, was inconsistent with Ḥanafī law, the father argued, the new provisions should be deemed void, and the Egyptian courts should apply the rule that would have applied if the amendment had never been enacted.

The SCC rejected the father's initial contention that Article 2 required Egyptian legislation to be consistent with Ḥanafī interpretations of Islamic law. Going further, it declared that modern Muslims were not bound by the classical juristic tradition. Accordingly, under certain circumstances, Islamic law permitted rulers to promulgate laws that were inconsistent with rulings accepted by all Sunnī jurists of the past.

---

[10] A divorced woman would have no right to child support for a son older than ten.

[11] Case No. 7, Judicial Year 8 (May 15, 1993), 285. For a discussion of these provisions of the law, see Fauzi M. Najjar, "Egypt's Laws of Personal Status," *Arab Law Quarterly* 10 (1988): 334–35.

[12] The father asked for custody to be granted by the ages given in the 1929 Code. Apparently, he did not ask for the even younger ages given by the Ḥanafī guild because he could not challenge the 1929 Code under Article 2, given that the personal status law of 1929 had been enacted before 1985 and was therefore not subject to challenge under Article 2 according to the SCC's 1985 decision. He could, however, challenge the law that extended further the period of *ḥaḍāna*.

At the broadest level, the Court vigorously asserted the modernist position that modern Muslims were not bound by classical interpretations and rejected the neo-traditional idea that contemporary interpretation should be performed by scholars with classical training. As Article 2 was a constitutional provision and as the SCC was the authoritative interpreter of the constitution, Article 2's principles of the *sharīʿa* would be those identified and interpreted by the SCC. Implicitly, the SCC rejected the neo-traditionalists assumption that modern Muslims should defer to the judgment of members of the *ʿulamāʾ*. Rather, the Court held that when applying Article 2, it was free to interpret Islamic law itself using its own modernist method. The method that it used was the pastiche of modernist methods that we described in the previous chapter. Applying that method, the SCC did not find any *sharīʿa* principle precluding judges from granting mothers custody of children past the age that the Ḥanafīs believed *wilāyat al-tarbiyya* began.

2. *The SCC's reasoning*

According to the Court, "the principles of the Islamic *sharīʿa*" include two types: (1) the rulings of the *sharīʿa* which are absolutely certain in their authenticity and meaning (*al-aḥkām al-sharʿiyya al-qaṭʿiyya fī thubūtihā wa-dalālatihā*); and (2) the principles requiring Muslims to act in a way that the SCC, using its own interpretive method, determines to be "goals" (specific or general) of the *sharīʿa*.

a. *Was the law inconsistent with an absolutely certain ruling of the* sharīʿa? The SCC found that there were no absolutely certain rulings establishing an age at which *ḥadhāna* must end and the father must take custody. In explaining its conclusions, the Court began and ended by looking at Qurʾānic texts. (It is not clear whether the Court examined *ḥadīth*s at all, or, if it did, how it evaluated their authenticity.) The Qurʾānic analysis is cursory. Ultimately, the SCC's conclusion that there was no absolutely certain scriptural ruling on point seems to be largely due to the fact that the jurists in the guilds (who presumably understood the scriptures as well as any modern court could) disagreed on when *ḥaḍāna* ended and *wilāyat al-tarbiyya* began.[13] The Court wrote:

[13] Case No. 7, Judicial Year 8 (May 15, 1993), 284. The SCC stressed particularly

> The Islamic *sharīʿa* in its universal principles—those that are absolutely clear (*qaṭʿī*) in their authenticity (*thūbṭihā*) and their meaning (*dalālatihā*)—do not fix a limit beyond which the age of *ḥaḍāna* cannot go.[14]

In the absence of any absolutely certain scriptural commands regarding the age at which custody must transfer, the Court held that the state was free to enact whatever rule would best serve the goals of the *sharīʿa*. The question of Article 20's unconstitutionality thus hinged on the question of whether it harmed people by preventing them from enjoying the "benefits" that God wanted them to realize.

> . . . [And to the extent that the legislature is not bound by any specific absolutely certain rulings its] *ijtihād* must occur within the framework of the Islamic *sharīʿa*'s general roots (*al-uṣūl al-kulliyya*) and [must] not go beyond them—by constructing practical rules by depending on deducing them from the indicators of the *sharīʿa* and intending to realize through them the general goals of the *sharīʿa* (*al-maqāṣid al-ʿāmma li-'l-sharīʿa*), among which are the preservation of religion (*dīn*), self (*nafs*), reason (*ʿaql*), honor (*ʿirḍ*), and money (*māl*).[15]

b. *Did the law impede the goals of the* sharīʿa?

Whenever there are no absolutely certain rulings on point, the SCC asks whether the law contradicts either the "roots" of the *sharīʿa* (which this book has referred to as the "specific goals" of the *sharīʿa*), or the "general goals" of the *sharīʿa*. With respect to the first, the Court assumes that God wants certain types of behavior to promote certain types of social result. Some rulings, therefore, reflect a desire to promote certain specific goals. When trying to establish the constitutionality of a law, the Court must determine what type of behavior is being governed and must ensure that the ruling advances the specific goals that God wants this type of behavior to promote.

> It is for the holder of power (*walī al-amr*) to perform *ijtihād* in the rulings that are probable (*ẓannī*), taking under consideration the true interest whose proof arises from Islamic legal (*sharʿī*) indicators.[16]

---

that among the divergent opinions on this question were the opinions of the Mālikī jurists who followed a rule very similar to the one adopted by Law 100. Case No. 7, Judicial Year 8 (May 15, 1993), 285.

[14] Case No. 7, Judicial Year 8 (May 15, 1993), 283–84, 285.

[15] Case No. 7, Judicial Year 8 (May 15, 1993), 283.

[16] Case No. 7, Judicial Year 8 (May 15, 1993), 285.

To determine this, the Court has in later cases examined all rulings that govern behavior in this area—not just the rulings that are absolutely certain with respect to authenticity or meaning, but those that are only probable with respect to authenticity or meaning, and the rulings that great jurists of the past have derived by analogy. It has tried to determine whether these rulings implicitly reveal a common understanding of the goals that God's law tries to achieve in the area of custody. In this case, the Court's analysis, atypically, looked for the "goals" only in the writings of the jurists. It first asked whether, in regulating the transfer of custody from mother to father, the classical jurists were primarily concerned with protecting a particular class of persons.

> Where there is no [Qur'ānic] text that is certain in its meaning and authenticity that determines an age for *ḥaḍāna*, it is not permissible for the holder of power (*walī al-amr*) to overstep them. He (the *walī al-amr*) must derive a rule that protects the broad interests of the parties involved as demanded by the goals of the *sharīʿa*.[17]

This passage raises a number of questions, the first being whose welfare is to be taken into account. In a custody battle, there are competing interests—those of the father, the mother, and the child. A ruling that benefits one person may harm another.[18] The question therefore must be how to balance the harms. Are custody rulings supposed to favor some people's interests over others or should they simply maximize aggregate welfare? The Court here noted that the classical jurists all agreed that a child must first be cared for by its mother and then by its father. Although the SCC did not stress the point, it was probably important that, among the jurists who did not establish a bright line rule for the transfer of custody, it was the child who gets to choose where to stay. The SCC concluded that the "goal" of the rules of custody is to serve the interests of the child. Although the principles of the *sharīʿa* do not require the gov-

[17] Case No. 7, Judicial Year 8 (May 15, 1993), 285.

[18] The SCC notes that some of the Muslim jurists have recognized that a father has an interest in custody because it allows him to protect his own bloodline. But even if this is true, the Court notes, the mother also has some other countervailing interest because she is entrusted with part of the custody, and ultimately the child's interest trumps both. See Case No. 7, Judicial Year 8 (May 15, 1993), 284.

ernment (the *walī al-amr*) or legislator (*musharriʿ*) to adopt any particular rule for the age of custody transfer, they do require the government to come up with a rule that will provide justice for the child and will maximize its welfare.[19]

> The *walī al-amr* must weigh what he sees as best and most beneficial for the little boy, taking into consideration [the fact that] his right to *ḥaḍāna* [i.e., to be cared for by a female custodian] is not considered to depend upon the request of the female custodian from whom he has the right to demand *ḥaḍāna*. . . . [A]nd the jurists indicated through their disagreement on the period of custody that the interest of the child sets the boundaries for the legal rulings [regarding the period in which a mother should have custody] and indicates that these legal rulings are one of the *ijtihādī* questions where views differ. Then, in each view, we must consider what is seen as most beneficial to determine what is most beneficial, each one [i.e., each practitioner of *ijtihād*] utilizing his own view to determine what is most likely to benefit the young child within the limits set by rights and justice.[20]

But how should humans define "welfare"? While the SCC did not in this case say explicitly how to do so, it implicitly seemed to assume that a person's "welfare" should be understood as the enjoyment by that person of the results God wants to promote more generally in society as a whole. Such results are axiomatically just and should be considered to be beneficial for humans; they include the promotion of religion, life, reason, property, and honor. In the passage already cited above, the Court explained that it would, to the extent possible, fill in the gaps in its understanding by "intending to realize through them the general goals of the *sharīʿa* (*al-maqāṣid al-ʿāmma li-'l-sharīʿa*), among which are the preservation of religion (*dīn*), self (*nafs*), reason (*ʿaql*), honor (*ʿirḍ*), and money (*māl*)."[21] Without any serious discussion, the Court concluded that the law served the interests of the child and thus advanced the specific goals that the custody rulings of the *sharīʿa* were created to achieve.

For reasons that are not entirely clear, there was no explicit discussion of the impact that the legislative provisions under attack would have on the general goals of the *sharīʿa*. Nevertheless, the

[19] Case No. 7, Judicial Year 8 (May 15, 1993), 284–85.
[20] Case No. 7, Judicial Year 8 (May 15, 1993), 285.
[21] Case No. 7, Judicial Year 8 (May 15, 1993), 283.

Court concluded broadly that the Egyptian rules governing the age of custody transfer were consistent with the goals of the *sharīʿa.*

Issue No. 2: Was the law inconsistent with the principles of the sharīʿa *if it permitted a judge to order a husband to provide compensation to his divorced wife?*

The husband challenging Personal Status Law 25 was aggrieved not only by the possibility that his wife might get extended custody of his child, but also by the possibility that he might have to pay her monetary compensation (*mutʿa*). The Court found that Egyptian law did not violate the principles of the *sharīʿa* when it permitted the judge to order such compensation. To understand the father's argument and the Court's reasoning, it is helpful to consider the evolution of Islamic legal thinking with respect to compensating divorced wives.

1. *Background*

The Qurʾān explicitly requires each man at marriage to provide his wife with a dowry (*mahr*) that is hers to control.[22] Jurists later concluded that the amount should be negotiated between the groom (or his guardians) and the woman (or her guardians). The groom may be required to deliver the entire dowry before the marriage, at which point it becomes hers to control, or he may simply enter into a contractual arrangement that obligates him to transfer a fraction of it, with the remainder due if and when he divorces her.[23] The institution of the dowry provides, in a sense, a safety net for the woman in case of divorce.

In Qurʾān 2:236 and 23:6, God commands men to pay their divorced wives some kind of consolatory gift or compensation (*mutʿa*), but does not specify exactly the nature or amount of this compen-

[22] See, e.g., Qurʾān 14:4. Traditionally, Muslim jurists believed that a number of other verses referred to the dower as well. See, e.g., Qurʾān 33:50; Qurʾān 2:236.

[23] Otto Spies, "Mahr" in EI2, vol. VI, 78. For a comprehensive survey of the rules governing the dowry in classical Islamic law, see De Bellefonds, *Traité*, III. 193–250.

sation.[24] Jurists had to decide whether this verse simply reiterates that men should ensure that their wives leave the marriage with their dowry (and, if necessary, with any outstanding balance on the dowry), or whether it instead requires men to make a separate payment to supplement whatever was promised in the dowry. Almost all the jurists in the traditional Sunnī guilds ultimately concluded that this *mutʿa* passage does not oblige a man to pay anything over and above the dowry.[25] It was reported that al-Shāfiʿī had held that a man can be required to pay a woman whom he divorces without fault some kind of additional *mutʿa* compensation.[26] As their master's position was equivocal, however, and as all other guilds were unanimously opposed to the institution of *mutʿa* compensation, later jurists in the Shāfiʿī guild concluded that al-Shāfiʿī had meant in the first case to refer only to a woman who had not received a dowry and whose marriage had not been consummated. Thus, they agreed that a man who has consummated his marriage is not legally obliged to pay his divorced wife *mutʿa* compensation in addition to the dowry.[27]

Following the unanimous doctrine of the four traditional guilds, Article 18 of the 1925 Personal Status Law initially precluded courts from ordering a man to pay his divorced wife *mutʿa* over and above the dowry if her marriage had been consummated. Over the course of the twentieth century, however, modernist Islamic legal thinkers rethought the classical position and came up with arguments in favor

---

[24] See, e.g., Qur'ān 33:6 and 2:236.

[25] For the ambiguities surrounding the husband's financial obligation to a divorced wife, see, e.g., Noel Coulson, *A History of Islamic Law* (Edinburgh: University of Edinburgh Press, 1964), 31–32. Note, however, the term "*mutʿa*" came to have very negative connotations in the Sunnī world. It was used to denote a "temporary marriage," a contractual arrangement, highly disfavored in the Sunnī guilds, in which a man "marries" a woman for a fixed period—perhaps an hour, perhaps a month—and pays her *mutʿa* on the completion of the term. This form of marriage, which seemed to allow for prostitution, was permitted only among the Shīʿa sect. See W. Heffening, "Mutʿa" in EI2, vol. VII, 759.

[26] It is also reported, however, that al-Shāfiʿī at another time stated that a man is not legally obliged to pay extra compensation to a woman divorced without fault, although it is morally praiseworthy for him to do so.

[27] See, e.g., the doctrine as summarized in Aḥmad ibn al-Naqīb al-Miṣrī, *ʿUmdat al-Sālik wa-ʿUddat al-Nāsik* (with commentary), ed. Noah Ha Mim Keller, printed in Arabic with facing translation as *The Reliance of the Traveler: A Classic Manual of Islamic Sacred Law* rev. ed. (Evanston, Illinois: Sunna Books, 1994), 536; There *mutʿa* is clearly considered to be a substitute when a husband has not provided a dowry or consummated the marriage.

of it. Accordingly, when the Egyptian government in the 1970s first proposed revising the personal status law to include *mutʿa* provisions, the government's official advisor on questions of Islamic law—the Chief *Muftī* of Egypt, Jādd al-Ḥaqq—justified the new provisions as "Islamic" through what seemed to be an exercise of utilitarian neo-*ijtihād*. According to Jādd al-Ḥaqq, the provision did not violate any clear Qurʾānic passage or any clear and unimpeachably authentic *ḥadīth*. In fact, it powerfully served the public interest because it put impediments in the way of hasty divorces and because it would prevent some divorced women from falling into poverty and perhaps prostitution.[28]

The husband's challenge to the *mutʿa* provisions of Law 100 relied on an argument similar to the one he had made when he challenged the custody provisions. By requiring Egyptian law to be consistent with the principles of the *sharīʿa*, Article 2 required Egyptian laws to conform to the doctrines of the Ḥanafī guild, which would not require him, under these circumstances, to pay *mutʿa*.[29] The SCC had already rejected the claim that Article 2 required Egyptian law to conform to Ḥanafī law, and it used its own modernist method of interpretation to determine whether the Egyptian laws permitting the judge to order *mutʿa* violated a principle of the Islamic *sharīʿa*. The justices concluded that it did not.

[28] Najjar, "Egypt's Laws of Personal Status," 332 (citing Jādd al-Ḥaqq). Note also that those who favored some form of neo-*taqlīd* could also make an argument for *mutʿa*. As the SCC notes, the Ẓāhirī guild required men to pay *mutʿa* compensation to their divorced wives. This comment betrays a modernist impulse in the Court's jurisprudence. Traditional jurists would not consider Ẓāhirī doctrine to be authoritative, because this guild came to be considered to be unorthodox in the fourteenth century. Yet some modernist jurists who tried to rehabilitate the Ẓāhirīs argued that their anathematization had been unfair and was due to jealousy rather than real dispute over the orthodoxy of the Ẓāhirīs' legal methodology. In fact, both Riḍā and Sanhūrī put the opinions of the Ẓāhirī jurists on par with the opinions of the jurists who belonged to one of the four traditional guilds.

[29] The plaintiff admitted that Islamic law requires a man to maintain his divorced wife after a three-month waiting period that immediately follows a divorce. He insisted, however, that it precludes judges from ordering any further compensation unless three conditions were met: 1) the marriage was not consummated; 2) there was no dowry fixed in her marriage contract; 3) he was never alone with her before the divorce (essentially the same as the first condition). Since his marriage had been consummated, the plaintiff argued, Islamic law bars a judge from ordering him to support his wife after the three-month waiting period. By this reading, Article 18 of Law 25, as amended in 1985, was unconstitutional and the courts should apply the provisions of Law 25 as it was applied prior to the 1985 amendment.

2. *The SCC's reasoning*

a. *Was the law inconsistent with an absolutely certain ruling of the* sharīʿa? To determine the constitutionality of Article 18 of Law 25, as amended in 1985, the SCC first asked whether the legal provisions of Law 100 governing compensation are inconsistent with any absolutely certain rulings of the *sharīʿa.* When looking for these rulings, the Court discussed Qurʾānic passages alone, and did not mention any passages from the *ḥadīth* literature. More strikingly, it made statements that could be interpreted to imply that, to its mind, Qurʾānic passages are the only scriptural passages that can be considered absolutely certain with respect to authenticity.[30] Ultimately, the Court identified three Qurʾānic verses that it found relevant to the question of compensation for a divorced woman. The first of these verses, Qurʾān 2:241, discusses the question of compensation for a divorced woman at a very general level: "for divorced women a provision [*mutʿa*] with kindness, [this is] an obligation on the God-fearing."[31] Qurʾān 2:236, states that men who marry women without promising any particular dowry, and then divorce them without consummating the marriage, must "make provision for them [the divorced wives], the affluent man according to his means, and according to his means the needy man—[This is] an obligation on those who [would] do good."[32] Finally, when the Prophet was considering divorcing some of his disgruntled wives, God told him, "Oh Prophet, say to your wives 'If you desire the present life and its adornment, come now! I will make you a provision and set you free with kindness'" (Qurʾān 33:29).

[30] In searching for absolutely certain legal rulings, it says, it was looking for rulings "rooted in principles laid down in Qurʾānic *nuṣūṣ*." Case No. 7, Judicial Year 8 (May 15, 1993), 287. It is unclear whether the Court means to suggest by this that absolutely certain legal rulings can never be found in the *ḥadīth* literature or whether it is merely asserting that in this case there are no relevant legal rulings in the *ḥadīth* literature.

[31] Cited in Case No. 7, Judicial Year 8 (May 15, 1993), 287. All English translations are based on the translation of A.J. Arberry, *The Koran Interpreted* (New York: Macmillan, 1955). I have checked the translations against the Arabic as printed in *The Glorious Qurʾān*, ed. and trans. Marmaduke Pickthall (1930; repr. Istanbul: Cihan Matbaasi, 1996). (Here, the translation is slightly modified by me.) All further references to translations from the Qurʾān will be from Arberry except as specifically noted.

[32] Arabic cited in Case No. 7, Judicial Year 8 (May 15, 1993), 287, 288.

Classical jurists did not consider this last verse to be a verse of general application. Rather, they considered it a verse creating a ruling to solve a problem unique to the Prophet.[33] It is unclear why the Court rejected the traditional, narrow interpretation and instead reads it as a verse of general application.

As the SCC pointed out, these Qur'ānic texts seem to require a man to pay his wife some sort of compensation but do not indicate whether a man satisfies this requirement by handing over the remaining portion (if any) of the dowry. Because these verses, taken together, were ambiguous, the Court found that there was no absolutely certain ruling precluding the state from requiring some compensation in addition to the dowry. Such a conclusion was confirmed, the SCC said, by the fact that the classical jurists disagreed about whether a man should be required to supplement his divorced wife's dowry with something extra. (It asserted that Shāfiʿī's doctrine was unclear on this question and that all the members of the Ẓāhirī guild agreed that it was required.)[34]

Where there is no absolutely certain ruling of the *sharīʿa* precisely on point, the *walī al-amr* is free to develop whatever rule he thinks best. In so doing, his discretion is limited only by the requirement that his law must not violate any constitutional provisions (including the human rights provisions) and not impede the realization of the goals of the *sharīʿa*.

> And whereas: It is clear from examining the doctrines of the jurists regarding the meaning of the Qur'ānic texts (*dalālat al-nuṣūṣ al-Qur'āniyya*) which have come to us in the matter of *mutʿa* that they differ on the scope of their application and on whether it [the giving of *mutʿa*] is, on the one hand, obligatory or, on the other hand, meritorious [but not required]. And this only means that since these texts are probable in meaning, they are unclear about the desire of God, may He be exalted. And thus the *walī al-amr* is permitted to practice *ijtihād* so as to develop a legislation (*naṣṣ al-tashrīʿī*) and to organize [the *sharīʿa*'s]

[33] The SCC's use of this verse is surprising, because authoritative *ḥadīth* traditions make clear that this passage gave instructions designed to tell the Prophet how to deal with a unique problem that had arisen among his wives. Thus, traditionally, this passage would not be considered a guide for Muslims in their dealings with their own wives. The SCC does not discuss this point and treats the *ḥadīth* as a source of general guidance. See Barbara Freyer Stowasser, *Women in the Qur'ān, Traditions, and Interpretation* (New York: Oxford University Press, 1994), 95–97.

[34] See Case No. 7, Judicial Year 8 (May 15, 1993), 287–88.

> rules by establishing the essence of the right (*aṣl al-ḥaqq*) in them. He [the *walī al-amr*] explicates its demand and unifies its application. He [the *walī al-amr*] establishes its edifice on a conception of equality with a view to removing all aspects of difference in it, and does not contradict the roots of the *sharīʿa*, or any of its principles.[35] . . . There is nothing in the Qurʾānic texts informing us that God, may he be exalted, decreed it [a particular type or amount of *mutʿa*] or set limits on it, inasmuch as they signify permission to organize it [the *mutʿa*] so that he[36] realizes for the people, their benefits [that are] stipulated by the *sharīʿa*. (*maṣāliḥahum al-muʿtabira sharʿan*).[37]

b. *Did the law impede the goals of the* sharīʿa?

To determine whether the law under attack violated the goals of the *sharīʿa*, the SCC first looked to the verse requiring men to compensate their divorced wives "with kindness." According to the Court, this verse establishes a specific goal for men in their dealings with their wives (or ex-wives)—namely, that men must act in a manner that benefits their divorced wives. "[B]eing compassionate to [the divorced wife] is part of the generosity (*murūʾa*) which is demanded by the Islamic *sharīʿa*."[38] As a result, legislation regulating men's behavior towards their divorced wives must advance the welfare of the wife. According to the Court, the legislation under review was consistent with this specific goal of the *sharīʿa*. Having determined this, the Court asked whether the law in question impeded the general goal of promoting general social welfare. In a quick, conclusory sentence, the Court concluded that the law did not impede them because it instructed the judge to determine the amount owed by the father on "an objective basis that does not create friction or hardship."[39] This sort of instruction, by itself, "guarantees more

---

[35] Case No. 7, Judicial Year 8 (May 15, 1993), 287–88.

[36] Gramatically, the "he" here should refer to God. However, the preceding sentences are focused on the jurists' elaboration through *ijtihād* of *fiqh* rules governing compensation. In context, I believe that the Court meant to say that in the absence of Qurʾānic rules, the *walī al-amr* (rather than God) is given permission to establish whatever rules realize the results that the *sharīʿa* tells humans are beneficial (i.e., the goals of the *sharīʿa*).

[37] The last sentence reads: *Wa-laysa fī al-nuṣūṣ al-Qurʾāniyya mā yufīd anna Allāh taʿāllā qad qadarahā aw ḥaddadahā bimā muʾaddāhu jawāz tanẓīmihā bimā yuḥaqqiq lī ʾl-nās maṣāliḥahum al-muʿtabira sharʿan*. Case No. 7 of Judicial Year 8 (May 15, 1993), 289.

[38] Case No. 7, Judicial Year 8 (May 15, 1993), 288.

[39] Case No. 7, Judicial Year 8 (May 15, 1993), 289.

friendship and allows for the renunciation of cleavages, and establishes human relationships on the basis of rights and justice."[40]

In sum, the SCC concluded the provisions of Law 100 that govern a husband's duty to support his divorced wife do not contradict any legal ruling that is laid down in a clear Qur'ānic text. Moreover, they advance both the specific goals of the *sharī'a* in the area of divorce, and they do not impede the general goals of the *sharī'a*. Accordingly, the SCC cannot strike down the provisions.

C. *Analysis*

This case, the Court's first lengthy Article 2 opinion, is unclear on several important points. The Court did not explain systematically how it went about analyzing scriptural texts and historical patterns of interpretation in order to isolate the absolutely certain rulings. For example, both when it investigated the question of custody transfer and when it investigated the question of support for a divorced wife, the Court failed to discuss any *ḥadīth*s. It was unclear why this should be so. Had the Court found no *ḥadīth*s on point? Had it concluded that all applicable *ḥadīth*s were of dubious authenticity or meaning? Second, it did not explain what tools it used to analyze the Qur'ān—an omission that was notable because its interpretation of some verses, while plausible from a "plain meaning" standpoint, departed from the interpretations of many classical jurists.[41] Third, the SCC claimed that the classical Sunnī tradition actually supported its reading of the texts, but it was unclear whether it had a systematic method of analyzing the tradition.[42] In searching for the absolutely certain rul-

---

[40] Case No. 7, Judicial Year 8 (May 15, 1993), 289.

[41] As noted above, in its discussion of a man's duty to his wives, the Court cited a verse that the classical jurists had interpreted to deal specifically with the Prophet's conduct, and it does not explain why it, in contrast, considers it to be a verse of general application.

[42] For example, the Court did not explain which texts it would consult in order to determine the doctrine of the Shāfi'ī guild. The analysis seemed, in places, somewhat self-serving. To bolster its claim that there is disagreement about whether a man might have to pay *mut'a*, the SCC points to a ruling that was attributed to Shāfi'ī, but was rejected by the majority of the Shāf'ī jurists as a statement of their master's position. Furthermore, it cited here the doctrines of the Ẓāhirī guild, a guild which died out early in Islamic history. Many modernists, to the extent that they look to the doctrines of classical jurists at all, consider the doctrines of the Ẓāhirī guild probative. Nevertheless, the SCC did not cite this guild in disposing

ings, the Court seemed to apply rigorous methods of textual criticism and exegesis, with the result that the Court did not, predictably, find any such rulings. The details of its methodology, however, were not clear.

As for its analysis of the goals of the *sharīʿa*, the SCC looked for clues to the "specific goals" in both the absolutely certain rulings of the *sharīʿa*, and in rulings that were less than certain. (These merely "probable" rulings include both ambiguous Qurʾānic passages and the rulings laid down over the years by classical Sunnī jurists.) The SCC determined that the specific goals of the *sharīʿa* are to ensure just treatment that will benefit specific classes of people. In the case of custody, the protected class are custodial children; in the case of *mutʿa*, divorced women. Having reached this conclusion, the Court must move on to a second stage of analysis. To understand whether a contemporary statute actually advances these specific goals, the Court must evaluate the impact of that statute on somebody's "welfare." People can naturally disagree about how to define welfare. To evaluate "welfare," the Court assumes that a person's welfare is to be equated with that person's enjoyment of the "general goals" of the *sharīʿa*. The SCC, however, does not discuss in this case how it identified these goals except to say that they include the preservation of religion (*dīn*), self (*nafs*), reason (*ʿaql*), honor (*ʿirḍ*), and property (*māl*).[43] It does not say how it arrived at these goals. Nor does it say what other general goals there might be. Finally, it does not indicate what method the Court would use to try to determine whether such goals are, in the aggregate, being promoted.

Finally, in analyzing the goals of the *sharīʿa*, the SCC seemed to assume that in most, but possibly not all cases, a statute which serves the specific goals of the *sharīʿa* will also meet the overarching requirement that all statutes advance the aggregate welfare of society by increasing the net enjoyment of general goals. Thus, after stating

---

of the custody issue and rarely cites it in later opinions. Why the doctrines of this guild are particularly relevant here (other than because they support the SCC's conclusion) is unclear.

[43] These five goals themselves raise some questions, because they echo, but are not exactly the same as, the five goals that Ghazālī and the majority of classical jurists recognized as "necessary" goals. The SCC departs from almost all the classical jurists in removing from the list the promotion of "progeny." See the discussion in Chapter 2.

that the Egyptian statutes requiring payment for divorced wives serve the specific goals of the *sharīʿa*, the Court asserts also that it establishes "rights and justice." It is not clear from the Court's discussion whether it believes laws that advance the appropriate specific goals should be assumed always to advance the general goals of the *sharīʿa* as well. The Court's next opinion did little to resolve these questions.

B. *Case No. 29 of Judicial Year 11, decided on March 26, 1994*[44]

In 1994, the SCC decided a second case involving an Article 2 challenge to Personal Status Law of 1929 as amended by Law 100 of 1985—the revised and re-enacted version of "Jihān's Law." As seen in the previous case summary, after a divorce, a mother was automatically given custody of infants. Case No. 29 of Judicial Year 11 (decided on March 26, 1994) arose out of a dispute over child support payments that a father was ordered to pay retroactively during the period that his infants resided with their mother.

Under the Personal Status Law of 1929, as initially enacted, a divorce could be finalized quickly and child custody quickly granted, but the law failed explicitly to address whether the father's obligation to pay child support began when the divorce was finalized or when a judge determined the amount of support that should be paid and issued an order to the father to commence payment.[45] Where the law was not clear, however, judges were supposed to follow the rules of the Ḥanafī guild of jurists, which had held that a father's obligation to pay child support began only when the judge issued an order determining the amount of the obligation, and this was the rule that judges applied. Thus, if a father could delay judicial proceedings, he could avoid for a considerable period the obligation to pay child support. On the other hand, Article 18, Section 4 of Law

---

[44] Printed in *SCC*, vol. VI, 231–56. For another analysis and a translation of this case into French, see Baudouin Dupret, "A propos de la constitutionalité de la Shariʿa," *Islamic Law and Society* 4 (1997), 91–113.

[45] In contrast, the Egyptian Personal Status Law of 1929 was clear about the rule that applied when a husband was in arrears on the maintenance due to his current wife. In this area, the law departed from Ḥanafī doctrine and stated that a husband's obligation to pay his wife maintenance existed even in the absence of a judicial order and thus became a debt upon the non-paying husband. See the discussion on this point in Aharon Layyish and Ron Shaham, "Nikāḥ: (II) In the Modern Islamic World: (1) The Arab, Persian and Turkish Lands of the Middle East" in EI2, vol. VIII, 31.

100 of 1985 required judges to depart from this practice and stated that a father had the duty to pay child support from the moment that a divorced mother took custody of children. If a father had been paying his wife less than the monthly sum that the judge declared to be appropriate, he would immediately have to make up the shortfall to the mother.[46]

The plaintiff in Case No. 29 was a father who had divorced his wife. The couple had had a child. Following the divorce, the mother retained custody of this child and supported the child until the child reached adulthood. For a period, she was not able to receive a court order requiring the father to pay her for the cost of supporting her child. When she finally did, the Court ordered the father to reimburse the mother for expenses previously incurred. The father refused to pay, arguing that the principles of Islamic law precluded courts from retroactively ordering a man to maintain his children. The SCC disagreed. To understand the father's argument and the Court's opinion, it is helpful to review some of the Qur'ānic texts dealing with issues related to child support and to consider the classical interpretation of these texts.

1. *Background*

The Qur'ān and *ḥadīth* literature contain a number of passages implying that a father must pay for the support of his children, and the classical jurists took the obligation for granted.[47] At the same time, most of the jurists in the traditional guilds had agreed that, although the moral obligation to provide child support accrues as soon as someone else takes custody of the child, the legal obligation arises only when a judge orders payment. In the fourteenth century, the Shāfiʿī jurist al-Miṣrī unequivocally summarized the preponderant doctrine of his guild as follows: unpaid support "does not become a debt" (*lā tastaqirr fī al-dhimma*).[48] The only exception to this rule

---

[46] A mother who had not sought an order of child support in the past could ask for reimbursement at any time in the future, even after the child was grown. Thus, as this case illustrates, a father could suddenly be faced with an order of retroactive support requiring him to pay very large sums of money.

[47] For an exhaustive survey of the doctrines of the four Sunnī guilds with respect to a father's obligation to provide maintenance to his children, see Linant de Bellefonds, *Traité*, 86–105. The following discussion draws on this work.

[48] See al-Miṣrī, *ʿUmdat al-Sālik*, 549.

occurred when the mother, with the permission of a judge, took out a loan in the father's name to pay for the expenses of raising the child. The jurists of the Ḥanafī guild agreed with the Shafiʿī jurists on these points.[49] The Mālikī jurists, however, took a different position. Khalīl Ibn Isḥāq summarized their position by saying that a judge could order a father to reimburse someone who had supported that child if that person had provided support without intending its support to be considered a gift.[50]

Following the established doctrine of the Ḥanafī guild of jurists—the doctrine that had traditionally been applied in Ottoman Egypt—the father argued that Islamic law recognized only a *moral* obligation to reimburse those who had cared for his child in the past. Because Article 2 prohibited the legislature from adopting a law that was contrary to the principles of the *sharīʿa*, he argued, it could not create a legal obligation to pay retroactive child support. This particular argument did not have much chance of success. The SCC had already rejected in the previous case the idea that, in applying Article 2, it was bound to defer to the Ḥanafī guild's interpretation of the *sharīʿa*. Rather, the SCC had asserted the right, indeed the obligation, to interpret Islamic law itself, using its own modernist approach to legal interpretation. Applying that method, the SCC determined that there was no explicit Qurʾānic ruling (or ruling in an indubitably authentic *ḥadīth*) that barred courts from ordering fathers to pay retroactive child support. Furthermore, it concluded that in the case at bar, such an order was consistent with the goals of the *sharīʿa*. Thus, the legal provision under attack was not inconsistent with any principles of the *sharīʿa*.

2. *The SCC's reasoning*

The SCC began its analysis by sketching again the broad outlines of its interpretation of Article 2:

> And whereas: That which the Constitution states in Article 2 [after its amendment in 1980] is that the principles of the Islamic *sharīʿa* are

---

[49] This, at least, is the undisputed position of the plaintiff in the case.

[50] See Khalīl Ibn Isḥāq, *al-Mukhtaṣar*, trans. G.H. Bousquet as *Abrégé de la loi musulmane selon le rite de l'imâm Mâlik* (Publications de L'Institut d'Études Orientales de la Faculté des Lettres d'Alger 17; Algiers: Éditions Algériennes En-Nahdha, 1956), vol. 2, 74–77.

> the chief source of Egyptian legislation. And this is a limitation which the legislative powers [of the state] must obey in legislation that is promulgated after the [date that] the aforementioned Amendment entered into force—among which are the rules of Law 100 of 1985 amending certain aspects of the laws of personal status. . . . The authority of the Supreme Constitutional Court is limited to supervising the adherence [of Egyptian legislation] to [the principles of the *sharī'a*] and to ensuring that they [these principles] defeat any legal provision that conflicts with them.[51]

The Court then reiterated its basic understanding of Article 2's command. Egyptian legislation must be upheld as consistent with the principles of the *sharī'a* so long as it meets two criteria: (1) it must not conflict with any absolutely certain rulings of the *sharī'a*; (2) it must serve the goals of the *sharī'a*. The SCC concluded that the statute in question did not violate either of these requirements.

a. *Was the law inconsistent with an absolutely certain ruling of the* sharī'a? The absolutely certain rulings are those laid down in an unambiguous Qur'ānic text or an unambiguous and authoritative *ḥadīth*:

> A legislative text is thus not permitted to contradict the Islamic legal rulings that are clear in their authenticity and their meaning (*al-aḥkām al-shar'iyya al-qaṭ'iyya fī thubūtihā wa-dalālatihā*)—considering that these rulings (*aḥkām*) alone are those [rulings] about which *ijtihād* is forbidden. For these represent within the Islamic *sharī'a*, its universal principles and established roots (*mabādi'ahā al-kulliyya wa-uṣūlihā al-thābita*) that cannot bear interpretation (*ta'wīl*[an]) or substitution (*tabdīl*[an]). Furthermore, it is inconceivable that their meaning will change with a change of time and place.[52]

The SCC found no unambiguous passage in the Qur'ān that dealt with the specific issue of retroactive child support. (Intriguingly, as in the previous case, the Court did not say whether when looking for absolutely certain rulings, it looked to the *ḥadīth* literature.) "Because there is no absolutely certain text (*naṣṣ qaṭ'ī*) providing a conclusive ruling (*ḥukm fāṣil*) about a child's need for support [from his father] for a period in the distant past, then, as regards this [issue], the path

[51] Case No. 29, Judicial Year 11 (March 26, 1994), 248–49.
[52] Case No. 29, Judicial Year 11 (March 26, 1994), 249.

of *ijtihād* has been left open."[53] The SCC held, the government was free to exercise *ijtihād* in this area—meaning that the government could enact and enforce whatever rule it felt best, so long as that rule did not impede the goals of the *sharīʿa*.[54]

b. *Did the law impede the goals of the* sharīʿa?

The Court began its analysis of the goals of the *sharīʿa* by asking what "benefits" were promoted by the absolutely certain Qurʾānic rulings dealing with questions of custody. It found two relevant passages in Qurʾān 2:233: "a father is obliged to provide for them [his children] and clothe them honorably"; and "a mother should not be made to suffer harm (*tuḍārr*) on account of her child, nor a father on account of his child."[55] The Court identified, in the first of these passages, a specific goal in the area of child support—namely, the promotion of childrens' welfare. The second verse simply qualified that a parent's obligation to their children ended when providing maintenance would cause more harm than good.[56] (Again, it is notable that the Court did not cite any *ḥadīth*s. Nor did it indicate whether it looked to the *ḥadīth* literature when trying to identify the principle or to establish its precise contours.)

How could the Court determine what constitutes welfare—either of the child or of a person dealing with the child? For the purpose of applying these principles, welfare is to be understood as the promotion of the results that constitute the general goals of the *sharīʿa*, which include, but are not limited to, the promotion of religion (*dīn*), self (*nafs*), reason (*ʿaql*), honor (*ʿirḍ*), and property (*māl*).[57] In fact, the SCC implies that the general goals of the *sharīʿa* include the promotion of anything that human reason tells us is beneficial. The question of whether a father must provide for his child is ultimately governed by the utilitarian principle established in the *ḥadīth* "do not injure or repay one injury with another" (*lā ḍarar wa-lā ḍirār*).[58] The

[53] Case No. 29, Judicial Year 11 (March 26, 1994), 251.

[54] "When there is no text about it [an issue], *ijtihād* is only limited by the universal rulings so as not to impede their general goals." Case No. 29, Judicial Year 11 (March 26, 1994), 252.

[55] Case No. 29, Judicial Year 11 (March 26, 1994), 254.

[56] Case No. 29, Judicial Year 11 (March 26, 1994), 254.

[57] Case No. 29, Judicial Year 11 (March 26, 1994), 250.

[58] Case No. 29, Judicial Year 11 (March 26, 1994), 254. As noted in Chapter

justices reasoned that to fail in one's duty to pay child support, whether deliberately or through negligence, is "unjust," and that a law that undoes an injustice *ipso facto* provides benefits. "Responding to the injustice of the father with justice, this is only a right that welfare requires and a duty that necessity imposes."[59] In this case, the Court concluded that the law under review does advance the welfare of the child without causing undue "harm" to the father.

Although the Court seemed to think that the balance of harms in this case was obvious, it was faced with the uncomfortable fact that many classical jurists had concluded that child support should *not* be applied retroactively. Implicitly justifying its decision to depart from the mainstream of classical doctrine, the SCC stressed that the Mālikī guild had, under some circumstances, permitted judges to order support retroactively.[60] It thus could not be unreasonable to think that such orders should be allowed. Furthermore, it argued, society has changed. It was reasonable to conclude that something advancing public welfare in, say, eleventh-century Baghdad, might not serve the public interest in twentieth-century Cairo.[61]

3. *Analysis*

In this case, the SCC failed to resolve the questions raised in its previous Article 2 cases. For example, in looking for rulings that are

---

Five, this *ḥadīth* was used by Rashīd Riḍā and other champions of utilitarian neo-*ijtihād* as justification for their utilitarian method of legal reasoning. The use of this *ḥadīth* thus suggests that a law advances the welfare of the child if it advances what reason tells us is good for that child, and advances the welfare of society if it advances what reason tells us is good for humankind.

[59] Case No. 29, Judicial Year 11 (March 26, 1994), 254.

[60] Case No. 29, Judicial Year 11 (March 26, 1994), 255.

[61] Case No. 29, Judicial Year 11 (March 26, 1994), 255. According to the Court, the Ḥanafī jurists and other jurists who had refused to order retroactive support established a juridical presumption that a person who had not sought an order of child support had not needed support. The court suggests that in the past, this might have been a justifiable assumption. At that time, the SCC claims, people were more religious and less willing to engage in immoral acts and thus, one supposes, would not ask for support they did not need. Furthermore, the justices asserted that courts were more efficient in the past and would therefore have quickly ordered child support in every case where they had been asked. In these circumstances, the wife's failure to get an order of child support might reasonably have led to the conclusion that the support was not needed. Yet, the Court said, this conclusion could no longer be accepted today. Court systems have become more complex, and a father has ample opportunity to abuse the process in order to delay the issuance of a support order. See Case No. 29, Judicial Year 11 (March 26, 1994), 255. Compare *id.*, 253.

absolutely certain with respect to both their authenticity and meaning, the Court in this case never explained how it established the authenticity of scriptures other than the Qur'ān—thus leaving uncertain the role that the *ḥadīth*s would play. In looking for absolutely certain scriptures, the Court looked only at Qur'ānic passages, but it cited a *ḥadīth* to justify the utilitarian aspect of its goals analysis. With respect to identifying the meaning of revealed texts, the Court also failed to clarify the hermeneutic methods to be used when establishing the meaning of a particular scripture. The Court's interpretation seemed decidedly impressionistic.

Because the SCC found no explicit texts on point with the specific question, the constitutionality of the law depended on whether the SCC believed the law advanced the goals of the *sharī'a*. Ambiguities, however, continued to plague the Court's goals analysis. In its analysis, the SCC began by looking to see if Qur'ānic texts and the exegetical tradition revealed the results that God wants custody laws to promote. The Court concluded that God wants fathers who have children to pay whatever is needed to advance the welfare of their children—up to the point where providing support would cause him unreasonable harm. In determining whether the harm involved in a support order was reasonable, the SCC seemed implicitly to balance the harms suffered by the father against the benefits enjoyed by the child. In measuring benefits and harms the Court apparently considered more than the five "necessary" benefits. Rather, it implied it was employing reason to determine what human welfare required and asking whether the law advanced the public good. How exactly it performed its utilitarian analysis was left unclear. The Court thus left itself ample room to argue that welfare required the promotion of justice and human rights as these had been defined in Court cases dealing with secular provisions of the constitution.

C. *Case No. 35 of Judicial Year 9, decided on August 14, 1994*[62]

In late summer 1994, the SCC issued its third opinion involving an Article 2 challenge to Law 100 of 1985. Law 100 had granted special rights to women whose husbands took second wives. Among the

62 Case No. 35, Judicial Year 9 (August 14, 1994), printed in *SCC*, vol. VI, 331–58.

new rights was a near-automatic right for her to receive, if she chose, a judicial dissolution of her marriage (*tafrīq*). The decision to grant this right was extremely controversial, and these provisions were quickly challenged in court.[63] To understand the controversy and the argument of the plaintiff in Case No. 35 of Judicial Year 9 (August 14, 1994), it is helpful to consider briefly the history of polygamy in the Islamic world.

1. *Background*

Before the rise of Islam, Arab society had permitted and may have encouraged polygamy.[64] The Prophet had a considerable number of wives, and Qur'ān 4:3 seems to permit Muslims other than the Prophet to practice a limited form of polygamy: a man other than the Prophet may not marry more than four wives, and he must treat them all equally:

> If you fear that you will not act justly towards the orphans, marry such women as seem good to you: two, three, four. But if you fear that you will not be equitable, then only one. (Qur'ān 4:3)

Cryptically, however, in verse 29 of the same sura, the Qurān adds an intriguing comment:

> you will not be able to be equitable between your wives, even if you wish to do so; but do not be altogether partial so that you leave her, as it were, suspended. (Qur'ān 4:29)

The classical jurists suggested that Qur'ān 4:29 was simply stating a truism. Although a husband might treat his wives equally from an objective standpoint (for example, by giving them the same dowry and allowance and by spending equal numbers of nights with them), he might still in his heart feel more strongly towards one of the wives. Reading this comment together with 4:3, the jurists concluded that this type of subjective impartiality was insufficient by itself to create a bar to second marriage. Accordingly, until the modern era, polygamy was permitted and practiced by Muslims in Egypt (and in

[63] For a discussion of the debates surrounding similar provisions in Jihān's law (which was voided on procedural grounds), see Fauzi M. Najjar, "Egypt's Laws of Personal Status," *Arab Studies Quarterly* 10 (1988): 328–31.

[64] For an interesting discussion of the pre-Islamic period and the gaps in our knowledge about it, see Linant de Bellefonds, *Traité*, II, 17–22.

other Islamic societies) who could afford the financial expense and could treat their multiple wives "equally" in such objective matters as maintenance and conjugal duties.

In the nineteenth century, however, the consensus behind the general permissibility (and advisability) of polygamy began to break down in many parts of the Muslim Mediterranean, including Egypt. Europeans viewed polygamy as an unjust practice that demeaned women and weakened a society, and some Muslims came to agree with them.[65] Thus, some early champions of utilitarian neo-*ijtihād* argued on utilitarian grounds that God's permission to practice polygamy had lapsed. They argued that polygamy was undoubtedly a correct practice for the early Islamic community, but modern men abused it in order to oppress women and sate their lust—with dreadful consequences for society at large. For example, Muḥammad ʿAbduh issued *fatwās* arguing vigorously that polygamy should be outlawed in the modern era.[66] These modernist criticisms of polygamy inspired a reaction by conservative Muslims.[67] Ironically, some conservative modernists employed utilitarian reasoning to bolster their conclusion that polygamy was permitted, even recommended, by God. Turning ʿAbduh's reasoning on its head, they argued that the practice of polygamy actually promoted the welfare of women and of society as a whole. Accordingly, they claimed that the state should promote polygamy.

The Egyptian government in the twentieth century attempted cautious regulation of polygamy. As potential reforms were debated, one possible approach was to permit women to seek judicial dissolutions of their marriage on grounds of harm whenever their husbands took a second wife. The idea of divorcing for harm, however, was controversial. The Qur'ān and *ḥadīth* literature clearly assume that men can divorce their wives in a number of different ways. Working from

---

[65] See, e.g., the opinion of Celāl Nūrī Ileri discussed in Günay Alpay, "Ileri" in EI2, vol. III, 1117; the opinions of Sir Sayyid Aḥmad Khan as described in Aziz Ahmad "Iṣlāḥ: (iv) India-Pakistan" EI2, vol. IV, 170; and those of Muḥammad ʿAbduh described in the text below.

[66] See Stowasser, *Women in the Qur'ān, Traditions, and Interpretation*, p. 21, citing, e.g., Muḥammad ʿAbduh, *al-Islām wa-'l Mar'a fī Ra'y al-Imām Muḥammad ʿAbduh*, ed. Muḥammad ʿAmāra (Cairo: n.d.).

[67] As Stowasser notes, "the topic of polygamy engenders a defensive reaction in modern conservative Muslims is partially due to Western criticism of that institution." Stowasser, *Women in the Qur'ān, Traditions, and Interpretation*, 121.

these texts, the classical Sunnī jurists came to agree that a man can divorce his wife at will and that sometimes a man and a woman could mutually agree to end their marriage. The classical jurists also agreed that, under a limited number of circumstances, a woman could ask a judge for a judicial dissolution of her marriage, although they disagreed about the circumstances that would justify the extreme remedy of judicial dissolution. The Ḥanafī guild established a restrictive doctrine, holding that dissolution was only possible in cases in which the husband was incapable of consummating the marriage.[68] The Mālikīs were the most liberal, permitting judicial dissolution on grounds of harm (*ḍarar*), so that a wife could have her marriage dissolved on grounds of cruelty or ill-treatment.

In the nineteenth and twentieth centuries, many governments in the Arab Mediterranean, including Egypt, tried to advance women's rights by adopting some form of the Mālikī rule permitting women to seek divorce on grounds of harm.[69] Such a right did not help women who were unhappy about their husband's decision to take a second wife. Judicial dissolution required a showing that a husband's marriage was causing a woman objective harm. Because polygamy had been sanctioned by the Qur'ān, however, courts could be reluctant to find that the taking of a second wife was a "wrongful act"—even when it made the wife unhappy. (It would, of course, require dissolution if a woman could show that her husband could not comfortably keep two wives and had thus cut the first wife's support.)[70]

[68] For a summary of the doctrine in the Ḥanafī guild, see Joseph Schacht, *Introduction to Islamic Law*, 164–166.

[69] With respect to Egypt, Article 11 of the Personal Status Law of 1929 had allowed women to receive a judicial dissolution of their marriage (*tafrīq* or *faskh*), if they had suffered from any type of cruelty or ill-treatment that constituted "harm" (*ḍarar*). For a general discussion of the reforms in Egypt, see David Pearl, *A Textbook on Muslim Law* (London: Croon Helm, 1979), 108–13. Egypt's example proved influential and other Arab countries adopted similar provisions. For a discussion of the modernist reforms in other Arab countries permitting judicial dissolution on grounds of harm, see *ibid.* and also Joseph Schacht and Aharon Layyish, "Ṭalāḳ, II: Reforms in the Modern Middle East and North Africa" in EI2, vol. X, 153–57; Nasir, *The Status of Women under Islamic Law*, 81–95.

[70] Upon allegation of this type of mistreatment or of cruelty, a judge would be required to appoint arbitrators who would first try to negotiate reconciliation. If the arbitrators agreed that the husband had committed some fault that caused his

Recognizing the difficulties facing women who wished to use "harm" as a means to escape polygamous marriages, the opponents of polygamy tried to have polygamy characterized as "harmful" as a matter of law. This meant that a wife could receive a dissolution of her marriage for "harm" simply by demonstrating that her husband had displeased her by taking a second wife.[71] Although this reform was tried early in some countries, conservative feeling about polygamy was sufficiently strong in Egypt that efforts to promulgate similar reforms failed repeatedly in the 1920s, 40s and early 50s.[72] In 1979, however, these reforms were enacted as part of the ill-fated "Jihān's law." After that law was declared unconstitutional on the grounds that it had been improperly enacted, the provisions relating to polygamy were re-enacted as part of Law 100 of 1985.[73] According to the provisions of Law 100, an Egyptian man who sought a marriage license was required to state in his application whether he was already married. If he was, the marriage official would notify the first wife before permitting the marriage. Within one year of the marriage, the first wife could seek a judicial dissolution of the marriage. A judge would be required to try to reconcile the parties. If he could not, he would have to grant the dissolution. As a practical matter, this law effectively allowed a woman to have her marriage dissolved if her husband had married a second wife. Upon dissolution, she could be awarded compensation just as if her husband had divorced her.[74]

---

wife objective harm, and if the wife refused to be reconciled to him, the court would be required to pronounce a dissolution. See Law No. 25 (1929), sections 6–11.

[71] In the 1950s a number of other Muslim countries modified their laws to state that taking a second wife was, in fact, a fault insofar as it caused insult or pain to the first wife. Since it was difficult for a husband to deny the wife's testimony that she found the presence of a second wife intolerable, the provisions allowed her essentially to dissolve her own marriage. See Aharon Layish and Ron Shaham, "Nikāḥ: (II) In the Modern Islamic World: (1) The Arab, Persian and Turkish Lands of the Middle East," in EI2, vol. VIII, 30.

[72] The Personal Status Law of 1929 included only one "reform." By engaging in *talfīq*, the legislature adopted a doctrine espoused in the pre-modern period by the jurists of the Ḥanbalī guild, which allowed women the right to include in their marriage contract a provision that permitted them to have their marriage dissolved in the event that their husband took a second wife. If women had not had the foresight or the bargaining power to have such a clause inserted into the contract, however, the law gave them no right to seek automatic dissolution of their marriage on grounds of polygamy.

[73] See the discussion in Chapter 9 above.

[74] As seen in the first case, once the marriage was dissolved, Law 100 allowed

In Case No. 35 of Judicial Year 9 (decided on August 15, 1994), a man challenged the 1985 amendments as unconstitutional. This man had taken a second wife, whereupon his wife was initiated a request for a judicial dissolution. In response, the man argued that the provisions of Law 100 at issue in the case were unconstitutional. The Qur'ān had explicitly invited Muslim men who felt they could treat multiple wives equally to marry more than one woman. The law allowing dissolution for polygamy prevented some of these men from accepting the Qur'ānic invitation. Accordingly, it was inconsistent with a principle of the *sharīʿa* and violated Article 2. In an intriguing opinion, the SCC rejected the plaintiff's argument.

2. *The SCC's reasoning*

In this case, the Court began by agreeing with the plaintiff that there was an absolutely certain ruling of the *sharīʿa* that recommends polygamy—at least under certain circumstances. Focusing on the circumstances under which polygamy could take place, the Court asserted that multiple marriages were only permissible when the marriage would advance the interest of all the man's wives and of society at large. This requirement created a back-door for non-textual considerations to enter. In determining whether the law advanced the women's interests, the Court relied on its own reasoned understanding of justice or utility. As a result, the Court interpreted the *sharīʿa* permission of plural marriage in a limited manner that jibed with international human rights norms. Working from this interpretation, the Court upheld the law under attack. The opinion is interesting because it shows how the SCC's method allows an interpreter to read scriptural texts in light of its pre-existing normative commitments. Notwithstanding the superficial textualism of the SCC's interpretive method, the Court's Article 2 opinions may ultimately be driven by its beliefs about the utility of the law under attack. And in this case, the SCC's understanding of utility seemed strongly liberal.

a. *Was the law inconsistent with an absolutely certain ruling of the* sharīʿa?

The SCC began by looking for absolutely certain rulings dealing with the question of polygamy. The Court identified two provisions

---

the wife (if she had children from the marriage) to retain custody of the children for a significant time, and allowed the judge to award the woman *mutʿa*. In addition, Law 100 permitted her to stay in the conjugal home so long as she had custody.

dealing with the issue. The first was Qur'ān 4:3, which obviously dealt with polygamy: "If you fear that you will not act justly towards the orphans, marry such women as seem good to you: two, three, four. But if you fear that you will not be equitable, then only one."[75] The second was Qur'ān 4:19 which dealt with the treatment of wives generally and thus of first wives: "Consort with them honorably." For reasons that are unclear, the Court did not cite Qur'ān 4:29, which could easily be interpreted as a limitation on the right granted in 4:3.[76]

According to the SCC, Qur'ān 4:3 grants an explicit, unambiguous permission to marry more than one wife *under particular circumstances*, and the legislature is flatly prohibited from passing laws that contradict this principle. That is to say, the Court actually found what it would consider an absolutely certain ruling that approved of polygamy under certain circumstances.

> It has been established that God, may He be exalted, declares a rule only to realize the interests/welfare (*maṣāliḥ*) of the people, and he has never neglected an interest/welfare (*maṣlaḥa*) that is necessitated by their conditions [of the people] without introducing a ruling concerning this thing. And it is likewise incontestable that what is fixed by a *naṣṣ* is a true interest that cannot be altered [i.e., something that will truly benefit men]. Doing what is contrary to it is to go beyond the boundaries of God. And the interest/aspect of human welfare (*maṣlaḥa*) that is incompatible with the Qur'ānic texts is not considered to be a true interest (*maṣlaḥa*). . . . And God when he permitted plurality [of wives] legislated this [plurality] for an aspect of human welfare. He decreed a response to the human soul. So he settled in a framework of moderation that adheres to the definition of moderateness by making plurality of wives—and this means marrying more than one wife and less than four—a right for every man.[77]

A blanket prohibition on polygamy would be unconstitutional. Some commentators have been struck by this passage, and have suggested that it might constitutionalize a rigid principle permitting

[75] Case No. 35, Judicial Year 9 (August 14, 1994), 349.

[76] It may be that because secularists often quoted Qur'ān 4:29 to support their criticisms of polygamy, the Court may pass over this verse in silence in order to avoid opening itself up to the same criticism leveled by conservatives at these modernists. It may also be, however, that the Court *wanted* to limit the right on the basis of harm and justice because such limitations permit, or indeed require, the Court to read their broader conceptions of human rights into the law.

[77] Case No. 35, Judicial Year 9 (August 14, 1994), 350.

polygamy.[78] The principle that the Court found, however, turns out to be less sweeping than it might at first appear. In interpreting the Qur'ānic command, the SCC noted that, although the permission to engage in plural marriage is conditional, it was allowed whenever a man does not "fear that he will treat [his wives] inequitably." This qualified permission was further limited by the command that men consort "honorably" with their spouses. In determining how the qualified permission should be applied in modern Egypt, the SCC concluded that the requirements of equity and honor require a man to refrain from marrying again unless he can be sure his actions will not lead to "injustice and favoritism" or to "the possibility of considering lawful injustice or harm to a wife who opposes the formation of a [marriage] contract between her husband and another woman . . ."[79]

The Court's exegesis here was clearly impressionistic. As in previous cases, the Court did not use *ḥadīth* analysis to support its interpretation,[80] nor did it look for a common attitude about polygamy among the classical jurists.[81] (Case No. 35 was thus important in suggesting that analysis of *ḥadīth*s or of the classical interpretations of a Qur'ānic command are tools to which the Court can, but is not compelled, to look.)[82] The Court also did not do a word by word

[78] See, e.g., Frank Vogel, "Conformity with Islamic Shariʿa and Constitutionality under Article 2: Some Issues of Theory, Practice, and Comparison," in Eugene Cotran, Adel Omar Sherif, eds., *Democracy, the Rule of Law and Islam* (CIMEL Book Series No. 6: London: Kluwer, 1999), 539–42.

[79] According to the Court, this verse prohibits "injustice and favoritism" and "the possibility of considering injustice lawful or harm to a wife who opposes the formation of a [marriage] contract between her husband and another woman. . . ." Case No. 35, Judicial Year 9 (August 14, 1994), 350.

[80] In this case, the SCC considers a *ḥadīth*, but it does so only in an aside, in a tangential discussion of why similar provisions that were written into the Personal Status Law of 1929 were consistent with the principles of the *sharīʿa*. The Court explains that the Ḥanbalī guild permitted a woman to include in her marriage contract a provision allowing her to divorce if her husband were to take a second wife. According to the SCC, the Ḥanbalī jurists justified this doctrine by referring to a *ḥadīth* of the Prophet. (Case No. 35 of Judicial Year 9 (August 14, 1994), 354.)

[81] This decision allowed the Court to sidestep the inconvenient fact that (as discussed above) most classical jurists did *not* make the Qur'ānic endorsement of polygamy conditional on the second marriage being harmless in every way. Rather, they conditioned it on a finding that a husband provide equal treatment to his multiple wives.

[82] To this extent, the Court's method of looking for absolutely certain texts apparently hews more closely to the method of Rashīd Riḍā and the champions of utilitarian neo-*ijtihād* than it does to the method of al-Sanhūrī and the champions of comparative neo-*taqlīd*.

exegesis of the Qur'ānic text. It simply looked to the apparent meaning of the words as understood in light of its own social values. This approach allowed it to argue that the constitutionality of the Egyptian legislation under attack rests on whether the legislation serves the specific and general goals of the *sharīʿa*. According to the Court, the absolute right to practice polygamy is a conditional right. It only applies so long as the contemplated marriage will serve the goals that God had in mind when he established the permission. According to the Court, these are the equal treatment of wives justly and the advancement of their welfare. The question of whether a piece of legislation actually advances the welfare of women must be understood in light of the general goal of the *sharīʿa*—which is to advance what reason tells us is good:

> the legislative text under attack contains a specific rule for divorcing on account of harm, and it is necessary that the legislative text that has been attacked be interpreted to bring its rules into agreement with God's speech, may He be exalted, "Consort with them honorably" [Qur'ān 4:19] and likewise in light of the universal rule (*al-qāʿida al-kulliyya*) that the Prophet, peace be upon him, formulated (*ʿāgha*) by saying "*la ḍarar wa-lā ḍirār.*"[83]

b. *Did the law impede the goals of the* sharīʿa?

If the SCC determines that a law does not violate an absolutely certain ruling of the *sharīʿa*, the Court must then ask whether it impedes the specific or general goals of the *sharīʿa*. In this case, the Court's goals analysis is integrated into its analysis of the absolutely certain rulings. According to the Court, the Qur'an explicitly permits polygamy only on the condition that the plural marriage results in "equitable" and "honorable" treatment. The SCC further assumed that these vague requirements are to be understood in light of the general utilitarian principle revealed in the *ḥadīth* "*la ḍarar wa-lā ḍirār*," because this principle:

> is a chief rule (*qāʿida ra'īsiyya*) from among the pillars of the Islamic *sharīʿa*. Its applications are many even if it is precise in its conciseness[84]. . . . And from this principle the jurists derived a number of rules

[83] Case No. 35, Judicial Year 9 (August 14, 1994), 354.

[84] The SCC goes on to note that "Qur'ānic texts of various provenance are discovered from it" and to quote Qur'ānic verses that advocate treating family members kindly.

> which are to be considered interpretations of it. Among these—and this is to be considered to be further an extension of the principle—is [the rule] that harm has to be pushed away as much as possible, and [the rule] that harm should be eliminated, and [that] harm must not endure through its likeness so that its extent will reach alarming proportions [in other words, one harm should not be repaid with another, thereby increasing the net harm]; and [that] the competition between two harms demands the choice of the lesser harm so as to push away the greater; and that one must bear the specific harm (*al-ḍarar al-khāṣṣ*) if it is necessary to ward off a general harm (*ḍarar ʿāmm*).[85]

In short, the SCC narrowed an absolutely certain scriptural ruling recommending men to marry polygamously and made the command contingent on realization of the specific goal to protect the rights of women already taken as wives. These rights for women include both the right to be treated justly and the right to enjoy what reason suggests is net improvement in their well-being. To determine whether the legislative provisions under attack are consistent with the principles of the Islamic *sharīʿa*, then, the SCC needed to ask whether they protected the wife from the general harms from which the *sharīʿa* wants to protect all Muslims. The Court concludes that the law does. Implicitly, the Court suggests that the law creates only a procedural mechanism that operates to ensure that the marriage is consistent with the Qurʾānic principle granting qualified permission for men to have up to four wives. The notice requirement permits a wife to press her claim that she has been harmed. And, the judge can grant a divorce only if the wife has been objectively "harmed."

The SCC's conclusion is not without its problems. The law apparently permitted a woman to use the existence of any second marriage to get a dissolution, without having to prove that it is objectively harmful. That is to say, the law created a legal presumption that if a wife complains about her husband's decision to take a second wife, this first wife has, indeed, been "harmed." If a first wife continues over the course of a year to maintain that she has been harmed, then she can receive a dissolution. Under the law, then, a judge grants dissolutions on the basis of a wife's assertion of harm without objective substantiation of her claim of harm. Is this not a grant of harm on the basis of subjective harm rather than objective harm?

[85] Case No. 35, Judicial Year 9 (August 14, 1994), 354–55.

To get around this argument, the SCC reasoned that polygamy, while not in itself harmful, inevitably gives rise to ancillary harms. For example, it always promotes "the natural jealousy between two women who share one man when he is not faithful to either one of them. This is, after all, a jealousy that the human soul cannot be cleansed of."[86] In essence, the SCC concluded that the Qur'ān permits a man to marry more than one wife under certain circumstances (if neither wife will suffer objective harm) and then concluded that these circumstances will never occur (because a first wife's inevitable jealousy of a second wife will always cause harm to her). Working from this premise, the Court casuistically concluded that a law granting a woman a right to annul her marriage on grounds of polygamy was consistent with the rulings and goals of the *sharī'a*.

3. *Analysis*

The SCC's theory of Islamic law requires the Court to interpret Islamic law, in the first instance, by interpreting scriptural passages that contain legal rulings. Such passages are the ultimate source of absolutely certain rulings of the *sharī'a*, which state legislation must respect. For the Court, these passages are also major indicators of the specific goals that God wants state legislation to promote in certain areas of the law—such as family law and property law. In its discussion of previous cases, this book has noted ambiguities in the Court's method of textual interpretation. We suggested that in earlier cases the Court failed to explain how it uses the *ḥadīth* literature. It tended not to cite *ḥadīth*s other than the *ḥadīth*, "*la ḍarar wa-lā ḍirār*," which it used as a proof text for its overarching utilitarian principle. Did it consider most other *ḥadīth*s to be suspect with respect to their authenticity? If so, why? The Court also failed to explain systematically what tools it believes should be employed to uncover the meaning of Qur'ānic texts.

The Court in this case did not answer these questions. Indeed, the opinion suggested that the Court's method of interpreting Qur'ānic texts was unapologetically impressionistic and that the Court was taking advantage of this to embrace, indirectly, a strongly utilitarian

[86] Case No. 35, Judicial Year 9 (August 14, 1994), 351.

approach to Islamic legal interpretation. The Court found Qur'ānic verses that on their face require men to treat their wives honorably and that suggest that men should not take second wives unless they are confident that they can be equitable. The Court interpreted these enigmatic caveats in light of what it believes to be the overarching utilitarian and rationalist spirit of the *sharīʿa*. It thus interpreted the verses to impose a broad prohibition on polygamous marriages that will cause wives "harm." And it suggested that "harm" was anything that reason tells us is harmful—including the jealousy that inevitably arises between two concurrent wives. Ironically, then, the explicit scriptural passage permitting polygamy is redundant; it reveals that, in questions of plural marriage (as in all other questions), the permissibility of an act depends entirely upon its consequences.

This opinion suggested strongly that the SCC's theory was not as strongly textualist or formalist as it might, at first, appear. The Court had repeatedly said that its method of interpretation required it to respect legal rulings announced in revealed texts and, when they were ambiguous, to interpret them in light of the juristic tradition. This case made clear, however, that the Court's interpretation tended to be shaded by its belief that rulings should be interpreted in light of the larger principle that all actions should promote the goals of the *sharīʿa*. It made clear that the Court's understanding of the *sharīʿa*'s goals was shaped by its commitment to liberal legal norms, including norms guaranteeing the rights of women.

Previous cases suggested implicitly that the Court had a utilitarian method of interpreting Islamic law, and that its evaluation of utility reflected a strong commitment to legal liberalism. The Court's opinion in the polygamy case provided the strongest evidence to date that this was the case. It is perhaps for this reason that the Court seemed worried about the possible reaction to its opinion—either to the utilitarian nature of its interpretive approach or to its decision to favor liberal visions of utility over traditional conservative ones. The opinion thus concluded with an unprecedented postscript reminding lower-court judges that, in Article 2 cases, they were obliged to accept the SCC's interpretation of Islamic law and to apply it faithfully.[87]

---

[87] As discussed above, this case was decided in the summer of 1994, shortly after

> When the SCC assigns—by various indications—a specific meaning to the content of a legislative provision, arriving thereby at a ruling and rejecting the constitutional challenges that are directed at it, this meaning [that the SCC has assigned it] is the ground on which the ruling [regarding constitutionality] was based. . . . Therefore no authority is permitted—even if it is judicial—to assign to this provision a different meaning, by going beyond the expectations of the sphere within which it [the authority] functions which is to articulate its framework in light of the judgment of the SCC [i.e., to articulate a framework by applying the legislative provision as it has been interpreted by the SCC].[88]

D. *Case No. 6 of Judicial Year 9, decided on March 18, 1995*[89]

On March 9, 1995, the SCC issued an opinion dealing with the constitutionality of a law that did not involve family law. In this case, the Court decided a challenge to Law 136 of 1981, which amended Article 29 of Law 49 of 1977 (henceforth "Article 29").

1. *Background*

Article 29, as amended, required a landlord under particular circumstances to extend a lease to relatives of a tenant after that tenant had died or had moved out of the dwelling. Under the law, a landlord would have to extend the lease to the wife, children or parents of the former tenant if they had been living with him at the time that he died or vacated the dwelling. The landlord would have to extend the lease to other relatives (direct or by marriage up to third cousins removed of the tenant) if they had been living with him (1) either for the year preceding his departure or (2) since he had first moved into the dwelling.

The plaintiff in this case was a landlord whose tenant had invited a brother-in-law to stay with him. When the tenant left, the brother-in-law sought to continue renting the house—as he was permitted to do under Article 29. The landlord refused to transfer the lease and challenged the law as unconstitutional. The landlord claimed

---

important members of the judiciary begun to issue opinions that reflected a staunchly Islamist position. The SCC may well have been concerned not only that the Islamist press would savage the Court, but that lower court judges would simply refuse to accept the SCC's strained interpretation of Islamic law. Case No. 35 of Judicial Year 9 (August 15, 1994), 357.

[88] Case No. 35, Judicial Year 9 (August 14, 1994), 357.

[89] Case No. 6, Judicial Year 9 (March 18, 1995), *SCC*, vol. VI, 542–66.

that it violated numerous constitutional provisions: Article 7 ("Social solidarity is the basis of society"); Article 32 ("Private ownership shall be represented by unexploited capital. . . . The manner in which it is utilized shall not contradict the general welfare"); Article 34 ("Private ownership shall be safeguarded and . . . may not be expropriated except for the general good and for fair compensation as defined by law"); and, finally, Article 2 ("The principles of the Islamic *sharīʿa* are the chief source of Egyptian legislation").

The Article 2 claim was an intriguing addition. The question of landlord-tenant law is not treated at any length in the Qur'ān or, to the best of my knowledge, in the *ḥadīth* literature. Over the centuries, the jurists of the guilds elaborated detailed bodies of *fiqh* governing the sale and lease of property, and the right to alienate property.[90] To date, however, I have not found instances in which the guild jurists specifically addressed the specific question of whether a landlord could be forced to continue leasing a house to people who had already been living with the tenant. Nevertheless, prior to 1993, the Court had issued several short opinions holding that to be consistent with the goals of the *sharīʿa*, a state law must respect private property rights. Apparently for this reason, the plaintiff appended an Article 2 claim to his property rights claim, and the SCC's disposition of this case was consistent with the results in these early cases.[91] The Court did, indeed, hold that the law under attack was inconsistent with the goals of the *sharīʿa* and, thus, unconstitutional.

---

[90] For example, the jurists of the traditional guilds discussed in some detail about preemption in the sale of land (*shufʿa*). The jurists agree that under some circumstances a neighboring landowner, by law, receives a right of first refusal when his neighbor sells land, although they disagree over the parameters of this right. A creative jurist might be able to find some insight in these discussions. For an example of a fourteenth-century C.E. explanation of the doctrine of the Shāfiʿī guild, see al-Miṣrī, *ʿUmdat al-Sālik*, pp. 432–35. For a tenth-century C.E. discussion of the doctrine in the Mālikī guild, see ʿAbd Allāh ibn Abī Zayd al-Qayrawānī, *al-Risāla*, ed. Leon Bercher, *La Risala*, 3rd ed. (Algiers: Jules Carbonel, 1949), 230. For an extremely abbreviated summary of the doctrine according to the Ḥanafī guild, see, e.g., Schacht, *An Introduction to Islamic Law*, 141.

[91] When analyzing the Article 7 challenge to the case, the SCC spends considerable time explaining that this Article prohibits the government from enacting laws that will permit one Muslim to exploit another. Some might be inclined to assume that landlords would be more likely to abuse their rights of ownership than lessees would be to abuse their rights of occupation. The SCC argues, however, that in this case such an assumption would be unjustified. The law in question, says the Court, puts a tremendous burden on landlords. By permitting so many people to

2. *The SCC's reasoning*

As in the 1993 cases, the SCC devoted most of its opinion to the disposition of the non-Article 2 claims, and it discussed the Article 2 challenge only in passing. In its Article 2 discussion, the SCC started by looking for absolutely certain rulings in the Qur'ān and *ḥadīth* that deal generally with the question of property. The SCC found only one Qur'ānic text that, it felt, provided any insight into God's attitude towards a landlord's rights with respect to his tenants. This verse, Qur'ān 57:7, tells Muslims to "spend of that unto which he has made you successors." Obviously, this verse did not contain an unambiguous ruling about the specific issue addressed in the Egyptian legislation under attack—the question of when a landlord may evict relatives of an absent tenant.[92] The SCC believed that Qur'ān 57:7 provided some information about the specific goals that the *sharīʿa* wants property regulations to promote.

The SCC found no absolutely certain ruling and no guidance as to the specific goals that this type of law should serve—no party whose interests are to be protected and no specific "benefit" that the law is supposed to promote. The SCC impressionistically interpreted this passage, however, to suggest that people had the right to use or dispose of their property as they saw fit—so long as their actions were not inconsistent with the general goals of the *sharīʿa*. Thus, a law that imposed on a landlord's leasing rights could only be tolerated if it was necessary to prevent the landlord from impeding the goals of the *sharīʿa*. Since the scriptures had not singled out any particular class of people for protection, the Court assumed that the legislation should not advance the welfare (and thus axiomatically the human rights) of a particular class, but should rather advance the welfare of society as a whole.

> Furthermore, the holder of power (*walī al-amr*) has a right to act so as to push away harm (*ḍarar*) as much as possible and also to prevent the causing of harm. . . .[93] If two harms (*ḍararān*) compete, it is neces-

succeed to a terminated lease, it created a very real possibility that once a landlord leased an attractive property, he would never be able to take possession of it for himself. By creating an undue burden on landlords, the Court found that the law violated the guarantee of social solidarity, and accordingly found that it was unconstitutional.

[92] Case No. 6, Judicial Year 9 (March 18, 1995), 560.

[93] In the ellipsis: "if it was pure retaliation increasing harm and does not benefit,

> sary to bear the lesser of them in order to ward off the greater. And included in this [principle] is the acceptance of the specific harm (*al-ḍarar al-khāṣṣ*) in order to repel a general harm (*ḍarar ʿāmm*).[94]

The Court's discussion is truncated but not entirely clear. It did define welfare in a very particular way. It did not equate general harm simply with a decrease in aggregate wealth or happiness in society. In determining whether a law promotes welfare as the *sharīʿa* commands, the only "goals that are worthy of consideration are those that are negated by spending money or circulating it frivolously or wastefully or hostilely or in a manner contrary to the communal welfare (*maṣāliḥ*) in a manner that violates the rights of others."[95] In short, the Court equated the goals of the *sharīʿa* explicitly with the guarantee of individual rights and "harm" with the violation of those rights. In the case at bar, a violation of the landlord's constitutionally-guaranteed individual rights was a "general" harm that the Qur'ān had commanded humans to avoid. By contrast, the incremental economic benefit to the relatives of his tenant was a specific harm that had to be borne. In imposing people's private property rights in order to advance the material comfort of a specific class of people, the government had violated the goals of the *sharīʿa*, and the legislation was unconstitutional.

3. *Analysis*

This case, like the polygamy case discussed earlier, makes clear that the SCC's method of textual criticism and interpretation was largely impressionistic. It left the justices great discretion to identify "authentic" scriptural texts and to interpret them to conform to their own reasoned assumptions about human welfare. As a practical matter, the Court often limited the number of texts that it thought relevant and/or interpreted them to be ambiguous—to identify a "goal" of the *sharīʿa* rather than a ruling. Thus, the constitutionality of a law would depend on whether it was consistent with the specific and general goals of the *sharīʿa*. In this case, the justices stated more explicitly than they ever had before that they viewed the goals of

only widening the area to which the harm extends. And he [the *walī al-amr*] should likewise rebuff the monstrous harm."

[94] Case No. 6, Judicial Year 9 (March 18, 1995), 561.

[95] Case No. 6, Judicial Year 9 (March 18, 1995), 560–61.

the *sharīʿa* through a liberal paradigm. The specific goals of the law generally required the government to promote the welfare of a particular class of people—but this meant that it required them to protect the rights of particular classes of people. The general goals of the law required the government to promote the welfare of citizens as a whole—but again the enjoyment of individual rights was an essential component of welfare. As a practical matter, the enjoyment of constitutionally protected rights was axiomatically considered to be a benefit, and the SCC was likely to find laws respecting these rights to be consistent with the goals of the *sharīʿa*. Conversely, a law that violated constitutionally protected rights that the Court had identified in the Constitution was likely to violate the controlling utilitarian principle of the *sharīʿa*, and thus to be unconstitutional under Article 2.

As this case makes clear, the SCC linked the goals of the law with the promotion of constitutionally protected rights (including international human rights). When interpreting "secular" provisions of the Egyptian constitution, the SCC has actively defended international human rights. In its Article 2 jurisprudence, the Court has implied that human rights are set down not just by international treaties, but also by God himself. Implicity, then the SCC could use Article 2 to shore up or, theoretically, to expand its existing rights jurisprudence. This case suggests that the Court might use Article 2 to overturn laws that it believed violated the rights of Egyptian citizens—either rights that had already been established or perhaps new rights that the Court identified.

In 1996, the Court decided a controversial case involving a ban on veils in public schools. Once again, the Court interpreted texts and applied the concept of the "goals" of the law in a rights-protective manner. Its interpretation of the *sharīʿa* again reflected the Court's existing jurisprudential commitment to women's rights as these had been defined in international human rights documents.

E. *Case No. 8 of Judicial Year 17, decided on May 18, 1996*[96]

In 1996, the SCC decided a challenge to a series of administrative rulings issued by the Ministry of Education, which regulated the

---

[96] Case No. 8, Judicial Year 17, decided on May 18, 1996, *SCC*, vol. VII, 657–79.

wearing of head coverings by girls in public schools. These administrative rulings were enormously controversial and the court challenges to the rulings were widely covered in the press.

1. *Background*

The Qur'ān contains a number of verses that require men and women to behave modestly and, more specifically, to dress modestly. For example, in one of the earlier revelations to Muḥammad, God commanded believers to interact with the Prophet's wives only when the wives were concealed behind some kind of barrier (*ḥijāb*). In the same verse, God goes on to command the Prophet's wives along with all Muslim women to

> draw close their cloaks when they go about. That will be better so that they may be recognized and not annoyed. (Qur'ān 33:59–60)

In a later verse, God reminds Muslims

> Tell the believing men to cast down their eyes and guard their private parts (*furūj*). That is purer for them. God is aware of the things they do. And tell the believing women to cast down their eyes and guard their private parts (*furūj*) and not reveal their adornment save that which is outward[ly apparent]. And let them cast their veils (*khumur*) over their bosoms and not reveal their adornment save to their husbands or their fathers or their husbands' fathers or their sons, or their brothers' sons or their sisters' sons or their women, or what their right hands own, or such men as attend them, not having sexual desire, or children who have not yet attained knowledge of women's private parts; nor let them stamp their feet, so that their hidden ornaments may be known. (Qur'ān 24:30–33)

The jurists in the classical Sunnī law guilds struggled to understand which parts of a woman were inherently sexual and should thus be concealed from men in public. Over time, they came to agree that Qur'ān 24:30–33 required women to cover their hair and to wear long dresses covering their ankles. They could not agree, however, about whether a woman had to cover her hands and face. According to most jurists of the Mālikī and Ḥanafī guilds, all parts of a woman's body except her face and hands were *'awra* (parts of the body that

---

Also printed in *al-Jarīda al-Rasmiyya* (*The Official Gazette*) No. 21 (May 20, 1996), 1026–41. All page references to this opinion will be to the version published in the Official Gazette.

had to be concealed). The jurists of the Ḥanbalī guild held that a woman's face and hands were also *ʿawra*. There were internal debates within the Shāfiʿī guild about this issue, but the Shāfiʿī jurists gradually moved to a position of increased conservatism. Although some early scholars held that a woman's face and hands could be uncovered, later Shāfiʿīs considered these parts of her body to be *ʿawra*.[97] Up through the rise of the modern era, it was accepted in Egypt and most other areas of the Muslim world that women should, if possible, cover at least their hair and their bodies.

In modern Egypt (and elsewhere in the Islamic world), the tradition of requiring women to cover themselves with either the *niqāb* or the *ḥijāb* was singled out for criticism by Europeans and indigenous secularists. In 1899, Qāsim Amīn, a French-educated Egyptian versed in the thought of Muḥammad ʿAbduh, published a short work on the emancipation of women that argued that Islamic society had fallen behind, while the West progressed, in large part because Muslim society has treated women as second-class citizens—a development that has led to tremendous moral corruption and social weakness.[98] Using a form of utilitarian neo-*ijtihād*, Amīn argued that no authoritative religious text explicitly required practices such as veiling and polygamy, and God would only want them to be adopted where they would lead to social welfare. In Amīn's eyes, these practices prevented women from leading productive lives and, ironically, increased lust in men. Because they harmed society, they should be considered to be contrary to God's command. Amīn's attacks prompted a furious response. Some neo-traditionalists argued that texts and the traditional interpretation of them made clear that veiling was

[97] On the disputes in the Shāfiʿī *madhhab*, see Stowasser, *Women in the Qur'ān, Traditions, and Interpretation*, 92ff. This would seem to be confirmed in the section on veiling in the twentieth-century C.E. annotated edition of Misrī, *ʿUmdat al-Sālik*, where the fourteenth-century C.E. text does not contain elaborate rules on the question of veiling, but the modern commentary interprets them in the most conservative possible manner.

[98] See the summary in Albert Hourani, *Arabic Thought in the Liberal Age: 1798–1939* (Cambridge: Cambridge University Press, 1983), citing Qāsim Amīn, *Taḥrīr al-Marʾa* (Cairo, 1899); Qāsim Amīn, *al-Marʾa al-Jadīda* (Cairo, 1901). For a more critical view of Amīn, arguing that he was not as "progressive" as scholars like Hourani have implied, see Leila Ahmed, *Women and Gender in Islam: Historical Roots of a Modern Debate* (New Haven, Yale University Press, 1992), 149ff.

required. Socially conservative practitioners of utilitarian neo-*ijtihād* turned Amīn's argument on its head and *defended* the practice of veiling on utilitarian grounds.[99] Stowasser suggests that

> [t]he *ḥijāb* has come to signify the sum total of traditional institutions governing women's role in Islamic society. Thus in the ideological struggles surrounding the definition of Islam's nature and role in the modern world, the *ḥijāb* has acquired the status of a cultural symbol.[100]

To understand the details of this case, it is necessary to understand not only the deep passions that the veil invoked, but also the difference between two types of "veil" that are worn in contemporary Egypt—the *niqāb* and the *ḥijāb*. The *niqāb* is the stereotypical "veil" made famous in orientalist literature and art. It is a head-covering that includes a piece of cloth that covers the face except for the eyes. The covering that is commonly referred to as the *ḥijāb* (a term that is also often translated as a "veil") is a less restrictive head-covering that conceals all of a woman's hair, neck and upper torso but not her face.

As Islamism spread in Egypt in the 1970s, an increasing number of women began to wear Islamic head-coverings.[101] The leading *ʿulamāʾ* generally embraced this trend,[102] and some secularists came to see the growing popularity of the *ḥijāb* and *niqāb* as an ominous sign of growing Islamist sentiment.[103] The Mubārak government, which was trying desperately to project an image of overwhelming strength against the conservative Islamic opposition, was deeply

---

[99] See e.g., Ahmed, *Women and Gender in Islam*, 149ff.; Stowasser, *Women in the Qurʾān, Traditions, and Interpretation*, 127–28 (discussing the arguments of the influential Indian thinker Maulana Maududi).

[100] Stowasser, *Women in the Qurʾān, Traditions, and Interpretation*, 127.

[101] This development was particularly startling, because even in pre-modern Egypt, few women outside of the cities wore the *niqāb* or the *ḥijāb*. Most women followed the traditional Egyptian fashion of covering their hair with a scarf knotted behind the back of their head or tied under the chin. See Andrea B. Rugh, *Reveal and Conceal: Dress in Contemporary Egypt* (Cairo: University of Cairo Press, 1989), 149–50.

[102] Most asserted that it was absolutely required for women to wear the *ḥijāb* and disagreed about whether Muslim women should wear the *niqāb*. See Jakob Skovgaard-Petersen, *Defining Islam for the Egyptian State: Muftīs and Fatwās of the Dār al-Iftā* (Leiden: E.J. Brill, 1997), 249–50, 258.

[103] See Rugh, *Reveal and Conceal*, 149. For a liberal Egyptian's view, see Judge Saʿīd al-ʿAshmāwī, "The Veil in Egyptian Law and Islam," *The Middle East Times*, Oct. 19–25, 1993, 3.

unhappy to see school girls attend school in the *ḥijāb* or *niqāb*.[104] In 1994, the Minister of Education issued edict No. 113 of 1994, which set up a standard uniform for school girls which precluded them from wearing the *ḥijāb* or *niqāb* in public school. Not surprisingly, the Ministerial act created a storm of controversy, and the Minister of Education hastily issued a second Edict No. 208 of 1994, "clarifying" the previous edict. It said that school girls would be allowed to wear the *ḥijāb* so long as they brought a written authorization to school in which the parent explicitly asked that their child be allowed to wear the *ḥijāb*. They would still not, however, be permitted to wear the *niqāb*.[105] According to the Minister, this new rule was designed to achieve two goals. As for the requirement that girls receive permission to wear the *ḥijāb*, this was necessary, it was said, to ensure that girls were not being pressured by Islamist teachers to wear the veil without their parents' knowledge. As for the outright prohibition on the *niqāb*, this was said to be necessary for classroom order because teachers might have difficulty distinguishing one girl in the *niqāb* from another. Lurking below these explanations seemed to be a desire to suppress symbols of conservative Islamism in the schools. According to the Minister himself, the decree was designed to make clear that "we will not let Egypt's schools become a well of extremism and terrorism."[106]

The modified ban on veiling still galled Islamists. Even the government's traditional allies among the *ʿulamāʾ* offered only tepid support for the Minister's edicts.[107] Shortly after the second ministerial

[104] In 1994, one newspaper estimated that 75% of girls wore the *ḥijāb* or even more concealing garments to school. "Court Throws Out Veil Ban," *The Middle East Times*, April 9, 1994.

[105] See Case No. 8, Judicial Year 17 (May 18, 1996), 1027–1030.

[106] Quoted in Yasmine Abou el-Kheir, "School Girls Veiled Without Consent," *The Middle East Times*, August 1, 1994, 1.

[107] Al-Azhar's *fatwā* council declared the new amendment unequivocally to be contrary to the principles of the *sharīʿa*. *Al-Sharq al-Awsaṭ*, August 1, 1994, cited in Ami Ayalon, "The Arab Republic of Egypt," in MECS XVIII (1994), 272. See also Kilian Bälz, "The Secular Reconstruction of Islamic Law: The Egyptian Supreme Constitutional Court and the 'Battle over the Veil' in State-Run Schools," in *Legal Pluralism in the Arab World*, Baudouin Dupret, Maurits Berger and Laila al-Zwaini, eds. (The Hague: Kluwer, 1999), 239 citing *al-Shaʿb* August 19, 1994. Slightly more comforting was the *fatwā* issued by Muḥammad Sayyid al-Ṭanṭāwī, Chief *Muftī* of Egypt, and the state's official advisor on questions of Islamic law. He had traditionally been skeptical about whether the *niqāb* was required or even advisable. See Skovgaard-Petersen, *Defining Islam*, 258, citing *fatwā* record 1329 number 461, dated October 28, 1992, and a *fatwā* on the *niqāb* that was printed in *al-Ahrām*,

edict was announced, a father with Islamist sympathies challenged the ruling in Court. This father had sent his daughters to school wearing the *niqāb* in violation of the Ministerial act. When they were suspended from school, he went to court seeking to enjoin enforcement of the order on the grounds that it violated Article 2. In August, an administrative appeals court found the father's claim to be plausible. It stayed enforcement of the order and referred the father's case to the SCC for a definitive ruling.[108] It is a sign of the sensitivity of this case that the SCC put the case on a fast track—deciding it roughly two years after the dispute first erupted. It held the minister's edict to be constitutional.

2. *The SCC's reasoning*

In its opinion, the SCC began with an extensive recap of its "theory" of Article 2, which echoes the summary given three years previously in Case No. 7 of Judicial Year 8 (the 1993 case in which the SCC first explicated its embryonic theory of Islamic law and Islamic legislation):

> And whereas: The judiciary of the Supreme Constitutional Court has been consistent regarding what the Constitution stipulates in its second Article—ever since [that Article's] amendment in 1980—namely, that the principles of the Islamic *sharīʿa* are the chief source of legislation. And it has been devoted to a requirement binding both of the two branches, the legislative and executive, to observe it and defer to it with respect to legislation issued after the amendment. Among those [acts of legislation that were issued after the amendment] are the provisions of the challenged [ministerial] Decision Number 113 of 1994, as explicated by [ministerial] Decision Number 208 of 1994. It is not permitted for a legislative text to contradict those Islamic legal rulings that are absolutely certain with respect to their authenticity and meaning (*al-aḥkām al-sharʿiyya al-qaṭʿiyya fī thubūtihā wa-dalālatihā*), considering

October 1987, p. 8. In this case, Ṭanṭāwī issued a lukewarm defense of the ruling, stating that the *niqāb*, though a custom, was not actually required, and the government rule that parents give permission to wear the veil was permissible insofar as it helped to guarantee that parents knew what their children were wearing in school. Ayalon, "The Arab Republic of Egypt," 272–73, citing the semi-official newspaper *al-Ahrām*, August 2, 1994; see also Bälz, "The Secular Reconstruction," 239, citing an article in *Ṣabāḥ al-Khayr*, September 13, 1994.

[108] "Court Throws Out Veil Ban," *The Middle East Times*, April 9, 1994; Ayalon, "The Arab Republic of Egypt," 273, citing *Middle East News Agency*, August 23, 1994; *Middle East News Agency*, September 15, 1994.

> that these rulings alone are those for which *ijtihād* is forbidden, because they signify the Islamic *sharīʿa*'s universal principles (*mabādiʾuhā al-kulliyya*) and its fixed roots (*uṣūluhā al-thābita*), which accept neither interpretation nor substitution. And accordingly, it is unimaginable that the understanding of [such rulings] would change with a change of time and place. . . . The presumptive rulings (*al-aḥkām al-ẓanniyya*) are not absolutely certain with respect to their authenticity, their meaning, or both. They fall within the realm to which *ijtihād* is limited and beyond which *ijtihād* does not extend. They develop by their nature—changing according to time and place, in order to guarantee their [own] flexibility and vitality, and to confront different events. They organize the affairs of the people (*al-ʿibād*) with an eye to protecting those interests of [the people] that are legally appropriate (*maṣāliḥahum al-muʿtabara sharʿan*) and should not interfere with their activities in life. *Ijtihād* must always fall within the framework of the *sharīʿa*'s universal roots (*al-uṣūl al-kulliyya li-'l-sharīʿa*) . . . adhering to [the *sharīʿa*'s] fixed controls (*ḍawābiṭuhā al-thābita*). It [*ijtihād*] must pursue methods of reasoning out the rulings (*al-aḥkām*) and binding supports (*al-qawāʿid al-ḍābiṭa*) for the branches of *sharīʿa* (*furūʿihā*), guarding the general goals of the *sharīʿa* (*al-maqāṣid al-ʿāmma li-'l-sharīʿa*) so that religion, life, reason, honor, and worldly goods are protected.
>
> And whereas: Use of the rule of reason, where there is no [scriptural] text, develops practical rules (*qawāʿid ʿamaliyya*) that are, in their ramifications, gentler for the people and more concerned with their affairs and [that] better protect their true interests (*maṣāliḥahim al-ḥaqīqiyya*). Legislative provisions seek to realize them [such true interests] in a manner that is appropriate for them [the people], affirming that the essence of God's *sharīʿa* is truth and justice, that being limited by the *sharīʿa* is better than widespread depravity, and that closing it [i.e., stopping re-interpretation of the *sharīʿa*] once and for all is neither acceptable nor necessary.[109]

Although the SCC asserted again that rules found in scriptures were binding only to the extent that they were authentic and clear, the Court was apparently still unwilling (or unable) to state explicitly how it would establish the authenticity or clarity of a scriptural text. Would the justices look primarily to the text's "plain meaning"? Or would they instead read texts in light of "external" factors, such as patterns of historical interpretation or a need to conform to the Court's interpretation of the "goals" of the law? With respect to the

---

109 Case No. 8, Judicial Year 17 (May 18, 1996), 1031–32.

goals of the law, how would these be identified? The Court continued to be coy about its answers to these questions.

Nevertheless, in the SCC's opinion, patterns of analysis echo those in earlier cases. For example, in looking for scriptural guidance, the Court looked to the Qur'ān rather than the *ḥadīth* literature. If it could not find clear rulings there, it turned to an analysis of the scriptures as interpreted over the years by the classical jurists—with an eye to identifying legal principles that were implicitly accepted in particular areas of the law (the "specific" goals of the law). To the extent that these could not be found or were ambiguous, the Court filled in the "gaps" in its understanding of God's command by asking what rulings would promote justice and human welfare. In so doing, it read into Islamic law its own reasoned understanding of justice and human welfare.[110] In short, the Court's opinion in the veil case provided further evidence that the Court was unwilling explicitly to clarify the ambiguities in its pastiche method of interpretation and to articulate a systematic method of scriptural criticism or of hermeneutics. Nevertheless, it suggested, the Court had implicitly adopted an interpretive approach that limited the number of specific *sharīʿa* rulings that had to be respected and narrowed their applicability. Thus, the constitutionality of legislation under Article 2 would depend upon the degree to which it advanced the specific and general goals of the *sharīʿa*—goals that were analyzed from a liberal, rights-oriented perspective.

1. *Was the law inconsistent with an absolutely certain ruling of the* sharīʿa? The SCC began its analysis by asking whether there were any explicit textual provisions in the Qur'ān or *ḥadīth* literature addressing the specific issue in this case: whether a girl is explicitly permitted or required to wear a *niqāb* or *ḥijāb*. The Court found four commands from the Qur'ān that provided guidance on the question of what clothes women should wear: Qur'ān 24:31, "[Tell Muslim women to] cast their veils (*khumur*) over their bosoms"; Qur'ān 24:31, "[Let them] not reveal their adornment"; Qur'ān 33:59, "[Tell Muslim women to] draw close their cloaks when they go about"; and finally,

[110] For a very different analysis of this case, see Bälz, "Secular Reconstruction," particularly 236–40.

Qur'ān 24:31, "let them [not] stamp their feet, so that their hidden ornaments may be known." As the SCC noted, these verses do not specify the type of clothing that women must wear. To check its conclusion that these do not establish a clear ruling, the Court asked whether the jurists in the past disagreed on the specifics of what women must cover.[111] Finding that the jurists disagreed, the Court concluded that there was no absolutely certain command or permission directly concerning the *niqāb* veil.

> The form of her clothes and appearance are not fixed by scriptural texts that have been determined to be certain either with respect to their authenticity or with respect to their meaning (*nuṣūṣ maqṭaʿa bihā sawāʾ fī thubūtihā aw dalālatihā*). These [i.e., the form of clothes and appearance] are matters of debate on which *ijtihād* never stops. They remain open within a fixed, general framework defined by Qur'ānic texts (*iṭār ḍābiṭ ʿāmm ḥaddadatihu al-nuṣūṣ al-Qurʾāniyya*). . . . [S]o long as they do not contradict an absolutely certain [scriptural] text, the *walī al-amr* has absolute authority to legislate practical rules within its/their boundaries, limiting the form of [a woman's] attire or dress in light of what prevails in her society among the people so that it is appropriate with their traditions and customs.[112]

In other words, if no absolutely certain rulings deal with the specific issue being regulated, then the *walī al-amr* is required to act in whatever way would advance the specific and general goals of the law:

> And whereas: the Islamic *sharīʿa* in refining the human soul and shaping the individual personality establishes only the essence of the rulings through which it builds a framework for defending the creed.[113]

Thus, the Court concluded that:

> The *walī al-amr* has—in disputed questions—the right to perform [his own] *ijtihād* so as to facilitate the affairs of the people and to reflect what is correct from among their customs and traditions, so long as [his legislation] does not contradict the universal goals of the *sharīʿa* (*al-maqāṣid al-kulliyya li-sharīʿatihim*).[114]

---

[111] Case No. 8, Judicial Year 17 (May 18, 1996), 1035.
[112] Case No. 8, Judicial Year 17 (May 18, 1996), 1035.
[113] Case No. 8, Judicial Year 17 (May 18, 1996), 1034.
[114] Case No. 8, Judicial Year 17 (May 18, 1996), 1038.

2. *Did the law impede the goals of the* sharīʿa?

In determining whether the administrative rulings at issue in this case served the specific and general goals of the law, the SCC asked first whether the authoritative texts dealing with the general question of women's clothing provide any guidance as to what specific results the Qurʾānic rulings regarding veiling were designed to achieve? According to the Court, it can be induced from the Qurʾānic passages cited above and from the *fiqh* rulings of jurists over the centuries that:

> Islam raised the share of the Woman [i.e., all women]. It inspired her to safeguard her chastity. It commanded her to protect herself from shame and degradation so that Woman would raise herself above those things that could sully her or dishonor her, especially through her attire, tenderness in speech, refinement in walking, bringing her allurements into view, tempting others, or revealing "adornments" that are concealed. [A woman] does not have the legal right to freely choose her dress as she desires, select it according to her fancy, or claim that her dress is only her personal concern. Rather, her nature must be upright and her clothing must support her in undertaking her responsibilities in the world.[115]

In other words, women have different obligations at different times. The specific goal of sartorial regulation is simply the promotion of dress that is as modest as possible, given a woman's responsibilities in the world. A regulation of women's dress will be unconstitutional if it does not serve this goal. The problem is, of course, that people have different ideas about the proper role for women in the modern world. "Modesty" also means different things to different people. It is not easy to identify the type of dress that is sufficiently "modest" given a modern woman's social responsibilities. The Court seemed to recognize that the question of whether dress is sufficiently modest requires a judgment call, and that people will inevitably reach different conclusions.

> The form of her clothes and appearance are not [however] fixed by scriptural texts that have been determined to be certain either with respect to their authenticity or with respect to their meaning (*nuṣūṣ maqṭaʿa bihā sawāʾ fī thubūtihā aw dalālatihā*). These [i.e., the form of

[115] Case No. 8, Judicial Year 17 (May 18, 1996), 1035.

> clothes and appearance] are matters of debate on which *ijtihād* never stops. They remain open within a fixed, general framework defined by Qur'ānic texts (*iṭār ḍābiṭ ʿāmm ḥaddadatihu al-nuṣūṣ al-Qurʾāniyya*).

So how did the justices think they should draw the fine line between that which is sufficiently modest and insufficiently modest? The Court seems to have started from the premise that women must enjoy the right to work enshrined in international human rights doctrines and, thus, incorporated into Egyptian constitutional law through the constitution's "rule of law" provisions. Furthermore, it apparently assumed veiling rulings must promote the general goals of the *sharīʿa*—meaning that these rulings cannot do grievous harm to the public welfare. Thus, covering is beneficial only if it allows a woman to play a full, active role in society, meaning that the goals of the *sharīʿa* were only served if women are protected from

> embarrassing situations, as would be the case if her whole body were considered *ʿawra*, with all the requirements [that pertain to *ʿawra*] with respect to knowledge of what makes her different [from men]. She must perform tasks that will involve her mixing with others. It is therefore unimaginable that life in all its aspects would surge around her while she would be specifically required to be an apparition clad only in black or the like. Rather, her clothing should be in accordance with the *sharīʿa*, displaying her piety in a way that does not inhibit her movement in life nor is limited to beautifying her and that is not an obstacle without her awareness. Nor [should her clothing inhibit] her performance of various activities that her needs or the good of her society impose on her. Rather, [her clothing] shall balance between the two [requirements], defined in light of necessity and safeguarding what are considered to be the appropriate customs and traditions.[116]

The SCC suggested that the stigmatization of full veiling would so immobilize women that they would not be able to serve themselves or serve society. To serve the goals of the *sharīʿa*, the legislator or governmental official must come up with laws that steer between the Scylla of titillation and the Charybdis of immobilization.

There is an interesting parallel between this case and the previous case. In the last case discussed, the SCC seemed not to defer to the political branches' views as to the likely effects of the law

[116] Case No. 8, Judicial Year 17 (May 18, 1996), 1036.

under attack. Here, too, although the Court upheld the Ministerial edict under attack, the justices managed to suggest that they had not shown any deference to the judgment of the legislator that the law advanced the welfare of women and/or of society as a whole. The law survived only because the justices had independently come to the conclusion that the law promoted social welfare without imposing upon women's rights. Indeed, the SCC came up with a fairly specific set of guidelines that limited the government's freedom to design uniforms for girls—including, apparently, a requirement that it cover her legs entirely:

> The *walī al-amr* has—in disputed questions—the right [to perform his own] *ijtihād* to facilitate the affairs of the people and reflect what is correct from among their customs and traditions, so long as they do not contradict the universal goals of their *sharīʿa* (*al-maqāṣid al-kulliyya li-sharīʿatihim*). [These universal goals] are not violated by the *walī al-amr*—acting in the sphere of his capacities—in regulating girls' dress.[117] For there should be no revealing of her *ʿawra* or legs, nor any informing about her body.[118]

The school dress code under attack fit neatly into the narrow window of acceptable regulations and thus was upheld.[119]

3. *Analysis*

In this case, the Court's explicit description of its Islamic legal theory and of its interpretive method remained the same as it was in 1993. The theory continued to bring together vocabulary and concepts from a range of modernist theories. At the broadest level, the Court continued to hold that state law must be consistent with universal rulings that met the criteria both of Rashīd Riḍā's universal rulings and of Sanhūrī's fixed rules. It also had to promote the goals of the *sharīʿa*—goals that seemed to be induced from the tradition in a manner that combined classical inductive approaches with Sanhurī's inductive analysis of the *fiqh* tradition and Riḍā's rationalist utilitarianism.

The SCC continued, however, to be cagey about the details of its interpretive approach. When it came to the Court's method of

[117] Reading *bidhātihā* as *badhlatihā* or *badhlātihā* My thanks to Robert Morrison for suggesting this reading.
[118] Case No. 8, Judicial Year 17 (May 18, 1996), 1038.
[119] Ibid.

looking for universally applicable rulings, it was unclear how it would identify the scriptural texts that were probative on a legal question, what hermeneutical tools it would apply to interpret these texts or how its interpretation would be influenced by the classical jurists' interpretations of these texts. When it came to the Court's search for goals, the opinions have never stated how the Court would isolate the specific goals that a particular law must serve. They have also been ambiguous on the question of the general goals that humans are commanded never to interfere with. As in the previous cases, the justices here identified five elements of general welfare, but they did not say why they believed these are essential aspects of human welfare. Furthermore, the opinion intimated that the question of whether a law advances the general goals can be determined through the exercise of unaided reason. The Court also failed to explain how (once it has identified the elements of human welfare that a law is supposed to promote) the justices can balance benefits and harms.

Although the Court shied from giving a full account of its interpretive method, its application of the theory repeats patterns that have been identified in previous cases. For one, the Court's interpretation of texts was impressionistic. As in previous cases, it interpreted texts and the historical trends in interpretation in such a way that it found no ruling or (as in this case) only a very narrow ruling that state law would have to respect. The ruling in this case was that women had to cover themselves modestly—including, it would seem, covering their legs.

The Court then drew from the texts and tradition indications of a larger "goal" of the *sharīʿa* that laws regulating women's clothes had to respect. In previous cases, the larger goal was sufficiently general that people would inevitably understand it differently. In this case, the goal of veiling laws was "modesty." As always, the law must not impede the general goal of public welfare. Thus when enacting laws, the government must ensure not only that women's legs are covered, but also that the laws do whatever is necessary to promote "modesty"—so long as these laws do not do grievous harm. As in previous cases, however, the Court views the specific goals of the *sharīʿa* (modesty) and the general goals (of public welfare) through a liberal, rights-oriented lens. "Modesty" is defined as whatever covering sufficient to save a woman from embarrassment without imposing upon her right to take part fully in society. General welfare is understood to require women's participation in society.

In short, the SCC has left parts of its theory unelaborated, with the result that its embryonic theory allows it to interpret the texts and tradition impressionistically. This leaves the justices considerable discretion, and as in previous cases, the SCC systematically exploits this discretion to interpret the *sharīʿa* in a liberal, rights-oriented fashion that is consistent with the international human rights doctrines that have been incorporated into Egyptian law.

Finally, by leaving ambiguous the degree to which it would defer to executive branch interpretation of the goals of the *sharīʿa* (or executive branch conclusions about whether a state law would promote those goals) the Court left itself considerable power. As a practical matter, most Article 2 cases have turned, directly or indirectly, on the question of whether the law serves the general goals of the *sharīʿa*—which apparently means the law advances what the justices consider to be public welfare. By reserving the right to disagree with the government about the utility of a law, the Court gave itself an independent ground on which to overturn laws that it finds repugnant to its liberal philosophy.

In short, the Court's jurisprudence could be used to reinforce its existing jurisprudence. Theoretically, it could even be used to create new constitutional rights which cannot easily be located in other provisions of the constitution. The next section will describe a series of cases from the late 1990s, in which the Court began to indicate that Article 2 analysis would play more than a mere supporting role in constitutional cases.

II. *Non-Article 2 cases that required the Court to consider the principles of the* sharīʿa

In the cases above, the SCC's interpretation of the *sharīʿa* was shaped by its commitment to Egyptian constitutional principles—including international human rights principles that the Court had incorporated into the Egyptian constitution. According to the Court, the principles of the *sharīʿa* must be interpreted to advance human welfare, and enjoyment of constitutional rights is an essential aspect of true human welfare. That said, the Court has been eager to make clear that it does not assume that principles of the *sharīʿa* are simply the same as the human rights principles that have already been incorporated into Egyptian constitutional law. In some cases, a law may violate constitutional provisions protecting human rights without violating the principles of the *sharīʿa*. In Case No. 5, Judicial Year 8 (decided on January 6, 1996), the SCC held that the legislation under attack did not violate Article 2, but it did violate the equal protection guarantees contained in Article 40.[120] In short, the Court was independently interpreting Islamic law, on the one hand, and secular constitutional provisions on the other. Though they often overlapped, they did not invariably do so.

The SCC has also been eager to demonstrate that Article 2 created constraints on the Egyptian government. The Court, to date, has never struck down a law on Article 2 grounds unless it also violates some other, "secular" provision of the constitution. The Court has suggested, however, that the enactment of Article 2 has changed the government's freedom of action, by forcing the Court to interpret "secular" provisions of the constitution in a new way.

In three separate opinions issued in 1995, the Court held that secular provisions of the constitution guaranteed Egyptian citizens' rights to behave in a certain way. In each case, however, it was difficult to understand the precise contours of the protected activity. To determine whether a particular act was protected, the Court returned to the principle that provisions of the constitution should be interpreted so that constitutional jurisprudence as a whole would be consistent. From this, it followed that the "secular" provisions should be interpreted in light of Article 2's command to the Egyptian government

[120] In this case, the SCC held that a provision of Law 100 of 1985 violated a secular provision of the constitution but did not violate Article 2. The provision at issue in this case provided that if a married man owned his home and then divorced his wife, he would have the choice either to let the wife and children remain in the house or to provide them equally good lodging elsewhere. If, on the other hand, a man simply rented his home and divorced his wife, a judge would decide which of the spouses should remain in the home. The Court found that this did not offend any absolutely certain principle of the *sharīʿa*, nor did it violate the specific goals of the *sharīʿa* in the area of maintenance. That is to say, the law did not do any particular harm to women or society at large. See the discussion in Nathalie Bernard-Maugiron, "La Haute Cour Constitutionelle Égyptienne et la sharîʿa islamique," *Awrâq* (Madrid) vol. XIX (1998), 123–24; compare her analysis with that of Nathan Brown, *Constitutions in a Non-Constitutional World, Arab Basic Laws and the Prospects for Accountable Government* (Albany: State University of New York Press, 2001), 184. Although the SCC found here that Article 2 created fewer restrictions to governmental action than did other provisions of the constitution, it left open the possibility that the converse might also always be the case. That is to say, in another case, the requirements of Article 2 might bar laws that would otherwise pass constitutional muster.

to respect the principles of the *sharīʿa*. In other words, the Court has held that to determine whether a state law violated the "secular" provisions of the constitution, the Court might have to consider whether this action was favored or disfavored under Islamic law.

Some examples may help illustrate how this principle operated in practice. First, in Case No. 23, Judicial Year 16 (decided March 18, 1995), a plaintiff challenged a law that barred members of the Council of State from marrying foreign women.[121] He argued that this violated a fundamental right to choose one's spouse. Although the constitution did not explicitly grant such a right, the plaintiff argued, the constitution contained broad rights-protecting language that suggested a subsidiary right to marry whomsoever one chose. To decide whether it should recognize this new constitutional right, the Court considered both whether the right was recognized in international human rights law and whether Islamic law permitted men to marry whomsoever they chose. Human rights documents recognized a right for men to choose their spouses. Based on its own reading of the Qurʾān, and using the interpretive method that it had developed in the Article 2 context, the Court concluded that the *sharīʿa* also permitted men to marry whomsoever they chose. The Court agreed that the legislation under attack violated a fundamental right and was unconstitutional.

In two other cases decided shortly thereafter in 1995, the Court looked again to Islamic principles to help understand the contours of ambiguous fundamental rights.[122] In a 1997 case it again stressed

[121] Case No. 23, Judicial Year 16 (decided March 18, 1995). For discussions of this case, see an article by the chief justice of the Court, Awad El Morr, "Human Rights as Perceived by the Supreme Constitutional Court of Egypt" in *SCC*, vol. VII, 1 (article is appended to the end of the Arabic cases). See also John Murray and Mohammed El-Molla, "Islamic Shariʿa and Constitutional Interpretation in Egypt," *Democracy, the Rule of Law and Islam*, eds. Eugene Cotran, Adel Omar Sherif (CIMEL Book Series No. 6: London: Kluwer, 1999), 521; Nathalie Bernard-Maugiron and Baudouin Dupret, "Les principes de la sharia sont la source de la législation': la Haute Cour constitutionelle et la reference à la Loi islamique," in "Le Prince et son juge: droit et politique dans l'Égypte contemporaine" eds. Nathalie Bernard-Maugiron and Baudouin Dupret, *Egypte/Monde Arabe* 2.2 (1999): 116; Bernard-Maugiron, "La Haute Cour," 127–28.

[122] Case No. 31, Judicial Year 16 (May 20, 1995), *SCC*, vol. VI, 716–39. For a summary of the case, see Maugiron and Dupret, "Les principes de la sharia," 117; Bernard-Maugiron, "La Haute Cour," 128. Case No. 25, Judicial Year 16 (July 3, 1995), *SCC*, vol. VII, 45–94. See particularly page 86 and the analysis of the case in Bernard-Maugiron, "La Haute Cour," 128.

that Islamic legal principles should be used to clarify ambiguities in "secular" provisions of the Constitution. In Case No. 74, Judicial Year 17 (decided on July 1, 1997), the Court stated in *obiter dicta* that provisions like "equal protection" were inescapably ambiguous and had to be applied in a matter sensitive to context. In understanding how to apply such provisions, the Court suggested the clearly-established principles of the *sharīʿa*, which permitted unequal treatment in certain narrow cases, should be considered.[123] The justices of the SCC thought that the principle announced in these cases was deeply important, and tried to publicize them.[124]

III. *Conclusion: The SCC's application of its theory of Islamic legal interpretation*

As discussed in Chapter 10 and again in this chapter, the SCC in its Article 2 jurisprudence has explicitly adopted several theses common to theories of Sunnī Islamic law: a government in power is permitted to enact whatever statutes it chooses, so long as it satisfies two tests. First, its legislation must not force Muslims to violate universally applicable rulings of Islamic law, which it defines as rulings that are certain "with respect to authenticity and meaning." Second, its legislation must advance the "goals of the *sharīʿa*." On questions where theorists of Islamic legislation have disagreed over the years, the Court has been much less clear. The Court's theory seems to be a pastiche and, in some fundamental ways, an embryonic theory. The theory could still evolve in a textualist, historicist, or utilitarian direction. Similarly, it might turn out to be progressive or conservative.

---

[123] In the case, the SCC barred a lower court from applying a law based on the traditional Coptic law of custody, which provided boys and girls with different rights. The Court stated that in cases where there was no absolutely certain scriptural ruling that required disparate treatment, a religious law must not be interpreted to violate the equal protection guarantees of the constitution. Noting that the Coptic law was not based on a clear Biblical command but rather on custom, the Court found that the law could not violate the equal protection guarantees of the constitution and was unconstitutional. For a fuller discussion of this case in Murray and El-Molla, "Islamic Shariʿa and Constitutional Interpretation in Egypt," 521–22, analyzing Case No. 74, Judicial Year 17 (July 1, 1997).

[124] I can personally vouch for the fact that several made a point to bring these cases to the attention of scholars who were studying the Court's jurisprudence.

Patterns in the Court's reasoning suggest that the justices of the SCC would prefer that their theory evolve in a progressive fashion and that it be applied to develop a liberal interpretation of Islamic law. The Court has recognized as certain and legally relevant only those specific rulings that meet the criteria of both Riḍā's "universal" and "absolutely certain" textual ruling and Sanhurī's "fixed" ruling—even though few rulings could possibly meet this test. Thus, the Court's conclusions about the constitutionality of legislation under Article 2 has inevitably turned on its second test—whether the legislation under attack is consistent with the goals of the law. The Court has also seemed to recognize two different types of goals: (1) specific goals of the law, which God wants certain types of law to advance; and (2) the general goals of the law, which God wants all laws to advance. The Court's interpretation of the specific goals of the *sharīʿa* is informed by historical patterns in the interpretation of Islamic law—a source of information that is accessed through a Sanhūrī-like analysis. In cases where there are no specific goals of the law, however, or where the requirements of the specific goals are unclear, the Court invokes a general principle that God always wants people to act in a way that advances the general goals of the *sharīʿa*. To determine whether a state law advances these general goals, the Court seems to ask primarily whether that law impedes what the justices consider to be the general welfare. The Court's method thus devolves, as Riḍā's did, into a largely utilitarian method of reasoning. Importantly, however, the justices have brought an established liberal philosophy to their analysis. They treat the enjoyment of human rights (as these have been defined by the Court) as axiomatically good, and the justices have thus been reluctant to consider just or beneficial any principles that would require (or even permit) the violation of international human rights norms. As a result, the Court has issued rulings that are consistent with conservative Muslim groups on the question of property rights, but it has rejected the traditional conservative interpretations of the *sharīʿa* in the areas of marriage, divorce, or veiling. In sum, the SCC has to date applied the theory, and exploited its ambiguities, to elaborate Islamic law in a way that does not conflict with—and indeed reinforces—the Court's existing jurisprudence, including their human rights jurisprudence.

Lest people accuse it of subordinating "Islamic" principles to "secular" principles, however, the SCC has issued opinions stating that ever since the adoption of Article 2, its interpretation and application of international human rights doctrine has taken "Islamic" rights principles into account. As a practical matter, the Court seems to suggest, Article 2 may have created important new constraints on the government. This is because the amendment of Article 2 has led the Court to rethink its understanding of fundamental rights. Since then, the Court's understanding of human rights has changed to take "Islamic" values into account.[125] The next chapter will look at reactions to the Court's theory and to the Court's liberal application of its theory. It will focus first on academic commentary—discussing the difficulty academics have experienced, to date, in characterizing the SCC's jurisprudence. Finally, it will explore the reaction of Egyptian judges to the SCC's theory of Islamic law and to the liberal assumptions that inform the Court's application of its theory.

[125] One might reasonably ask how much independent Islamic principles are likely, in practice, to inform the Court's understanding of fundamental rights. The degree to which the Court's new turn to Islamic legal principles would actually affect the Court's interpretation of fundamental rights in the future necessarily depended on the number of Islamic legal principles that the Court finds and the degree to which they are considered clear. In our discussion of the five Article 2 cases above, the Court rarely found clear principles of the *sharīʿa* and when it found ambiguous principles of the *sharīʿa*, it clarified them by referring to rights principles.

CHAPTER TWELVE

THE RECEPTION OF THE SCC'S ARTICLE 2 JURISPRUDENCE

The SCC has developed an intriguing theory of Islamic law, which draws rhetorically upon a wide range of Islamic legal theories but which is ultimately quite new. The theory has left the justices considerable discretion to decide cases based on their personal views about what is best for humans. As a practical matter, the justices have exercised this discretion to interpret Islamic law as consistent with the liberal values already enshrined in its jurisprudence. Yet the Court has declined to elaborate its theory in a manner that explicitly requires later courts to read liberal values into the constitution. This creates the possibility that future courts may turn in a more conservative direction.

This chapter will briefly consider why the Court has declined to clarify all aspects of its interpretive approach. It will then examine the Egyptian judiciary's response to the SCC's theory. Although lower courts have generally accepted the Court's theory and its liberal implications, these courts have subtly indicated that they believe it must pay more attention to the *ḥadīth* literature and show more deference to traditional interpretations of law—even if these are, in places, inconsistent with the SCC's current theory. Finally, this chapter will discuss the reception of the SCC's theory in the academy.

I. *Ambiguity in the SCC's theory of Islamic law and Islamic legal interpretation*

The SCC has written its Article 2 opinions in dense language. Although it has elaborated the basic skeleton of its approach, it has not explicitly articulated all the steps that it is taking to reach its liberal conclusions about the *sharīʿa*'s command. While it is possible to piece together some patterns in the Court's approach and to suggest that the Court has implicitly adopted a particular approach, the Court has not systematically described this approach. The SCC's decisions provide guidance to other courts and even to later panels of the SCC. Why has the Court been so cagey about the approach it is using? Why have members of the Court not clearly described and thus prescribed their approach for later judges to follow—thereby mandating their preferred liberal approach to interpretation?

It is unlikely that there is one simple answer. The justices may be uncertain themselves about whether their approach is appropriate and may thus be "trying it on for size." Alternatively, justices may have disagreed, and it is possible that the only way to achieve a majority opinion would be to leave open for a later date some of the details of its method. An intriguing possible answer is that anyone who wishes to interpret Article 2 will have difficulty constructing quickly a theory that will be widely accepted. Indeed, this challenge may be particularly acute for the justices of the SCC, who were appointed on the basis of their expertise in civil, constitutional and international law rather than Islamic law. If justices with this type of legal training had suddenly imposed in 1989 a novel, systematic, and strongly progressive approach to Islamic legal interpretation, then Islamists would have probably have stopped using the courts and might even have been tempted to use violence against its judges.[1] Worse, the Court's theory might have been rejected, not just by Islamists who preferred alternate and more conservative approaches to legal reasoning, but also by the public at large who would challenge their expertise and even by the lower courts.

In short, if the SCC's theory were to take root and legitimize state law (including the constitutional law established by the SCC itself),

[1] The 1990s were a time in which Islamists threatened or actually perpetrated violence against those who were considered disrespectful to Islam—including judges who questioned Islamist approaches to Islamic legal interpretations. For example, the internationally celebrated novelist Naguib Mahfouz was nearly killed in 1994. In 1995, Islamists tried to assassinate President Mubārak while he was in Ethiopia. Islamists accused the well-known professor Nāṣir Ḥamīd Abū Zayd of apostasy in 1996 on the grounds that his metaphorical interpretation of the Qur'ān was heretical. They used an obscure provision in Egyptian family law to have his marriage annulled. As a result, Abū Zayd left the country. In 1998, a reporter for the *New Yorker* magazine who visited Sayyid Ashmawy, a judge notorious for his progressive method of interpreting Islamic law, was shocked to find him protected by armed guards and to learn that Islamists had threatened him with death. On Ashmawy's predicament, see Mary Ann Weaver, "Revolution by Stealth," *The New Yorker*, June 8, 1998.

then the Court would have to "sell" this theory. The Court's approach may represent an attempt to suggest a progressive theory of Islamic law and to demonstrate its merits. The Court explicitly stated only the less controversial aspects of its theory, and it has pursued only implicitly its more progressive approach. In essence, the SCC may have been establishing the skeleton of a theory of Islamic law, and thereby allowing the public to see how it might grow into a progressive theory of Islamic law.

The SCC's cautious articulation of a liberal theory of Islamic law has allowed its theory slowly to take root in Egypt. Islamists may not like the results that the SCC has reached in its decisions, and they certainly would not like the SCC to crystallize its liberal approach. Nevertheless, the SCC provides one of the few public forums in which Islamists can argue about whether Egyptian law is consistent with Islamic law, and in which they can be confident that their arguments will be publicly noted and (notwithstanding the censorship of Islamist works) will quite likely be reported. Furthermore, the Court's theory is sufficiently flexible that if there is a tremendous public backlash or a change in personnel, the Court might start to apply its theory in a more conservative fashion. Islamists have thus had incentive not to reject the Court's theory outright, but rather to come to the Court and ask it to apply the theory it has articulated in a more conservative fashion.

Islamists and the SCC have benefited in the short term from the SCC's elaboration of an ambiguous theory. Islamists have gained a public forum and the possibility of a long-term victory for their conservative vision. The SCC has gained something too. The SCC's approach allowed justices who are best known for their prowess in civil and international law (rather than Islamic law) to establish themselves as credible voices in questions of Islamic legal theory. The fact that conservative Islamists have been willing to argue respectfully with the justices has helped to legitimize the Court as a serious voice in the debate about the proper interpretation of Islamic law in the modern world. Furthermore, the SCC has been able to monitor the degree to which its theory is accepted and if there is severe resistance on the part of the public or other judges. It remains free to modify its approach just enough to maintain public support for its vision of an "Islamic law" that is consistent with its liberal constitutionalist philosophy.

II. *The reaction of the Egyptian judiciary to the SCC's Article 2 jurisprudence*

The response of Egyptian courts to this delicate dance has been largely favorable. As noted in our discussion of the polygamy case, the SCC in 1994 was sufficiently worried about the judicial reactions to its approach to Islamic legal interpretation that it explicitly warned judges not to reject its theory. As the matter turned out, however, there was no widespread judicial revolt against the SCC's decisions; and indeed, some appeals courts have accepted the basic structure of the SCC's theory, and it would seem, its general liberal thrust. At the same time, judges in the regular courts and administrative courts do seem inclined to apply the SCC's theory in a slightly more conservative fashion. Judges outside the SCC tend to rely more heavily on the *ḥadīth* literature as a source of guidance on questions of Islamic law than the SCC has done, and when they make subjective judgments about the impact of a law on human welfare, they have favored more socially conservative outcomes than the SCC.

The most striking pattern in the judiciary's application of the SCC's theory is the implicit resistance to the SCC's use (or non-use) of the *ḥadīth* literature. As noted many times above, the SCC has never clarified its method of identifying "authentic" texts, but it seems to be such a stringent test that the *ḥadīth* literature is largely ignored. This is apparently unacceptable to some judges, as is evident from Appeal No. 5257/43 (decided on December 28, 1997), in which the Supreme Administrative Court evaluated the constitutionality of an administrative regulation issued in 1996 and found it consistent with the principles of the *sharīʿa*.[2]

The administrative regulation challenged in Appeal No. 5257/43 effectively banned female circumcision. As Kilian Bälz has demonstrated, the Supreme Administrative Court in this case followed a line of analysis that echoes in almost all respects the SCC's interpretation of Article 2.[3] Its differences, however, are revealing. While

---

[2] See Supreme Administrative Court of Egypt, Appeal No. 5257/43 (decided December 28, 1997).

[3] Kilian Bälz, "Human Rights, the Rule of Law and the Construction of Tradition: The Egyptian Supreme Administrative Court and Female Circumcision (Appeal no. 5257/43, 28 December 1997)," *The Rule of Law in the Middle East and the Islamic World: Human Rights and the Judicial Process*, eds. Eugene Cotran, Mai Yamani (London: I.B. Tauris, 2000), 35–42.

nothing in the case is incompatible with the theory that the SCC announced, the case departs from an implicit pattern of previous SCC cases—it contains a detailed and informed discussion of the *ḥadīth* literature. The Supreme Administrative Court systematically examined *ḥadīth*s that had been used to support the practice of female circumcision. In deciding not to follow these *ḥadīth*s, it pointed out that many jurists considered these *ḥadīth*s "weak" and therefore unreliable. The Court suggested that doubts about authenticity, rather than textual ambiguity, explained why the classical jurists disagreed about the legality of the practice.[4]

In its jurisprudence, the Court of Cassation has also implicitly echoed the Supreme Administrative Court's implicit appeal for more systematic use of the *ḥadīth* literature.[5] Such a development, if carried through, would lessen to some extent the discretion of judges to decide the legal status of acts entirely on the basis of "goals" analysis. It would also limit the discretion of the judges who engaged in goals analysis, making it harder for judges to declare a law consistent with the "goals of the *sharīʿa*" simply because that law promoted results that the justices subjectively thought were beneficial. Nevertheless, the Court of Cassation seems to accept that goals analysis will be informed by judges' subjective normative values. It is significant that the Court of Cassation has apparently embraced a more socially conservative interpretation of justice or welfare than the SCC.[6]

---

[4] See Bälz, "Human Rights," 38–41.

[5] As it said in one case, "The Sharīʿa texts are the Qur'an and Sunna, the latter being the second source of legislation . . . Qur'anic verses order us to obey God's Prophet (peace be upon him), which is like obeying God himself." Court of Cassation, Nos. 475, 478, 481, Year 65, Aug. 5, 1996, trans. Maurits Berger and Baudouin Dupret, "Jurisprudence Abu Zayd: Extrats des arrests du Tribunal d'Instance de Giza, de la Cour de l'Appel du Caire (traduit vers le français) et de la Cour de Cassation (traduit vers l'anglais)," *Droits d'Egypt: Histoire et Sociologie, Egypt Monde Arabe* (Paris: Centre d'Etudes et de Documentation Economique et Juridique, Second Seminar, 1998), 195. English translation follows Ousamma Arabi, *Studies in Modern Islamic Law and Jurisprudence* (Arab and Islamic Law Series vol. 21; The Hague: Kluwer, 2001), 187.

[6] See, e.g., Maurits Berger's analyses of the Islamic component in judicial interpretation of public policy. Maurits Berger, "Public Policy and Islamic Law: the Modern *Dhimmī* in Contemporary Egyptian Family Law," *Islamic Law and Society* 8 (2001): 88–122. The most notorious example of the Court of Cassation's potential for conservative interpretation came in its opinion in the apostasy trial of Abū Zayd. The Court of Cassation implicitly adopted the general premise of the SCC's theory—namely that in issues not governed by an indubitably authentic and clear

III. *Academic reactions to the SCC's Article 2 jurisprudence*

A number of historians, anthropologists, political scientists and legal academics have examined SCC opinions, but they have reached different conclusions about how to characterize the SCC's approach to interpreting Islamic law.[7] Oussama Arabi has claimed that the Court's theory is to be understood, "basically in terms of classical Islamic legal methodology,"[8] and he refers to their jurisprudential approach as "a version of state Shāfiʿism."[9] It is not clear exactly what Arabi means by this. He is an accomplished scholar of Islamic legal history, and he seems to recognize that the SCC's theory is not strictly classical. ʿArabi may simply be trying to emphasize that (1) the justices, like al-Shāfiʿī, differentiate between areas in which God's rule is clearly stated in scripture and other areas in which it is not; (2) in these "other" areas, Muslims must try to use a method called *ijtihād* to reconstruct what God wants humans to do; and (3) people who perform *ijtihād* will reach different conclusions about God's command. Accepting that, at this broad level, the SCC's theory and al-Shāfiʿī's theory have something in common, one should not downplay the Court's departures from al-Shāfiʿī's assumptions

scriptural text, interpreters could be expected to disagree. Not only did the Court of Cassation specifically assert that the *ḥadīth* literature should be considered a source of absolutely certain rulings, but it seemed implicitly to be willing to consider many of these *ḥadīth*s "clear." Thus, the "sphere of *ijtihād*" was much smaller than the SCC assumed it to be. Concluding that Dr. Abū Zayd's conclusions went beyond what that "sphere" the Court found Dr. Abū Zayd to be an apostate. For an analysis of this case, see, e.g., "Apostasy and Public Policy in Contemporary Egypt: An Evaluation of Recent Cases from Egypt's Highest Courts," *Human Rights Quarterly* 25.3 (2003): 720–40, particularly 728–33.

[7] Some important writing on Article 2 comes from legal scholars who do not specialize in Islamic legal theory. These scholars have, for obvious reasons, shied from parsing the nuances of the Court's use of technical terms or of critiquing its methodology. Instead, they have described in broad terms the Court's approach, and then analyzed, often perceptively, the patterns in the disposition of cases. See, e.g., Hatem Aly Labib Gabr, "The Interpretation of Article 2 of the Constitution: Islamic Sharia Principles as a Source of Law," *Human Rights and Democracy: The Role of the Supreme Constitutional Court of Egypt*, eds. Kevin Boyle and Adel Omar Sherif (CIMEL Book Series 3; London: Kluwer, 1996), 217–27; John Murray and Mohammed El-Molla, "Islamic Shariʿa and Constitutional Interpretation in Egypt," in *Democracy, the Rule of Law and Islam*, Eugene Cotran and Adel Omar Sherif, eds. (CIMEL Book Series No. 6; London: Kluwer, 1999), 507–24. For the purposes of this book, however, it is more useful to look at the writings of scholars who specialize in Islamic legal theory.

[8] Arabi, *Studies*, 174.

[9] Arabi, *Studies*, 195.

about texts and the proper way to interpret them. Al-Shafīʿī and other classical jurists accepted far more texts (including *ḥadīths*) as authentic and clear (and thus legally probative) than the SCC does, and thus they recognized far fewer issues as being open to *ijtihād*. Furthermore, in the areas where laws were to be determined by *ijtihād*, al-Shāfiʿī sharply criticized the type of intuitive consequentialist reasoning that the SCC seems to embrace. As most commentators have made a point to point out, there is something distinctly untraditional about the SCC's theory. Yet those scholars who have highlighted the distinctively modern tone of the SCC's Islamic legal theory have been reluctant to place it in any particular line of modernist thought.

In a seminal 1999 article, Frank Vogel described a number of the ways in which the Court uses traditional terms in untraditional ways.[10] Looking at the Court's claim to be performing *ijtihād*, he suggests that "their references to *ijtihad* may be no more than a careless use of words or conceptions, especially since they are usually bolstered by purely utilitarian arguments for assigning power to decide to the state."[11] Conceding that the SCC seems to be trying to establish a new theory of Islamic law and legal interpretation, he does not feel comfortable characterizing it as an analogue of any existing modernist theory and suggests that it is *sui generis*.[12] Similarly, in an insightful 1997 article, Baber Johansen stressed that the SCC has clearly *not* embraced a traditional method of identifying the principles of the Islamic *sharīʿa*.[13] Furthermore, he notes, the Court has not adopted

[10] Frank Vogel, "Conformity with Islamic Shariʿa and Constitutionality under Article 2: Some Issues of Theory, Practice, and Comparison," *Democracy, the Rule of Law and Islam*, particularly 535–38.

[11] Vogel, "Conformity," 538.

[12] "The Court may have begun to develop its own theory of Islamic constitutionalism and legislation. A key element so far is devotion to fixed but highly general principles established either by a clear text or by their pervasive influence on fiqh . . . coupled with an openness to a free-wheeling *ijtihad*, even when that *ijtihad* diverges entirely from the views, even the consensus of past scholars." Vogel, "Conformity," 543–44.

[13] Baber Johansen, "Supra-legislative Norms and Constitutional Courts: The Case of France and Egypt," *The Role of the Judiciary in the Protection of Human Rights*, eds. Eugene Cotran, Adel Omar Sherif (CIMEL Book Series No. 5; London: Kluwer, 1997), 347–76. The point was later pursued in more detail in a presentation delivered to a conference of Islamicists.

wholesale any of the most important modernist methods either: "Given the wording of this Article [2], the legislator and the Court could have boldly re-interpreted the term 'principles' in light of the Islamic modernism of Muḥammad ʿAbduh or ʿAbd al-Razzāq al-Sanhūrī. But apparently neither the legislator nor the constitutional court had the ambition to do so."[14] It was outside the scope of Johansen's article to describe in any detail, the method that he thinks they use to interpret the *sharīʿa*. He does note with approval that the SCC's theory permits it to interpret the principles of Islamic law in a way that renders them consistent with constitutional principles that the Court has already identified.[15]

In fact, some scholars have found the SCC's approach so perplexing that they have questioned whether the Court's theory can comfortably be placed in the "Islamic" legal tradition at all. They suggest that the Court, possibly in bad faith, has taken constitutional principles that are established in "secular" parts of the constitution and apologetically declared them to be Islamic principles. Thus, Kilian Bälz has asserted that Article 2 jurisprudence "is nothing but a strategy used by the secular order of secular law to maintain its autonomy."[16] Ran Hirschl has described the SCC's Article 2 jurisprudence in similar terms, calling it a "secularizing" theory of Islamic law—created in response to the rise of political Islamism.[17] Other social scientists have proposed a more elaborate version of this idea that there is something inherently "secular" and by implication un-Islamic about the SCC's theory.[18]

---

[14] Johansen, "Supra-legislative Norms," 369.

[15] Ibid., 370.

[16] Kilian Bälz, "The Secular Reconstruction of Islamic Law: The Egyptian Supreme Constitutional Court and the 'Battle over the Veil' in State-Run Schools," in *Legal Pluralism in the Arab World*, Baudouin Dupret, Maurits Berger, and Laila al-Zwaini, eds. (The Hague: Kluwer, 1999), 229–43.

[17] Ran Hirschl, "Constitutional Courts in the Field of Power Politics: Constitutional Courts vs. Religious Fundamentalism," *Texas Law Review* 82 (2004): 1822–28.

[18] See, e.g., Nathan Brown, "Islamic Constitutionalism in Theory and Practice," photocopy, 17. [My thanks to Professor Brown for providing me with a copy of his paper]; Baudouin Dupret, "'La Charīʿa est la source de la législation': interprétations jurisprudentielles et théories juridiques," *Annuaire de l'Afrique du Nord* 34 (1995): 261–68; Baudouin Dupret, "Entre le droit et la loi. Le juge et le jeu de la normalization islamique du droit positif," *Droits et Cultures* 30 (1995): 47–64; Nathalie Bernard-Maugiron, "La Haute Cour constitutionelle Égyptienne et la sharīʿa islamique," *Awrāq* (Madrid) 19 (1998): 653–80.

As this book has made clear, it is important to stress the degree to which the SCC's theory differs from classical theory. It is also crucial to note that the SCC's theory does not fit neatly into any particular line of modernist thought and that the Court's interpretation of Islamic law has been influenced by its assumption that human welfare requires protection of international human rights. Interpreted in this way, Article 2 has reinforced the Court's existing jurisprudence in the area of economic rights and other fundamental rights.

At the same time, I would argue that the SCC's theory can be placed more clearly in the line of modernist thought than previous writing has acknowledged. The modernist Islamic legal tradition is diverse and fluid. Modernist Islamic legal thinkers have appropriated the same classical concepts, but have used them in very different ways. In many cases, however, modernist theories share a common tolerance for subjectivism. While drawing rhetorically upon classical theory, and its methods of *ijtihād* and *taqlīd*, they reject the textualism and/or formalism of classical interpretive method. Their approaches tend to limit the number of rulings that jurists will find and thus increase the importance of broad principles that can be applied differently in various times and places. The SCC's theory as elaborated to date is best conceptualized as a pastiche of theories espousing utilitarian neo-*ijtihād* and theories espousing comparative neo-*taqlīd*. It is designed to appeal rhetorically to a wide range of Islamist factions—and, at the same time, to preserve the subjectivism that leaves the courts discretion to interpret Islamic law as consistent with the justices' assumptions about the nature of human welfare. For the current justices, these assumptions are consistent with their liberal constitutional jurisprudence.

Although this theory is ambiguous in places, it is not incoherent and, in its current form, can plausibly be located within the modernist tradition. It may yet evolve into a systematic and compelling theory. I suggested above that, notwithstanding the elements that the SCC's theory of Islamic law and legal interpretation shares with classical theories, it would be deeply misleading to characterize it as "classical." Similarly, the SCC's Article 2 jurisprudence draws much from the jurisprudence that grows out of the Court's interpretation of provisions other than Article 2, provisions that might be termed "secular." It would equally be a mistake to describe the SCC's theory as "secular" or to imply that it is somehow less authentic than the theories of some modernist Islamic groups whose good faith is rarely, if ever, questioned. Many modernist Islamists, including some members of the Muslim Brotherhood, have been willing to embrace extremely flexible utilitarian methods of Islamic legal reasoning. In so doing, they are willing to rely on Islamic methods of interpretation that are no less subjective than those used by the SCC. If a person accepts that "Islamic" legal judgments will depend upon a subjective preference for certain outcomes, then there is nothing inherently un-Islamic about a judge's belief that legal judgments should depend upon the degree to which human rights are preserved. To put it differently, a subjectivist theory should not lose its claim to be "Islamic" simply because the Court imports progressive assumptions rather than conservative ones.[19]

The SCC has created an embryonic new theory of Islamic law—one which represents a pastiche of influential modernist Islamic legal theories and is capable of being elaborated in a number of different ways. The generally favorable reception of the theory to date by Egyptian judges in the regular court system suggests that they too see the theory, as articulated so far, as plausibly Islamic—although they would prefer that it evolve in a slightly more conservative direction.

IV. *Conclusion: The reception of the SCC's Article 2 jurisprudence*

In sum, over the last twenty years, the SCC has elaborated a skeletal theory of Islamic law that can be (and indeed has been) applied to create a liberal theory of Islamic law. The promise of a liberal

[19] For a slightly different critique, see Arabi, *Studies*, 208–9 and accompanying footnotes. Finally, the claim that Islamic law is being secularized might arise from the fact that Islamic law is being interpreted by officials of the government, namely judges who have received a secular education rather than a classical religious one. But I am not sure this can be considered a compelling case. The leading modern *ʿulamāʾ* who have been educated and teach at al-Azhar receive a very different training than the classical jurists and their degree. Their degree is issued by a state-run university rather than an independent institution, and many of them are state employees who receive a paycheck from the state. Furthermore, as noted already, many Islamist theories assume that the *ʿulamāʾ* have no unique authority to interpret Islamic law. Thus, it is hard to see why an interpretation controlled by judges is inherently less "Islamic" than one controlled by members of the modern *ʿulamāʾ*.

interpretation of Islamic law has tantalized many Islamic legal scholars and politicians over the years. In spite of its ambiguities (and perhaps because of them), the Court's theory has been tested and seems to be gaining acceptance. It has been imposed without provoking serious public outrage, and Egyptian appeals courts seem generally to be adopting it, although they are relying more heavily on the *ḥadīth* literature and tempering the extreme progressivism inherent in the SCC's interpretation of the concepts of justice and welfare. The SCC apparently hopes that its vision of Islamic law will convince the next generation of Islamists and the next generation of judges alike that a constitutional Islamization provision can and should be applied in progressive fashion. Conservative Islamists today probably hope that this next generation of Islamists and judges will turn farther to the right. The results, though as yet undecided, are worth watching.[20]

[20] Johansen, "Supra-legislative Norms," 376.

CONCLUSION

By reflecting on the history and interpretation of Article 2, it is possible to understand better the challenges and opportunities facing governments which incorporate *sharīʿa* provisions into their constitutions. The idea that a government has legitimacy because it applies only laws consistent with *sharīʿa* has a long history in Egypt, and in the Sunnī Islamic world in general. This history helps to explain why, as constitutionalism spreads in the Muslim world, Muslims have shown a deep interest in constitutional Islamization.

In the early modern period, however, consensus broke down on the basic question of how to identify and interpret the applicable rulings and goals of Islamic law. Partly for this reason, governments in countries like Egypt chose to assert their legitimacy not in Islamic terms but instead in terms of secular ideologies, such as nationalism or pan-Arabism. Nevertheless, when these alternate ideologies lost their luster, states like Egypt were tempted to revisit the question of Islamic legitimacy. They acceded to the demands to measure the state's legitimacy in Islamic terms. Some, like Egypt, indicated their new commitment to Islamization by including a constitutional Islamization provision in their national constitutions.

A country, particularly a one-party state like Egypt, can easily adopt a constitutional provision for *sharīʿa*. As Egypt's experience with Article 2 reveals, however, it can be very difficult for a country that has adopted such a provision to develop a policy implementing its command. If a government wishes to convince the public that its law is consistent with Islamic norms, it must find (or generate) consensus on complex and hotly disputed questions: who can interpret *sharīʿa*, what methods the authoritative interpreters may use, and what assumptions they should make about the nature of human welfare.

In Egypt during the 1970s, the government of Anwar Sādāt was apparently confident that it could use the political process to negotiate and generate support for an official version of Islamic law. It loosened restrictions on Islamist organizations, began formal and informal consultations with various Islamist factions, and eventually began to draft Islamic revisions to its law. Believing that it was generating consensus around an acceptable theory of Islamic law, the government arranged for Article 2 of the Egyptian constitution to be amended in 1980 to state that "the principles of the Islamic *sharī'a*" were to be "the chief source" of Egyptian legislation. Shortly thereafter, however, the regime came to suspect that their proposed Islamic codes might not give their state the Islamic legitimacy for which they had hoped.

Official plans for Islamization were shelved. Once they had constitutionalized the *sharī'a*, they could not simply stop Islamization. By shelving the draft codes and abandoning their policy of executive-sponsored Islamic legal reform, however, the executive and legislative branches left the problem of Islamization in the hands of the increasingly independent judiciary. Faced with an increasing number of cases challenging laws as unconstitutional under Article 2, the courts were forced to issue opinions exploring whether (and ultimately how) Egyptian law should be measured against *sharī'a* norms.

The justices of the Supreme Constitutional Court seemed initially reluctant to take on the responsibility of deciding Article 2 cases. Starting in the early 1990s, however, they began systematically to articulate a theory—or at least the basic outlines of an intriguing Islamic legal theory, seemingly crafted to appeal to a wide spectrum of Islamists. The Court seems implicitly to suggest that constitutional Islamization clauses should be seen to impose, constitutionally, an analogue of the classical model of *siyāsa shar'iyya*. The SCC apparently envisions the judiciary functioning like the classical *madhhab*s, as the institution uniquely authorized to apply a generally-accepted method of legal interpretation to establish the Islamic norms to which the state's law must conform. Decisions of the authoritative members of the judiciary (here the SCC) will bind later panels of the SCC and, of course, less authoritative members of the judiciary—such as the judges on the lower courts.

In describing its method of Article 2 interpretation, the Court has drawn vocabulary, concepts and interpretive techniques from a number of competing modernist theories of Islamic legal interpretation. At the same time, it seems deliberately to have left aspects of its theory undeveloped. By establishing a theory that is subject to further clarification and evolution, the SCC gave Islamists incentive to come to court, accept the basic theory, and argue about its future elaboration.

At the same time, the SCC has implicitly shown a preference for a rationalist and utilitarian approach to its interpretation of the *sharī'a*.

The Court checks laws under attack for consistency with specific rulings that God has established. These rulings, however, must be interpreted and sometimes qualified by an overarching command that humans act in a way that is beneficial to themselves and others. In elaborating upon this utilitarian command, the justices have looked not only to the Islamic tradition, but also, implicitly, to reason. And the Court has apparently reasoned that the enjoyment of constitutional rights (and international human rights) are a fundamental component of the good life. As a result, the Court's interpretation of the *sharīʿa* has so far preserved and even reinforced the liberal constitutional doctrines which the Court has already developed, particularly in the area of women's rights.

As a result, some scholars have dismissed the Court's jurisprudence as apologetic. Such criticism, however, seems to overlook an essential point. Classical Islamic legal theory itself had an apologetic component—and was used in many cases to justify interpretations of Islamic law that had not previously been explained adequately in Islamic terms. Most would agree that this does not take away from the achievements of classical jurists or from the power that Islamic legal theory had to create legal order and legitimize states.

For those interested in evaluating the SCC's theory and understanding its impact on contemporary Islamic legal and political thought, the most important questions are whether the theory is coherent, and whether it has created in the eyes of contemporary Egyptian Muslims a compelling case for the legitimacy of a progressive, liberal jurisprudence. The SCC's theory is coherent, but not fully developed. The question of whether it will be widely embraced is one that remains to be seen. Only time will tell whether the SCC will succeed in its attempt to forge consensus around its liberal interpretation of the *sharīʿa*. Although some judges initially resisted the Court's decision which held Article 2 to be non-retroactive, there has been little, if any, overt disobedience to the SCC's orders or its precedents since the early 1990s. Thus, at some broad level, the SCC's liberal interpretation seems to have been accepted. On the other hand, the embrace of the Court's jurisprudence theory has not been unqualified. Judges in lower courts have often used their opinions implicitly to suggest that they would prefer to interpret *sharīʿa* in a manner that reflects more traditional notions of Islam—even at the expense of liberal constitutional principles. Thus, when called upon to interpret *sharīʿa*, the Court of Cassation and the Supreme

Administrative Court have drawn extensively upon the SCC's theory, but they have also used the *ḥadīth* literature more than the justices have, and this has led them to reach more conservative results.

As stressed many times in this book, the SCC has chosen not to elaborate every aspect of its interpretive method. For example, the Court has not been forthcoming about the method that it uses to identify which scriptural texts are absolutely certain to be authentic—and thus valid sources of knowledge about God's rulings. Nor has it fully described the hermeneutic tools it uses to interpret these texts. The theory could thus develop in a number of directions, including the more conservative direction favored by some Egyptian courts. The caginess on some of these issues may reflect the Court's concern that it has gone too far ahead of Egyptian society. To maintain support for its jurisprudence, it must leave some room for the theory to evolve, if necessary, to take account of the public's more conservative inclinations.

The qualified reception of the SCC's implicitly liberal interpretive assumptions suggests that the Court may indeed have past the point that the next generation of Egyptians feels appropriate. Then again, Egypt may simply be digesting the SCC's theory before it commits itself. This may have some interesting implications for the broader appeal and long-term consequences of the SCC's theory. The Court's Article 2 jurisprudence to date—both its theory and the implicit assumptions that it makes when applying this theory—may provide a model for countries that are trying to integrate Islamic law into the constitutional fabric of a liberal society. On the other hand, courts in other countries may come up with very different ways of selecting and combining various competing approaches to Islamic legal interpretation.

At the broadest level, Egypt's experience tells us interesting things about the evolution of Islamic law in the modern world. In Egypt, as in the rest of the Sunnī Islamic world, the debates raging about the methods of Islamic legal interpretation and the content of the *sharīʿa* have created a chaotic situation. I do not mean 'chaotic' in the popular sense, which has a pejorative connotation. The debates over Islamic law are chaotic in the classical Greek sense of a jumbled and disordered state that provides the raw material for a new order.[1]

[1] "Chaos: . . . (2) the disordered state of unformed matter and infite space believed,

Out of the building blocks of modern Islamic thought, the SCC has shaped a liberal theory of Islamic law—albeit one that will continue to evolve.

Islamic legal theory and law continue to inspire serious Muslim legal thinkers throughout the Muslim world and to provide them with a reservoir of powerful concepts and vocabulary. From the SCC's Article 2 jurisprudence, we learn that, in the hands of judges committed to democracry and human rights, these concepts and vocabulary can be put to different uses. Under the right circumstances, constitutional Islamization can help to reinforce Western notions of a liberal rule of law.

---

according to some religious or cosmological views, to have existed prior to the ordered universe." *Webster's II New Riverside University Dictionary* (Boston: Houghton Mifflin, 1995), 187.

BIBLIOGRAPHY

Abbreviations

EI2: *Encyclopedia of Islam*, New Edition (Leiden: Brill, 1971–).
MECS: *Middle East Contemporary Survey*, annual, Tel Aviv University
SCC: *al-Maḥkama al-Dustūriyya al-ʿUlyā* [Court Reporter of the Supreme Constitutional Court], vols. I–VIII.

Selected Legislation from the Arab Republic of Egypt

Arab Republic of Egypt, *Dustūr Jumhūriyyat Miṣr al-ʿArabiyya* (1971).

Arab Republic of Egypt, Law No. 25 (1929). For partial English trans., see David Pearl, *A Textbook on Muslim Law* (London: Croon Helm, 1979), 254–55.

al-Qānūn al-Madanī (Egypt), Law No. 131 (1948).

Arab Republic of Egypt, Law No. 48 (1979). For English trans., see Awad El-Morr, "The Supreme Constitutional Court and the Protection of Human Rights," in *Human Rights and Democracy: The Role of the Supreme Constitutional Court of Egypt*, Kevin Boyle and Adel Omar Sherif, eds. (CIMEL Book Series 3; London: Kluwer, 1996), 323–39.

Arab Republic of Egypt, Law No. 100 (1985).

Books and Articles

ʿAbduh, Muḥammad, *Risālat al-Tawḥīd*, Rashīd Riḍā, ed. (Cairo: Maṭbaʿat al-Manār, 1346 A.H.).

—— *Risālat al-Tawḥīd*, trans. B. Michel and Moustapha Abdel Razek, *Risalat al-Tawhid: exposé de la religion musulmane* (Paris: Paul Geuthner, 1925).

—— *Risālat al-Tawḥīd*, trans. Kenneth Cragg and Ishaq Masaʿad, *The Theology of Unity* (London: Allen and Unwin, 1966).

ʿAbduh, Muḥammad and Rashīd Riḍā, *Tafsīr al-Manār*, 12 vols. (Cairo: Maṭbaʿat al-Manār, 1346–1353 A.H.).

Abou-Talib, Soufy Hossain (Sūfī Ḥussain Abū Ṭālib), *Le Periculum Rei Venditae en Droit Roman et en Droit Musulman* (Cairo: Imprimerie Université du Caire, 1958).

Abu Lughod, Ibrahim, *The Arab Rediscovery of Europe* (Princeton: Princeton University Press, 1963).

Abu-Rabiʿ, Ibrahim, *Intellectual Origins of Islamic Resurgence in the Modern Arab World* (Albany: State University of New York Press, 1996).

Adams, Charles C., *Islam and Modernism in Egypt: A Study of the Modern Reform Movement Inaugurated by Muḥammad ʿAbduh* (1933; repr. New York: Russell and Russell, 1968).

—— "Muhammad ʿAbduh and the Transvaal Fatwa," in *The Macdonald Presentation Volume* (London: Oxford University Press, 1933), 13–29.

Altman, Israel, "Islamic Legislation in Egypt in the Early 1970's," *Asian and African Studies* 13 (1979), 199–219.

—— "The Arab Republic of Egypt," in MECS III (1978–79), 389–432.

—— "The Arab Republic of Egypt," in MECS IV (1979–80), 325–91.

Anderson, J.N.D., "The Shariʿa and Civil Law," *Islamic Law Quarterly* 1.1 (1954), 29–46.

—— *Law Reform in the Muslim World* (London: Athalone Press, 1976).
Ansari, Hamid, *Egypt: The Stalled Society* (Albany: State University of New York Press, 1986).
Amer, S., "Public International Law" in *Egypt and its Laws*, Nathalie Bernard-Maugiron and Baudouin Dupret, eds. (Arab and Islamic Law Series 22; London/The Hague/New York: Kluwer Law International, 2002), 377–92.
Arabi, Oussama, "Al-Sanhūrī's Reconstruction of the Islamic Law of Contract Defects: Error and Real Intent," *Journal of Islamic Studies* 6.2 (1995), 153–72.
—— "Intention and Method in Sanhūrī's Fiqh: Cause as Ulterior Motive," *Islamic Law and Society* 4.2 (1997), 200–23.
—— "The Dawning of the Third Millennium on Sharīʿa: Egypt's Law No. 1 of 2000, or Women May Divorce at Will," *Arab Law Quarterly* 16.1 (2001), 2–21.
—— *Studies in Modern Islamic Law and Jurisprudence* (Arab and Islamic Law Series vol. 21: The Hague/London/New York: Kluwer Law International, 2001).
al-Ashmāwī, Muḥammad Saʿīd, *Against Islamic Extremism: The Writings of Muḥammad Saʿīd al-Ashmāwī*, Carolyn Fluehr-Lobban, ed. (Gainesville: University Press of Florida, 1998).
Ayalon, Ami, "Egypt," in MECS V (1980–81), 413–57.
—— "The Arab Republic of Egypt," in MECS VI (1981–82), 441–79.
—— "The Arab Republic of Egypt," in MECS VII (1982–83), 413–46.
—— "Egypt," in MECS VIII (1983–84), 353–86.
—— "The Arab Republic of Egypt," in MECS IX (1984–85), 345–77.
—— "The Arab Republic of Egypt," in MECS XI (1987), 323–57.
—— "The Arab Republic of Egypt," in MECS XIV (1990), 314–49.
—— "The Arab Republic of Egypt," in MECS XVI (1992), 364–94.
Baer, Gabriel, *Studies in the Social History of Modern Egypt* (Chicago: University of Chicago Press, 1969).
—— "Islamic Political Activity in Modern Egyptian History: A Comparative Analysis," in *Islam, Nationalism and Radicalism*, Gabriel R. Warburg and Uri M. Kupferschmidt, eds. (New York: Praeger, 1983).
Bälz, Kilian, "Shariʿa and Qanun in Egyptian Law: A Systems Theory Approach to Legal Pluralism," *Yearbook of Islamic and Middle Eastern Law* 2 (1995), 37–57.
—— "Submitting Faith to Judicial Scrutiny Through the Family Trial: The Abu Zayd Case," *Die Welt Des Islams* 37 (1997), 135–75.
—— "La construction séculière du droit islamique: la Haute Cour constitutionelle égyptienne et la 'bataille de voile' dans les écoles publiques," *Droit et Société* 39 (1998), 277–91.
—— "Human Rights, the Rule of Law and the Construction of Tradition: The Egyptian Supreme Administrative Court and Female Circumcision (Appeal no. 5257/43, 28 December 1997)," in *The Rule of Law in the Middle East and the Islamic World: Human Rights and the Judicial Process*, Eugene Cotran, Mai Yamani, eds. (London: I.B. Tauris, 2000), 35–42.
—— "The Secular Reconstruction of Islamic Law: The Egyptian Supreme Constitutional Court and the 'Battle over the Veil' in State-Run Schools," in *Legal Pluralism in the Arab World*, Baudouin Dupret, Maurits Berger, and Laila al-Zwaini, eds. (The Hague: Kluwer, 1999), 229–43.
al-Banna', Hasan, *Five Tracts of Hasan al-Banna': A Selection from the Majmuʿat Rasa'il al-Imam al-Shahid Hasan al-Banna'*, trans. Charles Wendell. (Berkeley: University of California Press, 1975).
Barraclough, Steven, "Al-Azhar Between the Government and the Islamists," *Middle East Journal* 52 (1988), 251–77.
Beattie, Kirk J., *Egypt During the Nasser Years: Ideology, Politics and Civil Society* (Boulder: Westview Press, 1994).

—— *Egypt During the Sadat Years* (New York: Palgrave, 2000).
Bentham, Jeremy, *An Introduction to the Principles of Morals and Legislation*, J.H. Burns and H.L.A. Hart, eds. (London: Atholone Press, 1970).
Bentley, John, Egyptian Legal and Judicial Sector Assessment: Report and Recommendations submitted to USAID/Egypt" (Cairo: Kamel Law Offices, 1994).
Berger, Maurits, "Public Policy and Islamic Law: the Modern *Dhimmī* in Contemporary Egyptian Family Law," *Islamic Law and Society* 8.1 (2001), 88–122.
—— "Apostasy and Public Policy in Contemporary Egypt: An Evaluation of Recent Cases from Egypt's Highest Courts," *Human Rights Quarterly* 25.3 (2003), 720–40.
Bernard-Maugiron, Nathalie, "La Haute Cour constitutionelle Égyptienne et la sharī'a islamique," *Awrâq*, 19 (1998), 653–80.
—— "La deuxième décennie de la Haute Cour constitutionelle égyptienne, 1988–1998," *Annuaire international de justice constitutionelle* (1998), 653–80.
—— "La Haute Cour constitutionnelle, gardienne des libertés publiques," in "Le Prince et son juge: droit et politique dans l'Égypte contemporaine," Nathalie Bernard-Maugiron and Baudouin Dupret, eds. *Egypte/Monde Arabe* 2 (1999), 17–54.
Bernard-Maugiron, Nathalie and Baudouin Dupret, eds., *Egypt and its Laws* (Arab and Islamic Law Series 22; The Hague/London/New York: Kluwer Law International, 2002).
—— eds., *Le Prince et son juge: droit et politique dans l'Égypte contemporaine* (special edition of *Egypte/monde arabe*; Cairo: CEDEJ, 1999).
—— " 'Les principes de la sharia sont la source de la législation': la Haute Cour constitutionelle et la reference à la loi Islamique," in Nathalie Bernard-Maugiron and Baudouin Dupret, eds., "Le Prince et son juge: droit et politique dans l'Égypte contemporaine," *Egypte/Monde Arabe* 2 (1999), 107–26.
Binder, Leonard, "Al-Ghazali's theory of Islamic Government," *The Muslim World* 45 (1955), 229–41.
—— *In a Moment of Enthusiasm: Political Power and the Second Stratum in Egypt* (Chicago: University of Chicago Press, 1978).
Botiveau, Bernard, "Islamiser le droit?: l'éxample égyptien," *Maghreb-Mashrek* 126 (1989), 10–25.
—— "Les juges égyptiens saisis par le doute," *Annuaire de l'Afrique du Nord* 28 (1989), 261–68.
—— "Le statut personnel des musulmans égyptien au XXe siècle: régulations autoritaires et réponses sociales," *Annales Islamologiques* 27 (1993), 77–93.
—— "Contemporary Reinterpretations of Islamic Law: The Case of Egypt," in *Islam and Public Law: Classical and Contemporary Studies*, Chibli Mallat, ed. (London: Graham and Trotman, 1993), 261–77.
—— *Loi islamique et droit dans les sociétés arabes* (Paris/Karthala/Aix en Provence: Iremam, 1993).
Boyle, Kevin, "Human Rights in Egypt: International Commitments" in *Human Rights and Democracy: The Role of the Supreme Constitutional Court of Egypt*, Kevin Boyle and Adel Omar Sherif, eds. (CIMEL Book Series 3; London: Kluwer, 1996).
Boyle, Kevin and Adel Omar Sherif, eds., *Human Rights and Democracy: The Role of the Supreme Constitutional Court of Egypt* (CIMEL Book Series 3; London: Kluwer, 1996).
Brown, Daniel, *Rethinking Tradition in Modern Islamic Legal Thought* (Cambridge: Cambridge University Press, 1996).
Brown, Nathan, *The Rule of Law in the Arab World: Courts in Egypt and the Gulf* (Cambridge: Cambridge University Press, 1997).
—— "*Sharī'a* and State in the Modern Muslim Middle East," *International Journal of Middle East Studies* 29 (1997), 359–76.
—— "Islamic Constitutionalism in Theory and Practice," in *Democracy, the Rule of*

Law and Islam, Eugene Cotran and Adel Omar Sherif, eds. (CIMEL Book Series No. 6; London: Kluwer, 1999), 491–507.
Burton, John, *The Sources of Islamic Law: Islamic Theories of Abrogation* (Edinburgh: University of Edinburgh Press, 1990).
—— *An Introduction to Ḥadīth* (Edinburgh: University of Edinburgh Press, 1994).
Calder, Norman, "*Ikhtilāf* and *Ijmā*ʿ in Shāfiʿī's *Risāla*" *Studia Islamica*, 58 (1984), 55–81.
—— "Al-Nawawī's typology of *Muftīs* and Its Significance for a General Theory of Islamic Law," *Islamic Law and Society* 4 (1996), 137–64.
—— *Studies in Early Muslim Jurisprudence* (Oxford: Clarendon Press, 1993).
Cappelletti, Mauro, *The Judicial Process in Comparative Perspective* (Oxford: Clarendon Press, 1989).
Carré, Olivier, "From Banna to Qutb to 'Qutbism': The Radicalization of Fundamentalist Thought under Three Regimes," in *Egypt from Monarchy to Republic*, Shimon Shamir, ed. (Boulder: Westview Press, 1995), 181–94.
Caspar, Robert, "Le Renouveau du Moʿtazilism," *Mélanges de l'Institut Dominicain d'Études Orientales du Caire* 4 (1957), 57–72.
Chehata, Chafik, "Le project de nouveau Code Civile," *Journal des Tribunaux Mixtes*, series beginning with no. 3579 (Feb. 25–26, 1946) and ending with no. 4015 (Dec. 22–23, 1948).
—— "Les survivances musulmanes dans la codification du droit civil égyptien," *Revue Internationale de Droit Comparé* 17 (1965), 839–53.
—— "Logique juridique et droit musulman," *Studia Islamica* 23 (1965), 5–25.
—— "L'equité en tant que source du droit hanafite," *Studia Islamica*, 25 (1966), 123–38.
—— *Théorie générale de l'obligation en droit musulman Hanefite* (Paris: Sirey, 1969).
Cole, Juan R.I., *Colonialism and Revolution in the Middle East: Social and Cultural Origins of Egypt's ʿUrabi Movement* (Princeton: Princeton University Press, 1993).
Cotran, Eugene and Adel Omar Sherif, eds., *The Role of the Judiciary in the Protection of Human Rights* (CIMEL Book Series No. 5; London: Kluwer, 1997).
Cotran, Eugene and Mai Yamani, eds., *The Rule of Law in the Middle East and the Islamic World: Human Rights and the Judicial Process* (London: I.B. Tauris, 2000).
Coulson, Noel, *A History of Islamic Law* (Edinburgh: Edinburgh University Press, 1964).
—— "The State and the Individual in Islamic Law" in *The Traditional Near East*, J. Stewart Robinson, ed. (Englewood, N.J.: Prentice Hall, 1966), 122–35.
Crecelius, Daniel, "Non-Ideological Responses of the Ulama to Modernization," in *Scholars, Saints, and Sufis: Muslim Religious Institutions in the Middle East Since 1500*, Nikkie R. Keddie, ed. (Berkeley: University of California Press, 1973), 167–90.
Crone, Patricia and Martin Hinds, *God's Caliph: Religious Authority in the First Centuries of Islam* (Cambridge: Cambridge University Press, 1986).
Cudsi, Alexander S. and Ali E. Hilal Dessouki, eds., *Islam and Power* (Baltimore: Johns Hopkins, 1981).
Dalacoura, Katerina, *Islam, Liberalism and Human Rights* (London: I.B. Tauris, 1998).
Dallal, Ahmad, "Appropriating the Past: Twentieth Century Reconstruction of Pre-Modern Islamic Thought," *Islamic Law and Society* 7 (2000), 325–58.
Dekmejian, R.H., *Islam in Revolution: Fundamentalism in the Arab World* (Syracuse: State University of New York Press, 1985).
Dessouki, Ali E. Hilal, "The Resurgence of Islamic Organizations in Egypt: An Interpretation," in *Islam and Power*, Alexander S. Cudsi and Ali E. Hilal Dessouki, eds. (Baltimore: Johns Hopkins, 1981), 107–18.
Dupret, Baudouin, "La shariʿa comme référent legislative: du droit positif à l'anthropologie du droit," *Revue interdisciplinaire d'études juridiques* 34 (1995), 99–153.
—— "Entre le droit et la loi. Le juge et le jeu de la normalisation islamique du droit positif," *Droits et Cultures* 30 (1995), 47–64.

—— *Au nom de quel droit? Répertoires juridiques et référence religieuse dans la société égyptienne musulmane contemporaine* (Paris, Maison des sciences de l'homme: 2000).

—— "'La Charīʿa est la source de la législation': interpretations jurisprudentielles et théories juridiques," *Annuaire de l'Afrique du Nord* 34 (1995), 261–68.

—— "La sharīʿa comme référent legislative: du droit positif à l'anthropologie du droit," *Révue interdisciplinaire d'études juridiques* 34 (1995), 99–153.

—— "Entre le droit et la loi: le juge et le jeu de la normalization islamique du droit positif," *Droits et Cultures* 30 (1995), 47–64.

—— "A propos de l'affaire Abu Zayd, universitaire poursuivi pour apostasie; le process: l'argumentation des tribunaux," *Maghreb-Mashrek* 151 (1996), 19–22.

—— "A propos de la Constitutionalité de la Sharīʿa: Présentation et traduction de l'arrêt du 26 Mars 1994 (14 Shawwāl 1414) de la Haute Cour Constitutionelle (*al-maḥkama al-dustūriyya al-ʿulyā*) égyptienne," *Islamic Law and Society* 4 (1997), 91–113.

—— "La récherche judiciaire d'une moralité conforme: La Haute Cour constitutionelle égyptienne et le voile," in *Urbanité arabe: Hommage à Bernard Lepetit* (Arles: Sindbad, 1998), 353–81.

—— and Jean-Noel Ferré, "Participer au pouvoir, c'est édicter la norme: À propos de l'affaire Abu Zayd (Egypte 1992–1996)," *Revue Francaise de science politique* 47 (1997), 762–75.

Eccel, A. Chris, *Egypt, Islam and Social Change: al-Azhar in Change and Accommodation* (Islamkundliche Untersuchungen 81; Berlin: Klaus Schwartz, 1984).

—— "ʿĀlim and Mujāhid in Egypt: Orthodoxy v. Subculture, or Division of Labor?," *The Muslim World* 68 (1988), 189–208.

Ehteshami, Anoushiravan, "Is the Middle East Democratizing?," *British Journal of Middle Eastern Studies* 26 (1999), 199–218.

El-Alami, Dawoud, "Law 100 of 1985 Amending Certain Provisions of Egypt's Personal Status Laws," *Islamic Law and Society* 1 (1994), 131–36.

El-Morr, Awad, "The Supreme Constitutional Court and the Protection of Human Rights," in *Islam and Public Law: Classical and Contemporary Studies*, Chibli Mallat, ed. (London: Graham & Trotman, 1993), 229–59.

—— "Human Rights in the Constitutional Systems of Egypt and Other Islamic Countries: International and Comparative Systems," in *Human Rights and Democracy: The Role of the Supreme Constitutional Court of Egypt*, Kevin Boyle and Adel Omar Sherif, eds. (CIMEL Book Series 3; London: Kluwer, 1996), 161–215.

—— "The Status and Protection of Property in the Constitution," in *Human Rights and Democracy: The Role of the Supreme Constitutional Court of Egypt*, Kevin Boyle and Adel Omar Sherif, eds. (CIMEL Book Series 3; London: Kluwer, 1996), 115–27.

—— "Judicial Sources for Supporting the Protection of Human Rights," in *The Role of the Judiciary in the Protection of Human Rights*, Eugene Cotran and Adel Omar Sherif, eds. (CIMEL Book Series No. 5: London: Kluwer, 1997), 5–34.

El-Morr, Awad and Adel Omar Sherif, "The Separation of Powers and Limits on Presidential Powers under the Egyptian Constitution," in *Human Rights and Democracy: The Role of the Supreme Constitutional Court of Egypt*, Kevin Boyle and Adel Omar Sherif, eds. (CIMEL Book Series 3; London: Kluwer, 1996), 63–73.

El-Morr, Awad, Abd el-Rahman Nossier and Adel Omar Sherif, "The Supreme Constitutional Court of Egypt and its Role in the Egyptian Legal System" in *Human Rights and Democracy: The Role of the Supreme Constitutional Court of Egypt*, Kevin Boyle and Adel Omar Sherif, eds. (CIMEL Book Series 3; London: Kluwer, 1996), 37–60.

El-Nahall, Galal H., *The Judicial Administration of Ottoman Egypt in the Seventeenth Century* (Minneapolis: Biblioteca Islamica, 1979).

Enayat, Hamid, *Modern Islamic Political Thought* (Austin: University of Texas Press, 1982).

El-Sawi, Ahmad, "Procedural Law (Civil Procedure, Criminal Procedure, Administrative Procedure)," in *Egypt and its Laws*, Nathalie Bernard-Maugiron and Baudouin Dupret, eds. (Arab and Islamic Law Series 22; London/The Hague/New York: Kluwer Law International, 2002), 181–96.

—— "Law Professionals," in *Egypt and its Laws*, Nathalie Bernard-Maugiron and Baudouin Dupret, eds. (Arab and Islamic Law Series 22; London/The Hague/New York: Kluwer Law International, 2002), 197–208.

Esposito, John L., *Voices of Resurgent Islam* (New York: Oxford University Press, 1983).

—— *The Islamic Threat* (New York: Oxford University Press, 1992).

Fadel, Mohammad, *Adjudication in the Mālikī Madhhab: A Study of Legal Process in Medieval Islamic Law* (Ph.D., diss.; University of Chicago, 1995).

—— "The Social Logic of *Taqlīd* and the Rise of the *Mukhtaṣar*," *Islamic Law and Society* 3 (1996), 165–92.

—— "'Istiḥsān is Nine-Tenths of the Law'": The Puzzling Relationship of Uṣūl to Furūʿ in the Mālikī *Madhhab*," in *Studies in Islamic Legal Theory*, Bernard G. Weiss, ed. (Leiden: Brill, 2002), 161–76.

Fahmy, Khaled, *All the Pasha's Men: Mehmed Ali, His Army and the Making of Modern Egypt* (Cambridge: Cambridge University Press, 1997).

Farhang, Michael, "Terrorism and Military Trials in Egypt: Presidential Decree No. 375 and the Consequences for Judicial Autonomy," *Harvard International Law Journal* 35 (1994), 225–36.

Gabr, Hatem Aly Labib, "The Interpretation of Article 2 of the Constitution: Islamic Sharia Principles as a Source of Law," in *Human Rights and Democracy: The Role of the Supreme Constitutional Court of Egypt*, Kevin Boyle and Adel Omar Sherif, eds. (CIMEL Book Series 3; London: Kluwer, 1996), 217–27.

Gerber, Haim, *State, Society and Law in Islam: Ottoman Society in Comparative Perspective* (Albany: State University of New York Press, 1994).

—— *Islamic Law and Culture: 1600–1840* (Leiden: E.J. Brill, 1999).

Gerges, Fawaz A., "The End of the Islamist Insurgency in Egypt?: Costs and Prospects," *Middle East Journal* 10 (2000), 592–612.

Gershoni, Israel, "Arabization of Islam: The Egyptian Salafiyya and the Rise of Arabism in Pre-Revolutionary Egypt," *Asian and African Studies* 13 (1979), 199–219.

Gershoni, Israel and James P. Jankowski, *Egypt, Islam and the Arabs: The Search for Egyptian Nationhood, 1900–1930* (New York: Oxford University Press, 1986).

—— *Redefining the Egyptian Nation: 1930–1945* (Cambridge: Cambridge University Press, 1995).

al-Ghazālī, Abu Ḥāmid, *Kitāb al-Arbaʿīn fī Uṣūl al-Dīn* (Cairo: 1344/1925), partially trans. James Robson, "al-Ghazālī and the Sunna," *Muslim World* 45 (1955), 324–33.

—— *al-Mustaṣfā min ʿIlm al-Uṣūl*, 2 vols., ed. Shaykh Ibrahim Muḥamad Ramaḍan (Beirut: Dar al-Arqam, 1970).

Goitein, S.D., "The Birth Hour of Muslim Law," *The Muslim World* 50 (1960), 23–29, repr. in *Studies in Islamic History and Institutions* (Leiden, E.J. Brill, 1966).

Goldziher, Ignaz, *Die Zahiriten*, Wolgang Behn, ed. and trans., *The Zahiris: Their Doctrine and Their History* (Leiden: E.J. Brill, 1971).

—— *Muhammedanische Studien*, 2 vols. (Leiden: E.J. Brill, 1896), trans. C.R. Barber and S.M. Stern, *Muslim Studies*, 2 vols. (London: Allen & Unwin, 1967–71).

Gomaa, Ahmed M., "Islamic Fundamentalism in Egypt during the 1930s and 1970s: Comparative Notes," in *Islam, Nationalism and Radicalism*, Gabriel R. Warburg and Uri M. Kupferschmidt, eds. (New York: Praeger, 1983), 143–158.

Greenawalt, R. Kent, *Conflicts of Law and Morality* (New York: Oxford University Press, 1987).

Haddad, Yvonne Y., *Contemporary Islam and the Challenge of History* (Albany: State University of New York Press, 1982).

—— "Sayyid Quṭb: Ideologue of Islamic Revival," in *Voices of Resurgent Islam*, John L. Esposito, ed. (New York: Oxford University Press, 1983), 67–98.
Hallaq, Wael, "Was the Gate of Ijtihād Closed?," *International Journal of Middle East Studies* 16.1 (1984), 3–41.
—— "On the Origins of the Debate about the Existence of Mujtahids and Gate of Ijtihād," *Studia Islamica* 63 (1986), 129–41, repr. in Wael Hallaq, *Law and Legal Theory in Classical and Medieval Islam* (Aldershot: Varorium, 1995).
—— "Notes on the Term Qarīna in Islamic Legal Discourse," *Journal of the American Oriental Society* 108 (1988), 475–80, repr. in *Law and Legal Theory in Classical and Medieval Islam.*
—— "Non-analogical Arguments in Sunnī Juridical Qiyās," *Arabica* 36 (1989), 286–306, repr. in *Law and Legal Theory in Classical and Medieval Islam.*
—— "Logic, Formal Arguments and Formalization of Arguments in Sunnī Jurisprudence," *Arabica* 37 (1990), 315–58, repr. in *Law and Legal Theory in Classical and Medieval Islam.*
—— "The Primacy of the Qur'ān in Shāṭibī's Legal Theory," in *Islamic Studies Presented to Charles C. Adams*, Wael B. Hallaq and Donald P. Little, eds. (Leiden: E.J. Brill, 1991), 69–90, repr. in *Law and Legal Theory in Classical and Medieval Islam.*
—— "*Uṣūl al-Fiqh*: Beyond Tradition," *Journal of Islamic Studies* 3 (1992), 172–202, repr. in *Law and Legal Theory in Classical and Medieval Islam.*
—— "Was al-Shāfiʿī the Master Architect of Islamic Jurisprudence?," *International Journal of Middle East Studies* 25 (1993), 587–605, repr. in *Law and Legal Theory in Classical and Medieval Islam.*
—— "Was the Gate of Ijtihād Closed?," *International Journal of Middle East Studies* 16.1 (1994), 3–41; repr. in *Law and Legal Theory in Classical and Medieval Islam.*
—— "From Fatwās to Furūʿ: Growth and Change in Islamic Substantive Law," *Islamic Law and Society* 1 (1994), 29–65.
—— "Murder in Cordoba: Ijtihād, Iftā' and the Evolution of Substantive Law in Medieval Islam," *Acta Orientalia* 55 (1994), 55–83.
—— Review of *The Search for God's Law: Islamic Jurisprudence in the Writings of Sayf al-Dīn al-Āmidī* by Bernard Weiss, *International Journal of Middle East Studies* 26 (1994), 152–54.
—— *A History of Islamic Legal Theories: An Introduction to Sunnī Uṣūl al-Fiqh* (Cambridge: Cambridge University Press, 1997).
—— *Authority, Continuity, and Change in Islamic Law* (Cambridge: Cambridge University Press, 2001).
—— "*Takhrīj* and the Construction of Juristic Authority," in *Studies in Islamic Legal Theory*, Bernard G. Weiss, ed. (Leiden: Brill, 2002), 317–36.
Haykel, Bernard, "Reforming Islam by Dissolving the *Madhhabs*: Shawkānī and his Zaydī Detractors in Yemen," in *Studies in Islamic Legal Theory*, Bernard G. Weiss, ed. (Leiden: Brill, 2002), 337–64.
Heinrichs, Wofhart, "*Qawāʿid* as a Genre of Legal Literature" in *Studies in Islamic Legal Theory*, Bernard G. Weiss, ed. (Leiden: Brill, 2002), 365–84.
Heer, Nicholas, ed., *Islamic Law and Jurisprudence: Studies in Honor of Farhat J. Ziadeh* (Seattle: University of Washington Press, 1990).
Heikal, Mohamed, *Autumn of Fury: The Assassination of Sadat* (New York: Random House, 1983).
Hill, Enid, *Mahkama!: Studies in the Egyptian Legal System* (London: Ithaca Press, 1979).
—— "Change and Continuity in an Egyptian Judicial Institution: The *Niyāba*," in *Law and Social Change: Problems and Challenges in Contemporary Egypt*, 2nd ed., Cynthia Nelson and Klaus-Friedrich Koch, eds. (Cairo Papers in Social Science 2.4; Cairo: University of Cairo Press, 1983), 117–37.
—— *Al-Sanhuri and Islamic Law: The Place and Significance of Islamic Law in the Life and*

Work of ʿAbd al-Razzaq Ahmad al-Sanhuri, Egyptian Jurist and Scholar, 1895–1971 (Cairo: American University in Cairo Press, 1987).

—— "Law and Courts in Egypt: Recent Issues and Events Concerning Islamic Law," in *The Political Economy of Contemporary Egypt*, Ibrahim Oweiss, ed. (Washington D.C.: Center for Contemporary Arab Studies, 1990), 240–64.

—— "Majlis al-Dawla: The Administrative Courts of Egypt and Administrative Law," in *Islam and Public Law: Classical and Contemporary Studies*, Cibli Mallat, ed. (CIMEL Arab and Islamic Laws Series 8; London: Graham & Trotman, 1993), 212–18.

—— "Establishing the Doctrine of Judicial Review in Egypt and the United States," in *The Role of the Judiciary in the Protection of Human Rights*, Eugene Cotran and Adel Omar Sherif, eds. (CIMEL Book Series No. 5: London: Kluwer, 1997), 323–334.

—— "The Supreme Constitutional Court of Egypt on Property" in *Le prince et son juge: droit et politique dans l'Égypte contemporaine*, Nathalie Bernard-Maugiron and Baudouin Dupret, eds., a special edition of *Egypte/Monde Arabe* 2.2 (1999), 55–92.

Homoud, Sami Hassan, *Islamic Banking* (London: Arabian Information, 1985).

Hourani, Albert, *Arabic Thought in the Liberal Age: 1798–1939* (Cambridge: Cambridge University Press, 1970).

Hourani, George, "The Basis of the Authority of Consensus in Sunnite Islam," *Studia Islamica* 21 (1964), 11–60.

Hunter, F. Robert, *Egypt under the Khedives, 1805–1879: From Household Government to Modern Bureaucracy* (Pittsburgh: Pittsburgh University Press, 1984).

Ibn Qudāma, Muwaffaq al-Dīn, *Rawḍat al Nāẓir wa-Junnat al-Munāẓir* (Cairo: al-Maṭbaʿa al-Salafiyya, 1385).

Ibn Rushd, Muḥammad ibn Aḥmad (al-Ḥāfid), *Bidāyat al-Mujtahid wa Nihāyat al-Muqtaṣid*, 2 vols. (Beirut: Dār al-Kutub al-ʿIlmiyya, 1997).

—— *Bidāyat al-Mujtahid wa-Nihāyat al-Muqtaṣid*, trans. Imran A.K. Nyazee, *The Distinguished Jurist's Primer*, 2 vols. (Reading: Garnet Publishing, 1994).

Ibn Taymiyya, Taqī al-Dīn, *al-Siyāsa al-Sharʿiyya fī Iṣlāh al-Rāʿī wa-'l-Raʿiyya*, trans. Henri Laoust, *Le traité de Droit Public d'Ibn Taimiya* (Beirut: Institut Français d'Archéologie Orientale, 1948).

—— *al-Siyāsa al-Sharʿiyya fī Iṣlāh al-Rāʿī wa-al-Rāʿiyya* (Beirut, Dār al-Kutub al-ʿIlmiyya, 1988).

—— *Masʾalat al-Istiḥsān*, George Makdisi, ed., Arabic text published as "Ibn Taimīya's Autograph Manuscript on Istiḥsān: Materials for the Study of Islamic Legal Thought," in *Arabic and Islamic Studies in Honor of Hamilton A.R. Gibb*, George Makdisi, ed., (Cambridge: Harvard University Press, 1965).

Ibrahim, Saad Eddin, "The Changing Face of Egypt's Islamic Activism," in *Security Challenges in the Mediterranean Region*, Roberto Aliboni, George Joffé, and Tim Niblock, eds. (London: Frank Cass, 1996), 27–40.

—— "Anatomy of Egypt's Militant Islamic Groups: Methodological Notes and Preliminary Findings," *International Journal of Middle East Studies* 12 (1980), 423–453.

—— *Egypt, Islam and Democracy: Twelve Critical Essays* (Cairo: American University of Cairo Press, 1996).

Imber, Colin, *Ebu's Suʿud: The Islamic Legal Tradition* (Stanford: Stanford University Press, 1997).

Halil Inalcik, et al., eds. *The Great Ottoman-Turkish Civilisation* (Ankara: Yeni Türkiye, 2000), vol. I, 181–83.

Jackson, Sherman, "From Prophetic Actions to Constitutional Theory: A Novel Chapter in Medieval Muslim Jurisprudence," *International Journal of Middle East Studies* 25.1 (1993), 71–90.

—— *Islamic Law and the State: The Constitutional Jurisprudence of Shihāb al-Dīn al-Qarāfī* (Leiden: E.J. Brill, 1996).

—— "*Taqlīd*, Legal Scaffolding and the Scope of Legal Injunctions in Post Formative Theory: *Muṭlaq* and *'Amm* in the Jurisprudence of Shihāb al-Dīn al-Qarāfī," *Islamic Law and Society* 3 (1996), 137–65.

—— "Kramer v. Kramer in a Tenth/Sixteenth Century Egyptian Court: Post Formative Jurisprudence between Exigency and Law," *Islamic Law and Society* 8 (2001), 27–51.

—— "Fiction and Formalism: Toward a Functional Analysis of Uṣūl al-fiqh," in *Studies in Islamic Legal Theory*, Bernard G. Weiss, ed. (Leiden: Brill, 2002), 177–201.

Jacquemond, Richard, "La Haute Cour constitutionnelle et le contrôle de constitutionnalité des lois," *Annuaire International de Justice Constitutionnelle* 4 (1988), 271–95, 549–79.

Jansen, Johannes, *The Dual Nature of Islamic Fundamentalism* (Ithaca: Cornell University Press, 1997).

Johansen, Baber, *The Islamic Law on Land Tax and Rent: The Peasants' Loss of Property Rights as Interpreted in the Ḥanafite Legal Literature of the Mamlūk and Ottoman Periods* (New York: Croon Helm, 1988).

—— "Legal Literature and the Problem of Change: the Case of Land Rent," in *Islam and Public Law*, Chibli Mallat, ed. (London: Graham & Trotman, 1993), 29–47.

—— "Supra-legislative Norms and Constitutional Courts: The Case of France and Egypt," in *The Role of the Judiciary in the Protection of Human Rights*, Eugene Cotran and Adel Omar Sherif, eds. (CIMEL Book Series No. 5: London: Kluwer, 1997), 347–76.

—— *Contingency in a Sacred Law: Legal and Ethical Norms in the Muslim Fiqh* (Leiden: E.J. Brill, 1999).

Juynboll, G.H.A., *The Authenticity of the Tradition Literature: Discussions in Modern Egypt* (Leiden: E.J. Brill, 1969).

—— *Muslim Tradition: Studies in Chronology, Provenance and Authorship of Early Hadith* (Cambridge: Cambridge University Press, 1983).

Keddie, Nikki R., *An Islamic Response to Imperialism Political and Religious Writings of Sayyid Jamāl ad-Dīn al-Afghānī* (Berkeley: University of California Press, 1968).

—— ed., *Scholars, Saints, and Sufis: Muslim Religious Institutions in the Middle East since 1500* (Berkeley: University of California Press, 1973).

Kedourie, Elie, *The Chatham House Version and Other Middle Eastern Studies*, new ed. (Hanover: Brandeis University Press, 1984).

Kepel, Gilles, *Le Prophète et Pharaon*, trans. Jon Rothschild, *Muslim Extremism in Egypt: The Prophet and Pharaoh* (Berkeley: University of California Press, 1985).

Kemke, Andreas, *Stiftungen im muslimischen Rechtsleben des neuzeitlichen Ägypten* (Frankfurt: Peter Lang, 1991).

Kerr, Malcolm, *Islamic Reform: The Political and Legal Theories of Muhammad Abduh and Rashid Rida* (Berkeley: University of California Press, 1966).

Khadduri, Majid, "The Maṣlaḥa and the 'Illa (Cause) in Islamic Law," *New York University Journal of International Law and Politics* 12 (1979), 213–17.

—— and Herbert Liebesny, eds., *Law in the Middle East: Origins and Development of Islamic Law* (Washington D.C.: Middle East Institute, 1955).

Khalīl (Khalīl Ibn Isḥāq), *al-Mukhtaṣar*, trans. G.H. Bousquet, *Abrégé de la loi musulmane selon le rite de l'imâm Mâlik* (Publications de L'Institut d'Études Orientales de la Faculté des Lettres d'Alger 17; Algiers: Éditions Algériennes En-Nahdha, 1956), vol. 2, 74–77.

Kienle, Eberhard, "More than a Response to Islamism: The Political Deliberalization of Egypt in the 1990s," *Middle East Journal* 52 (1998), 219–35.

Kramer, Martin, "The Divided House of Islam," in MECS VII (1982–83), 235–55.

Lambton, Ann K.S., *State and Government in Medieval Islam* (Oxford: Oxford University Press, 1991).

—— "Changing Concepts of Authority in the Late Ninth/Fifteenth and Early Tenth/Sixteenth Centuries," in *Islam and Power*, Alexander S. Cudsi and Ali E. Hilal Dessouki, eds. (Baltimore: Johns Hopkins, 1981).
Laoust, Henri "Le Reformisme orthodoxe des 'Salafiyya,' et les caractères généraux de son organization actuelle," *Revue des Études Islamiques* 6 (1932), 175–224.
—— *Le califat dans la doctrine de Rasid Rida* (Beirut: Institut Français de Damas, 1938).
—— *Essai sur les doctrines sociales et politiques de Takî-d-dīn Aḥmad b. Taimîya*, (Cairo: Imprimerie de l'Institut Français d'Archéologie Orientale, 1939).
—— *Contribution à une étude de la méthodologie canonique de Takî-d-Dīn Aḥmad b. Taymîya* (Cairo: Imprimerie de l'Institut Français d'Archéologie Orientale, 1939).
—— "Le reformisme d'Ibn Tamiyya," *Islamic Studies* 1 (1962), 27–47.
—— *La Politique de Ghazālī* (Paris: Paul Geuthner, 1970).
Layish, Aharon, "The Contribution of the Modernists to the Secularization of Islamic Law," *Middle East Studies* 14 (1978), 263–77.
Levtzion, Nehemiah and Voll, John O., *Eighteenth-Century Renewal and Reform in Islam* (Syracuse: Syracuse University Press, 1987).
Lewis, Bernard, *The Political Language of Islam* (Chicago: University of Chicago Press, 1988).
—— *The Emergence of Modern Turkey* (New York: Oxford University of Press, 1968).
—— "Siyāsa" in *In Quest of an Islamic Humanism*, A.H. Green, ed. (Cairo: American University of Cairo Press, 1984), 3–13.
Libson, Gideon, "The Development of Custom as a Source of Law," *Islamic Law and Society* 4 (1997), 131–155.
Linant de Bellefonds, Yves, "The Formal Sources of Islamic Law," trans. M. Khalid Masud, *Islamic Studies* 15 (1976), 187–94.
Lombardi, Clark, "Islamic Law as a Source of Constitutional Law in Egypt: the Constitutionalization of the Sharia in a Modern Arab State," *Columbia Journal of Transnational Law* 37.1 (1988), 81–122.
Lowry, Joseph, "Does Shāfiʿī have a Theory of Four Sources of Law?" in *Studies in Islamic Legal Theory*, Bernard G. Weiss, ed. (Leiden: Brill, 2002), 23–50.
Mahmassani, Sobhi, *Falsafat al-Tashrīʿ fī al-Islam*, trans. Farhat Ziadeh, *The Philosophy of Jurisprudence in Islam* (Leiden: E.J. Brill, 1961).
Mahmoud, W. "Civil and Criminal Justice," in *Egypt and its Laws*, Nathalie Bernard-Maugiron and Baudouin Dupret, eds. (Arab and Islamic Law Series 22; London/The Hague/New York: Kluwer Law International, 2002), 315–24.
Makdisi, George, *The Rise of Colleges* (Edinburgh: Edinburgh University Press, 1981).
"The Guilds of Law in Medieval Legal History: An Inquiry into the Origins of the Inns of Court," *Zeitschrift für Geschichte der Arabisch-Islamischen Wissenschaften*, 1 (1984), 233–252.
—— "The Juridical Theology of Shāfiʿī: Origins and Significance of ʿUṣūl al-Fiqh," *Studia Islamica* 59 (1984), 5–47.
—— "Ethics in Islamic Traditionalist Doctrine," in *Ethics in Islam*, R.G. Hovannisian, ed. (Malibu: Undena Publications, 1985), 47–63.
—— "Freedom in Islamic Jurisprudence: Ijtihad, Taqlid, and Academic Freedom," in *La notion de liberté au moyen age: Islam, Byzance, Occident* (Penn-Paris-Dumbarton Oaks Colloquia; Paris: Société d'Edition des Belles Lettres, 1985), 79–88.
—— "La corporation à l'époque de l'Islam," in *Présence de Louis Massignon: Hommages et témoignages* (Paris: Maisonneuve and Larose, 1987), 35–49.
—— *The Rise of Humanism in Classical Islam and the Christian West* (Edinburgh: Edinburgh University Press, 1990).
Makdisi, John, "Legal Logic and Equity in Islamic Law," *American Journal of Comparative Law* 33 (1985), 63–92.
—— "Formal Rationality in Islamic Law and Common Law," *Cleveland State Law Review* 34 (1985–1986), 97–112.

—— "Hard Cases and Human Judgment in Islamic and Common Law," *Indiana International and Comparative Review* 1 (1991), 191–219.
Mallat, Chibli, "The Debate on *Riba* and Interest in Twentieth Century Jurisprudence," in *Islamic Law and Finance* (London: Graham & Trotman, 1988).
—— ed., *Islam and Public Law: Classical and Contemporary Studies* (London: Graham & Trotman, 1993), 69–88.
—— *Constitutional Law in the Middle East: The Emergence of Judicial Power* (SOAS Law Department Working Papers; London: SOAS, 1992).
Marlowe, John, *Cromer in Egypt* (New York: Praeger, 1970).
Marsot, Afaf Lutfi Al-Sayyid, "The Beginnings of Modernization among the Rectors of al-Azhar," in *Beginnings of Modernization in the Middle East,* William R. Polk and Richard L. Chambers, eds. (Chicago: University of Chicago Press, 1968), 267–80.
—— "The Ulama of Cairo in the Eighteenth and Nineteenth Centuries," in *Scholars, Saints, and Sufis: Muslim Religious Institutions in the Middle East since 1500*, Nikkie R. Keddie, ed. (Berkeley: University of California Press, 1973), 149–65.
—— *Egypt in the Reign of Muhammad ʿAli* (Cambridge: Cambridge University Press, 1984).
—— *Protest Movements and Religious Undercurrents in Egypt: Past and Present* (Occasional Papers Series; Georgetown: Center for Contemporary Arab Studies, 1984).
—— *A Short History of Modern Egypt* (Cambridge: Cambridge University Press, 1985).
Masud, Muhammad Khalid, *Islamic Legal Philosophy: A Study of Abu Ishaq al-Shatibi's Life and Thought* (Islamabad: Islamic Research Institute, 1977).
—— *Shatibi's Philosophy of Islamic Law* (Islamabad: Islamic Research Institute, 1995).
Masud, Khalid, Brinkley Messick and David Powers, eds., *Islamic Legal Interpretation* (Cambridge: Harvard University Press, 1996).
Mayer, Ann, "The Sharīʿah: A Methodology or a Body of Substantive Rules?," in *Islamic Law and Jurisprudence*, N. Heer, ed. (Seattle: University of Washington Press, 1990), 177–198.
McWhinney, Edward, *Supreme Courts and Judicial Lawmaking: Constitutional Tribunals and Constitutional Review* (Dordrecht: Martinus Nijhoff, 1986).
Melchert, Christopher, *The Formation of the Sunnī Schools of Law* (Leiden: E.J. Brill, 1998).
—— "Qurʾānic Abrogation Across the Ninth Century: Shāfiʿī, Abū ʿUbayd, Muḥāsibī, and Ibn Qutaybah," in *Studies in Islamic Legal Theory*, Bernard G. Weiss, ed. (Leiden: Brill, 2002), 75–98.
Meron, Yaʿakov, Review of *Loi islamique et droit dans les sociétés arabes* by Bernard Botiveau in *Islamic Law and Society* 6 (1999), 122–27.
Messick, Brinkley, *The Calligraphic State: Textual Domination and History in a Muslim Society* (Berkeley: University of California, 1992).
Merryman, John Henry, *The Civil Law Tradition: An Introduction to the Legal Systems of Western Europe and Latin America*, 2nd ed. (Stanford: Stanford University Press, 1985).
Mez, A. *Die Renaissance des Islāms*, S. Khuda Bukhsh and D.S. Margoliouth, trans., *The Renaissance of Islam* (London, 1937).
Middle East Watch, "Egypt: Human Rights Abuses Mount in 1993" (New York: privately printed, 1993).
—— "Violations of Freedom of Religious Belief and Expression of the Christian Minority" (New York: privately printed, 1994).
al-Miṣrī, Aḥmad ibn al-Naqīb, *ʿUmdat al-Sālik wa ʿUddat al-Nāsik* (with commentary), Noah Ha Mim Keller, ed., trans. *The Reliance of the Traveler: A Classic Manual of Islamic Sacred Law*, rev. ed. (Evanston, Illinois: Sunna Books, 1994).
Mitchell, Richard P., *The Society of the Muslim Brothers*, reprint with new intro. (New York: Oxford University Press, 1993).
Mitchell, Timothy, *Colonizing Egypt* (Cambridge: Cambridge University Press, 1988).
Moustafa, Tamir, "Conflict and Cooperation between the State and Religious

Institutions in Contemporary Egypt," *International Journal of Middle East Studies* 32 (2000), 1–21.
—— "Law Versus the State: The Judicialization of Politics in Egypt," *Law and Social Inquiry* 28 (2003), 883–927.
Murray, John, "Techniques of Constitutional Analysis in Egypt and the United States," in *The Role of the Judiciary in the Protection of Human Rights*, Eugene Cotran and Adel Omar Sherif, eds. (CIMEL Book Series No. 5; London: Kluwer, 1997), 377–92.
Murray, John and Mohammed El-Molla, "Islamic Shariʿa and Constitutional Interpretation in Egypt," in *Democracy, the Rule of Law and Islam*, Eugene Cotran and Adel Omar Sherif, eds. (CIMEL Book Series No. 6; London: Kluwer, 1999), 507–24.
Najjar, Fauzi M., "Egypt's Laws of Personal Status," *Arab Studies Quarterly* 10 (1988), 319–44.
Naveh, Immanuel, "The Tort of Injury and Dissolution of Marriage at the Wife's Initiative in Egyptian *Mahkamat al-Naqd* Rulings," *Islamic Law and Society* 9 (2002), 16–41.
Nielsen, Jorgen, *Secular Justice in an Islamic State: Mazalim under the Bahri Mamluks* (Leiden: Netherlands Institute for the Near East, 1985).
Nosseir, Abdel Rahman, "The Supreme Constitutional Court of Egypt and the Protection of Human Rights," DePaul University Law School, 1992. Photocopy.
O'Kane, J.P., "Islam in the New Egyptian Constitution," *The Middle East Journal* 26 (1972), 137–48.
Peters, Rudolph, "Idjtihad and taqlid in 18th and 19th century Islam," *Die Welt des Islams* 20 (1984), 132–45.
—— "Divine Law or Man-Made Law?," *Arab Law Quarterly* 3.3 (1988), 231–53.
—— "Murder on the Nile: Homicide Trials in Nineteenth-Century Egyptian Sharīʿa Courts," *Die Welt des Islams* 30 (1990), 8–116.
—— "Islamic and Secular Criminal Law in Nineteenth-Century Egypt?: The Role and Function of the Qadi," *Islamic Law and Society* 4 (1997), 70–90.
—— "Sharia and the State: Criminal law in nineteenth century Egypt," in *State and Islam*, C. Van Dijk and A.H. de Groot, eds. (Leiden: Research School CNWS, 1995), 152–77.
—— "State, Law and Society in Nineteenth-Century Egypt: Introduction," *Die Welt des Islams* 39.3 (1999), 267–71.
—— "'For His Correction and as a Deterrent Example for Others': Meḥmed ʿAlī's First Criminal Legislation (1829–1830)," *Islamic Law and Society* 6 (1999), 164–92.
Podeh, Elie, "The Arab Republic of Egypt," in MECS XVII (1993), 282–316.
Polk, William R. and Richard L. Chambers, eds., *Beginnings of Modernization in the Middle East* (Chicago: University of Chicago Press, 1968).
Powers, David S. *Studies in Qur'an and Ḥadīth* (Berkeley: University of California Press, 1986).
—— "On Judicial Review in Islamic Law," *Law and Society Review* 26.2 (1992), 315–41.
—— *Law, Society and the Maghreb, 1300–1500* (Cambridge: Cambridge University Press, 2002).
Qassem, Y., "Law of the Family (Personal Status Law)," in *Egypt and its Laws*, Nathalie Bernard-Maugiron and Baudouin Dupret, eds. (Arab and Islamic Law Series 22; London/The Hague/New York: Kluwer Law International, 2002), 19–36.
Qudūrī, Abū'l al-Ḥusayn, *al-Mukhtaṣar*, selections published in Arabic with French trans. by G.H. Bousquet and Leon Bercher, *Le statut personnel en droit musulman hanéfite* (Paris: Recueil Sirey, 1952).
Quṭb, Sayyid, *al-ʿAdāla al-Ijtimāʿiyya fī al-Islām*, 1st ed. (Cairo: Dār al-Shurūq, 1975/1390).

—— *Social Justice in Islam* (*al-ʿAdāla al-Ijtimāʿiyya fī al-Islām*), trans. John B. Hardie, rev. trans. Hamid Algar (Oneanta, New York: Islamic Publications International, 2000).
Rahim, Abdur, *The Principles of Muhammadan Jurisprudence* (Tagore Law Lectures, 1907; repr. Lahore: All Pakistan Legal Decisions, 1958).
Rahman, Fazlur, "Islamic Modernism: Its Scope, Method, and Alternative," *International Journal of Middle East Studies* 1 (1970), 317–33.
—— "Towards Reformulating the Methodology of Islamic Law," *New York University Journal of International Law and Politics* 12 (1979), 219–224.
—— *Islam and Modernity: Transformation of an Intellectual Tradition* (Chicago: University of Chicago Press, 1982).
—— *Islamic Methodology in History*, second printing (Islamabad: Islamic Research Institute, 1984).
al-Rāziq, ʿAlī ʿAbd, *al-Islām wa-Uṣūl al-Ḥukm* (Cairo: 1925); French trans. Leon Bercher, "L'Islam et les bases de pouvoir," *Revue des Etudes Islamiques* 7 (1933), 353–91, and 8 (1934), 163–222.
Reinhardt, A. Kevin, "'Like the Difference between Heaven and Earth:' Ḥanafī and Shāfiʿī Discussions of Wājib and Farḍ in *Studies in Islamic Legal Theory*, Bernard G. Weiss, ed. (Leiden: Brill, 2002), 205–34.
Reinich, Jacques, "The Arab Republic of Egypt," in MECS II (1977–78), 367–410.
Riḍā, Rashīd, *Yusr al-Islām wa-Uṣūl al-Tashrīʿ al-ʿĀmm* (Cairo: Maṭbaʿat al-Manār, 1341 A.H./1923 C.E.).
—— *Tārīkh al-Ustādh al-Imām al-Shaykh Muḥammad ʿAbduh* (Cairo: Maṭbaʿat al-Manār, 1933).
—— *Al-Khilāfa aw' al-imāmat al-Uẓmā* (Cairo: Maṭbaʿat al- Manār, n.d.); also publ. *al-Manār*, vols. xxiii–xxiv (1341/1922); French trans. Henri Laoust, *Le califat dans la doctrine de Rašīd Riḍā* (Beirut: Institut Français de Damas, 1938).
Robson, James, "al-Ghazālī and the Sunna," *Muslim World* 45 (1955), 324–33.
Rosberg, James H., *Roads to the Rule of Law: The Emergence of an Independent Judiciary in Contemporary Egypt* (Ph.D. diss.; Massachusetts Institute of Technology, 1995).
—— "Information and Liberty: The Development of the Rule of Law in Authoritarian Regimes," available on-line at http://web.mit.edu/web~rjames/www/ruleoflaw.pdf
Rosenthal, Erwin I.J., *Political Thought in Medieval Islam* (Cambridge: Cambridge University Press, 1958).
—— *Islam in the Modern National State* (Cambridge: Cambridge University Press, 1965).
—— "Some Reflections on the Separation of Church and State in Modern Islam," *Islamic Studies* 3 (1965).
Roy, Olivier, *The Failure of Political Islam,* trans. Carol Vol (Cambridge: Harvard University Press, 1994).
Rugh, Andrea, *Reveal and Conceal: Dress in Contemporary Egypt* (Cairo: University of Cairo Press, 1989).
Safran, Nadav, "The Abolition of the Shariʿa Courts in Egypt," *The Muslim World* 48 (1958), 21–28, 125–35.
Saleh, Nabil A., *Unlawful Gain and Legitimate Profit in Islamic Law* (New York: Cambridge University Press, 1986).
al-Sanhūrī, ʿAbd al-Razzāq, *Le califat* (Paris: Librarie Orientaliste Paul Geuthner, 1926).
—— "Le droit musulman comme élément de refonte du code civil égyptien," in *Introduction à l'Étude du Droit Comparé: Recueil d'études en l'honneur d'Édouard Lambert* (Paris: Librairie Générale de Droit et de Jurisprudence/Librairie de la Société Anonyme du Recueil Sirey, 1938), 621–42.
—— "La responsabilité civile et pénale en droit musulman," *Majallat al-Qānūn wa-'l-iqtiṣād* 155 (1945), 1–26.

—— *Maṣādir al-Ḥaqq fī al-Fiqh al-Islāmī* (Cairo: Jāmiʿat al-Duwal al-ʿArabiyya, Maʿhad al-Buḥūth wa-al-Dirāsa al-ʿArabiyya, 1956).
Schacht, Joseph, *The Origins of Muhammadan Jurisprudence* (Oxford: Clarendon Press, 1950).
—— "Classicisme, traditionalisme et ankylose dans la loi religieuse de l'Islam," in *Classicisme et declin culturel dans l'histoire de l'Islam*, R. Brunschwig and G. von Grunebaum, eds. (Paris: G.P. Maisonneuve, 1957).
—— "Islamic Law in Contemporary States," *The American Journal of Comparative Law* 8 (1959), 133–48.
—— "Problems of Modern Islamic Legislation," *Studia Islamica* 12 (1960), 99–129.
—— *An Introduction to Islamic Law* (Oxford: Clarendon Press, 1964).
al-Shāfiʿī, Muhammad b. Idrīs, *Al-Risāla fī Uṣūl al-Fiqh*, Muḥammad Shākir, ed. (Cairo: Muṣṭafa Bābī al-Ḥalabī, 1940).
—— *Al-Risāla fī Uṣūl al-Fiqh*, trans. Majid Khaduri, *Treatise on the Foundations of Islamic Jurisprudence*, 2nd ed. (Cambridge: Islamic Texts Society, 1987).
Shaham, Ron, *Family and the Courts in Modern Egypt: a Study Based on Decisions by the Sharīʿa Courts, 1900–1955* (Leiden, E.J. Brill, 1997).
—— "Judicial Divorce at the Wife's Initiative: The Sharīʿa Courts of Egypt, 1920–1955," *Islamic Law and Society* 1 (1994), 217–61.
Shalakany, Amr, "Between Identity and Redistribution: Sanhuri, Geneaology and the Will to Islamize," *Islamic Law and Society* 8 (2001), 201–44.
Sharabi, H., *Arab Intellectuals and the West: The Formative Years, 1875–1914* (Baltimore: Johns Hopkins University Press, 1970).
Shamir, Shimon and Ran Segev, "The Arab Republic of Egypt," in MECS I (1977–78), 284–329.
Shamir, Shimon, ed., *Egypt from Monarchy to Republic: A Reassessment of Revolution and Change* (Boulder: Westview Press, 1995).
Shepherd, William, "The Development of the Thought of Sayyid Qutb as Reflected in Earlier and Later Editions of Social Justice in Islam," *Die Welt des Islams* 32 (1992), 196–236.
Sherif, Adel Omar, *Al-Qaḍāʾ al-Dustūrī fī Miṣr* (Cairo: Dār al-Fikr al-ʿArabī, 1995).
—— "The Freedom of Judicial Expression, The Right to Concur and Dissent," in *Human Rights and Democracy: The Role of the Supreme Constitutional Court of Egypt*, Kevin Boyle and Adel Omar Sherif, eds. (CIMEL Book Series 3 London: Kluwer, 1996), 137–58.
—— "The Origins and Development of the Egyptian Judicial System," in *Human Rights and Democracy: The Role of the Supreme Constitutional Court of Egypt*, 13–37.
—— "An Overview of the Egyptian Court System," *Yearbook of Islamic and Middle Eastern Law* 5 (1998–99), 3–28.
—— "The Rule of Law in Egypt from a Judicial Perspective: A Digest of the Landmark Decisions of the Supreme Constitutional Court of Egypt" in *The Rule of Law in the Middle East and the Islamic World: Human Rights and the Judicial Process*, Eugene Cotran and Mai Yamani, eds. (London: I.B. Tauris, 2000), 1–34.
—— "Constitutional Adjudication," in *Egypt and its Laws*, Nathalie Bernard-Maugiron and Baudouin Dupret, eds. (Arab and Islamic Law Series 22; London/The Hague/New York: Kluwer Law International, 2002), 325–44.
—— "Constitutional Law" in *Egypt and its Laws*, Nathalie Bernard-Maugiron and Baudouin Dupret, eds. (Arab and Islamic Law Series 22; London/The Hague/New York: Kluwer Law International, 2002), 315–24.
Shoukri, Ghali, *Egypt: The Portrait of a President, 1971–1981* (London: Zed Press, 1981).
Sivan, Emmanuel, *Radical Islam: Medieval Theology and Modern Politics* (New Haven: Yale University Press, 1985).

Skovgaard-Petersen, Jakob, *Defining Islam for the Egyptian State: Muftīs and Fatwās of the Dar al-Iftā* (Leiden: E.J. Brill, 1997).

Smith, C.D., "The 'Crisis of Orientation': The Shift of Egyptian Intellectuals to Islamic Subjects in the 1930s," *International Journal of Middle East Studies* 4. 4 (1974), 382–410.

Smith, Wilfred Cantwell, "The Concept of *Sharīʿa* Amongst Some Mutakallimūn," in *Arabic and Islamic Studies in Honor of Hamilton A.R. Gibb*, George Makdisi, ed. (Leiden: E.J. Brill, 1965), 581–602.

Snouck Hurgronje, Christiaan, *Selected Works*, G.H. Bousquet and Joseph Schacht, eds. (Leiden: E.J. Brill, 1957).

Steppat, Fritz, "National Education Projects in Egypt before British Occupation," in *Beginnings of Modernization in the Middle East*, William R. Polk and Richard L. Chambers, eds. (Chicago: University of Chicago Press, 1968), 281–97.

Stewart, Devin J., *Islamic Legal Orthodoxy: Twelve Shiite Responses to the Sunni Legal System* (Salt Lake City: University of Utah, 1998).

—— "Muḥammad b. Dāwūd al-Ẓāhirī's Manual of Jurisprudence: *al-Wuṣūl ilā maʿrifat al-uṣūl*," in *Studies in Islamic Legal Theory*, Bernard G. Weiss, ed. (Leiden: Brill, 2002), 99–158.

Stone, Alec, *The Birth of Judicial Politics in France: The Constitutional Council in Comparative Perspective* (New York: Oxford University Press, 1992).

Tignor, Robert, *Modernization and British Colonial Rule in Egypt* (Princeton: Princeton University Press, 1966).

Toledano, Ehud R., "Law, Practice, and Social Reality: A Theft Case in Cairo, 1954," *Asian and African Studies* 17 (1983), 153–73.

Tyan, Emile, *Histoire de l'organisation judiciaire en pays d'Islam*, 2nd ed. (Leiden: E.J. Brill, 1960).

Udovitch, Avram, *Partnership and Profit in Medieval Islam* (Princeton: Princeton University Press, 1970).

Vatikiotis, P.J., *Nasser and his Generation* (New York: St. Martin's Press, 1978).

—— "Islamic Resurgence: A Critical View," in *Islam and Power*, Alexander S. Cudsi and Ali E. Hilal Dessouki, eds. (Baltimore: Johns Hopkins, 1981), 169–96.

—— *The History of Modern Egypt*, 4th ed. (Baltimore: Johns Hopkins University Press, 1991).

—— ed., *The Middle East from the End of the Empire to the End of the Cold War* (New York: Routledge, 1997).

Venkatraman, Bharathi Anandhi, "Islamic States and the United Nations Convention on the Elimination of All Forms of Discrimination Against Women: Are the Sharīʿa and the Convention Compatible?," *American University Law Review* 44 (1995), 1949–2011.

Vogel, Frank, "Conformity with Islamic Shariʿa and Constitutionality under Article 2: Some Issues of Theory, Practice, and Comparison," in *Democracy, the Rule of Law and Islam*, Eugene Cotran and Adel Omar Sherif, eds. (CIMEL Book Series No. 6; London: Kluwer, 1999), 525–44.

—— *Islamic Law and Legal System: Studies of Saudi Arabia* (Leiden: E.J. Brill, 2000).

Wakin, Jeanette, "Interpretation of the Divine Command in the Jurisprudence of Muwaffaq al-Dīn Ibn Qudāma," in *Islamic Law and Jurisprudence: Studies in Honor of Farhat J. Ziadeh*, Nicholas Heer, ed. (Seattle: University of Washington, 1990), 33–52.

Warburg, Gabriel and Uri Kupfershmidt, *Islam, Nationalism and Radicalism in Egypt and the Sudan* (New York: Praeger, 1983).

Weiss, Bernard, "Interpretation in Islamic Law: The Theory of *Ijtihād*," *American Journal of Comparative Law* 26 (1978), 199–212.

—— "Language and Tradition in Medieval Islam: The Question of *al-Ṭarīq ilā Maʿrifat al-Lugha*," *Der Islam* 61 (1984), 92–99.

—— "Knowledge of the Past: The Theory of *Tawātur* According to Ghazālī," *Studia Islamica* 61 (1985), 81–105.
—— "Language and Law: The Linguistic Premises of Islamic Legal Science," in *In Quest of an Islamic Humanism: Arabic and Islamic Studies in Memory of Mohammed el-Nowaihi*, Arnold H. Green, ed. (Cairo: American University of Cairo Press, 1986), 15–21.
—— *The Spirit of Islamic Law* (Athens: The University of Georgia Press, 1988).
—— "Exotericism and Objectivity in Islamic Jurisprudence," in *Islamic Law and Jurisprudence: Studies in Honor of Farhat J. Ziadeh*, Nicholas Heer, ed. (Seattle: University of Washington Press, 1990), 53–71.
—— *The Search for God's Law: Islamic Jurisprudence in the Writings of Sayf al-Dīn al-Āmidī* (Salt Lake City: University of Utah Press, 1992).
—— ed. *Studies in Islamic Legal Theory* (Leiden: Brill, 2002).
—— "Uṣūl-Related Madhhab Differences in Āmidī's Iḥkām," in *Studies in Islamic Legal Theory*, Bernard G. Weiss, ed. (Leiden: Brill, 2002), 293–314.
Wheeler, Brannon M., *Applying the Canon in Islam: The Authorization and Maintenance of Interpretive Reasoning in Ḥanafī Scholarship* (Albany: S.U.N.Y., 1996).
Wiederhold, Lutz, "Legal Doctrines in Conflict: The Relevance of *Madhhab* Boundaries to Legal Reasoning in the Light of an Unpublished Treatise on Ijtihād and Taqlīd," *Islamic Law and Society* 3 (1996), 234–304.
Winter, Michael, "A Seventeenth-Century Arabic Panegyric of the Ottoman Dynasty," *Asian and African Studies* 13 (1979), 130–56.
Yadlin, Rivka, "Militant Islam in Egypt: Some Socio-Cultural Aspects," in *Islam, Nationalism and Radicalism*, Gabriel R. Warburg and Uri M. Kupferschmidt, eds. (New York: Praeger, 1983), 159–82.
Yanagushi, Hiroyuki, "Judicial Function of the Sultan in Civil Cases according to the Mālikīs up to the Sixth/Twelfth Century," *Islamic Law and Society* 3 (1996), 41–74.
Zaman, Muhammad Qasim, "The Caliphs, the Ulama, and the Law: Defining the Role and Function of the Caliph in the Early Abbāsid Period," *Islamic Law and Society* 4 (1997), 1–33.
Zayd, Muṣṭafā, *al-Maṣlaḥa fī al-Tashrīʿ al-Islāmī wa-Najm al-Dīn al-Ṭūfī* (Cairo: Dār al-Fikr al-ʿArabī, 1953).
Zebiri, Kate, *Maḥmūd Shaltūt and Islamic Modernism* (Oxford: Clarendon Press, 1993).
Zeghal, Malika, "Religion and Politics in Egypt: The Ulema of Al-Azhar, Radical Islam, and the State," *International Journal of Middle East Studies* 31 (1999), 371–99.
Ziadeh, Farhat, *Lawyers, the Rule of Law and Liberalism in Modern Egypt* (Stanford: Hoover Institution, 1968).
Zysow, Aron, *The Economy of Certainty* (Ph.D. diss.; Harvard University, 1984).

INDEX OF NAMES

INDEX OF SUBJECTS

STUDIES IN ISLAMIC LAW AND SOCIETY

Edited by

RUUD PETERS and BERNARD WEISS

1. Jackson, S.A. *Islamic Law and the State.* The Constitutional Jurisprudence of Shihāb al-Dạn al-Qarāfạ. 1996. ISBN 90 04 10458 5
2. Saeed, A. *Islamic Banking and Interest.* A Study of the Prohibition of Riba and its Contemporary Interpretation. 1996. ISBN 90 04 10565 4
3. Shaham, R. *Family and the Courts in Modern Egypt.* A Study Based on Decisions by the Sharạğa Courts 1990-1955. 1997. ISBN 90 04 10742 8
4. Melchert, C. *The Formation of the Sunni Schools of Law, 9th-10th Centuries C.E.* 1997. ISBN 90 04 10952 8
5. Khalilieh, H.S. *Islamic Maritime Law.* An Introduction. 1998. ISBN 90 04 10955 2
6. Hoexter, M. *Endowments, Rulers and Community.* Waqf al Ḥaramayn in Ottoman Algiers. 1998. ISBN 90 04 10964 1
7. Johansen, B. *Contingency in a Sacred Law.* Legal and Ethical Norms in the Muslim *Fiqh.* 1999. ISBN 90 04 10603 0
8. Vogel, F. *Islamic Law in the Modern World.* The Legal System of Saudi Arabia. ISBN 90 04 11062 3
9. Gerber, H. *Islamic Law and Culture 1600-1840.* 1999. ISBN 90 04 11939 3
10. Müller, C. *Gerichtspraxis im Stadtstaat Córdoba.* Zum Recht der Gesellschaft in einer mālikitisch-islamischen Rechtstradition des 5./11. Jahrhunderts. 1999. ISBN 90 04 11354 1
11. Leeuwen, R. van. *Waqfs and Urban Structures.* The Case of Ottoman Damascus. 1999. ISBN 90 04 112995
12. Gleave, R. *Inevitable Doubt.* Two Theories of Shīʿī Jurisprudence. 2000. ISBN 90 04 115951

13. Donaldson, W.J. *Sharecropping in the Yemen.* A study in Islamic Theory, Custom and Pragmatism. 2000. ISBN 90 04 11490 4

14. Brockopp, J.E. *Early Mālikī Law.* Ibn ʿAbd al-Ḥakam and his Major Compendium of Jurisprudence. 2000. ISBN 90 04 11628 1

15. Weiss, B.G. (ed.) *Studies in Islamic Legal Theory.* 2001. ISBN 90 04 12066 1

16. Layish, A. and G.R. Warburg. *The Reinstatement of Islamic Law in Sudan under Numayrī.* An Evaluation of a Legal Experiment in the Light of Its Historical Context, Methodology, and Repercussions. 2002. ISBN 90 04 12104 8

17. Ergene, B.A. *Local Court, Provincial Society and Justice in the Ottoman Empire.* Legal Practice and Dispute Resolution in Çankırı and Kastamonu (1652-1744). 2003. ISBN 90 04 12609 0

18. Hennigan, P.C. *The Birth of a Legal Institution.* The Formation of the Waqf in Third-Century A.H. Ḥanafī. Legal Discourse. 2004. ISBN 90 04 13029 2

19. Lombardi, C.B. *State Law as Islamic Law in Modern Egypt.* The Incorporation of the *Sharīʿa* into Egyptian Constitutional Law. 2006. ISBN 90 04 13594 4

20. Yanagihashi, H. *A History of the Early Islamic Law of Property.* Reconstructing the Legal Development, 7th–9th Centuries. 2004. ISBN 90 04 13849 8

21. Van den Boogert, M.H. *The Capitulations and the Ottoman Legal System.* Qadis, Consuls and *Beratlıs* in the 18th Century. 2005. ISBN 90 04 14035 2

22. Masud, M.Kh., R. Peters and D.S. Powers (eds.) *Dispensing Justice in Islam.* Qadis and their Judgments. 2006. ISBN 90 04 14067 0

23. Maghen, Z. *Virtues of the Flesh – Passion and Purity in Early Islamic Jurisprudence.* 2005. ISBN 90 04 14070 0

24. Layish, A. Sharīʿa *and Custom in Libyan Tribal Society.* An Annotated Translation of Decisions from the *Sharīʿa* Courts of Adjābiya and Kufra. 2005. ISBN 90 04 14082 4

25. Powers, P. *Intent in Islamic Law.* Motive and Meaning in Medieval Sunnī *Fiqh.* 2006. ISBN 90 04 14592 3

26. Jaques, R.K. *Authority, Conflict, and the Transmission of Diversity in Medieval Islamic Law.* 2006. ISBN 90 04 14745 4

27. Ahmad, A.A. *Structural Interrelations of Theory and Practice in Islamic Law.* 2006. ISBN 90 04 15031 5